Gender Thinking

Gender Thinking

STEVEN G. SMITH

Temple University Press

PHILADELPHIA

To
Anne Simpson Lawton
(1892–1988)
and
Elise Lawton Isleib
(1924–1992)

Temple University Press, Philadelphia 19122
Copyright © 1992 by Temple University. All rights reserved
Published 1992
Printed in the United States of America

The paper used in this publication meets the minimum requirements of
American National Standard for Information Sciences—Permanence
of Paper for Printed Library Materials, ANSI Z39.48-1984 ∞

Library of Congress Cataloging-in-Publication Data
Smith, Steven G.
     Gender thinking / Steven G. Smith.
        p. cm.
     Includes bibliographical references (p.) and index.
     ISBN 0-87722-963-5 (cloth : alk. paper). — ISBN 0-87722-964-3
(paper : alk. paper)
     1. Sex role. 2. Philosophical anthropology. 3. Race. 4. Ethics.
     5. Mind and body. I. Title.
HQ1075.S58 1992
  305.3—dc20   91-47720

Photograph on p. 196 courtesy of The Museum of Modern Art/Film Still
Archive.

Humanity is something that must be overcome.
There are many ways of overcoming: see to that *yourself*!
But only a jester thinks: "Humanity can also be *skipped over*."
—Nietzsche, *Thus Spoke Zarathustra*

Contents

Preface

Black and white children started going to school together in the American South when I was in high school. On the school bus one morning in 1968, a black girl about my age asked me, a white boy, if I was "prejudiced." No, axiomatically not! What could be more hateful, stupid, and hindering than being against people because of their racial identity? How *awkward* race was, anyway; wouldn't it be better if we could blend the races forthwith to create an undivided world of medium-brown people? Meanwhile, why should skin color portend more than shirt or skirt color? (Or as much? At least you can read people's taste in their clothes.) What did my race matter to me? Wasn't the true principle of human relations always *knowing the individual*?

I might have been dimly aware that a medium-brown world would be in some way impoverished. Black people were more interesting to look at than whites (whose whiteness was not something I could see). Although I had only the slightest acquaintance with qualities of life associated with blacks and so could have little sense of what there might be to lose in a raceless world, I must have been able to see that, in principle, human diversity is a richness, a good. But I would have argued that the absence of racial diversity, supposing we could bring it about, would surely be a lesser evil than racism; by the same token, the loss of cultural diversity in any dimension—linguistic, political, religious—should be a lesser evil than cultural conflict. What could be more obvious than that we are all basically the same? And that individuals are all different?

While I entertained these democratic ideals, my thoughts about girls followed a different logic. Of course it was crucial with members of a sex, as with members of a race, to know them as individuals. But all one's dealings with girls assumed that they were basically, whether or not understandably, girl-like; for what could be more obvious and *moving* (and of greater practical consequence) than the difference between female and male humanity? No greater prejudgment could possess one. If a girl I liked deviated from feminine stereotypes, that did not upset the prejudgment about girls; that is how I knew she was special.

In those days, the problems of sexism were again beginning to be remarked widely, and I discovered that with the awakening to sexist injustice comes the very same thought, thinkable even as one stays immersed in familiar feelings: if our sex offend us, pluck it out! Or since we cannot by any amount of breeding get rid of femaleness and maleness, let us do away with the stereotypes of character and behavior that have been hung on physical sex, as these are the real supports of sexism. If we change the way we raise our children—trusting their plasticity, or their individuality, or their fundamental sameness, or some combination of these attributes—we can *abolish gender*.

Can we, though? That is a serious question; the difference between femininity and masculinity is intimately bound to the physical structure of procreation, which appears to be one of the great practical axes around which human affairs must always turn. So we need to establish exactly what gender is and how such a thing would be related to sex, procreation, and the ordering of life.

But even supposing that it lies in our power to abolish gender: May we? Should we? Can we make such a choice when the gender system gives us benchmarks of personal identity and worth along with primary channels in which to pursue the rewards of love? Had I sufficiently appreciated black distinctiveness in my high school days, I might have had second thoughts about the abolition of race. With the profound investment so many of us have in appreciating the female–male difference, how could we ever project a utopia without gender? To clarify our valuation of gender we need to see how it is implicated in love and personal character.

I have undertaken the study of these questions so that I will know better, as one who must make his way in a gendered world, what to think about gender—also about other human kinds, like race, age, class, culture, temperament, and sexual orientation—and I invite you into it for the same purpose. The purpose should bring us together even when much else divides us. There is an obvious limitation: the author cannot jump out of his own feet, his social and epistemological location, and when it comes to gender and sex relations a heterosexual white male author can perhaps *see* where the coals are awfully hot but still is not standing on those coals. It is all-important that such an author understand what the people on the hot coals are saying; but it is also important that he tell them what he is able to see from his own position. My first premise and final claim is that human truth will arise from an inclusive communalizing effort—that no subject or class (and no mode of reasoning) can adequately realize humanity on its own, in philosophy or politics or anything else. In spite of this ideal of sharing, of course, circumstances will pull us apart in our basic visions and commitments. The last thing one can say is: let us try to be humane about this thwarting of humanity.

The present work is a composition of conceptual maneuvers. I want to form a thought that is commodious, durable, and instrumental to a better life. I want to be able to think together a large, complicated set of considerations that (I now realize) all condition each others' meaning and so constitute a network, a network heretofore studied and exhibited only in fragments, misleadingly. My method is part survey and synthesis, interpreting what has been thought and said about human kinds in such a way as to maximize and exploit the cumulative insight in it, and part imaginative exploration in search of postures we should want to adopt and forms we should not miss beholding.

Of all the demands to which a thought has to stand up, the toughest is unrestricted sharability. I accept the principle that if what one thinks is not publicly acceptable, ideally speaking, then one should not think it. Now human kinds is an exceptionally hard topic on which to enforce this standard, but it is also a topic on which our thoughts matter very much and very directly to each other, so that the standard is more than usually pertinent.

The search for an adequate thought of gender leads me to give much attention to a gender principle and gender ideals. To readers who are mainly occupied with the pain and practical problems associated with our actual sex relations, this aspect of the work may seem irrelevantly or dangerously abstract. But more than one kind of abstractness threatens gender thinking. It is dangerous to set aside issues of character and value while theorizing political structure, because we thereby veil the question of how intentional beings are able to inhabit political structures (old or new); and it is dangerous to ignore the data of positive gender experience while elucidating gender malaise, because we thereby make our huge self-investment in gender incomprehensible. The first false move that sets up these abstractions is the identification of gender with sex, or sex-as-socially-constructed, or sex role, when in fact ordinary talk of "feminine" and "masculine" is not necessarily or even most often about any of these things but instead has to do typically with intentional qualities and, indeed, ideals. The intentional realities of gender are certainly related to the sexes, sex conceptions, and sex roles in a systematic way, but they are most interesting (for ordinary and critical thinking alike) precisely insofar as they are distinct. Thus readers are forewarned that their idea of "gender" may be contested in this work. I do this not for the love of multiplying conceptual possibilities but to secure that better view of the relevance of sex to human life that we all presumably wish to have.

It is not for me to say, finally, how far we will succeed with the approaches I offer, but there is bound to be reward in any effort to move toward the goal. Reflection on gender leads to fresh examination of problems that philosophers have always found especially interesting, including universals, "nature," embodiment, personhood, virtue, love, and the fundamental structures of thinking and valuing. In trying to get to the bottom of gender, I think we open up every great issue in a profitable way—which is a sign that human differentiation is a central question for us, like the polis in Plato's time or God's power in the Middle Ages. We will find ourselves (in that crazy philosophical way) reinventing the wheel, conceptually, over and over again. Reader, I hope you agree, or come to agree, that this is a great happiness of the mind.

Acknowledgments

No one in the world is less sympathetic to generalizations about people than Elise Lawton Smith, to whom I am indebted for a constant bracing battle over the ideas of this book. For much of what I can see of the cultural landscape of gender I have to thank Nona Fienberg, Richard Mallette, Judith Page, and Kathleen Spencer above all. The members of my Millsaps seminars in "Gender and Human Nature" awakened me to many of my questions. For valuable criticisms of the work as it progressed and for pointers along the way I thank Ted Ammon, Tim Coker, Vincent Colapietro, Jane Cullen, Victoria Davion, Lorne Fienberg, Catherine Freis, Richard Freis,

Allan Gurganus, Robert H. King, Marcy Lawton, Robert McElvaine, Michael Mitias, Elizabeth Peeler, Harrylyn Sallis, Nancy Snow, Donald Symons, and Richard Watson; please do not assume, however, that any of these persons endorse any of my arguments. I am grateful for additional help with the project to Walter Lowe, Andrew Tallon, and Edith Wyschogrod, and to Millsaps College for summer research grants and special leave arrangements in 1990–91. And I would like to thank Matthew and Katherine Smith for not once interrupting my meditations.

An earlier version of Chapter 2 appeared in *Public Affairs Quarterly* 3 (April 1989): 67–80, as "Gender and Humanity." Part of Chapter 3 was read to the Mississippi Philosophical Association in April, 1990, as "Gender and Embodiment"; parts of Chapter 4 were read in April, 1990, to the American Philosophical Association (Central Division) and Society for the Philosophy of Sex and Love as, respectively, "Principles of a Gender Aesthetic" and "The Attractions of Gender."

Steven G. Smith
Jackson, Mississippi
February 1992

Gender Thinking

A Prologue
on Democracy

Human differentiations are all burning issues because a certain communal project is underway. For that project, the most potent name we know is Democracy. The name has been invoked for different programs and has borne different connotations, yet it always points somehow to the universal sharing of power or rule.

Although "people's rule" is in the first place a political principle, it applies to more than what we call politics: it is a way of maintaining and advancing a culture. It is the first thing we should think about if we are to understand the significance, for us, of human kinds.

Politically, Democracy is rather an indeterminate principle. Who rules whom? Does the group rule its parts or do the parts rule the group? (How is "part" defined? What are the boundaries of "the people"?) If the group is thought to "rule itself" in the sense that the group qua group rules the group qua group, doesn't the distinction between ruler and ruled collapse, and with it the very notion of "rule" along with the possibility of allocating liberties and obligations? Democracy might mean, then, "the power of the people," its spontaneous self-expression, and an unforced mutual accommodation among its members. In that light it looks more like a culture than a government.

But what counts most is not, in any case, the *means*, be it "rule" or acculturation, but the *aim* of building the richest possible life in com-

1

mon. In a democratic society, both communing and individualizing are to be maximized, each limited only by the demands of the other, each interpreting the other—responsiveness becoming conscious, consciousness becoming responsive. Everyone is to swell and bloom past all prediction; everyone is to be concerned in every possible way with everything about everyone. (In our era, having the vote is posited as the chief instrument and symbol of this power-cum-responsibility, while education is posited as its great enabler.) No limit on universal love and respect is finally tolerable.

You can't argue against Democracy, when it carries this meaning. Proof: you understand the ideal; you can't think of one more alluring; and, even if our historical development can be interpreted otherwise than as a saga of democratic progress, you cannot deny that democratic progress is feasible from any historical point. (I say this, not to show that our thinking is historically constrained in a certain way, but instead as a reminder of what is really our brightest light, really our best path.) What we can argue about is how specific living arrangements realize Democracy or move toward it. We can argue for social constraint or liberty, competition or cooperation, challenge or support, as long as we speak to the aim.

Our actual arrangements, governmental or otherwise, are always marked by an element of coercive regulation. Here we find ourselves rulers and objects of rule—and inevitably somewhat confused about our ambiguous occupation of both positions. But we are also always borne along by a collective spontaneity by virtue of which we are exempt from regulation, a self-accomplishing togetherness without which regulation could not even take hold. Here—one might say, as "cultured" beings—we are what we want to be simply because we can be. Democracy, with its inordinate and dissolving trust in the potentials of government and human nature alike, calls on both kinds of order. It demands that we apply every conceivable technique to progress toward our ideal and simultaneously demands that we experience ourselves, together and separately, as infinitely (therefore equally) valuable, just as we are. We have to be unreservedly active in communing and individualizing, yet we can believe that each of us is already, in fact, fundamentally like the others and at the same time fatefully unique in her or his particularity.

So far from being crippled by the contradictions among these elements, Democracy, like a strong metaphor, gets its vitality from their provocative conjunction. And it makes us avid for news of "human nature." Sometimes we want an inspiring reading of human nature to support our hopes of progress; sometimes we set up a human-nature defense against demands for change. Always we are sheerly curious to think ourselves, since we are in motion.

As Democracy frames our view, differences among human beings must appear both as resources for an enriched collective life and as barriers to the sympathy and collaboration we require for that life. If we were content to let diverse people inhabit diverse worlds, the problem would not arise; but in the democratic frame, our frame, we are bound to be frustrated in our practice by human differentiation and confused about the meaning of human equality, since we are required to observe principles that are in some fashion opposed.

Political and cultural theory in the modern era have mainly wrestled with Democracy as an equation relating "individual" and "society." Our political ideologies are, for the most part, still officially preoccupied with the problem of harmonizing social and individual interests. Questions about generic human differentiations like gender and race, the human kinds, insistently arise because these are in fact salient features in the landscape of everyday life; yet the questions are shaped to fit the familiar equation. Race, for example, appears on our horizon as an issue for the two main given reasons that (1) racial stereotypes are a hindrance to fair dealing with *individuals,* or (2) there is (or isn't) a compelling *social* interest in removing racial discrimination to assure race-blind equality, that is, equal participation by individuals in the society. So it goes too for age, ethnicity, creed, and socioeconomic class.

One reason that gender is an especially accessible theme for an inquiry into human kinds is that it is more resistant than any other generic human identity to this reduction of the diversity issue into individual versus society terms. Race and other group identities are similarly resistant *within* the thinking of a self-affirming minority, and to a lesser extent in the majority that realizes it has to deal with that minority; but gender identity, linked to the virtually universal division of sex, organizes everyone's life in obvious and deeply felt ways, so that here the experience of participating in a human differentiation is typically profound—more profound even than the experience of being young or grown-up or old, since gender identity's hold on us is nearly life-long.

Gender is a super-familiar aspect of our life, yet it is the worst of our perplexities insofar as it intrudes on the democratic project as a dark spot. It stands apart from the "people" as a sub-universal, a partiality, not the definitive locus of the "common"; on the other hand, it stands apart from the person as a "type," compromising individual authenticity. Thus it can seem to block fulfillment on both of Democracy's fronts. If we regard it in this light, we are bound to want the nullification of gender. The converse point is that anyone who wants to be able to affirm gender after reflection must discover how gender does, after all, advance communion and individualization.

I foresee that the question underlying all others in our investigation will be whether the infinitizing program of Democracy can be reconciled with the essential limiting implications of human kinds.

Chapter 1

The Two Sides of Gender Thinking

Gender thinking in Western culture runs in two quite different channels, which I propose to call positive and critical. Positive gender thinking both assumes and trades on what it takes to be an apprehensible differentiation of human character by sex. It might do this in a crude and popular way ("Boys will be boys") or in a finely elaborated or exceptional way. Goethe's line at the end of *Faust*, "The Eternal Feminine draws us on," is an extreme form of the positive thought of gender: while it embodies a great deal of reflection and abstraction and belongs to a larger gesture of moral dissatisfaction with the workings of the actual gender system, it nevertheless subjects itself and us to an experience of feminine qualities. Critical gender thinking means to withdraw from this sort of subjection. It moves in a conceptual space in which the relation between humanity or personhood, on the one hand, and gender qualities, on the other, is contingent and alterable. Perhaps close examination reveals impurity in most specimens of the critical and positive approaches; would-be critics of gender may very well continue to trade unconsciously on their participation in gender, while celebrations of gender may ring hollowly, critical detachment lurking within them or in their implications. Still we recognize the opposed principles.

The antagonism between the two kinds of gender thinking gets represented, both confusingly and tellingly, as the question of the

5

"naturalness" of gender. For the positive thought, gender is not so much a natural fact as a transcendental structure, a hinge on which life turns at any given moment rather than an alterable arrangement in life. Gender critics dwell on the variability in gender systems as a proof that no particular form of gender is "natural," meaning necessary. But the positive thought is not committed to the view that women and men eternally match their gender-system portraits (though one can make this rash assertion) or to denying that a particular set of gender ground rules can change; it requires only that gender be acknowledged at any given moment as a structure enabling us to encounter each other and negotiate with each other. In other words, it requires that we be subjected to gender. The critical thought requires that we not be.

Often the kind of thinking I call positive is seen as something less than authentic thinking. Consider this assertion by Michel Foucault: "Thought is not what inhabits a certain conduct and gives it meaning; rather, it is what allows one to step back from this way of acting or reacting, to present it to oneself as an object of thought and question it as to its meaning, its condition, and its goals. Thought is freedom in relation to what one does, the motion by which one detaches oneself from it, establishes it as an object, and reflects on it as a problem."[1] Now thought assuredly *does* inhabit and inform some certain conduct, in every case; nevertheless, Foucault is right to say that it must amount to more than simple indwelling of conduct, for in thought there is always something of gazing, which assumes a step back, and a questioning posture. We find such "objectivity" and curiosity in positive gender thinking. But the freedom in this thinking (without which it would not be thought) is not freedom *from* gender, not "detachment," but rather a free play *in* and *of* gendered conduct. There is a job of determining gender to do, even if it is not the determination whether to be gendered. Questioning is not always doubting.

Positive gender thinking

I will draw on some well-known writings to illustrate the forms and complexities of positive gender thinking that are of greatest continuing importance for us. They will also remind us of the depreciation of the feminine that has characterized our culture.

Concerning the fictional evidence, I would suggest prefatorily that artistic specimens of gender thinking are always ambiguous with respect to the positive–critical distinction. They are typically positive inasmuch as the attractions and norms of gender contribute powerfully to their felt liveliness and truth. At the same time, they are always at least latently critical just because they are artificial and free rearrangements of life's elements—whether or not they take advantage of their opportunity to pull our minds away from what we take for granted.

The shape of men's and women's lives: Homer

The strong-armed men and fragrant-breasted women of Homer's *Iliad* inhabit the first dimension of gender, a division of human excellences by sex in which there is implicit confidence that individuals are fulfilled in their gendered forms. We go deeper into gender when we hold up for contemplation a difference in the overall shapes of women's and men's lives. For example, when Hector reminds Andromache of the separate fates of the sexes in war (*Iliad* 6:370–500), we are given a sense of what the two situations are *like*. It is also suggested that the woman and the man are differently sensitive to their situations, and (in part) why that is: Hector notes that he has "learned how to be brave, how to go forward always and to contend for honor," so that he feels shame at the thought of avoiding battle (6:441–46); and when he takes off his chief insignia, the flashing war helm, to quiet his baby, we are made to feel that the martial personality is a layer of his self.

The notion of men's masculinity and women's femininity may be hinted at in the extraordinary scene just mentioned, but it rears its head unmistakably in cross-sex comparison. It is only meaningful to say that a man is a man-like person if the possibility needs to be ruled out that he is, exceptionally or wrongly (at some distance from what we take for granted about him or want from him), a woman-like person. The foremost circumstance in which woman-likeness is liable to be imputed to men is war. Since a soldier's imponderable valor is of the greatest practical importance in war, it is always at issue, always subject to challenge, and so the cross-sex judgment most certain to be made is the old taunt that one's enemies or unreliable friends are "women," nonfighters, at heart.[2] Homer, whose vocabulary for male worth does not include *manliness,* does have Achilles speak a memorable version of the womanliness reproach. The Trojans have carried the fight to the Greeks' ships, and Patroclus comes to plead with Achilles for help, "streaming warm tears":

> Achilles watched him come, and felt a pang for him.
> Then the great prince and runner said:

> "Patroclus,
> why all the weeping? Like a small girlchild
> who runs beside her mother and cries and cries
> to be taken up, and catches at her gown,
> and will not let her go, looking up in tears
> until she has her wish: that's how you seem,
> Patroclus, winking out your glimmering tears."[3]

The insult is artfully elaborate. Even the most rudimentary woman taunt is artful in the sense that it feigns a judgment to make a point analogically; one doesn't believe that the male object of the remark may actually be a woman. (For that matter, one doesn't have to believe that women are necessarily weak or irresolute to use a womanlikeness convention.) But Achilles carries the feigning to an extreme by shrinking "woman" to "small girlchild" and giving the girl's image such a degree of poetic reality—so much, in fact, that we enter sympathetically into the two human conditions of wishfulness, that of the girl and that of Patroclus. Patroclus is, after all, Achilles' dear friend, as the tenderness of the simile makes us feel. It is Achilles' own pang that sets it in motion and causes Achilles himself to appear within the simile as a mother.[4]

A crucial variable is seriousness. The woman taunt is never serious about women, though it may become a serious criticism of a man. It is not a serious psychology in the sense that it pretends to capture something essential in a person's identity. Achilles is not remarking a "feminine trait" in Patroclus; still less does he worry about "effeminacy." The girl simile is ad hoc. Homer is playing with neglected resemblances among human beings and situations, perhaps to intensify the feeling of strangeness or uncertainty in a situation, or perhaps to redefine a situation in a fresh, more forceful way (as the *Odyssey*'s cross-sex descriptions of Penelope help to convey the special quality of her relationship with Odysseus);[5] yet there is no commitment to a conception of anyone's enduring nature. The same approach runs through the tradition of sex-reversal comedies.[6] We notice by contrast, however, the more serious descriptive pretentions of the statements about a man's "feminine delicacy" or a woman's "masculine forthrightness," and so on, that seem to abound especially in nineteenth-century writing.

The girlchild simile is polyvalent in reference as well as equivocal in tone. Man-confronting-femalelikeness is not the only structure summoned up in this passage. We are equally aware of adulthood facing childhood (for the girlchild makes us think of the young in general) and power facing weakness, or possession facing petition. Achilles' simile captures what it is for Patroclus to be in the position of the entreater. But in this gender system, the overlap of "child" and "entreater" with "female" is not accidental. As Hector's speech to Andromache reminded us earlier, females are understood to occupy a vulnerable and dependent position. The connection can be made in either direction: females can be expected to weep and plead because that behavior accords with their position; at the same time, femaleness is the apt reference of a simile that would describe a man in that position. (And a woman who acts independently can be credited with a "masculine mind.")[7]

Ethical gender prescription: Paul

Ethical and legal language is more serious and univocal because it wants to prescribe specific behaviors for classifiable persons and situations. Ideally, it is not ad hoc. In tailoring its mandates to the different lives of women and men, it contributes to the formation of an explicitly normative version of the thought of gender whenever it relates its ordering of behavior to character. The biblical book of Proverbs, for instance, goes beyond the purely outward sexual discrimination of the ancient Torah laws by telling women in particular to be "gracious" and not "contentious or fretful" (11:16, 21:19), men not to be "violent" or "wrathful" (16:29, 22:24).[8] (The normative vision of woman as man's gracious companion then supports the feminine personification of peaceful, hospitable Wisdom [9:1–6].) Generalizations about woman's and man's nature and propositions like "Frailty, thy name is woman" (whether sincerely or ironically advanced) all come in the train of the ethical gender thought.

Paul, the New Testament writer, presents the Bible's most reasoned gender legislation in his first letter to the Corinthians. He is evidently disturbed by sex-role innovations in the new Christian communities.

I want you to understand that the head of every man is Christ, the head of a woman is her husband, and the head of Christ is God. Any man who prays or prophesies with his head covered dishonors his head, but any woman who prays or prophesies with her head unveiled dishonors her head—it is the same as if her head were shaven. For if a woman will not veil herself, then she should cut off her hair; but if it is disgraceful for a woman to be shorn or shaven, let her wear a veil. For a man ought not to cover his head, since he is the image and glory of God; but woman is the glory of man. (For man was not made from woman, but woman from man. Neither was man created for woman, but woman for man.) . . . Does not nature itself teach you that for a man to wear long hair is degrading to him, but if a woman has long hair, it is her pride? For her hair is given to her for a covering. (1 Cor. 11:3–9, 14–15)

We know we are in the ethical realm because of the words *dishonor, disgrace,* and *degrade;* and all are given sex-specific application. But what is most interesting to us here is Paul's attempt to represent a foundation for these norms. Before nature is called in as our teacher—that is, before Paul appeals to a direct apprehension of gender qualities—a couple of tenuous theological arguments try to rationalize women's subordination. There is a play on *head* that suggests that the open display of the human head might fittingly symbolize a dominant social position. In working out the symbolism, are we to take it as a bare positive fact that women are subordinate to men? No, the fact is not bare; one can read in it a meaning put in with the order of humanity's creation. (This reading does not recognize that the woman of Genesis is created as the man's companion, not his subordinate, and that the husband's rule over the wife belongs to the curse and to sin [Gen. 3:16], not to creation.)[9]

Paul's thought seems thoroughly twisted. Whereas in real life it is women who give birth, we say that in the beginning man gave birth to woman; woman, made from man, is "man's glory," and man, made from dust, is "God's glory," hence woman is the glory of God's glory—apparently a doubled cause of rejoicing—yet she is of lower rank *for this reason;* the token of woman's inferiority and normative modesty, her long hair, is called her pride. Only one of these twists is Paul's own invention, but no matter where they originate, they all bear witness to the extraordinary leverage of the gender thought, "what nature itself teaches," which dictates how to read religious texts, how to link premises in an argument, and how to talk about everyday experience. For the propriety of longer hair and modesty for women, and of shorter hair and public prominence for men, is among the first of givens for Paul. He works from it toward a reasoned view, so that his reasonings are, now in a different sense, profoundly ad hoc. Although he puts this nature-talk in tension with a higher perspective—"Nevertheless . . . all things are from God" (1 Cor. 11:11–12), "In Christ there is neither male nor female" (Gal. 3:28)—he is not, and does not pretend or want to be, free of the natural presupposition about gender. That is not a peculiarity of Paul's; it is characteristic of positive gender thinking, sometimes jarringly so when an ethical or legal or (we can now say) theological context calls for argumentation to justify it.

I have put the gender ideology of 1 Corinthians 11 in an unfavorable light, but the possibility exists that this sort of reasoning, which is really about what Paul feels to be natural, could justly represent a human reality to which Paul's feeling responds. Perhaps the contradictions in the reasoning trace complexities in the reality. It has often been true, after all, that women's activity has depended on male sponsorship, that only male-mediated value has accrued to women and that women have been self-defeatingly proud of their tokens of subjection.

Spiritual gender: Proust

After the seriousness and practicality of Paul, we return in Marcel Proust's *Remembrance of Things Past* to an imaginary world where we might expect playfulness and irony to leaven gender judgments. But we have also moved forward to an age marked by an obsession with sexuality as the secret of personal identity.[10] Gender imagining is affected.

> One might have thought that it was Mme. de Marsantes who was entering the room, so salient at that moment was the woman whom a mistake on the part of Nature had enshrined in the body of M. de Charlus. Of course the Baron had made every effort to conceal this mistake and to assume a masculine appearance. But no sooner had he succeeded than, having meanwhile retained the same tastes, he acquired from this habit of feeling like a woman a new feminine appearance, due not to heredity but to his own way of living. . . .
>
> Although other reasons may have dictated this transformation of M. de Charlus, and purely physical ferments may have set his chemistry "working" and made his body gradually change into the category of women's bodies, nevertheless the change that we record here was of spiritual origin. By dint of thinking tenderly

of men one becomes a woman, and an imaginary skirt hampers one's movements.[11]

The thought directing Proust's description of M. de Charlus is that a person inwardly *is* a gender specimen—not *like* women or men in some action or situation, not female or male simply by virtue of possessing a female or male body, but *substantially,* "spiritually." If Homer stands at one end of the range of positive gender thinking, where men are men and women are women, with varying degrees of intensity, linked sometimes by resemblances; and if Paul stands at the ethically troubled midpoint where one has to reckon with the fact that women can wrongly act like men, and vice versa; then Proust stands at the other extreme, a postethical position where it is again true that men are men and women are women, but in a "spiritual" sense, so that the male or female body has become a metaphor of personal identity rather than its literal presence.

In this version of the thought of gender, we do not have the kind of solidarity with "what nature itself teaches" that Paul presumed on. M. de Charlus's gender is Nature's mistake. But he is, for all that, a creature of Nature, one who is true to his own unfortunate nature rather than one who errs by defying Nature. Paul would have blamed Charlus for choosing to think tenderly of men, but Proust removes his character from the reach of that criticism—"Nature's mistake" began, no doubt, with the tender thinking. Now, in any case, it is a gender fait accompli. Charlus's "spiritual" identity is as much a posit of the thought of gender as the norms for which Paul spoke: it follows from the premise that gender qualifies my true selfhood that I might, in an exceptional case, find myself in a body of inappropriate sex. Thus, having taken flight in the cross-sex comparison of the woman taunt, gender description now comes home to roost in the cross-sex *being* of the woman, M. de Charlus.

The thought of gender becomes most difficult at this point. If Charlus *is* not a man, how can "he" *be* a woman? We shrink from saying this; we would prefer to say that "he," or perhaps the gender-transcending "person," is *like* a woman, but Proust means precisely to rule out these less disturbing possibilities. Womanhood goes all the way down. Is "woman" then a kind of person that is usually, though not invariably, found inhabiting female bodies, exhibiting her nature through them? Is womanhood constituted by liking men? If so, does "men" refer to "physical" men, or more properly to "spiritual" men? It would seem more consistent to say "spiritual" men, yet Charlus's erotic attention is captivated entirely by male bodies. The entanglement of gender with what we nowadays call sexual orientation is easy to see, though hard to understand. Trying to get to the bottom of it, Proust's contemporary, Freud, starts an inevitably tortuous and inconclusive line of theorizing about identification and "object choice."

Critical gender thinking

When we turn to Paul's other gender proposition, "In Christ there is neither male nor female," we see that the notion of a separate spirit world or "resurrection" has opened a conceptual space in which gender might qualify no one. The same possibility is indicated also in Jesus' claim that women do not marry in heaven (Matt. 22:30). But to think of gender as a condition from which humans might be separated is to adopt an entirely different intellectual relation to it.

Since positive gender thinking predominantly shows up in our written record as thinking about *women* and *the feminine*—because men have done most of the writing, because we could expect men to sit more comfortably in a gender system that confirms the social restriction of women, and possibly because of something about the structure of gender itself—it is not surprising that the pioneers of critical gender thinking are mainly women, to whom we shall now turn for guiding examples.

Wollstonecraft's appeal to virtue

Especially fertile soil was prepared for the critical thought of gender in the eighteenth century with an increase of attention to the distinction between "nature" and "society" or "culture." This created a framework in which "masculine" and "feminine" could be interpreted as products of education and critically peeled away from the "human nature" and "reason" in which truth and value were anchored. At the same time, however, the rise of humanitarianism and the cult of sentiment brought a certain movement toward parity in the valuation of masculine and feminine, whence arose the rival Romantic thought that women's humanity, *as* feminine, is in principle as original, authentic, and worthy as men's, if not more so.[12]

The classic Enlightenment expression of critical gender thinking

is Mary Wollstonecraft's *Vindication of the Rights of Woman* (1792).[13]
She hits the nerve, the ethical gender distinction, by attacking "preju-
dices that give a sex to virtue" (11). The unity of virtue, she argues,
is grounded in the principle of "humanity," or, in religious language,
"soul": "Yet it should seem, allowing [women] to have souls, that there
is but one way appointed by Providence to lead *mankind* to either
virtue or happiness" (19). If humans are distinguished from brutes
by reason and reason-based virtue, and if the character of women be
found deficient or deviant in these respects (we note that the "frail,"
"fascinating" sex is defined into such a position), then it must be
allowed either that women are not entirely human or that a false system
of education has kept them from realizing their humanity. Wollstonecraft's argument succeeds in proportion to her audience's unwilling-
ness to say right out that women are less than human. Her trump card
is the principle that any human being must be maimed by the lack of
any genuinely important human excellence.

Rationality and virtue are linked, for Wollstonecraft, with strong
individuality. Persons who cannot judge opinion and fashion with
critical independence cannot be virtuous; therefore, a social institution that is unduly detrimental to individuality cannot be accepted. In
the following passage she talks of "profession," but bear in mind that
genders resolve into "professions" on her analysis.

> It is of great importance to observe that the character of every
> man is, in some degree, formed by his profession. A man of sense
> may only have a cast of countenance that wears off as you trace
> his individuality, whilst the weak, common man has scarcely ever
> any character, but what belongs to the body; at least, all his opin-
> ions have been so steeped in the vat consecrated by authority, that
> the faint spirit which the grape of his own vine yields cannot be
> distinguished.
>
> Society, therefore, as it becomes more enlightened, should
> be very careful not to establish bodies of men who must neces-
> sarily be made foolish or vicious by the very constitution of their
> profession. (18)

Shrewdly, Wollstonecraft makes it appear that the military profession
(nearer to embodying the essence of masculinity than any other social
position) is terribly enfeebling in just this manner, indeed, that it promotes follies and vices much like those associated with femininity (17,
23–24).

Wollstonecraft's wide-ranging account of the social distortions of human nature is necessary not only to dramatize the issue of virtue but to make credible the premise that genders are social artifacts rather than immutable essences. For example, by explaining in her seventh chapter how real women do and do not participate in the virtue of modesty according to their social experience, she exposes the hollowness of the "feminine modesty" stereotype.

The most substantial objection to Wollstonecraft is to fault her for being insufficiently critical of gender bias in the dominant norms of reason and virtue that she accepts, that she even cheerfully acknowledges to be masculine in token of the fact that society has given males a privileged relation to them. Instead, it might be claimed, we need a redrawing of the gender map in such a way that neither gender is dehumanized. Perhaps a rehabilitation of the feminine can go hand in hand with Enlightenment humanism: the latter-day androgyny ideal, which tries to combine critical freedom from gender with normative investment in it, expresses Wollstonecraft's principle that nothing humanly good can be held alien to any human de jure. Undercutting this move, however, there will be a further development of Wollstonecraft's suspicions of a basic inhumanity in the principle of gender, as we shall see presently.

In the nineteenth century, speculation and polemic are joined by theories based on methodical observation of human behavior. The social sciences come on the scene as interpreters of the dislocations brought on by Western industrialization and imperialism. The concepts of "roles," then "sex roles," and finally "gender" (as an analogue to "class" in Marxian social analysis) are all introduced as theoretical reflections of women's and men's experience of ever increasing variability.[14] (Think how the word *role* typically appears in phrases like "the changing role of X.") Gendering is more consistently interpreted as a "cultural" process, that is, a cultivation of human "nature" determined by the vicissitudes of early childhood or the customs of one's community; or as a "social" artifact, that is, a purely conventional formation of plastic humanity. Psychology investigates a postulated "mental difference" between the sexes and later comes to appraise feminine and masculine personality traits in both men and women as resources for effective function and happiness, even recommending an androgynous mix of such traits.[15] (In this last instance we circle back to the positive ethical thought of gender, albeit with revised content.)

Then, most momentously, feminism's explicitly partisan gender critique appears in the form of something like a discipline, enabling a systematic questioning of the premises of knowing and valuing as well as of the phenomena of gender. From this new feminism, which with unprecedented insight knows itself to be embroiled in the problematic actuality of gender, we draw the most penetrating expressions of critical gender thinking.

Critical gender thinking today: three theses

What drives the feminist gender critique is not simply having noticed the gender system's structure, but having suffered from it. Whether gender is really harmful is the sharp question that makes our inquiry urgent; it also constrains us, if we do not begin with the vision that arises from the experience of being harmed, to enter into it as far as we can. That actual gender systems have functioned oppressively, and still do, is past doubt, but whether the evil is rooted in the principle of gender itself rather than in other sources of evil corrupting it is a uniquely painful question *for we who are* (happily or unhappily) *gendered*.

Critical discussion of gender typically depends on the ground-clearing proposition that genders are not natural facts but "arbitrary" social constructions. *Arbitrary* is a loaded word, connoting lack of rhyme and reason, and sometimes these overtones are rendered explicit, as by Sandra Bem: "Largely as a result of historical accident, the culture has clustered a quite heterogeneous collection of attributes into two mutually exclusive categories, each category considered both more characteristic of and more desirable for one or the other of the two sexes."[16] Other gender critics might not think that the genders are so accidental and heterogeneous but would still call gender formation arbitrary in the sense that it transcends the constraint of physical facts. Thus the *Arbitrariness Thesis* minimally claims that gender is produced, at least in crucial part, by our own choices that could be made differently. But perhaps this is not so controversial a point. Even Paul admits that people can vary their choosing with respect to gender. Fuller-blooded versions of the Arbitrariness Thesis would be that we can *just as well* choose different gender schemes than the one we inhabit, or that we can *just as well* choose not to care about gender at all. The "just as well" condition refers, at one level, to practical possibility and facility—as when Margaret Mead concludes in *Sex and Temperament in Three Primitive Societies* that "men and women are capable of being moulded to a single pattern as easily as to a diverse one"[17]—and, at another level, to the issue of goodness. Humans are claimed to be free in this respect *from* practical constraint and *for* an equally worthwhile or better life on different terms. When we think of it as containing all of these dimensions, we see that the Arbitrariness Thesis is virtually a direct expression of the critical perspective on gender.

As far as the Arbitrariness Thesis goes, we might be fortunate enough to live in the best of all possible gender worlds. The thesis takes on greater consequence, of course, if we are unhappy with gender, because it opens the way to amelioration. If this gate were not open we would be pressed only into despair, not into constructive action, by two further theses that set us at odds with gender.

The most general cautionary claim, the claim that gender is harmful to whoever is gendered, I shall call the *Impairment Thesis*. It was there in Wollstonecraft, but now a Dinnerstein can sweepingly assert that our "bodily complementarity . . . works to maim us" under the gender system. "Traditionally, it has carried with it a social and psychological complementarity, a division of responsibility for basic human concerns, a compartmentalization of sensibility, that makes each sex in its own way sub-human."[18] This thesis is not merely an objection to a particular gender culture; it applies to virtually any arrangement that we would call gender.[19] It especially contests the belief or assumption that individuals are fulfilled through gender. The great assumption that the Impairment Thesis makes, in turn, is that, as regards the qualities affected by gendering, completeness in the human individual means the same as human completeness realized in community—that any "division of responsibility for basic human concerns" would make individuals "sub-human." The individual is judged as the human microcosm.

A variation of the Impairment Thesis holds that genders are cultural standards that prevent our realizing (in practice or in knowledge) a much wider range and greater complexity of desires, perspectives, and styles. Here it is human diversity rather than common humanity that is the casualty of gender.[20]

The *Asymmetry Thesis* is the view that the essential purpose of a gender system is to devalue and constrain members of one human kind, with reference to sex, in such a way as to maintain the members of another human kind in a superior position. A gender system is a power differential, and the core of each discriminated gender is its power advantage or disadvantage. One supposes that a system of domination is harmful to everyone in some way, that it must stunt the communal life,

and so one interprets asymmetry as a form of general human impairment; but the main point of the Asymmetry Thesis is that one gender
is worse off than another. Sandra Harding writes:

> [An] inadequate conception of gender involves the assumption
> that masculine and feminine are simply partial but combinable
> expressions of human symbol systems, ways of dividing social
> labor, and individual identities and behaviors. Many feminist crit-
> ics seem to say that it is possible to strip away the undesirable
> aspects of masculinity and femininity and thus arrive at attractive
> cores which, while partial, are morally and politically symmetri-
> cal. But femininity and masculinity are not so easily combined;
> central to the notion of masculinity is its rejection of everything
> that is defined by a culture as feminine and its legitimated control
> of whatever counts as the feminine. . . . Femininity is consti-
> tuted to absorb everything defined as not masculine, and always
> to acquiesce in domination by the masculine. . . . Gender is an
> *asymmetrical* category of human thought, social organization, and
> individual identity and behavior.[21]

Harding's mode of critique opens up the question of how the
meaning of a gender gets constituted. On this account, the gender
system is really a masculinity system, a project of masculine self-
distinction. The feminine has no power or value of its own; it consists only of whatever masculine beings can dominate. (If, on the other
hand, an original feminine reality does exist, then masculinity derives
its own meaning from the feminine parasitically, *construing* the feminine as the Other and the to-be-ruled so that the masculine can be
the Same and the ruler.)[22] A further question is whether, if a gender
really is constituted by some such operation, positive gender thinking
is oblivious of this or is aware of it in its own way.

The terms of the Asymmetry Thesis prove that gender egali-
tarianism is an important part of contemporary gender thinking. It
introduces us to the problem of measuring "equality" and "symmetry."
What if genders *value* differently—then, mustn't we see "asymmetry"
between them whenever we look from one to the other? Or is there a
transgender point of view from which the judgment of asymmetry can
be made neutrally? What is "desirable," as Harding confirms in passing,
is set by the feminist project, but where are the valuational grounds of
that project if not in a gender?

Social science wants value to be a neutral category, but critical study of gender runs into the double problem that its object is a deep fissure in the realm of valuing and that the criteria of study might themselves be gendered. Let us illustrate the problem from ethnology. Sherry Ortner and Harriet Whitehead conclude from their survey of research that gender systems typically have the prime function of locating persons "in a hierarchical scheme of culturally ordered prestige," where "prestige" itself is a male or male-centered concern.

> The tendency to define women relationally, in turn, must be seen as a reflex of their exclusion from—yet crucial linkages with—the world of male prestige. If it were simply a matter of there being two parallel value-equivalent domains—domestic and public, female and male—then the categories of womanhood might appear as parallel to the categories of manhood. Women might be described, for example, primarily as "childtenders" or as "hostesses," categories derived from their primary activities or role performances in their (domestic) domain. In fact, however, the categories of femaleness are not generated in terms of some sort of abstract symmetry with masculinity, but in terms of women's relationships with men, and terms of the relevance of those relationships to male prestige.[23]

Insofar as value means prestige, then masculinity and femininity are unequally valued. On a prestige scale, symmetry would mean equal access to individual distinction. But femininity is precisely a different, more "relational" scale. Hence we face the riddle: How is it possible to determine whether feminine value is as humanly important and fulfilling as masculine value or instead is just what women generally have to settle for, *faute de mieux,* under male domination? Is *asymmetry* only a biased word for difference, or is *difference* only a euphemism for asymmetry? Is a critic of femininity a mislocated masculine thinker or a true witness to a feminine (or human) predicament?

Implications for our study

The thought of gender stands shakily poised today between, on the one hand, a positive conception that responds to what it takes to be masculine and feminine with unprecedented sympathy and fairness—

fostering the historical illusion that people have always felt and talked thus—and, on the other hand, a critical conception that makes possible a more thorough exposure of our gender system's unfairness and harmfulness than it has ever received, with profound alienation from gender as a consequence. Both ways of thinking have now appropriated the term *gender*, so that the dividedness of our mind, a pivotal uncertainty about how to identify ourselves, inhabits this word.

Both ideas of gender are hostage to a set of facts, to how people actually are perceived and valued under such aspects as feminine and masculine in various real and imaginary settings. Without these facts, or a selection of them, gender thinking would lack content and orientation. But each idea is truly a conception, not a mere perception or reaction, and so each embodies a general principle that can be confronted with the facts. Each can be thought disingenuously, or confusedly.

If we seriously consider the possibility that gender is at bottom a phenomenon of impairment, domination, and dissimulation, a cause rather than a casualty of wrong, then we must hold up to our human-kinds inquiry the warning that any reading of gender into human nature might amount to collaboration in an enormous evil, rationalizing it or masking it. But there is an opposite pitfall. If we fail to trace the implications of gender all the way into human nature, we may thereby fail to understand the thing whose harmfulness we fear. The critical theses should not stop us from thinking out the meanings of gender in its traditionally stipulated givenness.

Regarded critically, gender is (in Foucauldian terms) a "discursive practice" or "regime" or "discipline" that is of fundamental importance in giving our life, our historically determinate configuration of "power," its basic character. Gender is to be contemplated as one of the largest and least escapable contours of meaning in human life, functioning more as a justifier than as a thing for which justification could meaningfully be requested. It takes an extraordinary act of distancing to put gender in question; one can even reasonably express skepticism about the feasibility of the move and expect to embarrass gender critics with the counter-question, How then do you suppose you value? (At the very least, thanks to the historical and cultural diversity that can be surveyed, one can make the critical move to the extent of recording the plurality and contingency of cultural forms.) The positive philosophical alternative to the critical view accords to gender the same fundamental structural role but calls it a *spirit*—that is, records its givenness as an in-principle validity, a norm norming, a priceless and imperious solution to the problem of community—and endeavors to think through its relations with other spirits and its practical consequences. Philosophical pneumatology stands to be embarrassed, for its part, whenever outsiders succeed in sustaining the sort of critical objection that unmasks a line of thought as the ideological cloak of an alterable practice.

The relationship between the positive and critical perspectives has important implications for our study of gender thinking:

1. We must sometimes suspend questions such as Are people really like that? and Does the system really work that way? while we elucidate the claims and presuppositions and consequences of positive gender thinking as we observe it in our culture. Of course it belongs to the positive idea of gender that "people really are like that," in some sense, and that "it really works that way," in some fashion; gender isn't thought to be either an arbitrary choice of lifestyles or a scam. We need to be able to register this thought without binding ourselves to it inescapably. Then again, human beings just are, in part, what they think; gender is a reality just in the existence of gender thinking, and we become qualified by gender to the extent that we let it live in our thoughts. A critic has reason to fear that we are playing with a dangerous drug.

2. In order not to fall too deeply into a gender dream, we need to rouse ourselves by asking skeptical questions about fact and necessity and value, appealing to criteria that are as independent of gender presuppositions as we can make them. But at the same time we need to keep critical distance from objections to the gender system by asking, Must gender be objectionable in that way?

3. We ought not to overestimate our objectivity. Gender thinking (both affirming and negating) is already running through us insofar as we are gendered or suffering from gender. We dare not pretend otherwise. The principal vantage point from which we take a critical perspective on gender is the category of the human, but the meaning of the human—according to gender thinking, which seems irrefutable on this point—is always qualified by gender. If humanity and gender really are tied in a Gordian knot, and if we are the knot rather than some sword-wielding Alexander, then we will have to learn to live with something less than a crystal-clear division of humanity's and gender's regimes.

4. Since we are thinking in the midst of a struggle between rival

interpretations of the human and are caught up not only in the democratic project but in a mixture of spirits that guide our judgments, any
claim made about gender and any inference drawn from reflections on
it will express and reinforce a certain politico-cultural direction. It is
obvious enough that ideas have consequences in life; what is equally
important to bear in mind is that ideas are themselves consequences of
how we are living.

In thinking, especially in philosophy, we fancy ourselves naviga-
tors on a calm and spacious sea, our questions and data surrounding
us on an infinite shoreline. But human thought is not a calm sea, it is
a river; in the river there are strong currents, and rapids; and in the
rapids there are big rocks that split the stream—all of which makes
some of our questions loom importantly but also cuts down our freedom to maneuver. Nowhere can the rush of circumstance be felt more
sharply than in thinking about gender. Gender theory is whitewater
philosophy. As, for instance, abortion-rights and fetal-rights proponents are swept today into different channels of valuation, each party
almost unable to hear the other, so too (in the deeper development)
the critique of gender has drawn away from ordinary gender thinking.
We can try to skip nimbly and understandingly between currents, and
we are bound to try to get an overview of the whole intellectual prospect, but we should realize that when we come down from questioning
into answering we must land in one current among several, having its
own history and its own meaning for everyone's future.

Insofar as we learn how to handle the difficulties of gender theory,
we should be able to handle ourselves better in other anthropological
rapids like the theories of race, ethnicity, culture, class, age, temperament, and sexual orientation. In all these domains, visions of essential,
fulfilling, and fair human complementarity clash with claims of arbitrariness, impairment, and asymmetry.

Is the thought not reassuring that all currents do, after all, belong
to one great flow through one great frame, Democracy? And that we
have the means of handling our questions in such a way that they can
be seen to concern everyone, namely, the category of human nature?
Thus do we stay within reach of each other even as we are pulled apart.

Chapter 2

On Conceiving the Human

Questions about gender have very different weights and implications depending on the intellectual context in which we ask them. Gender in linguistics is one thing, in sociology another, in a beer commercial something else. This chapter defines the context in which gender questions have the greatest *theoretical* importance, the context I propose for our thinking. It is traditionally called philosophical anthropology. The shape that our curiosity takes, in the frame of philosophical anthropology, is: How does gender pertain to human nature? How would such a thing as gender be involved in the most profoundly definitive shaping of our lives?

The presumption that one can make significant assertions about human nature requires explanation and defense. To this end, an analysis of the concepts of the human and the natural is carried out. The analysis yields two findings that structure the whole sequel. First, humanity is a generic nature that stands in two chains of mutually qualifying categories, one physical (which includes sex) and the other intentional (which includes gender). Second, for the purposes of philosophical anthropology there are four different important meanings of *natural*. What is claimed to be natural for us might be that which we have received as an *endowment,* an unalterable starting-point for human life; it might be a reliable *consistency* in human conduct or experience; it might be our optimal condition, our *métier;* or it might be a larger *harmony* of coexistents in which we are involved. And this implies that gender might pertain to human nature in four different ways (to be discussed in Chapters 3 through 6).

The "human"

We are asking what it means to be human, in the respect that one is or may be a certain kind of human being, especially in relation to sex. The charm of this pursuit is that it cultivates our self-acquaintance; we will be able to declare ourselves; we will bring forth an anthropology. The hitch in it is that we will be unable finally to determine what sort of being we are.

We cannot *see* what we are because, as the ones who see, we are at the wrong end of the line of sight running from seer to seen. Nor can the problem be solved by mirroring, for when I look at myself in a mirror I see what I look like rather than what I see like. The mirror experience is fascinating, certainly, because it takes me right up to the edge of seeing myself seeing, fudges an approximation of this, a kind of *Doppelgänger* experience, but it never quite delivers myself.

We cannot *say* or pass judgment on what we are, because we are ourselves the grounds of judgment. By analogy, the drafters of a national constitution cannot decide whether or not a suggested provision is constitutional, since constitutionality does not exist before they make their determination. And their constitution can always be overthrown or amended for extraconstitutional reasons. Now we may discover a superior constitution, as it were, to judge ourselves by, some divine or cosmic standard, but we cannot stand apart from our own act of constituting that standard as superior.

Most perplexing of all, we cannot even *be* what we are, because in raising real questions about ourselves—and if we are really questioning, then we are bound to suppose that our questions are real—we are opening ourselves up to novel determinations. In reinterpretation we must change, since interpretation is not just about us but is us; but this means that we can never catch up with ourselves. Questioners cannot have a fixed nature. But in spite of that condition, or because of it, we cannot keep from relating ourselves to the horizon of thinkability, the "Absolute," which in surpassing us tells us what our limits are. Since we take part in the surpassing by thinking that very thought, we must read ourselves as "image of God" or "shepherd of Being," distending our identity toward a transcendent First or Highest.

All such limitations inhere in the structure of inquiry. If we were to escape them, we would no longer be anything like human beings, and there would be no more discourse on the human.

That we can have no fully adequate awareness or definitive construal of ourselves does not mean, however, that there is nothing to be learned by asking about human nature or that we can keep from asking. There are observable human phenomena that give definite shape to our openness, and there are conclusions about human existence that must be thought out just to navigate from today to tomorrow. Our need for conscious orientation is such that we become paralyzed if we do not have some view of what we take to be our true capabilities and constraints. We must interpret ourselves to live, and we can no more interpret our experience without a working anthropology than a surgeon can operate without a working knowledge of anatomy.

If we are not put off by the inconclusiveness of self-interpretation, there are still other serious difficulties of principle to reckon with. The ideal "we" of "our" thinking is always subject to challenge, when some subjects believe themselves to be left out of its assumptions or presumptions; correspondingly, claims to discern the human "in general" are constantly shadowed by doubt whether one person's or community's experience is like another's or commensurate with it. It is important to recognize that any would-be reasonable discourse is an experiment that supposes the possibility of acceptable publicity, on the one hand, and accurate and useful generality, on the other. It may never pretend to succeed, only trust that it can make meaningful progress—precisely in rectifying human relationships—by trying to correct its flaws.

Granted this license, we are allowed, if not to say just anything, at least to begin.

The classic form taken by a conclusion about the sort of being we are in general is an attribution to human nature. To say that X belongs to human nature is to say that X is "how we are" in general, or that X is among the criteria by which a life or life-part is given its fullest identification as a member of the class "human." (How we play the classing game can be an important problem, but for our purposes the reference group for setting class criteria can be all members of the biological species *Homo sapiens* who are not thought by the majority of their conspecifics to be extraordinarily impaired or deprived.) We discuss human nature to strengthen our seeing-together of human beings: to appreciate individuals, it is necessary to grasp the resemblances off which their individuality plays.

Human nature is interpreted by a variety of categories. One group of categories has to do with observable shape. To know that human life is mammalian, for example, is to know a great deal about our organismic design and also patterns in our relationships and emotions. Likewise we have vertebrate, animal, living, and entitative shape. It seems that the mammal-to-entity progression of categories has less and less to do with our identity, that it concerns how we are, or the means of our existence, all that in which we "find ourselves," rather than who we are, or our end. The humanity of who we are is centrally interpeted by categories that organize us inwardly rather than outwardly. A human being is one kind of person, that is, a consciously relationship-oriented, linguistic being; and a person is one kind of intentional subject, that is, a sentient being aiming at other beings.[1]

We humans require a double definition, then, along the lines of the traditional formula "rational animal," because we come into two distinct yet (through us) mutually qualifying series of categories. The chief Western creation story introduces us in double aspect: we are made in the divine image, and we are made male and female (Gen. 1:27).[2] Whatever is true of person-as-such is true *for us* only in the way that it can be true of sexually reproducing animals; *animal,* more specifically *mammal,* names a particular field of intentional relations in which human subjects find themselves. That is the other side of the familiar point that we are a distinctively personal sort of animal.

To say we are persons is ambiguous, for we may mean by this nothing other than human persons, but then again we may be thinking of features that are relatively abstract and not specifically human, like rationality (unless we mean to think of specifically human rationality). On the other hand, when we say "human being" we may actually mean the more abstract "person." Statements purporting to be anthropological often tacitly mislead in this way. To take an example at random, Hegel once declared that the "fundamental characteristic of human nature is that man can think of himself as an ego."[3] Thus humans are distinguished from the "lower animals," as Hegel intended, but we learn nothing about what makes for a specifically human realization of self-consciousness. The anthropology is abstract. It is like saying that the fundamental characteristic of primates is that they nurse their young: this is indeed a point of fundamental importance for primates and in the absence of other mammals for comparison might well be their most striking characteristic, but it leaves out much of the heart of the primate story.

Another source of confusion is to mean by "human" only that which is the same for all humans without regard for differences among them. The legitimate purpose in this is to contemplate our commonality, but in abstracting from our differences we forget that being subject to differentiation is part of everyone's humanity. The literature of philosophical anthropology is pervasively marked by this forgetfulness.[4] Perhaps it is caused by the wish to create an ideal model of humanity as a sort of public utility—an inclusive apotheosis.

Let us give the designation of *anthropomorphism* (in an honorific sense) to the pursuit of full concreteness, the enforcing of all pertinent categories, in representing humanity. That our thinking about ourselves so often slides off into zoomorphism or theomorphism, observational biology or idealized psychology, shows that maintaining an anthropomorphic balance is not easy. (In general, positive gender thinking tries to strike a balance with respect to sex, while critical gender thinking maintains that no such balance is possible.)

*

Since it is sometimes argued that "nature" is the wrong scheme in which to display the meaning of "human"—that we ought rather to speak of a human condition or a human project—we should try to get a view of the relations among these conceptions.

"How we are," or "human nature," and "how it is with us," or "the human condition," are distinct yet mutually entangled notions. Knowing something of how we are is assumed by an insight into how matters stand with us, since we must be aware of what it is that faces a situation or what possibilities might or might not be realized in a theater of action. On the other hand, the enduring features of our situation stamp us so strongly that we cannot readily conceive ourselves apart from them. Does death pertain to human nature, or to the human condition? In which of these two categories are we speaking when we say we are mortal? (In which category were we speaking when we said, "We cannot know ourselves"?) It is impossible to choose one or the other. If we regard ourselves as capable of living in a fundamentally different situation, we become then other than human—for instance, we imagine ourselves in heaven as angels. To put the point in the most general terms: insofar as we abstract from *Homo sapiens'* emplacement in the world, separating our nature from our condition, we shift toward a wider genus than the human, such as the personal, and humanity is thought of as what happens when persons inhabit human circumstances.[5] This is not an unmeaningful idea. It conveys insight, as much as in saying, "A bat is what happens when a mammal has to fly." But there is still batness; it is *like something* to be a bat, and also to be a human; and that returns us to our more specific nature.

Among the ingredients of human nature are desires (say, appetite and our "spirited part") and capacities of awareness (the senses and the mind). Correlative with these are the ingredients of the human condition: we are given a certain array of happy and unhappy transactions to engage in, a certain array of aspects the world can wear. Taking all of this together as a living whole, we conceive a human project or perhaps a bundle of characteristic projects. What we are up to is surely the crucial revelation of what we are as well as where we are.

Whatever is generally determining for the interpretation of human life belongs to anthropology, so we must attend to human nature (as a dimension of individual beings and as a specification of being a person and being a mammal), human condition, and human project alike. But it is right to give preeminence to human nature, for in that category we inspect ourselves most directly and intimately, in our portentous obscurity. Our very intentions are drawn into what is in question about ourselves, and possibilities of imagining different kinds of human life stand only as open as they appropriately can.

The notion of "nature" is so rich and slippery, however, that we should pause to try to foresee where it can lead us if we adopt it for our self-interpretation.

"Nature"

My "nature" is what I am; my "human nature," what I and other humans commonly are. Whatness is a form of being. Our human whatness is the ideally knowable form you can match against other forms in determining whether something is or isn't one of us, or how fully or with what slant an individual represents us. Anything identifiable has a nature in this sense. When the words *I* and *you* are spoken to rip Self and Other loose from the already-woven fabric of experience, precisely to introduce new grounds of identification, then at that moment and in that aspect we have no natures; we are transcendences, holes in being. But we also always have a comprehensible aspect.

A thing's *whole* nature governs everything about it for the trivial reason that it includes everything about it; but since we never know everything about anything that is empirically actual (like ourselves), and in our own case have the extraordinary difficulties of knowledge already mentioned, we will not foolishly try to treat our nature, with its decently limited predictiveness, as an absolutely predictive essence.[6] If there are necessary implications of our conception of a thing's nature, the necessity will belong to our thinking, not to the thing we are thinking about.

Nature-as-such is all that really is, the totality of whatnesses, which we must conceive to possess some sort of internal structure or "system" of real and logical compossibility.

We did not, of course, demolish the prospect of human form in our opening arguments. Much can be seen in ourselves, without everything being seen; much can be said about us, despite the absence of a clinching judgment; and our living cannot but realize our form, even if we are continually changing it. (Still, the significance of our form's hidden aspects is never measurable.) But granting the possibility of doing anthropology, what does it matter, anyway, what we say about the form of humanity? What is at stake? Let us review the ways in which we line ourselves up in relation to what, if anything, we believe to be the form of humanity—what molecular structures are formed when the atoms of what we *mean* join with the atoms of what we think we *are*.

As endowment

We encounter our nature as an already-given involuntary factor in our lives, an origin not subject to shaping by us. Even if we think of human nature as pure creativity or an open site of radical transformations, we take that embroilment in novelty to be the involuntary horizon of our lives. The involuntary is also an invulnerability. If we can say, "We're the type that . . . ," our identity is secure, inalienable, in the given respect.

We feel, in always finding ourselves with our nature, that we have received it, and we readily speak of what we have received as an *endowment*—but this is not so small a step, because with endowments there is the issue of conservation and prudent use versus waste, and even a question of appropriate gratitude and respect for the endowing source. An endowment becomes the matter, the about-which, of piety. So far as the givenness of our nature goes, what counts is that the fundamental order of our lives is really settled in some way, and settled, one might say, all the way down, not open to significant questioning; we know that not this but other matters are to be determined by our thought and action, and that helps us decide how to point our attention. We also have a genealogical sense of who we are.

For some purposes, we trace our endowment on the slope of what comes naturally, that is, easily, to us—the fact that it is much easier to walk on our feet than our hands reads as a sign of what is natural to humans in the matter of locomotion—while for other purposes we look to what is difficult (wisdom, courage, or even walking on our hands) as most fully revealing of our given potential. Clearly, what we recognize as our endowed potential depends on what we want to do and how we are able to harmonize our efforts.

As consistency

For more direct and active self-orienting, our nature amounts to whatever we can make evident about ourselves and reliably refer to when we have to include ourselves in our calculations. The surgeon knows the anatomical part of our nature; the industrial psychologist knows how we are likely to behave under a given set of working conditions; the theater director can predict how we will react to stimuli from the stage; more deeply and indefinitely, everyone knows (up to a point) what everyone is like, for everyday purposes. Human nature is what we are able to hold, like a guide rope, or an anchor chain. It is the *consistency* of our life, what we generally expect to be possible or impossible, connected or unconnected, easy as "with the grain" or hard as against it. (From the stress on the fixed comes the equation of "nature" with "law," and from the stress on the tangible comes the use of "nature" to mean "physical nature," or "matter opposed to spirit.")

One could point out that such useful knowledge about humans always pertains to certain people rather than to humanity-as-such; and indeed many recipes cannot be exchanged between communities. But there are two reasons to go ahead and qualify what is known of "certain people" as human nature. One is that any particular person could, for all we ever know, be any other person at all, if the other were placed in the very same circumstances. The theatergoers of Peking might not react to plays as New Yorkers do, but they very probably would if they had been raised in New York by New Yorkers. A second reason is this. When we cross community lines and have to guess how to deal with strangers, we operate by two rules—to expect them to be different from the sort of people we know, and to expect them to be basically our own sort of being. The second rule reflects a presumption that community with the strangers can, should, and will be realized, and the first is subordinate to the second inasmuch as we are sensitive to difference *for the sake of* making any adaptations that are necessary for community. We normally want to maximize mutual understanding and cooperation with strangers, and so while we are ready in general to be surprised by them, we are committed to finding everything we know to be true of our own people to be true in some way of them as well, and everything we learn of them to be true in some way of ourselves. The rule is not always vindicated, but no other fundamental heuristic points to the payoff we are aiming for. (Seekers of the "exotic" are not really an exception to this rule; they are adventurous explorers of their own humanity.)

As métier

We took up a relation with our past when we regarded human nature as the already-given; we took up a relation especially with the present when we regarded it as a definite, accessible reference point for our calculations; we also use the notion in taking an attitude toward the future, as our freedom requires. To what account shall we turn our endowment, to what end use our hold on human consistency? The natural appears in this light as the fulfillment of the best promise of our given selves. We have distinctive and valuable potentialities—whether as human, as kinds of human, or as individuals—that it would be contrary to our nature, a "natural shame," not to actualize. The cultivation of beauty or power or serviceableness may be called "virtue," and the meaning of selfhood may be identified very closely with it. A most solid kind of happiness comes in finding one's métier.

Now this can be a mischievous idea. Is a young man, strong, well coordinated, and seven feet tall, who chooses not to play basketball guilty of a crime against nature, a "vice"? One doesn't rush to that judgment. All the same, one is irrepressibly curious to know what else he is doing with himself. One hopes he is doing something else he is good at, and so one continues to impose the category of the métier, though without holding him to a particular one. Suppose that even though he lacks a good color or design sense, he persists in cultivating himself as a painter. That is a mistake. The more strongly we believe that he is in a position to be aware of his mistakenness, the likelier we are to judge him deviant not only in action but in interpretation, hence "perverse."

Seven feet of height are not self-evidently and intrinsically dedicated to playing basketball. We can let this example reveal the absurdity of all claims that natural attributes are ordered to chosen goals by anything other than choice. But we cannot bring our awareness of the seven feet of height into relation with our planning and evaluation of life without caring whether it is put to some intelligent use. Other things being equal, and admitting that many other features of the person are worth caring about more, we will be gratified if the seven feet play a part in what he achieves (maybe as a lifeguard).

The métier norm is two-sided and ambiguous. Partly we use it to appreciate an individual's life for its own sake and on its own terms, but partly we use it to call for responsible role playing. We will ask the seven-footer to be a basketball player if we believe that the community will profit more from what he does in this area than from what others would do. But the question of community benefit is not really separable from the question of individual fulfillment. Flourishing individual and flourishing society require each other; ideally speaking, imperfection in either dimension impairs the other. (And of course there is the further difficulty that all conceptions of flourishing are debatable and subject to change.)

If nature as métier already relates the individual to a larger system, there is still another aspect of the notion of nature that touches this issue more directly.

As harmony

Nature-as-such, we already noted, is the sum of things. But things can coexist only if they are compossible in principle and mutually adjusted in fact. Thus, to speak of Nature is implicitly to speak of a "natural harmony," an order of things, and we call "natural" for us, with reference to nature-as-such, whatever accounts for the possibility of our coexistence with everything else in the universe, along with whatever actually adjusts us. The contemporary destruction of the world's forests is an "unnatural" human act in that it changes an order of things on which our own existence depends. (Once again, no conception of natural order is immutable or indisputable. We even hear arguments that human engineering is the ultimate principle of order in this universe; if we learn to manage our atmosphere and ecosphere differently than by relying on forests, that will only prove that all merely found orders are properly subordinate to our ordering.)

Natural harmony is always a fact given to observe, but it can be apprehended in more intense fashion as the holding- and belonging-together of the elements in the harmony, a unifying presence, what Emerson called "the integrity of impression made by manifold things."[7] The natural in us would then be especially the feelings, judgments, or actions that participate in this larger "integrity." One important implication of adopting this posture is that harm of other beings becomes a sin against ourselves: all are jointly defined by this present nature.

This last sense of nature leads back to our first. The harmony on which our own existence rests is our origin, seen in its full extent. To be unsociable toward the universe is felt as ingratitude and impiety.

In sum, we find four important dimensions of human nature: as an already-given constitution serving as a platform for our present and future acts; as a checkable reference point for calculations involving ourselves; as a goal for self-cultivation; and as a larger harmony that we can support or interfere with. We have here four kinds of light in which to appraise any human qualification.

Following nature

Though we never said outright, "Follow nature!" the uses of *nature* that we discussed were generally prescriptive. The apparent purpose of nature-talk is to call for conformity to a pattern. The reader will be aware, however, that the propriety of making any such move has been contested.

Partisans of reason have sometimes affirmed nature as the concrete expression of rationality, mixing in selected features of real living conditions to lend stability and weight to their visions. We see this in seventeenth- and eighteenth-century "laws of nature," although they still trade rhetorically on the older view, classically expressed by Aquinas, that human reason is but the dependent reflection of a divine reason expressed in the universe's nature. But Hobbes's "laws of nature" are set over a violent "state of nature": we are to look to convention, rather than our given condition as such, for our norms. Thus is foreshadowed the ultimate liberal revulsion from the "natural."

The revolution that puts human reason on the throne is consummated by Kant. Kant can grant no moral force to empirical anthropology, for natural facts about ourselves can always be otherwise and thus cannot absolutely bind judgment, as the concept of morality requires; but he wants to include among his formulations of the moral law, "Act as if the maxim of your action were to become through your will a universal law of nature."[8] By this he means to impose the moral test question, What if things always had to happen this way? He does not seem to be interested in determining whether a law of occurrences dictated by willing is compatible with regularities that we already observe in the world. If it is not—if, for instance, people always do a certain amount of lying according to a social-psychological law—then so much the worse for the immoral world. It is enough that we can *conceive* without contradiction a world where only truth is told. Only rational consistency matters.

For all of that, Kant's law-of-nature formulation does prompt us to investigate the larger framework of nature. It turns out that moral reasoning is very often decisively affected by this sort of consideration. For instance, if for the sake of the rational goal of peace I propose to give up all forms of recourse to harming others, it is not reasonable to imagine my pacifist natural law operating in a vacuum. To complete the moral gesture, I must conjoin my idea with known probabilities of aggression, conflict, and the consequences thereof. I realize then that even if I can conceive of a peaceful world, I can't plan on one, and that my peace policy had better be appropriately qualified if I am not to admit unacceptable results. Moral consistency is both rational and real.[9] Even if its premises were different, Aquinas's natural-law thinking nevertheless brought us to the same balancing point between reason and nature, for it presumed that our way of realizing fullness of being in our given form must involve the use of our intelligence.[10]

More carefully relating and to some extent reconciling moral thinking with observation of the whole system of nature in his "Critique of Teleological Judgment," Kant still declares that for the *final* purpose commanding our obedience "we must not seek within nature at all."[11] (Published in the same year was Burke's *Reflections on the Revolution in France*, with its many expressions of horror at the Revolution's "war with nature.") [12] Mill, more radical, does not try to conserve any of the meaning of the Enlightenment's "best of all possible worlds"; for him, nature is not only not a moral norm, it no longer provides any reliable clues to right action. Mill can paint nature the way Burke painted the Revolution, red in tooth and claw. "The physical government of the world being full of the things which when done by men are deemed the greatest enormities, it cannot be religious or moral in us to guide our actions by the analogy of the course of nature." [13] Nature is for amending rather than imitating. Emerson, still trying to hold nature and reason together, restates the Pauline claim that "the world lacks unity, and lies broken and in heaps . . . because man is disunited with himself"; [14] but Mill has let go of this vision and blames no one (except, tacitly, those who have rationalized injustices by dressing them in the gown of nature). His is the progressive spirit overleaping all the barricades of piety.

On either Kant's or Mill's view, and on liberal views continuous with theirs (including contemporary liberal attitudes toward sex, race, and age), "follow nature" becomes at best a hollow, at worst an offensive piece of advice. I do not aim to overthrow either the liberal view or its radical existentialist offshoot—they belong integrally to the project of Democracy carrying us all along—but I want to point out, on the basis of our earlier survey, what is here forgotten or forsworn that belongs to the thought of nature.

1. We have no "origin" beyond our own present discernment of the good. We have no past; we always constitute our identity right now, in our reasonings or negotiations. Thus we don't really have a history, we only have this one constant scenario.

2. As our anchor chain consists of reason only, we have no solidarity with our flesh and gain no support from our tangible surroundings. The natural world can set problems and we can use it to illustrate solutions, but it has no intrinsically meaningful moral form of its own and in that sense is enigmatic. We hear it on the moral wavelength only as static.

3. Clues to the fulfillment of personal character are entirely inward and thus individual. A person's métier is discoverable only by experiment and identifiable with some confidence only when extraordinary talents come into play (since unique capabilities remain hidden in lives of an average type).

4. The fact of adjustment between natural beings is not worth

consideration in its own right; it is overshadowed by questions such as How can we make life better? and How can we implement our ideals? As progressives, our worry is that we might not make the best use of our opportunities, as against the conservative worry that we will fail to preserve the built-up order that secures a good life.

The upshot of the liberal turn is that anthropology, as a mode of normative thinking, dissolves without remainder into ethics and politics. We should expect, then, that if we experiment with anthropology while keeping the great normative questions alive—and how could we not, since that is precisely what excites our interest in ourselves?—we will inevitably reintroduce in some way the aspects of nature that are excluded by liberalism.

Gender as an anthropological theme

The kind of human kind that will primarily occupy our attention, giving us an opening onto all the conceptual issues that pertain to human kinds, is gender.

To say that humans are gendered is to say that they are subject to description and evaluation as "feminine," "masculine," or in any other terms that have the same dual reference to sex and character. How exactly the reference works, and what sort of validity the describing and evaluating might have, is for us to find out. But our starting point is the massive fact that we are continually *subjected* to gender attributions in all phases of our lives and that the gender scheme has more orienting force for most of us, most of the time, than any other human differentiation.

Our culture's gender scheme is now the object of concerted criticism, epitomized in the theses of Arbitrariness, Impairment, and Asymmetry. It is the critical project that brings "gender" out as a focal theme of discourse; thus, the rise of gender as a category of our conscious self-interpretation coincides with a crisis in anthropology, or at least a rejection of anthropology in its traditional form—officially gender-blind, pervasively gender-biased. If you peeked under the plain robe of the philosophers' *anthropos* (and sometimes you didn't even have to peek), you found maleness. This state of affairs has recently been flooded with scholarly illumination.[15]

We may be disappointed in *anthropos,* historically, and due to other biases besides the sex-linked one, but the concept of "human being" is something like a tar baby in that we cannot but revive it when we criticize some specification or use of it. And we cannot use it without giving it content and thus conceiving a human nature. One would like to remain open to whatever humans are going to show of themselves and not restrict them with a defining formula; but then the very thought of this openness is an attribution to human nature, both in the sense that it is an inescapable norm defining the good or ill of our lives and in the sense that we believe or at least posit that we human beings all have the real availability of awareness and will to be responsive to each other.

Being human is not just having the body of *Homo sapiens* but feeling, judging, and acting as we do. The structures of our feeling, judging, and acting, when they are indeed constitutive of the sort of life we generally have, belong to "what it means to be human," or our "nature" in the full sense. Genders and other human kinds belong to human nature insofar as we do actually find generic differentiations of being human. They are not eternally fixed, for we can trace their historical evolution and their cultural variation; and they are not empirically deterministic, for they are only a qualification, and not the sole qualification, of persons who can still be understood as unique and free. But they are something we have to reckon with, something that affects us whether we choose to acknowledge it or not, and not just in our external circumstances but within ourselves.

If a human attribute like gender is variable according to historical circumstances, perhaps we can think seriously, supposing new circumstances, of a genderless life, as the Arbitrariness Thesis encourages us to do. The important question arises, whether this life would be human. How much will we let the "human" change before it becomes "alien"?

In Joanna Russ's powerfully imagined all-woman world, Whileaway, the structure of people's lives and personalities has been so changed that one is deprived of gender clues and is profoundly disoriented for that reason, and yet—what is all the more disorienting, when one reflects—feels fully responsive to the Whileawayans' humanity.[16] Do we accept the Whileawayans' co-humanity only because we tacitly read into them the whole structure of the life we know, including the gender part that happens to have lost its ordinary moorings? Treating them, that is, as eccentric mothers, sisters, wives, and daughters, as *we* mean these terms? If we do fully accept the revolution that is Whileaway's root premise, must we regard the Whileawayans (whether we find them attractive or repulsive) as aliens? Would becoming While-awayan be a leap out of the human, like becoming an angel? The question seems undecidable.

One rather too easy answer is to say that the Whileawayans must be human since a human so sympathetically imagined them. It is true that in the rationale offered in *The Female Man* for a Whileawayan's visit to our own world, Russ makes sure we remember that Whileaway is an actual woman's utopian projection. So Whileaway is essentially related to the present, in some way; but still it has great fictional integrity and only gets its due force if we regard it as a genuine alternative mode of life.

There is another solution to consider. If some of the contents of human nature are regarded as potentialities that may or may not be realized in a given community rather than as indispensable components of our form, then perhaps the Whileawayans do not realize their gender potentiality but do realize some other features that stay largely hidden among us, or realize familiar features to a more impressive degree. Then we would recognize the Whileawayans as neither less human nor less flourishing than ourselves. They would be, in short, another culture, albeit a unique one in lacking gender. The difficulty here is that once we admire any cultivation of human potentiality, we are bound to consider our life lacking in some way if we fail to make it our own. The situation as described makes us identify ourselves prescriptively with a higher synthesis of our own and the genderless Whileawayan virtues; meanwhile, neither we nor they flourish maximally. (Could we ever accept the reply that not all human virtues are compossible? Listening to Margaret Mead tell about free South Seas sexuality, could we totally reject the prospect of somehow digging this channel of joy into our own culture?)

Or reconceive. Suppose that the defining human potentialities do have to be realized in all humans, but that gender is not among them; instead, gender is only one of many forms that human self-expression and human love can take—perhaps not even an especially apt form. The Whileawayans then are at least as human as we are, and gender drops out of our portrait of the human-as-such, although it keeps a place in ethnology.

Is this the conclusion we should draw? For the duration of the present experiment, so long as we are dedicated to the full acknowl-edgment of gender, no. The Whileawayans, living in a world with-out heterosexual procreation and thus without sex difference and sex-related generic personal differences, are not (while that condition lasts) members of our kind. In effect, they are angels. As long as we are not angels like them, it is terribly dangerous to leave gender out of reflection on our defining characteristics, for that blinds us to the sort of bias that colors the supposedly gender-free anthropologies of the past and perhaps even the postgender utopias of the present.

To count gender as proper to human nature is, however, to disallow the judgment that gender-as-such is harmful to human beings. And to rule out that judgment is to close our minds to the very thoughts that take us out to the vexed frontier of anthropological inquiry. This we cannot do. Whether we can resolve the dilemma of answering to these opposite requirements depends on how we map the dilemma. On the premise that gender pertains to humanity, it isn't nonsensical to say that gender harms us if we are prepared to admit that humanity itself is an impaired condition for "us," supposing that "we" are subjects with a transhuman destiny. Thus a possible outcome of our experiment is that our unquenchable suspicions about gender will mature into a critique of human nature itself. And the queerness of humans criticizing humanity could be resolved by a new self-identification on our part: we could say we are "persons," for instance, with a new scruple, knowing that we meant something other than "humans" by that term.

*

Although I propose to filter anthropology through questions about human differentiation, I have to concede that the emphasis on difference has some unhappy precedents. Writers on human nature have at times taken race or sex all too seriously and centrally, with results that make us shudder. Racist and sexist views of human nature are defined, however, not only by their (often confused) attention to difference, but, more crucially, by their repression of the category of common humanity. In other words, they are inhumane. The remedy is to bring perceptions of race or sex fully into relation with the question of the form of humanity as such.

Perhaps this sounds like an abstract and leisurely move; but while it is true that "those who speak largely of the human condition are usually those most exempt from its oppressions," as Adrienne Rich observed,[17] it is also true that the oppressed have to win some exemption if they are to grasp their situation adequately and formulate a valid program.

Whether or not pursuing self-understanding "anthropomorphically" within the horizon of "anthropology" will ultimately satisfy us, it seems at any rate that what has yet to be successfully realized in the portrayal of humanity—which may look like a difficult trick but which we now see has to be attempted—is to inquire both ways at once, about humanity as differentiated into kinds and about kinds of people as human.

Chapter 3

Gender and Humanity

How is it that some people can see in gender a crushing impairment of humanity while others see in it a human glory? Does gender get in the way of properly respecting human beings? Is it possible to respond to a person's gender and to her or his humanity at the same time?

If we are to have satisfying answers to these questions, we require a definition of gender (with a careful redrawing of the sex–gender distinction) that makes clear the logical relationship of gender to humanity. This is a point on which critical gender thinking often diverges widely from positive gender thinking, with confusing results: gender is defined as an external encrustation on humanity like "sex role," for instance, rather than as the qualification of humanity itself (as well as of personal character) that people have in mind when they speak appreciatively of femininity and masculinity. While positive gender thinking is not necessarily justified in the way it conceives gender, we cannot neglect to pay attention to the positive thought's shape. Because we are members of a culture that is built on this thought, it is always ours, whatever else we might be thinking, and so we need to understand it to put our minds in order.

The strategy of this chapter is to presume that gender and humanity stand in a relationship of mutual qualification and then ask how the qualifications take place. This approach allows us to exhibit the kind of intimate and complex connection that positive gender thinking assumes and on this basis to make sense of some of the key tenets of gender idealism—for instance, that while members of different genders realize humanity in complementary ways, so that some dividing of humanity is involved, nevertheless each gendered person, even as gendered, is fully (though not unproblematically) human.

Once we possess a model of the gender–humanity relationship, we have much to learn by testing the possible analogies between gender and the other prominent human kinds. We discover important logical similarities between, for instance, the sex–gender, breed–race, and chronological age–spiritual age relationships; and we can map an intricate web of metaphorical construals and misunderstandings in the crossing of human-kind principles with each other that takes place both in ordinary discourse and in critical theories.

These investigations bring us to the point where we can answer one part of the question concerning how gender pertains to human nature. Gender and the other human kinds are indeed unalterable *endowments* providing us with basic resources for all possible versions of human life; however, the content of these endowments is not in any case a definite intentional character but is instead the fact and principle of a character-type *diversity* coordinated with various differences in our physical constitutions.

The problem: how to behave

As a young man, I once traveled back to Spain from Buenos Aires on a great liner. Among my fellow passengers there was a small group of American ladies, young and extremely beautiful. Although my acquaintance with them never even reached a footing of intimacy, it was obvious that I spoke to each of them as a man speaks to a woman who is in the full flower of her feminine attributes. One of these ladies felt rather offended . . . she said to me, "I insist that you talk to me as if I were a human being." I could not help answering: "Madam, I am not acquainted with this person whom you call a 'human being.' I know only men and women. As it is my good fortune that you are not a man but a woman—and certainly a magnificent one—I behave accordingly."

—*José Ortega y Gasset*[1]

What is one to say? When I imagine myself in the place of the woman, I feel a desire (now gender-anomalous?) to answer by punching Señor Ortega in the nose. But we want a more articulate and generally useful answer, toward which I offer these considerations:

1. "Full flower of feminine attributes" names something apprehended in women that is bound up with a prescribed way for men to deal with women. That is, Ortega's perception of the situation is not (privately) fanciful or arbitrary.
2. Nevertheless, we know what the woman meant who said, "Talk to me as if I were a human being." The category "human being" also corresponds to a reality and is relevant to the occasion. Thus, Ortega's calculated obtuseness about "humanity" is an important mistake.
3. The relations that accord with the category "human being" can interfere with the kind of "behavior" that Ortega says accords with men as men being together with women as women. Ortega's "behavior" reinforces a differential role prescription, as can be seen in the gloating flattery of "my good fortune" and "magnificent"; the lady's appeal to the "human" is meant to set aside or deny differentiation in favor of some sort of commonality.
4. The problem that Ortega has with the young American woman, and she with him, can be resolved in principle only by, first, ascertaining the relationship between the two realities of gender and humanness and, second, formulating a protocol for practice in awareness of this relationship. Our question becomes, How can beings who are both gendered and human know and get along with each other in both of those characters?

How gender qualifies humanity

The currently prominent sense of *gender,* that is, a sex-related mode of human existence, is transferred from the grammatical sense. In grammar, genders are sex-related systems of syntactical concord: various parts of locutions will take forms prescribed by a gender category to agree with substantives belonging to that category.[2] Similarly, the human genders work as systems of concord insofar as distinctive ways of speaking and acting are assigned to persons of different sexes. Within a culture's frame of reference it will be "ungrammatical" for, say, a woman to fight or a man to cry. The analogy between human and grammatical gender is not perfect, however, notably because while every known society is humanly gendered, many languages lack grammatical gender. Gender is one of the "secondary" features (like tense and number) that a language can do without.[3] Several questions are provoked by this fact. What does a language gain from gendering, and how much light does this consideration shed on human gendering? Why would human gender not be a dispensable feature of human systems?

It is hard to see the gain in linguistic gendering, since we experience it as a source of difficulties. Gender makes French harder for English-speakers to learn, for example; nor are English-speakers free from gender problems in their own relatively de-gendered native tongue, as their pronouns trip them up when they try to avoid sexism. But if we now encounter gender as an obstacle, how could it ever have been a way of going right?

Start by supposing the obvious, that speakers have all along been impressed by different sexual characteristics in at least some things and wanted to mark this in their language.[4] The point would be, in the first place, to make language more informative. Certainly cattle raisers would always want different words for heifers and bulls. But for true gendering we need not only *heifer* and *bull* in the lexicon but distinct pronouns for them, with associated distinct formations of other words. What then is gained, from a formal point of view, by inflecting adjectives to agree with nouns according to gender? There are statements in French that are less ambiguous, more clear regarding which part connects with which, thanks to gender agreement. On the other hand, French-speakers run into problems they would not have if all their adjectives were neutral.[5] It seems impossible to tell whether, all things considered, they enjoy an advantage in their gendering.

But the question of advantage may be misguided. Instead of looking case by case at a language's capacity to inform and discriminate, we might consider the hypothesis that in language, as in other aspects of human life, there is a potential (and under favorable conditions a tendency) for networks or "domains" to be established by means of orienting devices.[6] Sex-related pronouns, very powerful in their logical range and emotional connotation, could serve as such centers in language just as well as queens or kings do in the order of conduct. (The novice struggling with French, thinking by things rather than pronouns, never knows what thing will turn out to be a "she," but the native French-speaker knows the whole family of feminine forms through the offices of *elle*, which touches them all.) When a language is ordered such that gendering has no syntactic contribution to make at all—as in an "isolating" language like Chinese, where word order determines the relations among parts of an utterance—these gender networks will not be supported.

However it arose, gender is, at any rate, essentially a centered order. A genuinely arbitrary classification that divided words and inflections into groups *A, B,* and *C,* with *A, B,* and *C* signifying nothing except their difference from each other, we would not conceive to be a gender system. There is, of course, arbitrariness in any gender system, both in sounds and in the assignment of nouns. Still, even though there is nothing sexually female about *la plume*—on the contrary—the pen, with the articles and adjectives accompanying it, is assigned to an order with a generic "she" identity that presupposes an experience of some eminent "she" (women? Mother?), the center of the gender. The logic of gender does not require the meaning at the center to pervade the gender, for the ordering of the pen to "she" is not a proposition about the pen but a prearrangement for propositions involving the pen. (Like other grammatical rules, gender is an order that precedes any ordering we do in the present.) To say ordinary things about pens, it is always taken for granted that pen talk is feminine; by choosing feminine forms to go with "pen," one is not thereby asserting that a pen is a feminine being. Gendered talk does not, of itself, say anything *about* gender.

A question about this claim of centeredness may be raised by the neuter gender, still fully present in German, for example. The notion of an eminent "it" is dubious. But whether or not "it" refers to an experienced reality in the way that "he" and "she" do, "it" can function perfectly well as the center of one speaking network among others. From whatever motive of differentiation, a noun can be enrolled in the "it" category and thus aligned with the neuter markers in the system of concord whose subsystem center is the impersonal pronoun.[7] (Even if the natural significance of this gender center is only privative, that significance could still be great, as Martin Buber proved in thematizing "the basic word I-It" in *I and Thou*.)[8] Contrast is assumed between the neuter and sex-centered subsystems.

Grammatical gender is an image of the order of human gender. Human gender schemes possess centers of meaning in (what are taken to be) sexed bodies. There are systems of markers around these centers, many assigned according to no natural necessity—what counts as "women's work" in one valley may well count as "men's work" in the next[9]—but each totality, however composed, constituting a do-

main for the central subjects or styles. The human gender order prepares for decision making without itself being subject to deliberation:
under ordinary conditions, men and women refrain from acting in each
other's fashion not because they think it would be difficult, or disagreeable, but because it would be absurd—a joke or an outrage, but, either
way, not a serious option. One doesn't decide what the core content
of the human gender system will be (although one may consciously
elaborate it in clothing, speech, ritual, and morality); one doesn't decide to have genders in the first place. Genders are not experienced
as "roles" in a theatrical or managerial sense, although these dimensions are present and may be given priority from a relatively detached
point of view. For gendered persons they belong to human nature and
the Way.

The *center of meaning* for a gender, consisting of the objects of
apprehension in reference to which all the parts of the gender network are gathered together, must be distinguished from the *central
meaning* of the gender, a fabric of resembling qualities or styles that
extend through much, if not necessarily all, of the network. This is
the best construction to put on the sex–gender distinction. "Female,"
for instance, pertains to women, the egg-producing human beings,[10]
while "feminine" pertains to certain ways of feeling, judging, and be-
having (along with ways of being approached and responded to) that
are deemed appropriate to women without being restricted to them,
which indeed are thought to radiate outward from women—that is,
from the generality of women—into other beings animate and inanimate, and even into men. The central meanings "feminine" and "masculine" are more a focus of attention, more subject to active construction, more an issue, than the centers of meaning "female" and "male,"
which are treated as simply given; and the deep reason for this is that
the genders are intriguing and elusive intentional realities, while the
sexes have the status of physical facts, almost always instantly and unproblematically ostensible. (One can show that gender influences the
construction of sex conceptions, but that does not change the ordinary
directionality of gender thinking from sex to gender.)[11]

For some purposes it will be important to distinguish between
the biological aspect of the sexual center of meaning (as with the egg-
producing criterion) and the socially and psychologically determined
aspect of it, which is a matter of believing oneself and being believed to
be female or male. I will call the latter "sex identity." *The word "gender"
is very often used to mean sex identity, with the result that central meaning*

and center of meaning are confounded.[12] But everyday references to femininity and masculinity generally assume a difference between gender and sex identity, if only because gender is measured as a varying degree (A is more masculine than B), while sex identity is a constant (A is a man). Thus ordinary gender thinking has one sort of perspicuity that much scholarly and critical discourse lacks.

Both center of meaning and central meaning may have centers in turn, and we would expect these to converge: the preferred examples of "man" should also be the fullest instantiations of "masculine." But this centering of the centers can happen in a variety of ways. One's favorite movie star is a sex–gender paragon in one way, and one's lover or spouse is (for better or worse) a sex–gender paragon in another way. More broadly, differences of temperament, culture, race, class, age, and sexual orientation determine for each subject which qualities and persons count as more central or less central.[13] (It is important, for instance, to be aware of the privileged position held in our culture by the femininity modeled by cheerful, white, affluent, young, heterosexual women and of the different kinds of impact this privilege has on subjects depending on their own personal characteristics and social position.) Rather than assume any one manner or pattern of centering, however, I will treat the two gender centers as more diffusely general, as indeed all these variations of centering presuppose, and collectively reinforce, a relatively diffuse "common language" of gender.

In both the center-of-meaning and central-meaning notions there is an ambiguity growing out of the double aspect of the gerund *meaning*. Meaning is an objective reality that one comes upon, that one can look up in the dictionary—"the meaning of a term"—and manipulate like a counter. But meaning is also something we do, an action or activity. Thus gender meaning must be conceived both as a kind of text and as a quality of our intending, an occurrence that we cannot be purely *out* of—for a text isn't even a text if it is contemplated in perfect numbness, without some intentional enactment of its meaning—or *in,* that is, without any awareness of *what* it is we are meaning. Rather, the meaning is always real for us in both ways, and this is true in both sites of meaning, that is, in the appearances made by women and men as such and in the complexes of gender qualities as such.

A pitfall in the sex–gender distinction is that it can be taken for an assertion of genders' complete independence of their centers of meaning. Judith Butler pushes it to this extreme, speaking of the possible "radical independence of gender" from sex, "with the consequence that *man* and *masculine* might just as easily signify a female body as a male one, and *woman* and *feminine* a male body as easily as a female one." [14] In this logical just-as-easily claim, the Arbitrariness Thesis runs amok. Central meanings could not survive with this freedom because a gender's central meaning, the meaning that makes it a gender, is eminently the meaning of its center of meaning. How could one keep a sense of what feminine and masculine mean, even maintain a fanciful view of the genders, without somehow referring to what women and men look like and do? (That Butler appreciates the anchorage of gender in sex is shown in her further argument that the assumed facts of sex are themselves culturally constructed and "might well be constructed differently.") [15]

Another misreading of the sex–gender distinction is to take an essentially arbitrary set of role assignments—roles that happen to be assigned by sex, for greater or lesser utility—for the ideal gender domain in which roles *belong* to beings by virtue of a centered, sex-related meaning that they participate in. Because sex role is not the same as gender, Margaret Mead could intelligibly claim that the Arapesh and Mundugumor have sex-role systems, in that they divide activities by sex, but no gender system in the sense of a sexual division of personality types. (At least, she could not elicit statements of belief in such a division from her informants). [16] Perhaps it is unlikely that a sex-discriminating society could actually be free from gendering, but it isn't impossible. On the other hand, since it is axiomatic that gender (if it exists) is referred somehow to a sexual center of meaning, it is indeed impossible not to have the gender–sex linkage that Sylvia Yanagisako and Jane Collier warn against: "Although we claim to analyze socially and culturally constructed systems of *gender,* unexamined assumptions about biological sex differences pervade our analytic concepts . . . because gender is defined as having 'some connection to sex differences.'" [17]

Our primary concern, from this point forward, will be with the logical shape of gender in the sense of central meanings like masculine and feminine. We will ask what is said and understood about a being when it is thus called and thought of. By *feminine being* and *masculine being* I will mean not women and men, simply, but women or men or other beings to the extent that they are feminine and masculine. I will advance three answers to the conceptual question about gender:

1. Genders are generic realities.
2. Genders are complementary kinds of a kind.

3. Genders are normative and valid organizations of intention-in-community.

Genders are generic realities

Whatever their relationship to actual behavior and experience, genders are *understood* to be real and gender talk makes descriptive reference to something encountered. "Femininity" is that about feminine beings that I meet whenever I meet them, their real resemblance. Because one is usually responding appreciatively or prescribingly to persons with respect to gender, and because people exhibit gender qualities in varying degrees and not always in accordance with an observer's expectations or desires, it is easy to lose sight of the fact that gender thinking understands itself to be perceptive, not merely constructive. Genders may be elaborated into ethical or metaphysical structures (Yin and Yang) or pinned to invisible causes; they may be experienced and even defined in conformity with schematic situational requirements (for example, for active–passive complementarity); but the apprehensible real resemblance is always at their core.

There are notorious evils and errors involved in stereotyping persons, so that we have become leery of evaluating, prescribing, or predicting on the basis of generic human features—as a matter of conscious principle if not practice.[18] We will not agree to say so much as "Sam is a man" if "man" has any implication that Sam is a different *person,* differently sensitive or motivated or competent than others, by virtue of his belonging to a "type" of persons. His own unique nature, rather than anything collective or anything typical about situations in which he finds himself, should be the explanation and the point of accountability for his performance in society. The concept of person, retaining always a legal tinge, seems to require this.

Yet generic human features are facts of immediate experience that cannot be ignored. The difference between dealing with feminine beings and dealing with masculine beings—along with other comparable differences, including purely individual ones—is usually felt as keenly as the difference between a warm and a cool bath. Now this great difference obviously lies in one's prejudiced responses to women and men, not in women and men abstracted from one's responses. But that is also true of warm and cool. The pertinent question is whether my different modes of dealing with feminine and masculine beings have a real basis, of an interesting sort. Such a basis would not be a mere trigger-stimulus (as for instance certain feelings might be evoked in me whenever I see a dress, no matter who is wearing it); it would continuously allow a fuller showing of the other. In other words, a real basis must serve a genuine relationship. It could be extremely subtle and yet infuse everything in the relationship with a certain taste.

To say that a conception orients one to a real basis of relationship with certain beings is different from claiming that it entails definite predictions about them or limits the scope of empirical generalizations about them. For there is no telling exactly where a relationship will go. But the conception that orients one to the relationship helps one not to miss what develops in it, the gifts that are given in it. A gender conception is a partly indeterminate promise rather than a controlling essence.[19]

Stereotyping is cause for concern not because individuals are necessarily disserved by the attribution of generic natures but because any given generic attribution can mask or distort other important features, generic or individual. A stereotype, in the pejorative sense, is a generic conception used to constrict rather than to expand awareness. It fossilizes resemblance, treating beings that resemble each other not as joint constitutents of a network of approximations but as interchangeable instances of a completely defined type. (Any instances that come under a type without being perfectly interchangeable with the type's preferred center of meaning, its "prototype"—for instance, a movie-star gender paragon—are relegated to a deficient status.)[20] Since this sort of type is an alien shell imposed on its victims, it must be read as a reflection of the interests of the stereotypers, not as a disclosure of the stereotyped—except to the degree that they "inauthentically" allow themselves to be determined by it.[21]

The opposite shortcut, however, is to assert individuality in such a way that real resemblances do not have to be reckoned with. Individuality then becomes, in turn, a kind of hollowed-out stereotype. To be sure, individualism has the great justification that it focuses attention on the being who is in truth the concrete anchor of relationship. Even in a heavily sex-affected dealing like romantic love, the paramount claim on my attention is, say, *this* woman, the particular one. But I cannot unpack the meaning of *this woman,* or even the pronoun *she* by which I think of my beloved, if I repress awareness of the human field of womanlikeness. I am dealing with *her,* the individual, but because the individual is "her" she is related to my apprehension of women and the womanlike. And "I" who love am a correlated "he" or "she" and thereby related to manlikeness or womanlikeness.

That *I* and *you* are ungendered pronouns does not mean that they are ungendered experiences. They do, in fact, designate the purely personal point sources of "one's own" and "the Other's" intentions, which transcend any objectifiable nature; and this transcendence is the sharp edge of personal presence, supremely real. But how it is to be "I" in the way that I am in the world, facing a certain "you"—that is, the concrete shape of personal relationship as it can be *understood,* even by me—necessarily extends into the third-person realm of "she" and "he." Individuals have gender natures as soon as they have natures.[22]

In order to reflect on how our awareness of persons can best be managed with respect to gender, try thought experiments like this one: imagine that someone has proposed to abolish the separate categories "actor" and "actress" in giving out theatrical awards, on the grounds that acting is a human and an individual accomplishment; that it makes no more sense to identify acting performances by sex stereotype than by race or any other human feature; that the comparisons on which appreciation is based should not be restricted—no one should be thought "good at acting, for a man" or "for a woman" only.[23] There can be as many different awards as we have presently, but they should be determined by aesthetic categories like "dramatic," "comic," and so forth. A counterargument might be that sex and gender are indeed categories of fundamental aesthetic interest; that the challenge of acting a human part is as much marked by the sex or gender of the character as by the tone of the story. (Note, however, that this reasoning could also support award categories for age and other variables, and that the categories have logically to do with the kind of person being performed rather than the kind of person performing.) Alternatively, it might be argued that women's and men's acting ought to be appreciated separately for the same reason that women's and men's sports are: not to keep men from dominating women, but because what can be done through female bodies is intrinsically interesting, and at the same time we want to see what males can do in a sporting domain suitable to them.[24]

We may resist the counterarguments for good reasons, but they draw force from the fact that we (because we are gendered) have great difficulty imagining human endeavor except as based in and inflected by male and female bodies. And this is another indication of how gender is ordinarily taken to be fundamental to personal identity. What sort of woman is she?—a question that contains the default meaning What kind of feminine human being is she?—is no less a valid question than What kind of person is she? and in fact is for some purposes more precise and therefore more pertinent. The gender clue to her identity may be misleading—she may be an "unusual" woman in ways that, when specified, will be seen not to accord with certain gender norms— but precisely in that checked expectation one is on to something. The conceptual point that gender is fundamental to the identity of the gendered person is paralleled by the psychological finding that the sexed aspect of one's sense of self is formed very early in life and cannot be altered without grave psychic disruption.[25]

On this view, the gender critic is put in an awkwardly divided position. Not that there aren't ample grounds for criticism in one's experiences of pain and incongruity in the gender system, but the "person" or "human being" who undergoes gender ills and who stands to be reclaimed from the contamination of gender is not the same as the concretely understandable self. A gender-transcending "me" is an abstraction from the "me–him" or "me–her" that a gendered being is. If I am sick of gender, I am sick of something about myself.

Genders are complementary kinds of a kind

Asking about a woman (qua feminine being) is not a way of asking about a human being in the same sense that asking about a chair is a way of asking about a piece of furniture. "Human being," unlike "piece of furniture," is amply specific; we know enough information for a host of important purposes if we know that a being is human, and we know it for every human. But consider how Ortega obscures this point in the continuation of his remarks. The poor young American, he says, "had suffered the rationalistic education of the time [that] had produced the hypothesis of the abstraction 'human being.' It should always be remembered that the species—and the species is the concrete and real—reacts on the genus and specifies it."[26] Ortega means *species* in a logical rather than biological sense, but the two senses are related in that a species is taken either way to have a certain independence or priority in the order of existence. The oddity, in biological perspective, of regarding men and women as separate species is a clue to a conceptual mistake. Gendering is a division internal to a species rather than true speciation. Genders are not simply kinds but subordinate kinds of a primary kind. It could be true as a matter of folk taxonomy that "man" and "woman" are more *basic* categories than "human" in the sense that we learn these categories earlier and invoke them more often, with a greater number of distinctive practical implications.[27] Ortega's use of the concept of species might rest on this social-psychological fact. But reflective, normative consideration must take "human" to be more basic.

That genders are kinds of a kind in this way is, in part, an ontological proposition: genders cannot exist except as qualifications of the primary kind, in this case humanity. (In contrast, human beings can be conceived as existing in the absence of other primates or mammals or vertebrates or animals.) That genders are kinds of a primary kind also has the important implication that they can be defined only with reference to each other. If only one kind of a kind existed, there would be nothing to mark. Discerning masculinity assumes that at least one other quality like femininity is also to be discerned. (But any species can be defined without mentioning any other. One does not need to know the other primate species to know what humans are, except for the purposes of a specialized sort of knowledge.)

Genders are *complementary* kinds of a primary kind in the strong sense that they require each other. Anatomical maleness and femaleness likewise require each other, but the simplicity of this parallel is misleading. One speaks readily of masculine aggressiveness and feminine receptivity, masculine preoccupation with principles and feminine concern for specific relationships, and so forth, all fitting together as neatly as male and female reproductive parts. But if gender makes a difference in attunement and appreciativeness, all by way of a fundamental shaping of selfhood, then masculine humans *cannot fully understand* feminine humans and cannot duplicate or predict their actions and reactions, and vice versa. Although masculine and feminine subjects use the same words and perform actions with the same names, they must mean these differently, not like ships passing in the night, but like docking platforms that meet not quite squarely.[28] Intragender communication is felt to go more smoothly. (Those who shift from heterosexual to homosexual relations often report that they are gratified to have their sexuality much better understood.)

Thus the complementarity of another gender is mysterious— Ivan Illich likes to call it "ambiguous," by which he means that it is productive of incongruities in the "fit" between genders[29]—and the experiences of different genders are partly incommensurable. Only a pseudocomplementarity would tailor one gender to the fantasies or needs of the other. The human specialization of being gendered means in part that complementary specializations are in some respect outside one's own orbit entirely, including even the *appreciation* of one's own gender that is peculiarly in the power of the other(s).[30] Accordingly, the purpose of the concept of gender is partly to mark a limit to comprehension. A gender that could be entirely specified would not be a gender. We can also see why quasi-religious attitudes of fear and reverence of gendering will always have some warrant in a gendered human community. (At the same time, we can see that hope for the sort of "salvation" or "regeneration" that can come only from a Beyond provides a motive for stipulating that the genders are mutually mysterious.)[31]

The other gender seems not so much complementary or mysterious as inadequate insofar as more is expected of it than it offers. Besides appreciation and awe there is exasperation: "Sometimes you wonder if they're human."[32] Ideally, this complaint is illogical, analogous to saying that sports cars are not fully cars because they do not carry as much luggage as station wagons. The positive thought of gender does not admit that gendering-as-such is an impairment of humanity. In this perspective, "wondering if they're human" will normally be dismissed, finally, as a lazy or crabby response to members of the other gender, unless it works as a constructive *question* in the manner exhibited by Karl Barth:

> Much that is typically masculine would have to be left unsaid and undone, or said and done quite differently, if man remembered that in it, if it is to be truly masculine, he must prove his humanity in the eyes of woman, to whom he constitutes so great a question mark. For example, might not the very dubious masculine enterprise of war become intrinsically impossible if the remembrance of the confrontation with woman were suddenly to be given the normative significance which is undoubtedly its due?[33]

It can be admitted that no particular realization of gendering need be maximally fulfilling for us, and that some forms might even be tragically stunting. The gender principle is not a carte blanche to differentiate men's and women's lives in any old way. "You wonder if they're human" is a critical question simmering within the gender system. Note, however, that it is gender itself that animates this question by confronting one human attunement with another as the speaker of its hidden "but . . ."[34]

Genders are normative and valid organizations of intention-in-community

We have to treat genders as mysterious only if we are, ourselves, gendered, that is, located in some part or other of the complementarity rather than surveying it from outside. Certainly, if gender is real, then we are gendered—but not merely because we are biologically male and female. The real reason we are unable to separate ourselves from gender is that it confronts us as more than a phenomenon to be observed. It is always a normative solicitation of our intentions. The "reality" of it is naturally mediated by perception but consists at its core of something other than an apprehensible form; it is a prior qualifying of one's intending, affecting not merely what one perceives but who one is—partly as a fact of one's life and partly as an issue dominating the meaning of one's life. Thus, a direct valuation of genders, as we find for instance in some Enlightenment writers' association of the feminine with the beautiful and the masculine with the sublime, or in the *écriture féminine* and feminine moral theories of our own time, is nearer to the reality of gender (whatever errors of valuation may be committed in this or that account) than any sociology of sex roles.[35] Probably most assertions of the "naturalness" of genders are motivated more by a sense of their validity, their serviceableness in the quest for right relationship, than by any belief about natural facts.[36] Validity is the hinge on which this kind of life, "spiritual" life, turns.

Conceived simply as a way of being human, gender could be mistaken for a lifestyle, to be adopted or discarded as one chooses. Unlike lifestyle, however, gender is positively thought to be nondiscretionary in two ways. First, it shares in the original forming of one's intentions and personal identity, so that one is in a position to acknowledge it but not to decide to add it to or subtract it from oneself (since it already qualifies all such decisions). Second, *what* one is acknowledging in this case is a way of being a member of a community of intentional beings, an interintentional style (a spirit), not merely a style in the sense that a figure skater has one. Being accompanied by others in certain ways and, above all, being alive to the issue of how best to accompany others are essential ingredients of this twist on humanness, so that all of one's decisions are qualified from the start as collaborations. A gendered being teams with all other gendered beings. Insofar as I am masculine I am representative of all masculine beings to each other, in one way, and to feminine beings, in another. All these reasons prohibit thinking of genders as arbitrary.

Then again, gendering *is* understood to be discretionary in the sense that the program of a gender is carried out intentionally, not by reflex. One is free to rise to the baits of gendered living with more or less energy and more or less skill. The "givenness" of masculinity for a masculine being is precisely the challenge to be masculine, the shining forth of masculinity (in its place in the gender system) as the most acceptable possibility.[37] The whole gender system stands before all gendered beings as a possible fulfillment of community and beckons to them as such, its normative force consisting of nothing other than its ability to answer the life-interpreting question of how intenders shall live together. No one can tell exactly what communal fulfillment means, since it rests on the imponderables of other persons' intentions (in their unknowableness as Others) and the total effect of their communal actualization. But the orientation to fulfillment still bears the meaning of a quest, which implies freedom to pursue a goal.

Suppose one wanted to assert one's independence from gendering. Then one would have to believe that, whatever may have been true in the past, gender is now not real, that is, not a norming norm. But if a gender critic does claim this under present conditions, someone else will answer that gender is indubitably real and that the denial of it can only be mistaken and willful. The critic can remain cold to this claim. In the end, the only proof of the reality of the disputed thing lies in our response to it, which might or might not obtain—like faith that does or does not arise as a witness to the divine. The contingency here makes the gender defense reminiscent of Anselm's argument with the fool who denies God. To conceive the disputed reality is perforce to acknowledge it, because the reality of that which is disputed just is (at least in crucial part) a certain orientation of our intentions—the orientation to the maximally affirmable being, in Anselm's argument, and to sex-linked ways of being human that together form an acceptable whole, in the case of gender. But just as Anselm's argument only has force for me if I have actually encountered a reality that can bear the name "that than which no greater can be conceived," so also the defense of gender presupposes an involving disclosure, the magnetism of the norm, which cannot be guaranteed in advance. To whatever degree our thinking *is* gendered, then, it is subject to the same kind of fundamental contingency and obscurity that theology typically admits to be defining of itself and tries to be lucid about.

How humanity qualifies gender

In relation to genders, the human is the more inclusive category, but it is important to remember that the inclusion can be achieved either by paring down human attributes to common denominators, so that everyone is human in just the same way, or by encompassing all variations, so that humanity transcends any one of us even while we all draw on it or breathe its atmosphere. Thus there are at least two relations of the gendered to the human, not one. To this point, we have been concerned with the relation of gender to humanity-as-a-whole; let us concentrate now on the sense of "human" that Ortega's interlocutor appealed to, a humanity owned by an individual and at the same time common to all.

Humanity, the primary kind to which genders give further specification, consists of ways of feeling, acting, and thinking that are bound to the bodily forms of the species *Homo sapiens*. We have noted that "person," even though often used interchangeably with "human being," is properly a broader category including all beings who are capable of having intentions with respect to their relationships with others. "Treat me as a person!" is the basic claim to standing in the community of beings who have conscious dealings with each other. There is a presumption of commonality in making this claim, but it is relatively abstract: the implicit assertion is that we are all able to communicate and to form and carry out policies of action affecting each other. Simply as persons, we might have no experience in common, no inclinations in common, and no common constraints on action except the correlated existence of each in the other's universe. But as human beings we share a particular form of life based on our bodily design, the activities it supports, and the problems to which it gives rise. "Talk to me as if I were a human being" implicitly means "Remember that like you I need certain provisions to maintain life and health; want certain physical competencies and liberties; want to possess certain goods; have both a need and an ability to cooperate with others in the accomplishing of certain practically important tasks; am liable to feel anger, disgust, fear, happiness, sadness, and surprise," and so on.[38]

Humanity is invoked to remind Ortega of a project or set of projects that he is supposed to be engaged in with all men and women. This woman has a human body that entitles her to make the claim, but she means to direct Ortega's attention to ideals of conviviality that his sexist manner falls afoul of. To some extent these ideals must already be known and followed, but it is part of the joint project of humanity that she can specify its meaning, occasion by occasion, in relation to herself. A fundamental feature of humanity that preorders the dealings of humans with each other is commonality as such—whatever is required to be acceptable all round. In this signification, humanity is a variable; one can be noted for greater or lesser humaneness, as a great human being or a poor excuse for a human being, according to how much sensitivity one has to the needs and desires of others. That one is subject to measurement on this scale is the already-given interintentional frame of reference (in its human specification), a set of questions fixing the dominant meaning of what we do as better or worse answers.

Except in the vexed cases of unborn life and quasi-death, we have no doubts at all about who lives humanly. Anyone with our sort of body has the privilege of joining us in defining humanity; the inescapable rightness of allowing that privilege is the foremost generic reality met in all owners of human bodies. An action that horrifies or harms so much as one ordinary man or woman is "inhuman" solely on that condition. We cannot say anything comparable of gender, for no division of humanity-as-a-whole can be essentially inclusive in this fashion. A woman dissimilar to most other women will probably not redefine the feminine but instead will oddly instantiate the masculine or some other category. Thus the horizon of a gender is more determinate and closed than the horizon of the human—which is reassuring under some circumstances, oppressive under others.

Given that gender and humanity are realized in the same object of attention, ourselves, the two identities must qualify each other, and we can now see that this reciprocal qualification will consist in part of a dialectic of closing and opening, acknowledging and negotiating. But the terms of this dialectic qualify each other even before they qualify each other. Just as we had to begin with the basic characterization of gender as a way of being human, so now we have to add that humanity itself is, among those who are gendered, entirely gendered—not only in the sense that humanity-as-a-whole divides into complementary genders, but also in the sense that common-denominator-humanity always comes variously gender twisted even as we can recognize the commonality in it. At least this is the point that Ortega was trying to make. A masculine human being and a feminine human being have humanity in common in the way that a man and a woman have the human body in common, or in the way that a brother and a sister who both resemble a certain ancestor have a sort of resemblance in common. Humanity as such is an abstraction (like human-body-as-such or ancestor's-likeness-as-such) in the sense that one cannot perceive it in isolation but at best only give a formal definition of it; yet common humanity is as concretely present in masculinity and femininity as that instantly recognizable human form or that striking resemblance—both as a natural reality and as an ideal project.

Ortega's remarks could be construed, then, as the claim that even in addressing each other as human beings he and the American woman must actualize humanity in the different masculine and feminine modes, imposing on them a significant noncommonality. While this claim stands up, supposing the reality of gender, nevertheless his rejection of the category of the human is in this instance a rejection of reasonableness itself. For reasonableness, among humans a function of human personhood, spans the division between genders, postulating togetherness and common perception among gendered beings alongside any separation and opaqueness entailed by gendering. The actualizing of humanity in the form of reasonableness is, like gendering, contingent, yet, in the event, indubitable. The American woman knew that it is possible and (for sanity's sake) necessary for masculine and feminine beings to converse reasonably, and that Ortega's determination to dance a gender minuet precluded this.

The requirements of humanity brook no infringement. The individuals from whom I receive gendered signals are entitled to assume that I will treat them as human beings, however else I take direction from them or try to affect them. I am always forbidden to discriminate against, that is, to make generic or individual difference a reason to limit or withhold human affirmation; I am required, however, discriminatingly to appreciate all distinctive qualities of character, so that comportment sensitive to generic and individual qualities can, as it were, fully implement humanity. It is well that I face warnings about stereotyping so that my benign responses are not of the confining sort ("She's so good with children").[39]

Interaction between gendered persons—on shipboard or in laboratories, in academic journals or at political conventions, in the workplace or in the nuclear family—follows a protocol embedded in our normative culture. The master rule of any such protocol is to respond properly to those with whom one deals. Now proper response depends on awareness of all the circumstances attending an encounter, including beliefs about roles, and assumes that all parties are already embarked on intelligibly related projects; but, in principle, the supreme governor of propriety must be the cue directly furnished by the other, in whose discretion it lies to slit his or her eyes and say "Let's dance" on one occasion and, staring, "Treat me like a human being!" on another. The protocol for relationships cannot be entirely settled in advance, or in the mind of one party, else relationships would become mere handlings of one by another. (Illustrating the worst case, the wife-killer of Tolstoy's story "The Kreutzer Sonata" argues that sexual desire fixes a purely instrumental relationship between men and women in which women's humanity is prevented from appearing to men. In this depraved order, a conscientious man may think, "Still, women are human beings," and yet be unable to live with them humanely.) [40] Ideally, however, gender relationships are already human, even before supervening requirements of humanity are brought into play, insofar as they follow the basic rule of cuing by the other's self-disclosure. Despite the handicap of bias, masculine beings as masculine can find out from feminine beings as feminine something of what femininity means, as they go. In turn, the fact that human relationships are gendered means that as we reason together about humanity we find out as we go how humanity adds up from the different twists with which it appears. Our theorizing about humanity sets up a capstone to the conscious segment of our protocol, while outside of consciousness the norming of gender gives orders to our thinking and speaking.

Gender and central human projects

We had recourse to the notion of human project in analyzing Ortega's wrongful use of the gender principle; his problem was not simply that he described someone mistakenly but that he derailed a humanly definitive enterprise. Once we think in these terms, we have to ask: What are the projects that define human fulfillment? And how, in each case, does gender qualify our engagement in a human project?

Dorothy Dinnerstein recognizes that if we are fully to understand either appreciative or critical claims about gender, we need to be clear about how humans-as-humans seek fulfillment. Accordingly, she posits "central human projects" against which we can measure the gains and losses that are realized in a given cultural arrangement.[41] Her chief interest is in the project of sexual liberty, that is, "liberty to reject what is oppressive and maiming in our prevailing male–female arrangements; liberty to restructure them to fit our conception of full humanity, and to restructure them again as that conception continues to develop" (11). Back of this is the project of projects, our self-creation (12). But what is full humanity, and whither does self-creation tend? For Dinnerstein, it is a matter of achieving collectively a stable and fruitful relation among given ingredients of human nature and the human condition: reconciling reason and emotion, ego and id; being at home in our bodies and in our natural environment; making peace with death; maintaining a bridge between the generations; and coming to terms with the delights and disappointments that attend our need for each other.

The map of essential human projects looks one way, if we are thinking mainly of our opportunities, and another way, if we are focusing on our limits. For example, because we are rational subjects, we have the opportunity of knowledge—maximally, of possessing all the forms of the universe in the microcosm of our minds. Because we are rational, cooperative agents, it is open to us in principle to administer the whole universe so that it abides in peace and to form a character for ourselves that fits us for this task. Because we are sensitive to beauty, we can fashion a way of living and an environment that abound in delights. And so forth. In the opportunity perspective, conditions like our mortality, our inordinate longings, and our interpretative discord are seen as problems to be solved. But in the limits perspective, we are up against these problems in a more fundamental sense: being up against them *defines* us. If we were not bound to face death, not liable to be rocked by unruly emotion, not always having to deal with disagreement among ourselves, we would be angelic or even divine instead of human. Such limits are just what we do not have the opportunity to overcome: they draw the boundaries within which specifically human opportunities exist, drawing a human face on the heart's desire.

Thus there are two different versions of the fundamental human project: to create ourselves ideally (heeding the call of the True, the Good, and the Beautiful), on the one hand, and to adjust to our acknowledged reality, on the other.

When Plato speaks of soul, when Jesus and Paul speak of a future heavenly condition transcending flesh and blood, when Mary Wollstonecraft appeals to reason, when Jean-Paul Sartre and Simone de Beauvoir proclaim transcendence, we have to do with the ideal project. This project is only equivocally humanistic, because its true object is to overcome the human. Yet it is authentically human insofar as it is true to say that to be human is to long to be divine.

We can say with as much justification that the realistic project's premise of humanly definitive limits is equivocal. For the notion of human limits implies a human perspective surpassing limits, and "project" assumes the presence of a transcending freedom that deals creatively with limits. Thus Aristotle wrote, "We ought not to follow the proverb-writers, and 'think human, since you are human,' or 'think mortal, since you are mortal.' Rather, as far as we can, we ought to be pro-immortal, and go to all lengths to live a life that expresses our supreme element."[42]

Our assessment of these projects would be dialectically incomplete did we not recognize that our grandest ideal opportunities take on the character of frustrating limits, insofar as they remain beyond our real grasp. For instance, it would not be painful and confusing to know that our knowledge is always incomplete, if we did not have a conception of divine knowledge. Likewise, our very limits take on the character of ultimately sweet opportunities—for instance, to serve the flourishing of other beings, or to die a Good Death—if we succeed in accepting our finitude. For only a limited being can participate in something larger than itself and be taken outside itself.

Dinnerstein is sensitive to both dimensions of the question of human projects and makes an exemplary attempt to balance them. Her proposed solution to gender problems is fundamentally neither idealist–utopian nor conservatively adjustment-oriented. As for the specific claim that a "project of sexual liberty" is emerging on an ever broadening front and will dissolve the familiar gender scheme, primarily as a consequence of equalizing the male and female contributions to early child care, one must accept it or resist it according to one's assessment of the possible meanings that can be bestowed on the male and female contributions to procreation, as part of "our conception of full humanity." It is remarkable that Dinnerstein pays as little attention to the enterprise of procreation as she does, for all her concern for child raising. But the capital point now is not what Dinnerstein relatively emphasizes but rather the challenge she issues us to articulate the human-project framework within which a gender scheme figures as a good or an evil, and to build both our freedom and our limits into that framework.

Supposing that gender always qualifies the human, any statable "human project" will be undertaken in gendered ways. By applying this principle to human projects, we will find out more about the content of the genders and what is at stake in them. Let us consider some examples, using simplified ideal gender orientations to fighting and to nurturance.

If being at home in our bodies and our emotions is an essential human project, then a fighting gender will dictate utterly one-sided terms to body and emotion: they should be apt instruments of conscious purpose, perhaps even have beauty and power ingrained in them, but they should have no influence of their own. In contrast, the nurturing gender will affirm flesh and emotion as water in which the human being swims.

If rendering mortality acceptable is an essential human project, then members of a fighting gender will claim the solution of fame, that is, memorable individual achievement—ultimately by choosing the Good Death—while those of a nurturing gender will make their accommodation with death in the actual life-giving process, choosing life in spite of death. The first gender specializes in giving meaning to death, the second in appreciating that death is overshadowed by actual life (not only by ideal meaning).

If coming to terms with our need for each other is an essential human project, then members of a fighting gender will affirm a free camaraderie of shared purpose, interpreting even natural ties in this light, while members of a nurturing gender will affirm relations of natural and emotional dependence, interpreting even utilitarian association in this light.

When stated so baldly and in such extreme opposition, these gender versions of human projects seem terribly inadequate. I don't want to treat my body as a tool, or swoon in my flesh, either; I don't want to search out a good death, or refuse to admit my mortality, either; I don't want relationships to be either purely voluntaristic or purely involuntaristic. But in actual practice these emphases have certainly shown themselves in the masculine and feminine twists on the human projects under consideration. How could anyone live out such twists? The answer is that just as human projects come gendered, anything we could specify as a gender project must come humanized. Because human beings cannot in fact be at home in their bodies treating them merely as tools, even masculine beings do not have to live that way, for they are also human beings. Humanity pulls on masculinity. But it pulls on masculinity in a masculine way. A masculine voice does not tell someone that it's all right to cry in the same way that a feminine voice does.

If humanity is really caught between these opposed ways of advancing the central human projects—if, for instance, we really are bound to veer between the extremes of embracing death and rejecting it, either because those are the psychologically stable attitudes or because we often find ourselves in extreme situations (like war and childbirth) to which one-sided attitudes are best adapted—then the genders would function as necessary reminders and correctives to each other. But if a synthesis of these opposites or a balance between them is thinkable in an ideally mature human individual, and if we can imagine such an individual learning all the sides of the human truth without the inspiration of gender exemplars, then we seem to lose the best possible reason for thinking that gender is humanly indispensable.

The central human project we are most concerned with in the present inquiry is that of coming to terms with human kinds, thought of as an important limit-and-opportunity ingredient in human nature and the human condition. Whether human kinds, or gender in particular, ought to be acknowledged as something to come to terms with is an issue always before us. But one way to resolve *this* issue is to find out, by seeing what would be involved in coming to terms with a given human kind, whether we can afford to admit its reality.

Gender and other human kinds compared

So far we have done little to weigh the human value of gender or to assess the actual genders. We have, however, marked within the large structure of gender thinking two principal avenues for further inquiry, the sexual center of meaning and the spiritual central meaning in a gender. These are the subjects of subsequent chapters, where we can come to closer grips with the contents of our gender experience.

Before we move on in those directions, however, we can profitably expand our analysis of human differentiation to the other human kinds, comparing them all with gender for reciprocal clarification.

Human kinds can be thought of as forming a system insofar as they correspond to the chief categories in which the "human" falls:

With the possibility of being a *subject* comes variability in the fundamental quality of one's engagement with the world, that is, in *temperament*.

Being a *person* implies communal life and its variable self-definition, *culture,* which sets one up with a scheme for interpreting experience and taking up a position in relationships. *Class* reflects the variability in a culture's definition of its members.

A set of variabilities is given with the fact that subjective and personal life is lived by a sexually reproducing *animal: race, age,* and the sex-based *gender* and *sexual orientation*.

My survey of human-kind notions is guided by a four-part hypothesis: first, that each kind has its own distinctive way of qualifying the human (which is why it stands out as a durable category in our thinking); second, that each kind is subject to qualification by all the others; third, that each kind's distinctive principle can be taken from its home base and applied to other kinds in thinking and talking about them, whether in confusion or as a matter of deliberate metaphorical assertion; and fourth, that such transfers happen chronically, both with and against the grain of the actual cross-qualifications of the kinds, complicating our everyday apprehension of each kind. If following this hypothesis does bring such complexities to light, then anyone trying seriously to interpret human experience through categories like gender, class, and race had better be aware of them.

Temperament

Temperament is an intentional disposition. Like my physical "constitution," it is pretty much fixed, but like my freer "attitudes" and "tastes," it is subjective. We think it is important because we detect it at the back of attitudes and tastes. It is often seen as overlaid by character types like "ambitious," "sympathetic," "introverted," and so forth, but the latter are more specific and accidental and more capable of varying through an individual's life, while the former is the more fundamental, "natural," unalterable qualification. (As a matter of fact, a temperament may be induced by early experiences and not literally innate, but it is apprehended, regardless, as already in place.) Temperament is the first (or last) human kind, the beginning (or end) of our discernment of resemblances among individuals, the generic nature most closely bound to our perception of individuality itself. One can say, "That's her temperament," without assigning her to any named temperamental categories; nevertheless, by invoking temperament one establishes a basis for seeing her together with others who might turn out to "have" it also. "That's her temperament" is one step toward the generic from the purely individualizing "That's her."

Attempts to conceive a system of temperamental types—whether as the classical foursome Sanguine, Melancholy, Choleric, and Phlegmatic, or in more recent Jungian approaches like the Meyers–Briggs system—bend the *semantics* of temperament toward the ordinary semantics of gender, limiting the possible assignments that persons can receive, but cannot alter the more flexible *logic* of temperament, according to which the difference between two versions of a temperament is of greater interest than the difference between two versions of a gender. That the point of temperament thinking is to make a near approach to knowing the individual subject is evident in the complex, nuance-seeking application of temperamental type-systems to individuals. The other side of this coin is that generic reality is felt more weakly in temperaments than in genders. If temperament were perfectly analogous to gender, we would meet in, say, cheerful people a more standard common cheerfulness in which we felt them to participate; we would have a sense of dealing with cheerfulness itself whenever we dealt with a cheerful individual; and, as the crucial support of this sense, we would be able to point to a certain group of human beings as a material center of meaning, like sexes for genders. (Faces ruddy for choler and pale for phlegm?)

But perhaps genders just are postulations of broadly opposed, complex temperaments linked to sex. After all, temperament is like gender in deeply and to some extent uncontrollably affecting one's attunements to other beings and what one can perceive, be persuaded of, and be expected to amount to. William James thought it important to recognize that people take intellectual positions to which they are temperamentally suited, and now feminist writers have shown how a number of dominant ways of thinking in our culture are emotionally tailored to males.[43] Temperament and gender both have a kind of cogency that solicits without simply predetermining one's will; a sanguine person can feel the quasi-objective pull of sanguinity itself, besides being for the most part spontaneously cheerful. Furthermore, the complementarity of temperaments, as of genders, is profound and intimate. Friendship between persons of contrasting temperaments strikes us as a sort of marriage.

The precise difference between gender and temperament will be grasped only if we bring into view the anthropological categories to which they correspond. Because temperament arises in the variation possible to subjecthood as such, its lines of difference run across cultures, classes, races, ages, and sexes, and the specifications it receives from these other kinds are only secondary in our discernment of it. A phlegmatic young Chinese girl is of the same temperamental type as a phlegmatic old Swedish man, whatever the difference in the temperament's expressions. For that matter, there is no absurdity in saying that they share their temperament with a phlegmatic rat. Gender, however, pertains to the variability of sexed personhood, which means that it is essentially related both to body types and to culture. We expect a Chinese man to be both like and unlike a Swedish man in respect of masculinity—like, in our reading of the active presence of physical maleness, and unlike, according to the different ways their cultures position them in a gender system to act and react in relationship with other persons. And a rat cannot be masculine at all, though we may joke that an aggressive rat is "macho" or a timid one "demure." To construe gender as temperament is, therefore, either a mistake or a metaphor.

Before passing from this subject, it will be worthwhile to consider Mead's argument in *Sex and Temperament in Three Primitive Societies* that the most interesting and important human differences pertain to temperament rather than sex.[44] Two of the New Guinean societies she studied seemed to promote a single character ideal for women and men alike, each taking the "clue" of a particular temperament that might be found in either females or males in any society. Since these two societies adopted virtually opposite temperaments as their models, the content of sex roles varied wildly between them. One could not see, for instance, a common maternalness in Arapesh and Mundugumor women; instead, one saw a common nurturing orientation in Arapesh men and women. In addition, temperament explained better than sex the phenomena of individual deviance: it was not women who were proportionally more unhappy in the Mundugumor regime of fierceness, but nonfierce individuals of both sexes.

While Mead made reference to the larger theme of "sex differences" rather than gender in the strict sense, one could say that gender was her true object of inquiry, that she created a space in which gender differentiation would be apparent to us if it was indeed present, and that a certain sort of sex-related difference failed to appear. What caused this nonappearance, however, was a pair of conceptual difficulties that Mead, in her time, could scarcely be expected to overcome. In the first place, the "sex differences" problematic ties genders too closely to sexes and sex roles; it prevents one from realizing how much like temperament gender is, even to the extent of being free of sex in a way. Second, Mead was looking for a relatively definite and innate determination of character—as definite as Western sex roles, as innate as sex—but since gender is a relatively more diffuse and open character type than temperament, and more culturally stipulative than either temperament or sex, it was sure to be eclipsed by temperament in Mead's findings. Thus obvious evidences of gender difference, like the childlikeness of Arapesh women in their relations with men, are reported by Mead without being registered as gender phenomena.[45]

When Mead asserted that all normal Arapesh are maternal, she intended an ironic reflection on American preconceptions about sex; in the event, though, she illustrated the difference between gender and sex attribution (since Arapesh men really are maternal in striking ways) as well as the difference between gender and temperament (the former open enough to serve as a plausible characterization of a whole society, the latter specific and fixed enough to be seen in a cross-culturally recurring ensemble).

Culture

Culture, we think, establishes a whole human world by cultivating human capacities in a particular, variable way. It has an objective aspect—a language, a set of customs, practical and artistic styles, an array of material artifacts, a history—and a subjective quality in what it is *like* to live in the world as someone thus cultured. It is not an influence upon consciousness but a shape of consciousness. Like other human kinds, culture influences our consciousness, but it alone is the very articulate form of consciousness—so that if we were to posit, say, "class consciousness" or "race consciousness" as species of consciousness, rather than as qualifications of consciousness, we would necessarily be speaking of class- and race-based cultures.

Culture and gender are both normative organizations of intention binding a group together, creating a space- and time-spanning "us," except that genders, as complementary kinds of a kind, are more like subcultures. One's culture is cognitively and valuationally global, so that one is a sort of prisoner in it; it is the map on which all maps must be located. (We can acknowledge this without denying culture the flexibility and openness needed to grow, to improve, and to translate the expressions of other cultures. We can also admit the possibility of the multicultural person who is equipped with alternative master maps: the fact that any culture is in a sense complete does not mean that it exhausts the human capacity that it cultivates.) But whereas culture is a self-sufficient whole, except in the respect that it contrasts itself with foreign cultures, temperaments always vary within a community, while genders actually articulate an internal structure of the community. Gender is bound in some way to manifest physical differences that are understood to be naturally given, but the physiognomy of a culture is much more diversified and is understood to be a product of our activity.

What happens when gender is interpreted as "cultural"? As a purely descriptive claim, this says, rightly, that gender is an objectified meaning and a shared form of consciousness, a perspective on the world. As a claim about cause, it says that our being gendered is the product of cultural process. Taken one way, the latter claim only draws an obvious conclusion from the principle that everything human is "cultural." Even the human body is an adaptation to the cultural opportunities of speech and extended learning. But what is meant is "culturally imposed within an individual's lifetime," as against "innate." Temperament would be the best example of relative innateness in the sense of this opposition. Is gender more like cultivated or innate qualities? Positive gender thinking is most comfortable saying "innate"; critical thinking would rather say "cultivated." But our earlier discussion of the sex–gender distinction implied that gender is not more like either one: its whole point is to be like both. The principle that gender is *based* on sex, has sex as a center of meaning, tells us that a gender-specific endowment awaits cultivation. That gender is a culturally engineered "central meaning" with a culturally influenced physical basis tells us that it is not thinkable apart from the cultivation.[46] (We will find a similar doubleness in the thought of race.)

Gender is "cultural," too, in the sense that it bonds its members together with a tradition-glue that one can either keep pouring on or try to dissolve. For instance, one woman celebrates feminine intuition and guile, while another shrinks in embarrassment from so corny and demeaning a stereotype. It is like the two sides of the assimilation question for a cultural minority.[47]

The concepts of "culture" and "race" both gained currency in the era of nationalism, and it is not always clear in which of these categories to locate talk of a "people" or "ethnicity." (There is a corresponding ambiguity in the concept of genocide.)[48] J. G. Herder meant by *Volk* a community united by language, that is, a culture, but Adolf Hitler meant by *Volk* a "culture-supplying" community of heredity.[49] To remove this uncertainty, or to appreciate it where we cannot remove it, we must be able to trace the logic of race thinking.

Race

Race is an "us" or "them" produced by breeding—either a discernible type resulting from patterns of breeding in the past or a prospect of likely (or licit) breeding in the future.[50] These two frameworks are not separable. If the males traditionally called Caucasoid were, in general, every bit as likely to have children with the females called Mongoloid or Negroid as they were to have children with the females called Caucasoid, then the Mongoloid, Negroid, and Caucasoid types would count for us not as races but as intraracial variations on the order of blond and brunet. But it is true at the same time that if breeding actually went this way, the distinctions between the Caucasoid, Mongoloid, and Negroid types would disappear in the genetic mixing.

Under ideally simple conditions the race community should coincide with the cultural-tradition community, providing each culture its own racial face, because the practical cooperation that sustains culture should extend to mating and thence to a more or less regular distribution of the communal repertoire of heritable physical traits, even as they vary over time. Things do not happen so simply, however. Often there is intersocial gene flow to break a culture's hold on distinctive traits, and within a society there are kin- and class-based constraints on mating. (In a "multiracial" society, people pay attention to race precisely to maintain a sense of different breeding affinities, if not an out-and-out taboo on cross-race breeding.) It remains possible to bring race and culture together by a coup: the members of a society can overlook physical-type differences among themselves if the primary move in their race thinking is a stipulation that they are commonly descended from worthy forebears.[51]

One can say that races furnish the human material for cultures in the sense that races, as reproductive processes, produce the human beings who become members of the cultures; but there need not be a one-to-one race-to-culture relationship. The cultures that inspirit races are perhaps "of" them in the way—one must choose this analogy carefully—that a painting is made "of" its colors. The room that there is to argue about how matter and form qualify each other in a painting, and their relative contributions to the painting's effect, is analogous to our uncertainty about the mutual qualification of races and cultures.

I have so far treated race as a collection of people, according to the most common usage. But if we are to be clear on the issues we confront under this heading we will have to draw a distinction, parallel to the sex–gender distinction, between physical–factual "breed" and social–personal "race" proper.[52] Nearly any time we speak of "race relations" or "the race question" or use categories like "black literature" or "white soul music," we construct transpersonal characters or spirits for which physical types are mere vehicles: we construct them, whether or not we started out envisioning them. And true racism is assuredly more profound, and more profoundly objectionable, than the silly breedism to which it is rhetorically reduced ("How can you dislike people for the color of their skin?"). Although talk of race very often purports to be about breed only, I think it must virtually always engage qualities of race (in the stricter sense) in some way.

Breed differences do not have a biological foundation as definite as that of sex difference and cannot be fixed to the same degree. As the deposits left by past breeding, they are only blurrily bounded (for the copulation opportunities have been somewhat open); as a menu for future breeding, they can of course be instantly redefined or even banished altogether, depending entirely on how we think about sexual eligibility. If it happens that people line up as strictly White or Black in a particular multiracial society, race difference will simulate the apparently natural or logical duality in sex–gender, and there will be a tendency to think of race genderishly—positively, as an appreciation of natural complementariness, and negatively, as a horror of sexual relations crossing the customary lines. The arrival of a third racial group in such a society poses a confusing new riddle of classification.[53] But overall there is no principle to be detected in the number or quality of salient breed/race types we now experience, except that they sketch for us some part of the range of physical possibility for humans and thus make us aware that a range is not to be denied. If confronting sex difference makes me realize that I need a partner to reproduce, confronting breed difference makes me realize that no finite reproducing community can have the category of the human all to itself. The gravity of these two realizations is fundamental to the meaning of gender and race, respectively.[54] At the heart of racism is a refusal to let oneself be decentered, to represent only one set of possibilities among others.

The racial central meaning has an even looser tie to the breed center of meaning than gender does to sex; its emotional roots are not ordinarily as deep, and individuals usually have more latitude to choose what to make of breed identity (or even whether to acknowledge it) than is the case with sex identity.[55] An easily seen proof of race quality's ability to travel beyond its breed base is the massive black American influence on Western and ultimately world culture, quite noticeably affecting the way millions of nonblacks talk, sing, and move their bodies, often with direct reference to the activities of blacks. One ought to assume that racial influences run constantly in all possible channels and directions, even if not always so strikingly (for this white observer) as the black influences cited.

How a race's qualities are based on a physical type should become more understandable once we have studied the basing of gender on sex in Chapter 4. It is worth observing now, though, that race, like gender, consists of a complex, infinitely variable fabric of personal qualities that no formula can perfectly define. As with gender, it is our lively sense of contrast in a certain dimension, rather than any definite perception, that makes race a palpable quality. The strangeness wants a name; it will be called something like "paleness" or "darkness" first and then given other characters. This explains the seeming paradoxes that (1) people can only imprecisely and inconsistently spell out the character of a difference that they feel to be the most obvious thing in the world, and (2) members of one group can lump diverse physical types into one or two racial categories that make no perceptual sense to members of another group.[56]

If hereditary differences within a breed are noted as sub-breeds like aristocratic "blue blood," or degrees of "color," or clan or family membership, then to these sub-breeds will correspond subraces. A subrace may very well be called a class, as in the case of the aristocracy, but to use this notion is to invoke a different logic.

Class

The Latin word *classis,* with the sense of "summons," was used by Romans for military levies on different income-level groups.[57] Since then class has always had the twofold implication of graded social rank and vital social function, with the latter usually receiving the greater emphasis in any ideal rationale for a class system. The flourishing of society is thought to require that a range of specialized tasks be carried out harmoniously—or, not to be too narrow, we could speak of an ideal that a range of types of life be lived harmoniously—and that a range of specialized human aptitudes correspondingly fit people for these tasks. The aptitudes might be naturally given, or they might be induced; but the functions, in any case, are perceived as necessary (some must produce; some must fight; some must rule). That justifies the stern requirement to shape one's whole life in devotion to a particular function. Class members' natures are determined positively by their capacity to make the contributions expected of them, negatively by their being forbidden to presume to share in the distinctive experiences of any other class.

A class both is and isn't a world unto itself. That it is set up to make a vital social contribution entails that its members interact daily with members of other classes; but that it deeply affects the personal character of its members entails that they will "naturally" find their friends and spouses within their class. Thus we can expect a class to hold itself together through generations, even without strictures based on race or subrace theory.

A class system is haunted by the legitimation question: If everyone really is socially necessary, then are institutionalized inequalities of power and privilege justifiable? If not, can classes exist without these inequalities?

Gender resembles class in being linked to function. We feel the resemblance strongly in the measure that we view gendered functions (like childbearing and fighting) as socially necessary and require that our lives be substantially adapted to them. Could we define gender as "sex class"? The principle of class is correlative with cultural, not biological, variability. A class system is a cultural answer to the question of how to maximize richness in collective life. This would be a fair description of the gender system, too, up to a point, yet in reading gender, body type is primary and function is secondary (implied by the body), while in reading class, function is primary and body type (for instance, the rough hands of laborers) is a consequence of it. (If class is rationalized with an aristocratic theory of "blood" or a Platonic myth that people are made of unequal metals, then the supposed physical data are more important; but in that case we have strayed into the category of race.) It follows from the lesser importance of the body for class that class is more readily understood as artificial, mutable, and open. Stories of class-crossing are much less disturbing than stories of gender-crossing.

Professions are something like subclasses or miniclasses, depending on the social position of the function involved. We often apprehend, though more faintly, that knowing members of a profession is knowing a kind of people. As Wollstonecraft pointed out, the constraints of professions give rise to character traits that might or might not be approvable.[58] The *déformation professionelle* is proverbial; perhaps it would be fair to pay more attention to professional *formation*, since virtues as well as vices are promoted by the practical challenges to which the professions correspond. Even in lawyers.

Age

Chronological age ranges are the physical bases of "young," "mature," and "old" as personal qualities. With the understanding that age is a human kind we can appreciate people as (say) "youthful," or deride them as "childish," whether or not spiritual and chronological age agree. One culture might adopt a universal directive to be young at heart; another might prefer emulation of the serene dignity associated with the old.

In the following example of age thinking from Hume's essay "Of the Standard of Taste," youthfulness and oldness are either treated as temperamental qualifications or run very closely together with them.

> A young man, whose passions are warm, will be more sen-sibly touched with amorous and tender images than a man more advanced in years, who takes pleasure in wise, philosophical re-flections concerning the conduct of life and moderation of the passions. At twenty, OVID may be the favourite author; HORACE at forty; and perhaps TACITUS at fifty. Vainly would we, in such cases, endeavour to enter into the sentiments of others, and divest ourselves of those propensities, which are natural to us. We choose our favourite author as we do our friend, from a conformity of humour and disposition.[59]

In the general area of "natural propensities," where we run into the variables of "humour" and "disposition," we might wonder where exactly age quality falls. I claimed earlier that temperament varies in-dependently of age, that young and old persons—I will now add, *as* youthful and august—can share a temperament. We could accommo-date Hume's sense of age by saying now that temperament partly does and partly doesn't vary in relation to it. Alternatively, we could carry over our reasoning about temperament and gender, maintaining that age, like gender, is fundamentally a personal variation. But this specific parallel fails the rat test. It turns out that rats *can* be youthfully flexible or agedly staid, and the reason is that like us they have aging bodies and a life of accumulating experience.

At first blush, age seems to differ decisively from race and gender in several ways; yet the differences shrink in reconsideration. It is especially clear in the case of age that what people believe about age's centers of meaning, the age ranges, varies a good deal. "Childhood" as a time of life with its own distinctive character and value is a recent thought for us, historically speaking, and a reconceptualization of "old age" is in progress right now; in both cases of paradigm shift, what we are able to notice about an age is greatly changed.[60] If we turn to the histories of race and gender thinking with this point in mind, we will indeed see significant variation in what people have construed to be the facts of breed and sex to which these human meanings refer.

Of all human qualifications that have something essential to do with the body, age seems the least affected by it: youthfulness is more a matter of openness and untrammeled enthusiasm than of small size or smooth skin. It is not so much the physical aging of the body as the building up of knowledge and personality over time that accounts for olderness. That is why it is common enough for a child to be precociously mature or a grown-up to be young at heart. But gender and race identities are similarly founded in experience, not just in the body. Feminine and masculine personalities crystallize out of a certain socially ordered set of interactions, and one could say the same of personalities like "white" and "black" whenever racial interaction occurs. One can say that the essence of youth is newness of *mind*, but one can also say that the essence of femininity is sympathy as a mental quality, or that the essence of European "whiteness" (in a particular race economy) is rationalist abstraction. In each case, physical quality is a symbol and not the human kind itself.

Because age identity is determined by a sliding position on the line from birth to death, which we are all supposed to travel, we feel every age to be freighted with the significance of the universal human condition. We have, at most, only glimmers of such a feeling about gender and race; but perhaps we ought to cultivate it, since the worst, most radical kind of genderism or racism is not a judgment that the Other Kind is of lesser value but rather is a disposition to *nullify* the Other Kind: *they do not concern me, I can understand myself without considering them.*

While inequities may exist in relations between age groups, at least everyone has to take a turn in each. To be sure, this minimal fairness is not automatic; it is violated when some people are kept from reaching certain ages or from having the characteristic experiences of certain ages, such as when young men are sacrificed in war. But gender and race, apparently lacking any equivalent to this fairness, pose more severe problems of justice. Now here is a second thought. The fact that virtually no one changes sex or breed does not make it impossible to "take turns" with gender- or race-specific *experiences* and in that fashion appropriate some of the qualities of which gender and race are constituted. We have a choice how to proceed, so that a sort of justice question does arise. Males could say that women are naturally superior nurturers, so that, like it or not, child care is not men's business; or they could take a turn with the children. Whites could say that the blues is black music, and so nothing to do with them; or they could learn to appreciate the blues. Which are the better ways?

To the extent that we think of ages as passing stations on a journey,[61] we are not very worried about the imprisoning effect of making generalizations about age, particularly about youth. Who raises an eyebrow when I say that "youth" is open and uninhibited? Yet my illustrative attributions to "feminine" and "white" are not likely to go unchallenged. Perhaps, rather than relaxing our guard, we should watch age definitions more vigilantly. Children, for example, are not free from the harm of child-stereotyping simply because they will one day no longer be children; in fact, it is not the case that children will one day no longer be the persons they were as children, for life is a continuation and development of self, not a succession of different selves. At any rate, even as children they are entirely human beings who stand to live well or poorly and ought to be enabled to live well. If, say, our view of children leads us to treat them as infinitely flexible and resilient when the truth is that they often suffer lasting emotional hurt, then we face here the sort of stereotyping problem that is familiar to us from gender and race thinking.

More positively, sensitive attention to age improves our ability to preserve and elaborate the *virtues* of the different ages as our age experience accumulates. Cultural endorsement of youthful character traits like curiosity and playfulness can help us realize the advantages of what biologists call neoteny, the retention of childhood forms by adults.[62]

Sexual orientation

There has always been variation in people's sexual tastes and attitudes, but the modern thought of sexual orientation supposes that significant human kinds are formed by partner-type preferences. As one aspect of the infinitely various potential called "sexuality," sexual orientation is an unclear notion at least to the degree that we are unsure what sexuality is—how desire, fear, pleasure, and power are at stake in it, how personality is affected by it, how biological and cultural factors interact in it, and how it is related to gender (a contested notion in its own right).[63] For all that, there has been a massive effort to think this thought, and we can and must try to get clear on its logic.

We encountered one version of the idea of sexual orientation in Marcel Proust's assertion that M. de Charlus had become a woman by thinking tenderly of men.[64] Sometimes Charlus is presented in the more old-fashioned way as a man who *has* particular tastes, that is, has developed or acquired these tastes, and whose indulgence of them is conventionally regarded as wicked or degrading or unnatural *activity;* but at other times he is called "the invert," the man who *is* "Nature's mistake." Historically speaking, Charlus is almost ready to walk out onto a public playing field where everyone will wear jerseys with "gay," "lesbian," "straight," and other more specific characters marked on them—and where suspicions will be voiced that each individual's locker contains a whole set of jerseys.[65] But we want to know whether these labels correspond to apprehensible variations of human nature. For instance, do all gays, or all persons insofar as they realize gayness, have a distinctive sensibility or style? Charlus's effeminacy is something of a red herring, for neither gays nor lesbians necessarily model themselves on their opposite sexes. Sometimes a publicly visible manner accompanies sexual orientation, sometimes not; indeed, part of the thrust of marking off sexual orientation from sex on the one hand and gender on the other is to target something about a person that is *not* on the surface, an utterly inner and soulish thing, desire, which one can only infer from the subject's activities of seeking, finding, and coupling with certain others.[66] With no other human kind could we ask, Is it overt?

Do sexual preferences flower forth in *cultural* expressions through which we apprehend their quality? It is not clear whether the formation of lesbian and gay "subcultures" more resembles the self-definition of interest groups within a common culture (like, say, environmentalists, who also have their own literature, their own organizational forms, and so forth) or the cultivation of distinctive endowments in the manner of ethnic groups or genders.

In order to grasp the anthropological significance of sexual orientation, we must begin by marking the kind of human variability that is involved in it. As sexually reproducing mammals we are set up with the male and female reproductive roles, and with more than that: since we are extremely sensitive and smart, we carry a kit of strong sex-associated emotions along with our reproductive equipment. To these emotions belongs a new variability, namely, to whom our longings and fears will refer, or where to seek sexual happiness. This variability is irreducibly real, no matter how it is or isn't articulated (that is, by innate endowment or individual experience or cultural process); and it is this issue that lies at the heart of the experience of difference in sexual orientation, giving that experience its characteristic quiver. We are making a great mistake if we assume a disjunction between the "culturally constructed" and the "real" in human identity.[67]

The interior variation of desire is not volition, although it is interpreted as perverse choice by those who feel threatened by it. Implicit in the variability of sexual preference is the alternative of either foregoing the combination of erotic life with procreation or not foregoing it, but homosexual preference as such is no more a choice against procreation than heterosexual preference is a choice for it. (Some nonheterosexual couples want children and some heterosexual couples don't.) Another alternative similarly implicit in sexual preference is whether one belongs to a social "mainstream" or to a minority, but this is not usually a matter of choice either—even though social conformism may help in suppressing nonheterosexual desires, while revulsion from the mainstream may propel one more forcefully into an overtly nonheterosexual mode of life.

Because sex is involved in both differences, we may be tempted to fit sexual orientation and gender together into one scheme. Bringing the sex–gender distinction to bear, one might think of a scheme such as this:

MALE OR FEMALE:

Homosexual masculine	Homosexual androgynous	Homosexual feminine
Bisexual masculine	Bisexual androgynous	Bisexual feminine
Heterosexual masculine	Heterosexual androgynous	Heterosexual feminine

But many nonheterosexuals, declining to be lumped under the homosexual rubric, would draw the significant differences differently. "Gay" is quite other than "lesbian," lovers of youth different from lovers of older persons, and so on. Revising to accommodate these perceptions, we will define more and more kinds of human being. Very well. Suppose for the sake of argument that we can make a map of this sort that is semantically acceptable all round; let us now consider its syntax. The map's layout has the merit of showing that orientations are not simply extra genders, and genders are not simply specifications of orientation by sex. But what do the conjunctions of gender and orientation mean?

At first it seems that orientation is a desire and an associated behavioral pattern that might be influenced by gender but need not be an influence on gender in turn. A gay man might be feminine to the degree that he fancies woman-associated ways of making love to men; but he might equally well prefer man-associated ways of making love to men, or like both ways. It is truer to say that insofar as a gay man is a feminine person he is more likely to enjoy the receptive part of sex, since the observed or presumed sexual receptivity of women is a source from which feminine quality is drawn. It was by being feminine that Charlus thought tenderly of men.

Such an approach leaves our understanding of gender undisturbed and asks for no new apprehensible qualities of "gayness" or "lesbianness" or "straightness." But it is too easy. Since positive gender thinking takes maleness and femaleness as paradigms and must include sexual behavior among the significant revelations of the nature of the sexes, variation in sexual orientation will crucially blur the meaning of "man-associated" or "woman-associated" and therefore of the genders. We cannot carry masculinity over from straight men to gay men unchanged, because man-associated sexual behavior among gays varies from the heterosexual norm consistently enough to generate rival conventions.

There are of course other components of masculinity that can characterize homosexuals and heterosexuals the same, making the two masculinities brothers, if you like. And there would be a reference to the sexual manner of heterosexual masculinity in the lovemaking of masculine gays or lesbians who acted the "man" part of a "man–woman" script. But there is more than one way to make the heterosexual reference, and there does not have to be such a reference at all.[68] What is fundamentally different about the homosexualities is precisely their grounding on a sex-based commonality, their rapprochement between sexual identification and desire—a kind of sexual meaningfulness more basic and universal than the highly variable psychological accompaniments that so often distract analysis of these orientations— as opposed to heterosexuality's postulated union of male and female specializations, *which is the basic premise of a gender system.* That is the way in which the homosexualities really are complementary to heterosexuality and why we might rewardingly think of the orientations as forming a genderlike scheme together even though the homosexualities are ungenderlike, in not affirming sexual complementarity, and also differently genderlike, in separately deepening the sense of "what it is to be a woman" and "what it is to be a man" along their same-sex paths.[69] (Wittig's ideal of the lesbian as one who departs from sex-marking altogether is a still more radical departure from gender, but this program can no longer be identified with any sort of "sexual orientation.")[70] Someone of a different orientation may very well strike me as a different sort of person in much the same way that someone presenting different gender quality does, but the difference is not that between masculine and feminine but instead a shift in the meaning of being sexed, and thereby a certain twist on gender. If I cannot bear the twist, I feel it to be "twisted."

From the heterosexual side, one powerful defense against the twist will be to put a Charlus in the familiar category of "woman"— now turning the old woman taunt inside out, using it to bring someone into an approved structure rather than to ostracize—so as to make his strangeness manageable. In homosexual perspectives, heterosexual preference is most intelligible as a perversion, not of gender (for gender in a sense *is* the perversion), but of humanity: heterosexuals may be seen as more sexually animalistic, or as lords or slaves in an order of sex-based domination.[71] Ideally speaking, the mutual disrespect between orientations is a serious problem for everyone, although it is a problem of health and livelihood just for the persecuted minority orientations. The special difficulty here lies in the lack of intimate relations across the sexual orientation boundaries, or in something actually the opposite of intimacy, a panicky aversion; for it is intimacy with each other, or disposition to intimacy, that generally leads heterosexual men and women to regard each other more as complementary than as deviant.[72]

A sex–sexuality–gender system cultivates women and men in such a way that the sexual centers of meaning and central meanings of the genders will be held fairly steady.[73] But the variability of sexual orientation unsettles the order of sexual behavior, which forms a crucial part of both centers. And this variability seems to invade from just across the threshold of personal or spiritual order as such, namely, out of the indeterminacy of subjecthood prior to spiritual qualification. It is not that I make conscious, intelligible, or morally assessible choices outside the spiritual frame of reference, which would be impossible. This indeterminacy is not "freedom." It is a question concerning which boxes in the spiritual post office I will arrive in. For example, "straight" and "gay" are equally personal structures, but which way I respond to other persons and participate in our communal self-definition will be determined by this obscure factor that is a sort of "taste" or "disposition," not by my sex. We want to think that the meaning of the lives of individual subjects is entirely regulated by spirits—that they are rational (or irrational), have appropriate loyalties (or cheat), measure up to (or fall short of) gender ideals, and so forth—but sexual orientation, like the better-domesticated variable "temperament," represents an elusiveness of the subject with respect to spirit, not an unruliness within it. That is why those who regard their own orientation as normal tend to view other orientations as horrifying treacheries and are prone to portraying deviants as tragically fouled-up people.

Although subjects come from outside the spiritual frame of reference in some sense, they have no exemption from spiritual norms; they cannot live either before or beyond good and evil. If we have a primordial liberty to endorse or to refuse the categories of good and evil, still the swings of our liberty have to be interpreted in those categories, for the spiritual order is the supremely concrete circumstance and authoritative principle of our existence; our self-interpretation is bound to it both de facto and de jure. Qua spiritual failure, one is an enigma. Yet one's liberty or variability might, without any possible advance justification, land one in a strange yet spiritually tenable place, thereby enriching or helping to rectify the spiritual state of affairs in the larger community. Perhaps this sort of event is always at the heart of moral progress: a new sensibility arrives in the world without warrant and shows a better way.

I mean to suggest, not that sexual orientations must be moral sensibilities, but that they are analogously unaccountable without being, for that reason, purely threatening. Now, to heterosexuals it seems that other-sex preference is eminently accountable because it corresponds to a practical necessity for species survival. But the very existence of homosexual preference without a comparable rationale opens up an abyss beneath heterosexuality's feet: if any given person might be homosexual, then what accounts for any given person not being homosexual?[74] (The tables can be turned. If it is self-evident to a circle of gentlemen that the nobler love is of boys, it is still true that any given gentleman might prefer women; how then can one finally account for the sort of gentleman one is?)

If the subject's variability is interpreted more positively as radical *freedom,* a Sartrean freedom in which "I have at my disposal an infinity of ways of assuming my being-for-Others,"[75] then sexual orientation, especially a nonconforming one, takes on the significance that it vindicates the subject against the social order. Although I have contended that there really is no knowable or valuable subject outside the social order, I admit that there is something in the subject that can be vindicated, namely, a new social possibility of which the subject is a bearer, and in this case sexual orientation indeed begins to look more like a moral sensibility. Thus it is not surprising that some contemporary women (for example) choose lesbian existence as the authentic radical alternative to a spiritually unacceptable participation in heterosexuality, and that an articulation of "lesbian ethics," not as a provincial adaptation of general ethics but as fundamental ethical insight, accompanies the formation of a self-conscious lesbian community.[76]

Hume's younger men and older men had different literary tastes because of a more basic age-based dispositional difference. Is sexual orientation, in contrast, *just* a sexual taste, not a "deeper" disposition— a taste that could attach to any disposition? If the taste is intensely emotional and profoundly involving because it shapes one's sexual life, on which so great a part of one's happiness depends, does that make it as fateful a thing as a character type or temperament? Just because they shift people off the conventional centers of gendered personality norms, the minority orientations do open up possibilities of being, let us say, an exceptionally aggressive woman or an unusually sensitive man. But if sexual orientation were in itself so all-determining a qualification of persons, one would expect "straightness" and "gayness" to be more consistently manifest than they are. One must conclude that orientation as a human qualification cannot be pinned down to one position on the spectrum between one's discrete "tastes" and one's most basic "disposition." Compounding the enigma, people differ in their positions on this tastes-to-disposition spectrum as well as in their objects of preference.

But even if taste is probably an inadequate category by which to define sexual orientation, still the old dictum that there is no accounting for tastes, or no meaningful disputation of taste, is our most familiar and clear window onto the variability of the subject where orientation is determined, and also onto the elusiveness with which this sort of difference makes itself felt.

Human nature as an endowment of diversities

Reviewing the human differences, I am decentered over and over again, provided that I stay mindful of who I concretely am. I am always just one of the planets. Had I taken the more usual approach to "human nature," I'd have been the sun; in the end I'd have admired a larger-than-life projection of everything I experience as though it were all proper to myself. "Nothing human is alien to me" would have meant: nothing is human that is really beyond me. But the major human variabilities are indeed beyond me, for I am in every case just one part of human variability, not the variability itself. (The clearest exception to this rule is age; still, I always am *an* age and a *certain* aging.)

I am not, however, off-center in just so many separate ways as there are human kinds. That they are all *human* kinds not only makes each of them subject to negotiation and mutual acceptance, it also holds their variations together in a system of complementary support. There is no human project that does not stand to be enriched or better balanced by the influence of every variation. I cannot be sure that I will never meet a situation in which a different gender, temperament, culture, race, class, age, or sexual orientation than mine will offer supremely apposite guidance. This diversity is a marvelous collective equipment for life, analogous to the strictly genetic diversity that makes living species resilient.

Variabilities *of* humanity form a peaceful system in which I have a noncentral place. Variabilities *from* me, lines of difference radiating out from myself as central point, form another sort of system, one of fear, violence, and domination.[77]

We cannot say that any particular shape of specifically human diversity, like gender as distinct from sex, is "natural" in the sense that it belongs permanently to the consistency of human life. For any such shape is culturally specified and therefore variable. The same is true of any specification of a human kind considered as a format for personal fulfillment or for interpersonal harmony. What is a universal and necessary feature of human life, however, are the diversities as such, present in all human affairs as a starting point. No matter who I am, if I am human, I can be certain that unless I take myself out of the human world I will be subject to decentering in the dimensions of sex, race, temperament, and so on. These variabilities of life in the human body, as much as any "positive" feature of life like reason or language, furnish the fundamental *endowment* for human life, the unchangeable setup for human life *par excellence,* and are proper objects of piety (or else despair). These variabilities give reason and language their mission.

Chapter 4

The Sex "Basis" of Gender

In each of the next three chapters we approach an aspect of the gender problem by first taking one large step backward into a more general philosophical problem. Here the question we want to be able to answer is, How is gender "based" on sex? The distinction between a gender's central meaning of character qualities and its center of meaning in facts of sexedness yielded clarity at one stage of our investigation, but it also opens up new questions. We said that the central gender meaning "refers to" the sex center of meaning in the sense that it is eminently the meaning of the center of meaning. But there is more in the ordinary thought of the sex–gender relation than was expressed in that formula. The ordinary thought takes gender to be "based" on, *and by,* sex; that is, it supposes not only that the benchmark expression of a gender character is found in the generality of people of a certain sex, but also that a chief reason for this is that sexedness really does, of itself, make a generic difference to character. How, then, would the difference be made? What can coherently be supposed about the influence of sexed bodily form on gender?

We cannot coherently suppose anything about a relationship between physical and intentional qualities if we do not have, first, a view of the relationship between descriptive and intentional concepts and, second, a general understanding of the phenomenon of embodiment.

The latter especially is a dark, difficult issue, and the darkness seeps into the gender discussion insofar as sex minimizers tacitly rely on an untenable dualist view of mind–body relation, while sex determinists rely for their part on an untenable materialism.

Without undertaking a treatise on embodiment, it is possible to outline a model of embodiment that is satisfactory in two crucial respects: (1) it promises to be free of the most obvious shortcomings of the familiar dualist and materialist accounts and (2) it furnishes a helpful framework in which to interpret the most important claims and concerns about the relevance of sex to character. The key idea in this account of embodiment is to construe intentional and physical phenomena as events of centering and extending, respectively.

Not every reader will care to follow the details of a priori reflection on the possible direct influences of sexedness on intention, but this exercise will show what there is in our sexed embodiment—to wit, *not nothing* in every major dimension of embodiment—that we use our discretion to make much or little of in our constructions of gender. These not-nothings are necessarily important for science, politics, and art.

Unfortunately, gender theorizing does not usually incorporate a thoughtful appraisal of biology. Embraces and dismissals alike tend to be naive. On the one hand, the intentional concepts that are central in human self-interpretation are fundamentally different from the descriptive concepts with which biology or any natural science works (a point that motivates dismissal of biology); on the other hand, humans are undoubtedly objects of biological study, that is, physiological structures that are products of evolution, and in this character are not simply different beings than the ones who form plans and who judge good and evil (a point that motivates biologism). It would seem that biology is neither all-competent to define us nor irrelevant to our definition. The challenge, then, is to develop an understanding of the relationship between humanity as an object of biological study and the humanity in which we fully recognize ourselves, and that is the task of the last three sections of this chapter.

The female and male bodies are the principles of *consistency* in our gender experience. It is because of its "basing" on sex that gender pertains to human nature in this aspect.

The problem of junction between intentional and descriptive concepts

We are dealing with a particular form of an old, profound puzzle, latterly known as the mind–body problem. We cannot expect to understand the gender–sex relation if we do not understand how intention is present in a body. The problem has a logical aspect as well: we will not understand the relation between gender talk and sex talk unless we understand the relation between intentional concepts and descriptive concepts in general.

Corresponding to the two aspects of "meaning" distinguished in Chapter 3, the intentional and the descriptive are ideally distinct orders of concepts serving two distinct fundamental purposes. Intentional concepts steer our practice; descriptive concepts identify observable objects. Descriptive concepts *have* meaning, insofar as they record the shape of experiences we have had and expect to have in the world, whereas of intentional concepts it would be more apt to say that they *do* meaning (though they naturally *have* meaning as well insofar as it is possible to get hold of them). The meaning of an intentional concept is eminently ourselves meaning, as in "She really means it." Biology employs descriptive concepts like "adaptive" and "maladaptive" (referring to the observable longevity of organic entities), "gene," and "behavior." Morality and politics employ intentional concepts like "good" and "bad," "motivation," and "conduct." We are constantly trying to effect a junction between the two orders of concepts, simply because we cannot live otherwise than in the world, that is, in an environment of perceptible beings, and we cannot be in the world except as alive, that is, as self-steering.

Most terms, of course, can represent either a descriptive or an intentional conception. The different sorts of conception can alternate in possessing a term. (With *human, woman,* and *man,* this happens all the time.) What counts is what we do with terms.

Descriptive concepts have no meaning apart from our tracing and reacting to the features of things, and so they already establish a kind of junction between intentional probing and the observable realm. But there is no self-awareness in them; for that we require intentional concepts. As the mental wake left by expressive, self-aware bodily action, intentional concepts "solve" the junction problem at this higher level, but only insofar as they directly express our embodied existence. They become puzzles when we make them themes of reflection, since there is room in abstract thought for estrangement between their distinguishable meanings. For example, "motive" identifies an aspect of our own agency with the natural phenomenon of motion. Thinking of myself, qua mover, as moved, I realize a junction between intention and the way of the phenomenal world. Reflection establishes, however, that the moving of intention cannot be the same as phenomenal displacement, for intending as such is not directly observable, not originally spatially extended, but only apparent as it enters space in its *expression;* furthermore, the moving of intention is always *aimed* and thus always involves satisfaction or frustration, unlike phenomenal movement as such. The doubleness in "motive" and our general double nature as intentional and observable beings now stand revealed. But the reflective problem of this doubleness now resists solution because, by getting clear on the distinction between the intentional and the descriptive, we have lost the tools with which we might overcome it: now all our concepts have to be assigned to one order or the other.

Sometimes the problem of junction is covered over by using concepts in an equivocal way. For instance, "motivation" might mean causation in a psychological experiment where the caused phenomenon happens to be a person's action. But confusion is apt to result from talking in this way, because the scientific observer qua observer is only coincidentally *dealing* with the "motivated" experimental subject, and the act of supplying a cause of a certain behavior (in order to check the effect) is not the same as the act of giving a reason for a certain action (in order to see how the reason stands up). Similarly, an elevation of testosterone level may observably cause more aggressive behavior, but it cannot directly serve as a reason to feel lordly, in the way that appreciating one's own power does. And yet what makes such experiments interesting is our concern for motivation as an intentional issue.

We have different systems of beliefs corresponding to these two kinds of concepts, beliefs like "Failure to feed one's young offspring is usually maladaptive," on the one hand, and "It's wrong to be inattentive to one's children's needs," on the other. An ambiguous middle sort of belief would be "Children are harmed by neglect" (since *harm* and *neglect* carry definite physical meanings at the same time that they predicate ills of intentional existence). Gender beliefs are typically expressed in ambiguous terms, the descriptive concepts "women" and "men" employed to mean the intentional characters "feminine" and "masculine" at the same time that they refer to female and male bodies. "Women are more nurturing than men" is a belief that depends on such ambiguity. More than anything, it means "nurturing is an ingredient of femininity"; the claim is not invalidated if it turns out that some women have less nurturing aptitude than some men, for it only expresses a practical expectation that one will find more nurturing aptitude in one's dealings with women, or that insofar as one conducts oneself in a womanlike fashion one is likely to be a better nurturer, or that the female body is the single most important qualification (that is, relevant capability) for nurturing. At the same time, all these expectations are, in the end, empirically vulnerable, because the meaning of womanlikeness is not independent of what women are observably doing. For instance, if I am presented with data showing that infanticide is routinely practiced by women in some societies, my normative conception of feminine nurturance cannot but be affected.[1] Thus the problem of junction between intentional and descriptive concepts is also the problem of the status of such ambiguous beliefs.

Once this problem has arisen in reflection, there are only two ways to address it honestly. One is to confess that the junction, though we realize it in everyday life, is theoretically unintelligible. As Descartes, the author of the "mind–body" version of our problem, wrote to Princess Elizabeth:

> Metaphysical reflections, which exercise the pure intellect, are what make us familiar with the notion of soul; the study of mathematics, which chiefly exercises the imagination in considering figures and movements, accustoms us to form very distinct notions of body; finally it is just by means of ordinary life and conversation, *by abstaining from meditating and from studying things that exercise the imagination,* that one learns to conceive the union of soul and body. . . . It seems to me that the human mind is incapable of distinctly conceiving both the distinction between body and soul and their union, at one and the same time; for that requires our conceiving them as a single thing and simultaneously conceiving them as two things, which is self-contradictory [emphasis mine].[2]

Applying this answer to our problem would let us off too easily, and too dangerously: if we cannot finally form a distinct conception of gender's centering or basing on sex, we may as well give up our inquiry without more ado and be resigned to having our minds pulled hither and thither by gender experience and the deliverances of biology.

The other answer is deliberately to form a conception of junction or union. Descartes had earlier suggested to Princess Elizabeth that "as regards the soul and body together, we have merely the notion of their union," and then had gone on to give more weight to this notion by appropriating the word *gravity* for it (which he later conceded to be a "lame simile").[3] As Descartes realized, the bare assertion of union is not a helpful conception of it. We want a conception that in some way displays or models the relation, so that we think it with some degree of insight.

Spinoza took the metaphysical high road of postulating a single reality that would be inclusive of intentions and appearances. On his view, the question about junction dissolves, except as a pedagogical problem caused by "inadequate knowledge."[4] Unfortunately, his view makes our topic dissolve as well. It is conceivably true that gender is a "thinking" expression of a metaphysically indivisible reality whose corresponding "extended" expression is sex, but if we declared a conceptual victory of this sort and went home, we would have failed to gain insight into the ambiguous and loose way in which we base gender on sex, and how our gender experience unfolds in a dialectical relation with our alterable beliefs about sex rather than directly as a function of sex. (That is not to deny that a Spinozan pedagogy might be capable of acknowledging and tracing the logic of our gender experience as accurately, in its own way, as any other approach can. It is only to observe that the ultimate Spinozan solution does not help us at this point.)

What is left, after the Cartesian timidity and the Spinozan tour de force are set aside? Only a conception that is composite, with a foot on each side of the junction that interests us; only a conception that goes beyond stating the bare fact of junction to suggesting something about it—more particularly, something about *how,* by what common measure, intentional and observable reality are joined; only a conception that is capable of relating "center" in the sense of gender's central meaning to "center" in the sense of gender's sexual center of meaning.

The familiar notion of embodiment best satisfies these criteria. It ties in a knot that which is distinct from body together with body. It can be read either as an action, as intention requires, or as a fact, as description requires. It appeals to the variable *in/out* as a common measure of intentional and observable reality: the principle of intention has an ascertainable location *in* a body, just as a body may be *in* a room, but the principle of intention is not thereby falsely represented as an extended thing. Finally, an embodied intender actualizes centrality by participating directly in the performance of a central meaning of character but also presents a phenomenal center of attention in her or his sexed body.

Embodiment is one dimension of a subject's *installation* in a particular position in a world.[5] That is a condition in which I find myself, and it can be stated as an intransitive proposition: I am installed. It is also an action of which I am the object, as I have in fact been installed in gender by the intentional community in which I have grown up: the community stipulates what counts as female and male bodies, what life will be like in a male body among these sorts of bodies, what norms (and latitudes) of character and conduct are associated with these bodies, and that I am a male. At the core of this installation is something that my community did not do, namely, put me in my body. (Perhaps I think of God putting me in my body.) But this embodiment is the centerpiece of the whole installation. And so it must be the hinge of my beliefs about my own intentional–observable nature.

To proceed further, we require a model of intention-as-embodied that will prompt some relatively definite insights into the differences sex would or could make to character. Of course our model must not only have applications to gender thinking, it must stay clear of the major pitfalls known to philosophy of mind. (That we can actually pursue both objectives at the same time is another indication of the special philosophical interest of gender thinking.)

The structure of embodiment

The mental acts and dispositions called intentional have in common the feature of directedness or aiming. The aiming might be at any sort of object, or at the possibility or absence of an object; the structure of the aiming might be that of a flitting glance or a held gaze, a flying away or a homing in. What intention grasps or fails to grasp is the content of experience, the observable and describable. In relation to what there is to grasp, intention's own life is a *discretion* of positioning, choosing, and reaching for things to grasp over a range of possible ways. The forms realized in the playing out of this discretion, not entirely determined by the natures of the things there are to know and value, are the interesting features of the realm of "character."

That which lives the intentional life, and which will be the subject of gender qualification, is the intender or aimer. What sort of reality is this intender?

The intender-as-such might be conceived as a soul, that is, a psychical "level" of reality consisting of a distinctive substance or class of events supervening upon an organic "level." There need be no relation of soul to sex. There might be a "lower" level within the soul that is especially close to bodily processes, like carnal appetite, but the lower part can be subjected to the rule of a higher part that is free of such contamination, or else it can be eliminated altogether in a new non-bodily existence. According to this stratified anthropology, sexedness would not reach as far as the authentic self, and gender would most naturally be regarded as a provisional or even a completely spurious qualification of character.

The strength of the stratified or dualistic view is that it captures the order of priority between intention and body. The body does serve as the means of intention—not in the sense that one would normally say, "She looked at the dog by means of her eyes," or, "He replied by means of his lips," but rather in the sense that when we attend to eye and lip actions as such, we understand them to be media for a subject, not subjects in their own right. The most important drawbacks of this view include difficulties in seeing how a soul could be identified apart from a body and in conceiving interaction between immaterial soul and material body. People who want to be treated without regard for their bodily characteristics, or who interpret themselves in that way, are implicitly caught in these difficulties. (I will take this up again presently in the context of my constructive proposal.)

According to the rival materialist view, the intender is just the bodily being that exhibits the behavior associated with perceiving, knowing, wanting, and so on. Of course, empirical study is required to know the specific correlations of sex with behavior, but it would be surprising, on the materialist premise, if a structurally important feature of the body were not determining of the intender's dispositions in an important way. Possibly the structure of language or other social customs override anatomical structure in determining this or that aspect of what we call character. Still, the materialist view, unlike the dualist view, allows for sex to run deep into human nature and encourages us to look for evidence of how it does.

Materialism solves the identification and interaction problems of dualism by not letting them arise. But it cannot tell where the commander is in the command relation between intention and body. Thoughts are quite different from brain processes, both logically and experientially. If "dispositions" or "functions" are introduced to expand the horizon within which bodily phenomena are viewed, we are forced in interpreting these things either to reduce them to the content of observation-predictions—which takes us back to implausibly identifying thoughts with physical phenomena—or else to let them count as an active factor not directly observable, such as the relating of perceptions to behaviors, as distinct from the observationally defined input–output relation—which restores something like mentalism.

In sum, it seems that the intender cannot be a being separate from a body but cannot simply be identified with the body either. It so happens, moreover, that precisely this distinction-in-inseparability is affirmed whenever gender is affirmed, for gender's mediation between intention and sexedness would be pointless if the two were not distinct and impossible if they were separate.

Now to develop a positive doctrine.[6]

That the intender is sentient means that physical actions upon it not only can have the effect of observably altering or moving it but also can be registered in their bearing in on it, taken into a "within," reduplicating outer-world complexities of extension as inner-world complexities of superposition and tension. The necessity of superposition for sentience constrains us to think of the intender as a monadic center point from which intentional relations radiate. *Here* and *there,* inescapable terms in the description of sentience, presuppose a center. But while this center point is the *sine qua non* of intentional life, it cannot be the whole intender. There must be something extended that is centered by this center, since otherwise we could not associate directions with it or trace actions to it—not, at least, by ordinary perception. If intentions did not leave characteristic traces in space, moving quickly or slowly toward or away from these or those things, they could not be identified and told apart. And if it were not possible to assign some of these characteristic traces to the point-source of intention as its own "body," then we could not be clear that we had an intender to deal with as distinct from a general pattern of intention. If the intender were only a point, it could not interact with spatial beings and could never be in relationship with other intenders (except possibly in the strained sense of "relationship" offered by a Leibnizian preestablished harmony). But in any case a center cannot exist without an extendedness to be the center of.[7]

Nor can an intentional center exist without its own ordered complexity, a system of mental or psychic forms. If we are now able to conceive the forms of physical nature bursting out of a Big Bang, perhaps we can also conceive that psychic forms are produced by an interiority-opening implosion in every living subject and accordingly suppose that the structure of the physical circumstances of the implosion is somehow continuous with the structure of the psychic result. Unless the existence of psychic forms and their coordination with worldly occurrences is to be written off as a perfect mystery, we must suppose that they are proximally produced by the body, most immediately by the brain. Many of these forms will be taken for duplicates of worldly, exterior forms in the context of our perceptual enterprise of reproducing aspects of the world interiorly; many more will be drawn out of our bodily engagement with the world and reoriented in metaphorical construction;[8] others will be hit upon just because they are arbitrarily realizable. And just as each of these forms can only become an item of awareness through a superposition of physical actions on a center, so they must all be gathered into a center if they are to belong to a subject's life. Whenever we try to understand or explain the behavior of a sentient being we will refer to these forms as centerings and as things subject to centering—that is, we will engage in some version of psychology.

While the convergence of intentional relations to a formed point centralizes the body's extension, the body extends the intender's centrality. The intender is expressive as well as sentient. Normally, when my hand touches you, *I* am touching you (handily); the hand's action is my expression. When you touch my hand, you touch me. When you observe what my hand does, you may very well be meeting me. The bodily sphere, though not identical with the point-source of intention, does furnish its setting in a specially intimate way, so intimate indeed that "setting" is a misleading word for it. As I feel or act, the body is my spatiotemporal realization. Unlike everything else in the world, my living body cannot be thought separate from my intentional center. (You know very well what my location is if you say that my thoughts are elsewhere.)

Traversing paths in space, intentions project their forms by means of bodies that are in space and that *do* the reaching out and drawing in; but the bodies inevitably do this in such a way as to exhibit characteristics they possess independently of the intentions they express. We know all too well that the body is not an entirely transparent or pliant medium. It forces its own (sometimes decentering) activity upon the subject in the form of sensations, it forces impulses or drives on the intender as components of action, and it always enforces its limitations. Over time, the body acquires manners of its own that are not perfectly harmonious with the built-up character of the intender's intention as such. We can feel rewarded by the body's independent materiality under certain circumstances (including even pregnancy, on Iris Marion Young's showing).[9] But whether we find it gratifying or frustrating, clearly the relation between intention and body is not simply an intimate collaboration but involves certain inevitable oppositions posing challenges of management; accordingly, some such metaphor as *riding* best expresses intention's employment of its body. The body is a steed—the one unswitchable steed, a zone of virtually immediate translation of impressions and movements between intender and world.[10] Our experience of the "riding" relation between intention and body is the main warrant of the notion of a separate soul. But of course the riding metaphor breaks down when we look for the body of the rider-as-such, for the rider-as-such is only the centralization on a point of intention, and the steed-as-such is not a separate animal but the core of the worldly installation of intention.

The intentional center cannot exist without at least one other center outside of itself, for aiming is impossible without a target. The world in which intention occurs must contain beings. Now everything we can call "a being" is at least a construable center, that is, can be organized as a unity by perception, since the integrity of an individual being requires that all its parts be perceived and dealt with together. But in the most interesting case, the being at which I aim is an active centerer like myself, not just perceived but met, not just coexisting in the universe with me but modeling another way to live. The intender's awareness of real alternative ways to live, and ultimately of the entire extra dimension of multicentered (intersubjective or communal) feeling, judging, and acting, transforms our problem: my "embodiment" is now a question not merely of my own spatiotemporal realization but of my relationships with other incarnations. My body is in play in a field of relations between bodies. These relations affect the kind of career my body can have and thereby my career and character—both my occurrent qualities of feeling, judging, and acting and (more profoundly and determiningly) the basic, total intentional quality that is seen as the kind of person I am.

No claim is made here that intentional "center," "form," and "character" are perfectly stable or capable of being stabilized once and for all. All that these concepts require is the possibility of recognizing some flirtation with stability in intentional life.

We can understand intentional life, then, as a complexly "characteristic" aiming and riding realized in a body in a system of bodies. (Some of these bodies are met as fellow intenders, which creates an interintentional frame of reference for the meaning of the intender's life.) As the taking of a direction, an aiming, we shall expect intention to have three main aspects: whither it aims, how it aims (that is, how it is refracted through its instruments and influenced by its situations), and whence it aims. The same aspects will be found in intention's riding, that is, its career in time: its prospect, how it is going, what its progress to this point has been. We could ask whither, how, and whence with respect to a momentary attitude, or an action, or a project, or a whole life, depending on how extensive an intentional qualification we wanted to consider. But at any of these points we can suppose that an intender's intention might have a character, that is, a structural consistency more specific than the universal structures of intentional possibility; and at each of these points we can ask what difference the sexedness of the body would or could make, and what is at stake in the difference.

Qualifications of intention by sex

It follows from the two-sidedness of embodiment, extending and centering, that the question of the difference that the body makes is two-sided. We can turn first to one side, thinking of the body's direct influence upon intention (like the handiness of my outreach to other persons and worldly objects), and then to the other, thinking of the construal of the body's meaning via intentional and interintentional structures (whether in ordinary, particular claims like "This is my hand" or in systems of belief formation like biology). We do have to take one side at a time for the sake of exposition and evaluation. But it is also implied by our model of embodiment that the two sides are parts of a whole in such a way that each is always subject to the qualification of the other. The center does not stop centering extension while it is being extended, nor does extension stop extending the center while it is being centered; my actual handiness and my understanding of my hand are always both parent and child to each other.[11]

Bearing in mind that our theme properly dwells in this dialectic, let us begin with the first side of the question, asking how in principle such a thing as intention could be qualified by such a thing as a sexed body type. (We will not try to identify all the important qualifications;

for this, the reader is referred to Margaret Mead's comprehensive discussion in *Male and Female*.) [12] In subsequent steps, we will review the kinds of difference that could be made by beliefs about the sexed body.

Intention's Whither

The Whither issue has two sides. What objects and ends are in my field of awareness? And what pattern of movement, what directionality, is there in my acts of attention? These questions are essential concerns of science in the broadest sense: a knowledge-seeking community does not want to miss noticing anything.

The premise that people who have different opportunities for paying attention will for that reason be different sorts of people plays a part in a wide range of inferences. For example, there is the old notion of a landscape- and lifestyle-based character difference between country folk and city folk, which can be broadened into a theory of different general characters possessed by inhabitants of different environments; there is the notion that distinctive virtues and vices flourish in each profession; there is the belief that one has been deeply reshaped by a wilderness vacation or a great book. While it is not possible in any of these cases to determine the exact extent to which people's dispositions are affected by their experiences, we will still insist on thinking that such influence can be significant because our interest in forming ourselves forbids us to treat our characters as inalterable. But supposing that some part of character difference is not determined by innate endowments, this part can only be attributed to practice and habituation in different kinds of acts, and different acts are permitted and required precisely by different objects and object fields.

Sex-related general character differences of this sort could come about in two ways, either as the artifacts of sex-role assignments—as when a community places most males in military pursuits and most females in child care—or as the concomitants of natural features of male and female embodiment, like male genital exposure and female menstruation, or even sex-specific "skin shocks" at birth.[13] The latter kind of character formation is often considered innate because it is controlled by the naturally given body, but there is a difference in principle between having an original gender endowment, in the sense of having a gendered character from one's conception forward, and becoming gendered through a series of experiences occasioned by the sexed body. This is an important point, because we can more robustly affirm our

common humanity and more richly develop our own individual personalities in the measure that we take our character divergences to be
the outcomes of experiences that can be imagined to befall anyone
(what if *I* had grown up in a female body?). Furthermore, sex patterns
in the behavior of newborns would not seem so massively important
for gender theory if the historical dimension of sexed embodiment
were better appreciated.

Field of view. By virtue of their bodies, members of one sex perceive different things, or the same things from a different perspective,
than do members of the other. A woman, for example, perceives the
distinctive processes of the female body itself, the self-image based on
such data, and also (under certain circumstances) important aspects
of fetuses and nursing babies. The female perspective is realized not
only in experiences with a female role, like childbirth and genital intercourse, but throughout life on the basis of the female body's morphological difference from the male's—which of course might have dimin-
ished significance if a woman's body deviates from the female average
or ideal, as when a six-foot woman finds herself looking down at most
men, or when a childless woman finds herself freer for professional
endeavor.

Females and males might also conceive different ideas or follow different intellectual standards, even if the difference is masked
and largely overridden by the common language they use to express
their thinking. Female brains are empirically distinguishable from male
brains, and different ways of forming and connecting ideas could arise
on the basis of brain difference.[14] Admittedly, brain facts have a special
status in that they do not belong to our ordinary experience of maleness and femaleness; our conceptions of male and female, masculine
and feminine cannot be cued by them as they are cued by everyday
appearance and behavior. But some of the intentional qualities that we
do grasp in our gender experience are probably objectively dependent
on brain structure, which accords with the ordinary supposition that
gender in some way emanates from sex.

Directions. Everyone must look in particular directions, following the map of their culture's interpretation of sex, if they are to deal
with a number of exigencies that inhere in sexual nature no matter how
it is interpreted.

First, the pattern of looks that one takes at *oneself* can be affected by actual sexual features and, perhaps more importantly, by the sexual and sex-related ingredients of one's self-image. These will be sources of pleasure and vulnerability for females and males alike, but not in just the same way. Females and males have different arrays of body pleasures to be aware of, and different qualities of pleasure, privation, and pain as well. (Whether these are made much or little of, kept separate or integrated with life's other adventures, is of course another question.) Any public discussion that points to or draws on such experiences will point the attention of a participating subject more toward self when the experience is that of the subject's own sex.

Second, insofar as I am to be aware of the structural *difference* given in human reproductive physiology, make judgments about it, and take actions with respect to it, women are the "different" class of people and men are the "same," if I am male, the reverse if I am female. Since women are not only physically different from men but (for this adopted reason) are to some extent differently placed and differently active in my part of the world, aiming at them as the different or same ones takes on different patterns than aiming at men as the different or same ones.

Third, because powerful *desires* and possible gratifications belong to the sexual part of my life, I will incline relatively spontaneously toward members of a specific sex according to the sex-linked "orientation" I take. (Bisexuality is not a counterexample. A female bisexual cannot aim at same-sex and other-sex objects of desire in the same way that a male bisexual does, because different sexes are respectively "same" and "other" for these two.)

Fourth, my feelings, judgments, and actions relating to *procreation*—hence to my role in society, my potentialities as a parent, and my death—must aim in some way or other at the sex other than my own.

Although the content of all these intentional relations depends on the highly variable meaning assigned to men and women in their cultures, we can see that the directional patterns of aiming are generally symmetrical for men and women for the elementary reason that sex divides humanity in half. If, in a given community, one sex is proportionally low in numbers or effectively secluded, the aiming patterns will probably be less symmetrical and could more plausibly produce a character difference. (The gender difference that purdah promotes in this way could even be as significant as the difference it creates in the images of the sexes.) Otherwise, though, the intentional symmetry will tend to make for commonality between the sexes in proportion to the strength of the sexual exigencies. For example, people will tend to be more alike the stronger is their common inclination to form a sexual attachment, and in fact most women and men are very decidedly inclined this way. We might have different reasons for seeking it (pleasure, security, power), and there might even be gender-related generic differences in the ways in which we seek it, but the directionality of the aiming is common.

*

Are anatomically based differences of view more consequential or less consequential than differences created by the division of activities and experiences in a society's gender economy? There has been some hope that social scientists could settle this nature-versus-nurture question. In truth, however, it can be treated as an empirical question only under the severely limiting condition that we define "consequentialness" by fixed specifications drawn from the culture under study. Anatomically based differences could be swamped by sex-role effects in one culture but fetishized and reinforced by sex roles in another. More important, no culture is simply fixed. Since we usually bring up this question of the relative importance of "nature" and "nurture" not so much to establish existing patterns in our culture as to envision possible new directions for it, we had best recognize that we are using discretion when we do this.

Intention's How

The How of experience presents two main aspects: how we find ourselves situated and how we find ourselves acting.

The interactional frame. In the foreground of any sort of awareness of a being is that being's own shape, trajectory, and so on. But the sides (as it were) of my intentional reach toward a being have a shape determined by all the possibilities of what I might do with respect to it and what it might do with respect to me. These possibilities might collectively be called the interactional frame. Ordinarily they function not as known things but as colorations of knowing. For example, women's and men's perception of each other is affected by their awareness that a kind of sexual event can occur between them. Not that they are constantly thinking of this possibility, or all thinking of it in the same way, but what they do and do not propose to each other often reflects its presence. That a woman would generally be dealing with men in this awareness, and a man with women, must qualify their characters differently (assuming that they *are* dealing with each other) in the measure that what a woman stands to give to or receive from a man differs from what a man stands to give to or receive from a woman in sex. This point applies not only to sex acts but to pregnancy, which is so great an impingement on a person's life that we must expect the interactional frame to be a prominent factor in any culture.

We try to become lucid about the interactional frame in our *politics*.[15] We now know, for example, that we are embroiled in a serious political problem reaching into our most intimate, "private" experience, as Andrea Dworkin indicates:

> Intercourse occurs in a context of a power relation that is pervasive and incontrovertible. The context in which the act takes place, whatever the meaning of the act in and of itself, is one in which men have social, economic, political, and physical power over women. Some men do not have all those kinds of power over all women; but all men have some kinds of power over all women; and most men have controlling power over what they call *their* women. . . .
>
> Intercourse as an act often expresses the power men have over women. . . . The uses of women, now, in intercourse—not the abuses to the extent that they can be separated out—are absolutely permeated by the reality of male power over women.[16]

Expression. The other side of my How is how I am—most interestingly, how I am expressing myself.

Intention is to body as tune is to instrument: conduct has the tone of the body that accomplishes it. Male and female bodies are profoundly similar instruments yet quite noticeably distinct, something like pianos and organs or banjos and guitars. The hairier and larger male face, for instance, is more apt to express ferocity, while the smoother female face lends itself better to expressing subtler moods like irony. Yet all the equipment of either face type is duplicated in the other, so that women can be ferocious and men ironic; but one feels these cases to be a bit off the standard, as far as face reading goes.[17]

What best accounts for all the images of ironic men and ferocious women that have crowded into the reader's mind by now is the overriding expressiveness of language, above all in what is said. Now sex-differentiated patterns in language use would be attributable to mental differences, not directly to the body as the instrument of linguistic expression.[18] But besides what is said, there is *voice,* a specially important refraction of intention by the body in that it is the dimension of self-presentation with which the intender is continually in touch. There must be a difference of force in women speaking and singing higher, men lower—apart from extrinsic effects of association, as when higher-voiced people remind me of my mother, lower-voiced people of my father—first, because auditory perception works differently, with different affect, in higher and lower pitch ranges and, second, because any contrast between persons provokes dramatic interpretation.[19] You will not necessarily hear opera sopranos as heavenly and basses as earthly, but given the magnitude of the auditory issue and the exigency of drama, you *are* bound to register their distinctness with some important-feeling difference of associations. It is more certain still that composers will exploit the possibility of hearing different person types in different voice types, as the effect enlivens their art.

Expression differs from the interactional frame in that it cannot be so readily objectified as a "factor" for the intender to deal with. As the intender's own self-revelation, it typically involves her or him too immediately for that. A man's voice, for instance, in its relative lowness, is ordinarily apprehended as a display of who he is, as his presence, not as a more or less adequate instrument by which his inner self communicates with the outside world. We may apprehend him differently at exceptional times, such as when his boy's voice is changing, or after an illness. Similarly when something goes funny in his relation with his limbs or with anything else that he lives in and through. But so long as expression functions as our window on a person, it is the very "front" of intention as it addresses situations and other beings. If you think critically about the self-expressive adequacy of a person's voice, you are contemplating alternative voices, not abolishing voice.

The effect of sex on preference. The Hows of intention affect the intender primarily by affecting preferences. Consider, for instance, how the female body supports a certain kind of liking for holding a baby. (A man might like holding babies, too, but if he feels femininely tender and nurturing toward a baby he cannot but regard the female breast as a valuable qualification he lacks.) On the other side, the male body more than the female generally supports a zest for certain tests of short-term strength. The male vocal apparatus produces a more satisfactory bellow, the female a clearer and crisper tone. Here we have generically different gradients of spontaneous enthusiasm and also of attractiveness supporting even more enthusiasm. The sexed body is more likely to be admired for the relatively greater aptitudes of its sex. What counts in this connection is not so much the being-liked in itself as the effect of being liked on one's own likings, as these form the heart of one's disposition. It is an open question how much relative weight such sex-affected preferences have, but their weight must be greater than zero for any human beings in any circumstances.

An objection to this reasoning is worth considering. Assume that an average male can perform an action that an average female cannot (say, lifting one end of a big piano). The preceding discussion implies that the male will more probably *like* to lend himself to tasks of heavy lifting, and probably to the whole range of tasks that can be linked metaphorically with heavy lifting, because of the encouragements of succeeding at it and being appreciated for doing it; and also that this liking will define the male's character in one way. The female's character could not be defined in the same way. But suppose that by snapping our fingers we instantly granted the female greater lifting strength. Would she not enjoy being able to lift a piano or being appreciated by others for rendering that service? But if the female is always ready to like and identify herself with that activity, must we not have gone too far in founding a character trait on physical aptitude? That is, must she not have been already like the male, in her readiness to have the malelike likings, even before we gave her the greater lifting strength that would promote the development of those likings?

The objection as stated is, I suggest, both wrong and right. It is wrong to minimize the challenge of integrating new likings into a stable ensemble with other established likings; that this challenge can be formidable is shown by the deep distaste many women feel for the idea of taking advantage of the muscular potential they actually have.[20] The objection is right, however, to deny that human spontaneity or responsiveness can be fixed once and for all by an appearance or conception of character type. Indeed, our ideals of moral accountability and perfectibility forbid us to think of characters as immutable. The claim that there are characterological consistencies in our experience, however, does not require us to accept the false premise that characters cannot be changed. That the characters of males and females are potentially feminine and masculine, respectively, since changes in equipment and situation would tend to cause dispositional shifts, does not dissolve the principle of sex-based character.

Intention's Whence

Behind its "front," intention's Whence is the third and most mysterious of its dimensions. I aim myself into situations in the world, aware of myself as the rider of a particular kind of body-steed that takes pleasures and strengths and pains and weaknesses from my various encounters; *and* my movement out of my center-point traverses through time a certain line or oscillation, at a certain complex rate, in a certain complex of vectors, all of which go toward constituting my disposition, or rather which at every moment have already constituted my disposition. We cannot change the Whence, even in thought experiments, as we can the How; to posit a different Whence is not to make a person different but to substitute a different person.

Part of intention's Whence is simply historical and lies on the surface for examination: because of the series of past experiences I have had, I arrive at this next experience in *this* posture. We rely on this accessible evidence when we theorize about people's characters. (The evidence may not be easily accessible, it may take psychotherapy to get at it, or it may never be gotten at; yet by referring to it we put ourselves on the way to a generally intelligible interpretation of an individual's character—generally intelligible because it pertains to the generic human subject that we ideally realize when we imagine ourselves reacting to all those situations, contemplating the same meaningful ends and acting in relation to them.) But intention comes from behind the scene of the present in a more profound sense than merely being past. It wells up with its own style, comes out of the invisible interiority of its center, which we can finally explain no better than by saying, "That's her" or "That's him."

As for why an individual would have a distinctive way of coming into situations, a distinction going beyond what a generally intelligible interpretation can account for, we have a decision to make. We could deny radical individuality in principle, insisting that if we only had all biographical information we would no longer have to settle for saying, "That's him" or "That's her," but rather could say with insight, in every case, "Thus it is with any person who has had such experiences." Paradoxically, this is a way of affirming the full range of human responsiveness while negating spontaneity. The true basis of the view seems to be repugnance to individuality as much as humane flexibility. Granting individuality, though, do we want simply to accept our inability to see the grounds of intentional style distinctions, or shall we assign them a material basis or medium?

Perhaps we have good reason to stay blind. If we wish to hold individuals morally responsible, it may be necessary to deny that their original principles of choice have knowable grounds in order to avoid the problems of determinism. For if we know all the grounds of behavior then there is no further rationale for a responsibility system except of a behavior-modifying sort we cannot but regard as cynical. On the other hand, it may be irrational not to deepen our explanation of intentional style by letting a material entity play the part of "basis" (at least presumptively), if a suitable entity is in the picture. Our bodies do seem suitable. They differ from each other both individually and generically in parallel with the individual and generic differences of intentional style that we want to understand. (To be sure, the stipulations of the community enforce differences along precisely these lines, and one can always say that physical differences are associated with character differences because they offer themselves as reference points for the playing out of social differentiation processes; or, more simply, because it is just reasonable to take different attitudes according to the body type and associated social position a person has to deal with.[21] But we are considering the premise that these stipulations and reasonings are naturally supported.)

The greatest difficulty in relating body as "basis" to character is that it seems to reverse an order of priority that is crucial to intentional life, even constitutive of it. If intention is the center and centerer of the life of the body, how could the body be a "basis" of intentional character?

It is true that the answer to the question, Where are my intentions coming from? must ultimately lie not in any extended medium but in the point of the intentional center. This consideration does not by itself entail that selves transcend generic character features, since people might fall into character types just because of the structural possibilities of character—for the same reason that there are definite types of atoms. It does entail that bodies or any other material entities cannot be the whole formal cause of character. Nevertheless, the effects of the body on intentional life must be pervasive, because nothing comes into or goes out of the intentional center except by the body's mediation. And if there is radical individuality in the intentional center, its existence can be explained only as the result of chance, miracle, or—most satisfactorily—the character of a physically unique body imploding into sentience in its unique way.

Mental life seems to transcend its installation in the body in many ways, but this is made understandable by distinguishing logical import from psychological reality and (more to the present point) by noting the autonomy and range of brain activity in relation to other bodily processes. Apart from brain activity there is no evident means by which impressing on the center and expressing of the center can really occur. Apart from "movement" of physical values in the brain there is no evident basis of the real event of "motivation" in the person—this is as certain as the principle that ideal forms are required to explain the meaning of motivation.

On this view, then, I find irresistible such a proposition as "He has his distinctive way of coming into situations partly because his body, in or through the processes of which his intentions occur, has a distinctive type of constitution and thereby directly affects his intentions." (This does not commit me to accepting a particular proposition about how the influence works—in hormonal action, for example—but it allows me to find such propositions meaningful.) Scarcely less resistible is the related proposition "People are more likely to share ways of coming into situations insofar as they share physical features, because of the direct influence of those features on the shaping of their intentions." The influence of my body on my character need not be conceived deterministically, either as blocking my availability to the kinds of solicitation from other beings that concern us in law, morality, and religion, or as preventing a spontaneous polymorphism of intention. An influence is a factor that helps account for something being the way it is, something lacking which the thing would be different, on which it in that relatively weak sense depends as a "basis"; it is the sole or sufficient explanation only of some aspect of a being, not of the whole being. Thus determinism is not an ethicometaphysical worry in this case (even if the *social* determinism of role prescription remains always an important practical concern).

With these clarifications, we have furnished ourselves with a way of representing the darkest part of the whence of intention. Because my intention occurs riding on and reaching through my body processes, it always enters a situation already disposed in certain ways, and the upshot of my disposition is that I notice and value things in an associated distinctive way, insofar as the structure of the things themselves and generic structures of perceiving and valuing leave room for this distinctiveness. For my consciousness, however, my disposition is necessarily hidden. Our behavior manifests our dispositions so that inferences about them can be drawn, yet they never come into the light as phenomena.

We would like to inspect this background of motivation directly, the better to understand valuing; but we have to stop with the recognition of its opacity, contenting ourselves with inferences about it. The only means of actually presenting it is *art*. Through the experience of art we become aware of our background not by seeing it but by resonating with it while perceiving well-chosen forms. And in our art criticism we do commonly recognize both individuality and gender as dimensions of artistic meaning.

Gender and biological facts

So far, we have explored the main ways in which physical sexedness could directly affect the structural consistency of our intentions. For the most part we could only point to general possibilities, since the influence of sex on intention would be, of its very nature, not something we see but something steering our seeing. In addition to our unconscious expression of sex, however, we dwell in sex by relating ourselves in various ways (including gendered ways) to what we can see or conjecture about the facts of sex.[22] We step now into the sphere of biology—or, to be more exact, into a cognitive–practical web woven of many sorts of takes on the world including an ideally distinguishable component, "biology," which holds the special authority of science and therefore a special interest.

Whenever we apply biological *meaning* (descriptively conceived) to ourselves, we appropriate it for our *meaning* (intentionally conceived). Human biology is bound to produce ambiguous or hybrid descriptive-intentional beliefs. We want to see how the process works. We will begin by studying the biological approach to the body's observable meanings as a collection and use of "facts"; then we will ask about the biological dimension of "human nature" in general, in order to understand the biological basis of gender in that broader sense.

*

The relevance of biological facts to gender can be exhibited in a grid. We locate along one axis two main kinds of biological information: physiological (in a broad sense), having to do with the structure and internal functioning of the body, and (also in a broad sense) ecological, having to do with the body's relations with other natural beings. Along the other axis are two kinds of difference biological information can make to us: first, it can shape our view of the sexual center of meaning that serves as a reference point for our understanding of gender and also guides the interintentional construction of our sexual installation sites; second, it can give us practical options.

	SEX THEORY	PRACTICAL POSSIBILITIES
Physiology	Genetic, structural, and hormonal effects on behavior	Physical interventions to alter experience and conduct
Ecology	Selection probabilities, reproductive "interests" and "strategies"	Alterations of environment and breeding practices

Physiology

Sex theory. Gender notions, while not identical with beliefs about sexual physiology, are tied to them. For example, the qualities of patience and unselfishness that have accrued to femininity in our culture came to be understood, especially around the turn of this century, as grounded partly in the supposed absence of sexual excitability in normal women. (This replacing an earlier view that women are sexually insatiable.) But twentieth-century sexological research rendered that belief publicly untenable. Thus biology can cut against a given ideology; it can even predict that we would say or do things for "real reasons" (causes that become reasons once they enter our consciousness) quite different from the reasons we are accustomed to cite.[23] If we are compelled to revise beliefs about sexual nature, the immediate effect is to weaken the bond between our understanding of gender and its sexual base. Our conception of gender then becomes, if not vaguer, at least more abstract, and our application of it necessarily more flexible.

I find an analogy in what happened to my notion of the "wise owl" when I learned that owls are not, in fact, very smart birds. I still know what is meant by calling someone a "wise owl," but there is a hollow ring to it; I have to specially recall my outmoded apprehension of owls to make the metaphor work. My grasp of wisdom itself becomes a bit more abstract if I can no longer rest my sense of it so much on real owls. (I shall concentrate on the visible qualities of stillness and a large-eyed steady gaze, and try not to think about their tiny brains; but this, again, abstracts from the real owls.) So too, given a dissonant contribution from sexual physiology we have to put on an attitude to make physical sex work as a manifestation of gender qualities. The difference between sex-based gender and owlish wisdom is that we can distinctly define wisdom without any reference to owls, while a gender defined without any reference to sex would not be a gender. Our gender notions are hostage to the facts of sex. Thus we have to say: either femininity does not include the kind of self-sacrificing disposition that could rest on sensual disinterestedness or else some other evidence and ground of this quality must be discoverable in the generality of female lives.

Practical possibilities. Knowledge of physiological facts could have immediate practical implications relevant to gender. Actually, we could say the same of historical and other sorts of facts, so let the following physiological example serve as an allegory of every practical challenge that might come about through sex–gender studies. Suppose that the biochemistry of aggression becomes well enough understood that any human individual's aggressive propensities can be medically altered to a significant degree.[24] Now say I am an "assertive" and, to that extent, "masculine" person, and say I realize that "aggressive behavior" is the publicly observable correlate in my own case of what I would avow to be "assertive conduct," generally matching outward surface for intention. Suppose further that my friends, fed up with my aggressions as such and/or my assertiveness as such, advise me to take one of the new hormone-blocking medications. (This is better than castration!) Now, consider what I *know* and how I shall *decide:*

1. I know that my assertive way of comporting myself, and my liking of this style, are dependent on certain hormonal actions in my body.
2. I know, thus, that to change these actions would be to change in one respect who I am. It would not immediately alter the receptive and active dispositions of my intentional center, but it would change the bodily refraction of the lines of intentional relation radiating from the center such that I would look and act differently henceforth, certainly with an accumulating effect on my character.
3. I do not want to change who I am in this respect, for I like

being this way. (I also want to keep my friends, though, so I do have a reason to change.)

How significant is the news that my disposition is changeable in this particular way? I knew all along that a person's character could change as the result of being knocked on the head, wounded, and the like. I may even have changed my own character on purpose, just temporarily, by drugging myself. The news is that an aspect of what I have regarded as my stable baseline character, indeed part of me that entered into such decisions as when and how much to use drugs, can be changed, in principle, for good. (I would be able to change back, but that would be another decision made from a new position.) The news is important because it puts part of my self into my power.

I had also known that by exerting myself to form and change habits I could act upon my own character, rather in the way that I could build up selected muscles with physical exercises. But I had understood character building to be an unfolding of my potential, a process of cultivation, and there seems little of cultivation in taking a pill.

Does learning that my disposition is changeable change the status for me of my liking of assertiveness? Apparently so. By presenting me with a decision to make about my own character, it objectifies my assertiveness (now the matter of the decision) and calls for the introduction of another principle to guide me. A gap is opened up between a liking of mine—I might well have called it a valuing or approving, and rightly so, since in it I concurred with many other persons' sense of the way a man should live—and a prospective attitude of superior validity, superior inasmuch as it better rectifies my position in relationship with other intenders.

4. I must therefore ask myself, Is it more justifiable to leave myself as I am or to change myself in this way? The justification question invokes the largest thinkable assembly of fellow intenders, both as co-deciders and as ones who stand to be benefited or harmed. To answer it, I have to pay careful attention to what everyone else says and to their interests so far as I can understand them. My superior justificatory frame of reference is the "human/humane," or what is acceptable and beneficial to humans qua humans. I ask, Will I be a more humane person if I am less assertive? It is purposeless to ask, Will I be more myself? because no one (except, one might wish to say, God) has knowledge of an essential destiny with which given realizations of my selfhood

could be compared. Note the general point that having to make decisions like this swings my apprehension of character away from gender and toward "humanity"; the authority of the gender format for personal fulfillment is undermined. (Yet if our self-understanding takes this turn, gender is not thereby completely neutralized, for we might still fall willy-nilly into groups who understand "humanity" differently, along gender lines.) Suppose then:

5. I decide to take the medication. My decision was *forced* by this gender-typical aspect of my disposition (since that's what the decision was about); my decision was *free* of this aspect of my disposition in that my relish of assertiveness was overruled; however, my decision is bound to be *conditioned* by assertiveness in another sense, for of course my final decision against assertiveness is assertively made, and I march to the drugstore and demand my pills.

The junction between the bodily and the intentional, my embodiment or worldly installation, was realized in this case in two ways. I *saw* that what for observers counts as aggressive behavior on my part is the same reality as conduct expressing my assertiveness (even though the meaning of its physical aspect is different from its intentional meaning), so that my theater of action came to include hormonal biochemistry in a new double sense, perceived on the scene and posited as a factor behind the scene; and I *acted* on my physical existence by taking the pills, in order to have an effect on my character. Putting these two links together, I have warrant for a hybrid descriptive–intentional belief by which I "base" myself on a fact: "Changing my hormonal state makes me less assertive." In such a sentence, *makes* means neither "is constantly associated with," simply, nor "motivates," simply, and this ambiguity mirrors the two-sidedness, extending and centering, of installed intention. On the extension side, *makes* does mean "is constantly associated with"—why would I take the pills if I were not counting on this? It also implies the centering event of motivation, as in statements like "Injustice makes me angry," because the changed hormonal condition is the same reality as a certain shaping of my intention in its traversal of my hormone-affected nervous system.

Ecology

Sex Theory. Existence is coexistence; a being's nature and survival depend on sustaining relations with other beings. Biology uses the principle of adaptation to interpret the interdependence of beings, showing that X is "adapted" by showing how the known structure of the whole ensemble of beings in X's world admits and requires X. (The larger structure must have some knowable constants of its own if invoking it enhances understanding.) Adaptation as a requirement of coexistence applies as much to intentions as it does to material entities. In gender, we feel ourselves caught in an ambiguous intersection of the two kinds of relation and adaptation. Masculine and feminine intentions follow the patterns of a cultural sex–gender system—a system wherein some intentions are compossible and "successful" in that they receive more confirmation than other possible intentions—while male and female bodies exhibit their continuing characteristics according to the structure of the community as biologically construed. The biological relations are then endowed with the meaning of the sex–gender system, while the sex–gender system gets form and anchoring from the biological relations.

So far, the most significant biological advance for the history of gender consciousness has been the conscious discovery of paternity.[25] If we believed reproduction to be an exclusively or predominantly female power, creativity would likely play little part, or at any rate a very different part, in our sense of masculinity, and the practical possibilities for the exercise of male power would be different as well. Given the knowledge of paternity, however, the disastrous illusion of a male monopoly on creativity becomes possible.

For a newer illustration of the influence of ecological knowledge, consider the possibility of a satisfactory evolutionary explanation of the fact that human females depart from the general mammalian plan of limited estrus periods for copulation. Currently there is not enough evidence even to decide whether this human peculiarity is a chance byproduct of evolution or is truly adaptive—whether, that is, it promoted the perpetuation of the genotype supporting it in the environment in which it appeared.[26] But suppose that enough ethological and anthropological evidence were gathered to show, not only that continuous female attractivity is adaptive, but which of the possible scenarios of adaptation is more probable. Then our gender understanding would be challenged or reinforced. For example, if expanding female sexuality was adaptive because it helped stabilize pair-bonds in a situation in which pair-bond mating was favored by natural selection, then our normative notion of womanlikeness or femininity would be cued to combine passion and loyal attachment, the very stuff of our romance novels. Or would it, necessarily? Aren't women able to carry on very differently than their forebears under modern conditions, and isn't femininity's observable basis independent, therefore, of findings about evolution?

We arrive thus at an antinomy. The thesis would be that fundamental value contours of our present life are determined by patterns to which the human physical constitution adapted over a long term of natural selection; and the argument would be that what counts as value for us cannot be independent of our physical constitution, of which natural selection is the ultimate formal cause, because in terms of either ideal valuation or practical feasibility no one generation can be wiser about the human good than the implicit wisdom of millennia's worth of natural selection operating to define the distinctively human good by fitting humans to their niche in the world, above all to community with each other. Our physical constitutions, like our customs, have prima facie validity as vehicles of communal life, since our irreplaceable achievements in communal living depend on them. And if we have come to live under "unnatural" conditions with reference to this constitution, then we have the weightiest possible reason to change those conditions. But then we must weigh the antithesis that natural history is not necessarily relevant to the evaluation of modes of living. The argument on this side would be that while human goods are shaped by human bodies, the filtering of intention through body structure is naturally affected by nothing other than the structure itself, as it exists at any moment, and as it might permit or provoke any number of experiences unrelated to natural selection pressures. Natural history is not relevant to character in the way that biographical history is. The latter constitutes meanings directly, but the former constitutes only the physical apparatus in which meanings are experienced. How a glass was made has nothing to do with the taste of liquid in it (unless knowing how it was made draws one's attention to a feature it presently has). We are liable to interpret natural history as news of what people did and how they shaped their living arrangements, that is, as history in the proper sense; and this it is not.

Each argument connects its claim to our supreme project of living as happily and approvably as we can. They both appeal to the ultimate criterion of interintentional feasibility; they disagree only about the conditions for it. The thesis (as advanced in the early Wilsonian sociobiology, for example) is not in good odor today but should not be entirely dismissed. Since any configuration of human life, whether physical or historico-cultural, cannot fail to be imbued with the consent of those who live in it—their very living amounting to a kind of consent, even if their practical options are narrowly limited—it becomes something analogous to a contract, and it is not entirely wrong (although it is surely misleading) to speak of "bargains" struck between females and males in the forming of humanity. So there is a minimal validity implicit in human evolutionary history that we are not free to disregard. At the same time, however, we are free and even required to overrule a norm derived from evolution whenever we are aware of overriding considerations, conscientiously tasting the liquids in our glass.

Practical possibilities. If it were true that the female body and emotional ground plan are adapted to the pair-bond—and supposing also, from the necessity of breeding cooperation between the sexes, that the parallel adaptation of males cannot be fundamentally inconsistent with the adaptation of females—then we would have *a* reason to promote monogamy, and that in turn would shape the orientation of masculine and feminine genders to each other in a particular way. Marriage serves as a model of wholeness achieved through gender complementarity. But the members of a marriage are committed to each other as individuals, not merely as gender exemplars, and to the extent that complementarity and wholeness are defined in a dimension other than sex and gender, the importance of sex or gender is relatively less. If, on the other hand, we were led to conclude that quantitative and qualitative (gene catching) reproductive opportunity, rather than the pair-bond as such, was the main advantage to which male and female sexuality adapted, then the situation would be different. Not only would we have *a* reason not to put all our sexual eggs in the monogamy basket, we would be moved to understand the genders differently, sexual fidelity appearing to be a less important ingredient in either.

Because I find no reason that would compel a more restrictive view, my surmise is that our actual natural history has blended these two scenarios. A well-known intentional ambiguity in gender could be "based" on this ambiguity in natural selection: we respond to gender both as instanced by a numerically indefinite collection of individuals and as decisively incarnated by one individual who claims our interest. In the first case, gender will be relatively more salient—individualities are variations on this general theme. In the second case, gender will be of subordinate interest because it figures as a qualification of individuality. This point should not be neglected in analyses of love and lust.

Human nature as animal nature: human biology and anthropology

To see the sense in which an intentional structure (in this case, gender) can have a biological explanation, it is first necessary to see how humanity itself can be an object of biological inquiry. In this section I am concerned with developing an alternative to the more or less standard philosophical practice of *terminating* analysis of this issue in a radical disjunction between the realms of rational, (fully) human life and nonrational, nonhuman life.[27]

Humans are animals. But the thought that humans are animals is incomplete, and therefore indeterminate. To a biologist, it poses the question: What *kind* of animals are humans, that is, what specifically do we find when we examine the structures and behaviors of *Homo sapiens* in light of what we know in general about animal life? And by what observable processes are the human phenotypes realized? An anthropologist, however, has to determine the thought in a different dimension: *How* are humans animals, that is, in what particular ways do we find human bodies and vital processes taken up into patterns of culture (spirits) and consciousness?

It seems that the two lines of inquiry should converge, faithfully delineating all the constants and variabilities that are apparent in the one human phenomenon; or else, owing to a difference in their definitions of the human, they should run on parallel tracks. There actually is such a difference (which we will consider presently), yet the two approaches do not divide neatly. Due ultimately to the two-sidedness of embodiment, biology and anthropology are dialectically entangled with each other so that neither can resolve itself on its own.

The object of biological interpretation is always *what we are seeing*, "phenotype," and since all vision is already interpretation (a centering of the extended according to some strategy), there is for us no pure evidence of the natural thing-in-itself—not even in the case of DNA molecules, but least of all in the case of human beings, whose phenomenal showing, the to-be-understood, comes culturally invested with meaning. There could not be a human biology that failed to ask about the biological basis of intentional structures like gender, inasmuch as these belong to the human phenomenon. But we can only pursue questions about intentional structures if we make assumptions that have no biological warrant—assumptions, namely, about what subjects are meaning, or what they could possibly mean, which biological investigation will then show the process or machinery *of*. Since human biology is always a prisoner of assumptions about its phenomenon, it should pay critical attention to debates in anthropology, for these will alert it to the effects of cultural forces on biological conceptualization and thereby widen its view.[28]

On the other hand, anthropology's interest is not in what we are seeing from the detached natural scientist's perspective but in *what is going on* in the richest and ultimately most observer-involving sense. Its main object of interpretation is interpretation itself—the clothes on human life, so to say, rather than the naked body. But clothes are no more independent of this body than the body is independent of clothes. The interpretation presents itself as the human reality; its projections go unquestioned in everyday life; but once we notice that different peoples have different interpretations of the human, how can we not ask about the unmistakably common *physis* (extension) on which these *nomoi* (centerings) are "based"? The question we now ask is an alien one, one that decenters and recenters extension. It is as though we are ripping clothes off the body. The biological question will not remain alien, however, for what we say about the stripped body must affect what we think about the clothes. For example, we will conceive of the marriage-and-kinship component of a culture not only in the culture's own terms, as a scheme of statuses and alliances, but also as a mechanism for optimizing reproduction under a given set of environmental constraints. Increasing biological awareness makes us think of ourselves more in biologicized terms.

Outside the disciplines of biology and anthropology, I am caught up in the problem of human animality in quite another way through my sympathetic relations with nonhuman animals. A dog and I have so much in common—and in saying this I indicate not merely a fond fancy but a real condition that shows itself in an extensive coordination between our attitudes and movements—that I cannot but conclude that I am *realizing* this commonality when I speak anthropomorphically of the dog's "loyalty" and also when I speak zoomorphically of people's doglike "submission signals" and the like.[29] A large number of intentional descriptions can apply rather squarely to both of us, like "happy," "lonely," "playful," "fearful," "pugnacious," and "vacillating." The more sensitive I am to dogs, though, the more I realize that whatever we have in common, they have in a different way—a recognizable yet unassimilable canine way.[30] (In spirit-related respects that matter crucially to me, I have to say it is a lesser way.) And because I grasp our commonality in my own distinctively human way, I cannot unequivocally define it in human language. I am fully entitled to say that the dog and I are both playful, yet dog play is not human play, and my word *play* cannot perfectly capture what we both are. Indeed, my basic feeling of sympathy for a dog already records this complexity, for sympathy is not simple identification with another but precisely an awareness that some quality of life is *shared* with an *other*.

If we look beyond dogs to simpler forms of life, we find fewer words to state the enormously important but almost-too-obvious-to-discuss features that we share with them, like irritability and motility, and we become increasingly offended or astounded by their alienness. Nevertheless, lines of affiliation connect us to all of them.

The scientific ventures of biology and anthropology both rest on, and answer to, our sympathetic solidarity with the rest of the natural world. This was a dimension of that original intentional probing that generated the descriptive concepts of the two sciences. Biology's charter is to construct a broadly zoomorphic model of humanity; to serve this end best, it needs to be wary of anthropomorphism. Anthropology's mission is to grasp the self-forming of *anthropos,* and it must always interpret animal description as one subordinate part of this master project—hence its mandatory distrust of zoomorphic substitutes for anthropology. Biologists and anthropologists can never be entirely happy with each other's representations of the human. But their concepts are drawn from a single continuum, a "scale of nature" (actually a scale of intentional richness) whose inner strings vibrate in my everyday sympathies. Both sets of concepts apply to me, the microcosm.

It is instructive, in this light, to examine the dissatisfaction of the anthropologist Clifford Geertz with Donald Symons's evolutionary-biology account of human sexuality.[31] We notice a scale-of-nature effect when Geertz complains that Symons's characterizations of female and male are "at about the level of descriptions of the Irish as garrulous and the Sherpas as loyal" (4). If there is such a thing as human biology, which supposes an observable human phenotype (or phenotypic range) with a determinate relation to physical structures possessed by the human animal as such, then the biological characterization of humanity cannot possess the richness of anthropological accounts sensitive to different peoples' discretion to make different things of their biological endowment. In biology there is a necessary and explicit search for cross-cultural human characteristics that may only be statistically discernible. While it would be an anthropological crudity to sum up the Irish as garrulous (even supposing that anthropologists did find a lot of talkers in the Irish population), it would be a biological failure *not* to sum up male and female sexuality in a zoomorphic formula that is simple relative to cultural complexity. The biological portrait is only oversimple if it is mistakenly treated as an anthropological portrait (a mistake Symons constantly warns against). Within anthropology, it would be a mistake even to ask Sarah Blaffer Hrdy's question, Why are human females more male-dominated than most of their primate cousins?—after all, think of all the different meanings *dominance* has to human beings!—yet this is an authentic and inevitable biological question, even if it must also be a controversial one because of the conceptual indeterminacy of its object.[32]

In principle, Geertz favors collaboration between natural and social scientists, but he will not allow an *analogical* relation between zoomorphic and anthropomorphic constructions of a human feature like sexuality: "What finally does Symons in . . . is his failure to understand that in human beings sexuality is not, like the opposable thumb, a biological fact with some cultural implications, but, like speech, a cultural activity sustaining a biological process. To explain it, 'ultimately' or otherwise, by looking through rather than at its meaning is rather like trying to understand language armed only with aural acoustics and the anatomy of the vocal tract" (4). In effect, Geertz insists on the anthropological view of humanity; in order to leave the field clear for the anthropological view, he insists on an indeterminate biology. Yet while human sexuality is indeed a meaning system like language, it is also, again like language, one among a multitude of animal adaptations to promote genotype reproduction. These are different aspects of the phenomenon of sexuality, but they are analogically related on a descriptive continuum, just as there is an intentional analogy between non-human and human sexual motivation. Biological and anthropological sexuality are the same in that they are both schemes of behavioral coordination, of failure and success in mating attempts, of propagation and selection. But the "self" and "world" described by social science are different from the "organism" and "environment" described by natural science, so that "behavior" becomes "conduct," "failure" becomes "evil," and "propagation" becomes "marriage" and "parenthood" as we bring ideal ends into view.[33]

The project of human biology is to look both "through" and "at" the human meaning of the human phenotype. Biologists have to be aware of what sexual issues concretely mean to human beings so as not to lose touch with what we want to account for. But biological insight is produced by isolating the foundations of human structure and behavior that are shared in principle with other animals; then, realizing a different perspective, we see how these are enriched and varied by culture.[34] We can arrive at the same appreciation from the anthropological side, if we are not illogically revolted by the descriptive poverty of the biological view with respect to culture. Anthropology, for its part, is committed to looking "through" as well as "at" cultural meanings insofar as it maintains its own counterpart to the notion of a human phenotype, namely, a human nature (this time a spiritual nature) that makes of cultures a universe. Much biological richness underneath the clothing of this human nature will remain invisible to it.

The present analysis implies that anthropology and biology ought not to think of fusing. There will be tension and a running misunderstanding in their dialogue. But they should consider themselves united in the sense that the meanings they give to terms like *sexuality* are always subject to influence from both directions on the scale of nature. Zoomorphism and anthropomorphism are not strictly separate frames of reference. Together with the theomorphic thinking that guides our project of transcending the human, they form a system of complementary ways of organizing our self-awareness.

In the equivocal encounter of different conceptual projects addressing the same object and sharing terms of discourse, we find ourselves on the same logical ground that we mapped earlier in our study of the complementarity of genders and other human kinds. But with genders and analogous human kinds, the sense of human impoverishment we sometimes get in looking at an imperfectly understood alien type is not due to its placement on a lower rung of the natural scale—even if the metaphor "lower form of life" can ungraciously describe one's fellow humans.[35] Gender ambiguation comes in at right angles to the scale of nature and further discomposes the notions of sex and sexuality, which now are split into feminine and masculine aspects as well as into human and lower-animal forms.

Human nature as animal nature: the Beast Within

> [God] took man as a creature of indeterminate nature and,
> assigning him a place in the middle of the world, addressed
> him thus: "Neither a fixed abode nor a form that is thine
> alone nor any function peculiar to thyself have we given
> thee, Adam, to the end that according to thy longing and
> according to thy judgment thou mayest have and possess
> what abode, what form, and what functions thou thyself
> shalt desire. . . . We have made thee neither of heaven nor of
> earth, neither mortal nor immortal, so that with freedom
> of choice and with honor, as though the maker and molder
> of thyself, thou mayest fashion thyself in whatever shape
> thou shalt prefer. Thou shalt have the power to degenerate
> into the lower forms of life, which are brutish. Thou shalt
> have the power, out of thy soul's judgment, to be reborn
> into the higher forms, which are divine."
>
> —*Pico della Mirandola*[36]

The scale of nature lies inside us as a scale of human possibility. "According to thy longing," says Pico's Creator: do our longings not include unchosen inclinations like those that move the brutes? "According to thy judgment": are we not able to consider the forms of goodness and decide with reference to these what life we ought to live? But can we consider anything except as moved by our longings, or decide on any other grounds than our longings? Do I not as surely compose myself out of my animal longings as out of spiritual idealizations? By what logic do I break these apart from my truer self under the label *animal longings*?

My intending comes from somewhere, not a spot I can point to but a "whence" pictured negatively as a "within" or "behind" in relation to the beings I am aware of and the field of view I can trace the boundaries of. In this within is the spring of self—"disposition," if I think of it as an attitude, and "motivation," if I think of it as energy or efficacy. When my intentions take a remarkable turn for the better or the worse, I want to be able to say what there is in my self-source (other than my ordinary self) to account for this. There can be something alien in the self-source, oddly enough, because even though it is me, closer than my jugular vein, it is also not me inasmuch as it is not in my ordinary self-apprehension. I can think about what I both am and am not by employing the nonhuman categories of existence that I both do and do not occupy, namely, the animal and the divine. Thus I will speak of the self-quality that troubles me as the Beast or the God Within. The Beast and the God are bound to be unverifiable, "metaphysical" postulations for the two complementary reasons that their location is my essentially invisible "within" and that they differ categorically from ordinarily knowable humanity in precisely the way that is required to explain the stranger features of my life.

Thinking about a divine element in our character can take the form of a theology that refers directly to God—as for instance Mary Wollstonecraft links human dignity to a perfectibility called "soul," which she defines in turn by the perfection called "God"[37]—or a theomorphic representation of Reason such as we find in Plato or Aristotle or Hegel. In regarding ourselves under the aspect of the divine, gender might survive or be erased, depending perhaps on how the Genesis 1:26 statement of "divine image and likeness" is read; but the crucial point for us is that there is room in theology to erase gender because of the kind of ignorance that theology speaks to, namely, the open question about the nature of the best life. (Pico gives us an "indeterminate nature" to open us up to the spiritual beyond.) Now it might be the case that we cannot ultimately conceive the best life fully without somehow incorporating all the natural ingredients of life as we experience it, with all their implications; sex and gender might turn out to be impossible to erase for this reason. All the same, it *is* possible to construct a prima facie intelligible theology without reference to gender, because the direction of theology's reference is away from natural facts, toward transformation. The God Within or angelic principle is a free-blowing spirit.[38]

With biology it is another story. The point of zoomorphic interpretation is to ground our experience on natural facts. The ignorance to which biology speaks has to do with how our invisible self-source might be continuous with such facts. Our expectation of the ultimate result of biological inquiry is roughly a reversed image of what we expected from theology: while we might determine in the end that an animal structure like sex has no effect on human character, the initially most plausible surmise is that sex does have a significant influence. Biology will now try to speak in an empirically well-founded way, not directly about sex's influence on character (for the transition to character transcends the biological sphere), but about the physical side of the "influence" transaction—the wrinkles in the fabric of the body through which intentional centering and extending occur.

In biology as in theology, what we want must be the ultimate object of our curiosity about our own constitution, since all our features take on their ultimate significance in relation to this. The phenomenological site of this mystery within ourselves, our feelable being-moved, we call emotion. Emotion always reflects our being-moved *inside* ourselves, that is, the part of our motion that is not subject to choice *because* (unlike adventitious bumps from outside) *it belongs to that which chooses*. Emotion is the vibration of wanting and fearing. Extraordinary emotions are incursions into our awareness of the wants and fears that belong to our alien natures.

In theological perspective, emotions are evaluated for their truth or falsity as indications of our real affinities with beings and Being (or the beyond-Being); an inherent lucidity may be discovered in the better, "enlightened" emotions contrasting with darkness in the worse.[39] In biological or zoomorphic perspective, however, the "darkest" emotion may be the most readily comprehensible, while motivations that count as religiously lucid (such as conscious, kinship-indifferent altruism) are obscure. Since I *am* animal and spiritual, my own motivations will never be simply plain or obscure to me, no matter which perspective I adopt. For example, the impulse of sexual desire obviously refers to a definite bodily gratification and is therefore easy to make zoomorphic sense of. But to say that sexual desire is an animal motivation is to narrow it unduly. For a human being, sexual desire is a kind of lust, and lust is a powerful possessive impulsion that can affect me with respect to any sort of thing.[40] What then is the relation between "lust" and "sexual desire" as events within *me*? Is sexual desire just lust with respect to sex (which I would experience in essentially the same way with respect to other coveted things), or is there an important distinctive quality in sexual desire owing to its bodily conditions? (If so, sexual desire could become a pungent metaphor for other sorts of desire.) But even supposing the body-based uniqueness of sexual desire, I cannot say that this desire is fully intelligible in relation to a certain bodily gratification. Not just bodily history but personal history lies behind sexual desire as *I* experience it, and not just bodily satisfaction but personal satisfaction is at stake in it.

Thus we readily find indications that it would be a mistake to view the more zoomorphically interpretable emotions as body-caused perturbations of self, or as impositions of a distinct animal self on a personal, fully human self. (We will not stop here to study the complementary mistake about theomorphic aspects of emotion.) I do often experience emotion as a disruptive force: fear keeps me from following my friends off the diving board, infatuation with chocolate cake takes me off my diet, and so forth. To the extent that I regard the human emotional nature as a source of threats to coherent personal life, I must think that civilization's task is to subdue this nature, and in externalizing it from my true self (or the truer part of my self), posing better self against worse self as its would-be conqueror, I picture the repudiated nature as the Beast Within. It is easy then to identify the Beast with my animal constitution, although my problems mostly arise in *my* possession of this constitution and not in the animal world at large. (If a distinctively human anxiety or self-love is the real Beast, then animal nature is implicated in beastliness only insofar as it furnishes the matter of perverse intentions.) With the animal aspect read as Beastly and held at arm's length, authentically human motivation is stripped of biologically approachable content, with the ironic result that contact with actual humanity is lost. The self breaks into an Angel and a Beast that are pure postulates of moral or theological reflection; left unsolved is the problem of relating these ideal constructs to the empirical universe of behavior.

More reasonably, however, we can accept our whole emotional nature as a necessary constituent of fully realized human life; and as we shall then take civilization's task to be the cultivation of all such ingredients in a harmonious ensemble, we will look to biology for important information about an animal within. Unlike the Angel-or-Beast dualist view, which casts the parts of human character as all-good or all-evil, the inclusive view is bound to inquire about morally neutral or proto-moral elements of character to see what morally acceptable role they do play, or might play, in the whole structure. To the extent that an animal nature caused moral problems for us, we would aim to cope with it rather than to pull ourselves apart from it.

The first biological contribution to this perspective is the fundamental thesis that emotions have adaptive significance as disposers and motivators. If it is clear that feeling pain when I touch fire helps me save my hands from present danger and also to remember not to hazard them so again, it should be equally clear in principle that having certain aversive emotions can help keep me out of more complex sorts of trouble that sensations cannot adequately warn me about. For instance, feeling disgust at the thought of sleeping with one of my siblings prevents inbreeding. That is not to say that particular emotions are innately determined to occur. Certainly my incest aversion is cued by my parents and friends as I grow up. Still, my readiness to feel revulsion from incest is a natural fact requiring biological explanation, and if the emotion does appear in my experience it is as an involuntary and opaque power, quite a bit stronger and less immediately intelligible than, say, my learned aversion to rival political parties or religious denominations.

Another biological thesis on emotion, more arguable, is that mental and behavioral plasticity will not develop without a complementary motivational structure to keep the organism well oriented. Symons writes: "Since mental plasticity increases the number of maladaptive, as well as adaptive, behaviors that can be learned, it can only evolve with concomitant mechanisms that evaluate stimuli and motivate the seeking of stimuli, thereby making likely the development of adaptive behaviors. These mechanisms of evaluation and motivation must be closer to the genes than are the behaviors they produce."[41] Closer to the genes means less likely to vary by situation, that is, more predictable from genotype. But to say that our emotions are closer to the genes is not to say that they are simple. We have a physical basis for our fantastic emotional complexity in an exceptionally developed limbic system.[42]

The sex-related emotions are among our strongest and evidently have a great effect on our reproductive behavior, so it would not be surprising if a selected heritable structure appeared here, if anywhere, in our emotional life. A further thesis would be that since females and males have had significantly different reproductive risks and opportunities over the period in which the present human genotypes developed, their guiding sex-related emotions must be sex-differentiated; that is, there must be different female and male "sexual natures."

A word of caution is in order before we go further with the notion of a "nature" as an object of evolutionary explanation. In this context, the core of a species-nature is a genotype, but a particular genotype can only be a snapshot or sample taken from a process of change in the relations between genes, organisms, and their environment. Thus the natural structural consistency of an organism or species is to some extent a measurable fact (as for example we measure human consistency in cross-cultural studies) and yet is ultimately intelligible only in relation to the organism or species' ability to succeed in the whole range of circumstances it has to face—or, alternatively, in relation to the biosphere's ability to sustain life forms. To say that a fact of structural consistency is intelligible only in relation to a larger system of facts and possibilities is to say by implication that any such fact is incomplete and untrustworthy. The fact is incomplete because we need to know its relation to evolutionary process to know its status, that is, what line of development it belongs to and how stable it is. (Symons stresses the point that insofar as the environment to which the human genotype adapted has vanished, it is an open question whether genotypic features are presently adaptive.[43]) The fact is untrustworthy because to know something about what human beings tend to be like under today's conditions is not to know what they will tend to be like under tomorrow's conditions—which we are busy creating. We *make* a fact of human nature trustworthy by *construing* ourselves as adapted to our world; and indeed that is what is going on in the interpretation of sexual facts as gender resources or ingredients.

Now I shall present the chief hypotheses about the human "sexual natures" that are formulated and tested in Symons's *Evolution of Human Sexuality*, the best-thought-out account of its kind.[44] The hypotheses have to do with female and male emotional tendencies relating directly to sexual behavior; he does not discuss the possible sex affiliations of emotions like maternal love or fighting rage, although they too are approachable in evolutionary perspective.

Men should more highly value sexual variety, because their parental investment in each offspring can be so small. Women have much less to gain from variety because their minimum investment in each of their children is relatively large, and they also have a vital interest in being helped by a partner in child rearing; thus they should favor long-term relationships rather than hit-and-run. Men should be most attracted to nubile women signaling the greatest reproductive potential (while, according to David Buss, women should be most attracted to men who signal the greatest command of resources).[45] Since any individual man is more likely than any individual woman to be shut out of reproductive success, men should be more anxious about access to women, hence more readily aroused by the sight of women with good reproductive potential, more importunate, and more jealously possessive.[46] Living in community with each other, men and women will partly mask their sexual natures with compromises in sexual behavior and ideology, but their difference will always be measurable. In the test case of male and female homosexual behavior, where heterosexual compromises are removed, we do see a much clearer manifestation of the difference, as gay men have a strong tendency to prefer multifarious and relatively impersonal sexual encounters, while sexual activity *per se* is a lower priority for lesbians, and long-term sexually exclusive relationships are more the norm.[47]

What matters for our purposes is not whether this view is true in any or all respects but whether a view of this type could be true. There are three ways to resist such claims: first, by adducing empirical counterexamples to them, which implicitly concedes that there could have been good enough cross-cultural evidence to establish them; second, by denying that a biological nature exists in humans, which is absurdly at variance with the premises that set up the enterprise of biology; third, by denying in principle that a biological nature has any relevance to human self-interpretation, which supposes an arbitrarily exclusive interest in theomorphizing or else a confused belief that animal and spiritual dimensions of human nature, since they are distinct, can be only equivocally related. But they can be analogically related. Thus I conclude that biological talk of human sexual natures is meaningful.

But there is still a difficulty in saying how a sexual nature is meaningful in relation to gender. A biological fact, regarded strictly as such, must belong to gender's physical center of meaning and affect my sense of gender via my beliefs, as we have already seen. Yet *this* fact has to do with my own valuation, for one of these sexual natures is very likely (if never certain) to be (to some extent) my own, according to my sex; and if it is, and to the extent that it is, it participates directly in the constitution of the central meanings I apprehend and uphold in the genders. Does biological insight break down the distinction between gender and sex in this case?

Let us pursue this question with reference to a specific emotional example.

The case of sexual jealousy

Jealousy makes a specially interesting case study of sex/gender "nature" for several reasons. For one thing, it is considered natural but at the same time is regarded with distaste. Although there may be powerful cultural signals encouraging and excusing jealousy, any approved role for it—for example, in the sort of story in which a woman saves her marriage to a distracted husband by exciting his jealousy—is subordinate and temporary. Thus it *seems* not to be a construct of our culture but a factor that our culture copes with or exploits; at least, our culture posits it so. Personal experience confirms this reading. We experience jealousy as a force carrying us away rather than as choice or judgment, even if we can, to some extent, control its intensity, its object, and its expression. Most important, jealousy is a sex-differentiated emotion in that it is thought to be more natural to men than to women; it is recognized, though, that women sometimes burn as fiercely with jealousy as men, and this is not considered unnatural. (A gender difference may yet appear upon careful comparison: women may tend to be jealous more about commitment as such than about sexual access as such, and more about reliability than about undivided attention.)

According to Symons, the sex difference in jealousy is reflected in the fact that polygynous human societies are common but polyandrous societies very rare, as well as in evidence that men have more emotional difficulty in polyandry than women have in polygyny: "Although circumstances obviously do exist in which men will become co-husbands, circumstances do not exist in which men will do so as contentedly as women will become co-wives. . . . The experience of sexual jealousy of a co-spouse seems to be a facultative adaptation [a capacity activated in some conditions but not others] in the human female but more of an obligate adaptation in the human male."[48] If polygyny and polyandry are unequal human possibilities owing to a sex difference in jealousy, then it would seem that jealousy must contribute much of the emotional basis of the whole sexual code known as the "double standard."

At the heart of the phenomenology of jealousy is its impersonal or prepersonal force that "carries one away." I *can't stand* someone else's access to my object of attachment because this shakes my *foundations*, and in a double sense: objectively, failure to control my object of attachment upsets a life plan predicated on control and, subjectively, the experience of this failure causes me overwhelming emotional upset. Now, as for the emotional upset, what sort of force could do this? Where would it come from? (How did a "foundation" with this sort of unsteadiness get built in the first place?)

To explain my sexual jealousy, the evolutionary argument proposes that I am endowed by natural selection with a set of strong emotional responses that are kept largely outside my conscious control so that my tremendous intellectual and behavioral plasticity will not lead me to act in a reproductively disadvantageous way. These emotions are the foundation of my felt orientation in the world. In this case, if I, a male, were not instinctively zealous to maintain exclusive access to my mate(s), I would more likely be the loser in sexual competition, either as a failed suitor or as a cuckold. Jealousy is an alarm bell that tells me when the future of my genes is threatened. It has to be a loud alarm (just as pain has to be sharp) to command my attention totally and rouse me to my greatest aggressiveness or tenacity; hence the sensation of upset. And women's jealousy tends to differ from men's because women's reproductive prospects do not depend nearly as much on controlling their mates' sexual activity.

Thus we can conceive an emotional nature in me which, on the occasions when it bewildered my calmer self, I might well have imagined as a Beast Within. The animal nature as such does not have the same meaning as the Beast figured by my fear (although the two conceptions might refer to the same reality), nor is it necessarily the same in any one respect as the nature of any other animal. It is just the nature of the human animal, zoomorphic in the sense that it is comprehensible in a framework in which all animal life can be thought about.

We should not fail to take note here of an equally powerful but apparently very different explanation of the jealous Beast that is offered in psychoanalytic theory.[49] On this view, the human infant's emotional nature, like its intellectual nature, is shaped by experiences during its long developmental period after birth, especially in its first few years. The strongest of all its attachments is to the person or persons who directly care for it the most, from whom all blessings flow—for us, the mother—and its corresponding greatest frustrations and fears are related to its inability to control the source of blessings. Girls, who belong to the same sex type as the mother, grow up identifying with this source, but boys identify themselves as different from it and therefore grow up to respond to women with irrational fear and longing as though they are all (like the original mother) problematic keys to happiness that need to be controlled. The beast of jealousy that roars within males has the dark force of *unconscious* feeling, its now-hidden structure forged in the intense joys and rages of unremembered childhood. I can't stand not commanding the attention of my beloved now because as a powerless infant I couldn't stand not commanding my mother.

The psychoanalytic explanation of male sexual jealousy is indeed a rival to the biological hypothesis of an emotional nature innately determined as to its objects, because if we found that making fathers primary caregivers also made girls grow up to be more prone to sexual jealousy than boys, we would confirm the former view and invalidate the latter. But the "ultimate" evolutionary explanation would not necessarily be overthrown by this result, because if human mothers were the primary caregivers to infants throughout the period in which humanity evolved, then it remains possible that the hypothesized psychology of infant–parent relations was the sufficient *proximate* cause of a male "sexual nature" that was ultimately caused by the male reproductive position. In that case, intensive fathering would "fool" the boys and girls by confronting them with a parent of a different sex than they were adapted to "expect," and over the long term—supposing that we were to be under the same constraints on reproductive success as operated in our evolutionary past—this behavior would be selected against, as it would give females and males disadvantageous emotional equipment. Reproductive interest would then cause a different mechanism of sex-appropriate emotions to arise, a different way of realizing our "sexual nature."

By whatever history and mechanism, jealousy is on the human scene, and because of its sex differentiation and its application to sexual behavior we expect it to be relevant to gender. Just how it is relevant depends on the relation between an "emotional nature" and a "character"—for we have defined gender as a qualification of character, that is, of people's intentional natures.

For biology, emotion is the presumed subjective aspect of an alteration of an organism's inner bodily state in response to stimuli that are aversive or attractive or both. (In this formulation, "inner" bodily state is contrasted with "behavior" or interaction with other beings in the environment; it need not be invisible to an observer.) Emotion is of biological importance to the degree that the subjective experience as such is a cause of behavior, although to deepen our insight at this point we invoke a distinct type of explanation, the psychological. An emotional nature, then, is the endowed capacity to alter one's inner bodily state in response to circumstances and to feel those alterations; the structural consistency in one's alterations and feelings of alteration that anyone can count on finding; the possibility of specializing and excelling in certain emotions, that is, a métier; and one's adjustment to a larger system to which one's emotional capacities and tendencies are suited and to which they make some contribution.

Our physical endowment for emotion includes the limbic system. Emotions such as general animation or depression, rage, docility, and a generic sort of bliss—the very emotions that strike a subject like a gust of wind or a strong undertow—can be produced by direct stimulation of various points in this area of the brain. These are at once the least personal and the least informative of emotions, so that we are least likely to identify ourselves with them or value them. But the limbic system is normally in communication with the entire cerebral cortex, so that we emotionally know the wealth of material registered in that larger, newer part of the brain. "Love is pleasure accompanied by the idea of an external cause."[50] Hence I love *her,* everything about her, or I am mad about *that,* the whole situation; and there are felt subleties and shifts in my inner body state corresponding to all the complexities recognized in these objects. The more fully integrated this emotional experience is, the more I must experience it as myself; there is no possibility of setting up a separate self over against the emotion. Therefore, "emotional nature" becomes "character," for better or worse, to the degree that it is integral to the intentional disposition with which I identify myself and am identified by others.

The feelings that are produced by electrode stimulation of the brain do not have emotional repercussions in character. But if we stimulate our brains by reading *Middlemarch* or *Crime and Punishment,* then our emotional experience attains an intensely, challengingly personal grade. We have risen from being moved involuntarily and blindly (in passion) to being moved by what we know *through* knowing (in judgmental emotion) and ultimately to being moved in response to that about the beings we encounter that transcends knowableness and that introduces us to the spiritual frame of reference in which the decisive forms of validity and justification are constructed (in reverential emotion). That the experimental techniques of biology cannot directly produce experiences of higher grade does not mean that the occurrence of such experiences is not, in one aspect, a biological phenomenon. Our emotions will, to be sure, escape a determining biological explanation, if differences and changes in emotional experience cannot be correlated with physiological or ecological differences and changes; but even our variability is an object of biological hypothesis.

Part of jealousy's fascination is that in being jealous one typically oscillates between identifying with it and dissociating oneself from it, that is, disapproving of it or wishing one could be free of it. The swings of this oscillation often correspond, on the one hand, to knowing and not knowing the *object* or *final cause* of the feeling—for if I am jealous of a lover whose perfidies are fully evident, my emotion seems to be well founded and to fit me into my situation appropriately, whereas if the emotion is blind it makes me feel rootless and out of place. On the other hand, my relation to the emotion depends on whether I am aware of an *efficient cause* of the feeling—for if I can attribute jealousy to a Beast Within, or merely to being overtired and overcaffeinated, then I can take a distance from it.

The oscillation in jealousy is a living experience of the sex–gender distinction. As an involuntary surge of relatively blind possessiveness —as, say, it hits me in the instant that I hear a man's voice on the phone when I call my well-trusted beloved—I can recognize it as a "programmed" psychosomatic event that I also know to be more characteristic of males than of females. (If males are not the more jealous sex in a different culture, or if they aren't even really more jealous in my own culture but I am encouraged in my culture to believe that they are, then what I take to be a sex fact would be, indeed, a cultural rather than purely biological constraint, but it would still be, for me, on the involuntary and impersonal side of a distinction that lets gender be distinct from sex. If we classed sex with gender here because of the artificiality of both, we would miss this crucial point.) In this way, I assign my experience of jealousy to the factual center of meaning of masculinity. I draw on this center of meaning when I think about masculinity and go about actualizing it. I may find myself to be unmanly if I do not experience an emotion that I believe to be typically experienced by men. Or I may excuse myself for ugly behavior by asserting that it is, after all, masculine, so that my beloved (supposing she wants a masculine lover) had better see that this is an essential part of the good bargain.

I actualize the central meanings of masculinity and femininity directly, however, in being jealous in a more voluntary and conscious way. I am aware of myself in the role of one who needs to control and can control—I posit myself as having this essential concern and the right to act on it—and I perceive my beloved in the dual role of foundation of my happiness and instrument of my interests. (One reason we find expressions of jealousy distasteful is that neither of these role relations are adult-to-adult. I am playing child to her as mother, on the one hand, and patriarch to her as daughter, on the other.) My exigent masculinity asks for her condescending or pliant femininity. My masculine *individuality,* requiring the sustenance of the undivided attention of others, expects to be granted priority in the serving of this need over a feminine selfhood that is not supposed to be so vulnerable in this respect.[51] Rather than being knocked over by my emotion as though by a gust of wind, I feel an expansion of myself into this extraordinarily strong feeling, which fits into a larger structure of motivation and behavior that I share with other masculine beings, complementing a similarly large structure inhabited by feminine beings. More than this psychic strength, there is a *spiritual* strength, that is, a perceived interintentional validity in my realization of masculinity: I sense that the personal community wants, or at least accepts, my feeling and acting this way. I am on track in my relationships with Others, justified, and thus nothing prevents me from investing myself (and being seen to invest myself) in this pattern normatively. It belongs to my character. In all these ways, the emotion of jealousy is part of the production of gender. Of course the jealousy depends on a cognitive scheme to have this effect—and such schemes can define sexual "rights" in very different ways—but we can say with equal justice that without the energy and directionality of such emotions, a cognitive gender scheme would seem unreal.

There is an analogy between an obligate adaptation of jealousy, which the evolutionary biologist predicates of a heritable emotional nature, and the righteous masculinity of my jealousy, which is predicated of my character in the gender system. Analogical relation assumes difference: what is an urgent need for me as a gendered personal subject is not the same as what is an urgent need for me as a prospective reproducer. It is true that when I appeal to an inherited nature to justify my masculinity, I might seem to collapse the two, but actually I am asserting connection, not identity, between my animal and personal jealousies. The sense of "natural" that is most apposite to the justification of a character quality is what we have called métier. Thus I regard righteous masculine jealousy, not merely as a personal analogue to the animal programming envisioned by the biologist, but as a cultivation of it: I consciously adopt the vocation of effectively expressing and fruitfully elaborating an endowment.

Now masculine jealousy is not, in general, a pleasant manifestation of gender. One of the most common forms of homicide, the murder of a woman by a suitor or husband or ex-husband who feels rejected by her (and who often plans to kill himself afterward), is a behavioral consequence of it.[52] A fully approvable elaboration of jealousy would have to transform it into a basically different attitude and behavior pattern. For that matter, one can judge jealousy to be ignoble and weak on strictly masculine grounds. It is a debasement of masculinity. But even though jealousy would probably not figure largely in anyone's ideal portrait of masculinity, it surely is an important part of actual masculinity, and this implies that it *can* appear as a justified attitude. If no one ever personally identified with jealousy it would just count as a predominantly male "problem," the emotional equivalent of baldness or heart disease. And even while we are looking at jealousy from outside, with distaste, it may yet count as approvable in the weak sense that males generally deserve permission to be ugly and weak in this way—up to some point. (It shows how grotesquely far the permission can be taken that juries have often excused from all punishment men who in jealous rage killed their adulterous wives.)

The extent to which gender *culture* can be explained biologically as the product of individual organisms' adoptions of available behavior patterns, those individual choices governed by factors like male sexual jealousy, has not yet been seen.[53] But our analysis of multiple aspects of human nature in the individual would lead us to expect similar ambiguities in culture. Many people mean to exclude the zoomorphic aspect of human affairs when they choose the word *culture* to talk about it, but even granting that stipulation, it remains true that human collective behavior is partly comparable to the collective behavior of ants, wolves, and baboons, just as my own motivation is partly like the urges that move these animals individually.

Human nature as sexual consistency: the racial parallel

Let us sum up what we have learned about the thought that sex is gender's basis.

Our self-interpretation travels around a circuit. It passes through the body (what is felt in the body and believed about the body) on its way to appreciating the structures of intentional life as such, and it passes through intentional structures on its way to forming a picture of the body. Therefore, the most important concepts that we apply to ourselves, including the concepts of the human and of each of the human kinds, are ambiguous: they can be given intentional or descriptive force by stipulation, depending on our purposes, but our fullest self-awareness depends finally on acknowledging rather than repressing their complexity of meaning. The supreme examples of this complexity should be gender, race, and age thinking, all of which represent centerings *of* the body that center *on* the body.

The best model of embodiment implies that differences in character can be directly caused by the body's sex in a variety of ways. The personal qualities that are caused by the human body in its always-sexed condition, qualities that show up as the trademark of specifically human personhood, make up the most fundamental culture- and history-spanning *consistency* of human life, the always-to-be-reckoned-with, and in this way belong to human nature. The consistency is not perhaps as definite as one would like, because its content is debatable (and even when we fix some part of its content we still disagree about whether it should be changed).[54] We know that the inner chemistry of sexual difference making cannot be open to inspection, and even if we *may* feel it powerfully in sex-linked emotions, we can never treat our interpretations of emotion as clear windows onto the influence of sex, so variable and interested are they.

On the other hand, we stand to be affected not only by sex itself but by beliefs about sex, and these can be studied in the same way that any ideology is studied. These beliefs may have a consistency of their own due to causes other than the human body, such as the structural requirements of social existence, and thus may deserve recognition as enduring features of human life; but they cannot have the title to human naturalness that consistencies arising from the human body do.

Gender culture is often analyzed as though its sole basis were beliefs about sex. But it is always possible that a gender culture exhibits some of the actual drift of sex's effect on character; that its forms are, to some extent, elaborations of this given; and that what we feel to be significant in the sex-linked aspects of our science, politics, art, and everyday emotions and behavior is sometimes a realization on our part of our being gendered by sex. To admit this is to admit the coherence of gender thinking that refers to sex as a causal basis of gender. (Now gender thinking can refer to the sexed body in a purely phenomenological or poetic way, without implying anything about causation, but the causation of sex is the most important assumption underlying expectations of consistency in the sex–gender linkage.) If believing something about a fact immediately magnifies the fact, intentionally centering the body's extension in such a way as to reinforce the sexed character of the body's extending of intention, that reveals a variable dimension in the fact, not that there is no fact. Note, in any case, that gender thinking also brings the natural difference of sex into relation with that real and ideal common humanity by virtue of which we try to rule such differences so that they enhance our common life, or at least don't disfigure it.

If we retraced the itinerary of our investigation of sexed embodiment, asking instead about the basing of race on breed or of personal age on physical age, we would find analogies at every point. We would also be able to interpret culture and class along the same lines to the extent that the culture- and class-determined forms of life (language or dialect, artifacts, arts) constitute a "body" that intenders live in and through and into which they read themselves, in continuity with their physical bodies.[55] Temperament, too, can be matched to body type— weren't red-haired people supposed to be fiery, "dark" people passionate or sensual?—but the fundamental correlation in this category is actually with the *individual* body. Finally, sexual orientation connects the invisible individual base of temperament with the sex-relational structure in gender's base.

Rather than spell out all the analogies, however, I would like to concentrate here on one issue relating to the physical basing of race.

Some sociobiologists have argued for a relatively fixed "race emotion" comparable to the sexual emotions we have discussed, namely, an uneasiness about people who look different from the "normal" physical type one takes to be one's own.[56] The implications of a "natural" basic repulsion between peoples would, it seems, be very grave in a world of political frameworks and economic communities that typically encompass racial and ethnic diversity. We might take some comfort from the fact that human history does not show a universal, across-the-board, undiscriminating repulsion from racial foreignness. Racial xenophobia is common, but so is xenophilia. Racial fear and distaste are usually found where there is competition between the racial groups (and so too, given competition, hatred bases itself on family resemblance or clothing style or any other perceptible generic quality); emotional racism is the subjective intensification of a perception of threat. There would only be cause to speak of a natural emotional racism if there were threats intrinsic to race. Are there?

What sorts of threats does race carry? First, the threat that *their* people will displace *our* people from needed life supports, if their numbers increase more than ours. (But this displacement could happen on a basis other than race, even if race puts the most genes at stake. The illogical homophobic feeling that homosexuals will "take over" if not suppressed shows better than anything else the breadth of this sort of fear.) Second, the threat that that other type of sexual attractiveness, the product of sexual selection in the other breeding community, will have more influence than we do over the people we want to attract. (Again, race is only one object of a more general anxiety. Much like the member of a different sexual orientation, the attractive member of another race changes the rules of sexual competition disturbingly, destroying my chances. This must be an emotional root of the horror of "miscegenation.") Third, the threat that the other type will manage superlatively to incarnate some virtue that I cannot but value, so that I cannot but lament my racial exclusion from it. (Obviously this is as much or as little likely to happen on the basis of gender, culture, etc.)

The reasonable conclusion seems to be that while humans show much evidence of innate mistrustfulness and hostility, as would be predicted from the competitiveness of human genotype propagation, the only factor that would give rise to an intrinsically racist version of these feelings is the difference between the average number of genes shared by individuals within a breeding community and the average number of genes shared between breeding communities. A "Chinese" genotype, say, might have been more favored by selection if it had been jealous of its identity vis-à-vis "foreign" genotypes. Notice, however, that everything depends on how individuals identify their breeding community. Selection may favor defining it inclusively rather than exclusively; sexual reproduction is, after all, a pursuit of genetic diversity as well as replication, and "interbreeding" is, in fact, an important cause of the presently observable distribution of human genes. Perhaps this suggests an instinctual basis for the lively and appreciative interest people often take in race difference, when they are relatively free from the sense of threat.

Thus if *Homo sapiens* has evolved a race-sensitive disposition—as is certainly possible, and seems likely—then the political and cultural challenge is to create a framework in which racial groups do not compete with each other as such. But since any breeding group does threaten in principle to displace any complementarily defined other, there are only two fundamental protections against racism. One is a stable apportionment of resources among recognized racial groups. The difficulty here is that such stability can be achieved and maintained only with extraordinary political luck. Government actions with respect to race groups (immigration policies, Affirmative Action, etc.) are usually felt to be destabilizing by the dominant group, while inaction allows the minorities to be oppressed and demoralized. The other protection against racism is to define the breeding community inclusively, which ultimately implies erasing any sharp lines of racial difference. Even when this is done, however, there may remain gradients of socially significant value, like a preference for "light" over "dark" or vice versa.[57] It may be impossible to separate physical looks entirely from the social stratification process.

For the humanization of race in a multiracial society, the most auspicious state of affairs I can imagine is a mixture of the two scenarios just identified. Freedom of interbreeding is desirable, not only to let individuals marry whomever they love but to relieve the broader psychic pressure of thinking of the races as breeding competitors. At the same time, the most effective equalizing mechanism in a democracy is the rule of interest-group representation—so that what happens in a polity does not get determined without the fairly empowered participation of representatives of the most important constituencies in it—and this mechanism can achieve justice in the realm of physical looks or body-based aptitudes only if there are distinct, stable reference groups to be represented. "Whites" could claim a certain number of seats in Parliament, but "lighter" people could not. And this political standing would support the "white community's" sense of its own dignity.

Plainly no political approach to racial issues can be either perfectly satisfactory or perfectly stable. Beyond politics, we should plan (as with gender) to try to ameliorate the malaise that always attends human differentiation by educating ourselves to be more appreciative of diversity and to make more mature judgments about it. The heart of the requisite attitude must be sheer affirmation of generic as well as individual diversity.[58]

*

Positive gender thinking makes much of a generic difference and is not illogical for doing so, even if one judges it to be ill advised. Critics of the positive thought of gender protest that sex-based intentional differences are not important relative to the other features of character that should concern us. They point out that when such differences are accurately measurable, they are often small relative to individual variability and other factors. Yet a gender system bases itself on sex by *treating* sex difference as important. We have the discretion to do this. We may do it as the unconscious instruments of social stratification processes, or (which concerns us more here) we may do it for statable reasons,[59] or we may do it consciously yet inarticulately as part of our entire valuational gesture in the dimension of life where we are necessarily alert to sexedness, namely, in all that concerns procreation.

Since the relevant reasons need to be assessed and the valuation clarified, our inquiry into gender must now adopt a more consistently anthropomorphic approach. Instead of sexual natures like continuing attractivity and jealous possessiveness, we will confront the beautiful and the noble, the sympathetic and the principled. Parts of sexual anatomy will become signifiers of cultural styles. Reproduction will become marriage and family.

Chapter 5

Gender, Valuation, and Selfhood

We shift now from the bodily center of meaning to the intentional central meaning of gender, which consists of character qualities. It was a concern with defining gendered character qualities that produced the first wave of modern gender theory in the eighteenth century. Early gender theorists like Burke, Rousseau, and Kant were aware that differences of character type had important implications for what are now called "value" issues—they knew, indeed, that deep differences in character are precisely deep differences of valuing and of valuableness, and they made it clear that the genders belong to human nature as *métiers,* or ideals to be cultivated—not simply as given facts. That these writers gave obnoxiously sexist accounts of the gendering of value makes it difficult to recapture the question they were trying to answer. But that question is central to the understanding of gender. Gender difference would simply not be very interesting if femininity and masculinity did not present rival paradigms of attractiveness and virtue. Though we may not always be comfortable admitting it, our gendered conduct constantly proclaims such paradigms, and honesty at least should compel us to give an articulate account of them.

To construe the genders as modes of valuing or types of valuableness presumes that values come in constellations—that we can non-arbitrarily group certain values together, thanks to their real affinities, and mark real divisions or even oppositions between such groups. Thus the general philosophical problem that interests us at this stage of the inquiry is, How is the realm of value structured? Could it be said of any gender scheme that it cuts the value realm at the joints? We find that value affinities do contribute to the cogency of gender thinking, though not in such a way as to make any particular division of value necessary. We also find that the genders are humanizers of romantic love insofar as they mediate between "finer feelings" of attraction to character and lust.

Turning to the new *locus classicus* for the question of gendered moral valuation, Carol Gilligan's *In a Different Voice*, we have to ponder the suspicious resemblance Gilligan's categories Care and Justice bear to Kant's sexist categories of female and male attraction; and, noting how Gilligan's vision of human development prompts us to entertain a vision of androgynous wholeness, we have to ask whether the gender division of humanity is morally tolerable. A related problem that stands in the way of affirming gender is the affiliation of the genders with pathologies of relationship (here designated "pornography" and "heterocracy") as well as with recognized degenerations of morality like sentimentalism and legalism. These are the worst sorts of impairment for which gender could be blamed. It is possible, however, to understand them as impairments of the genders rather than as impairments of humanity that are present just insofar as humanity is gendered.

Gender is often thought to be alienating for individual selves: "true self," like true humanity, would be compromised by gender typing. Meanwhile, at another critical pole that holds suspect the very notion of identity, the discourse that produces "selfhood" would be rejected along with the discourse that produces gender. But it turns out that the concept of "true self" is an indispensable means of thinking pertinently about oppression and happiness, and that gender norms can function as windows onto individual identities provided they are cast as questions about people rather than as definitions of them. This methodology is put to the test in my interpretation of the gender plot of *High Noon*. I use the gender icons from *High Noon* to make acceptable sense of the claim that distinctively feminine and masculine virtues are, in general, the best utilizations of our resources of femaleness and maleness—that is, are humanly natural as métiers.

The attractions of gender and "finer feelings": Kant

How do humans appear to each other to be good? They can be good *at* doing interesting things, like talking or dancing or building; they can be good *for* important purposes, like collaborating in work or play or politics; they can be good *to* each other as benefactors or kindly presences. Or they can be appreciated more directly and globally as good examples *of* their kind—good-looking, well conducted, and so forth.

Calling people "good" expresses a logical satisfaction in their fulfilling some assumed criteria; beyond this, it often also expresses a psychic satisfaction in *seeing* people as good, an attraction to their flourishing. One enjoys attending to human excellences like bodily grace, balance of mind, and steadiness of will. For analysis, these features can be isolated as good-ats, good-fors, and good-tos, but they are apprehended as constituting their bearers' selfhood; and they are attractive apart from instrumental calculations, even though one would point out what the excellences are good for if one were asked to explain them.

What is it, then, to be good as a feminine or masculine being, and what is it to be attracted to these types?

We came upon one point of reference in our study of the sex basis of gender. It appears in biological perspective that the important, specifically sex-linked way in which females impress males is by signaling reproductive capacity, that is, by a nubile look, combined with expanded sexual receptivity; meanwhile, males impress females with indications of their power to command resources to help females and children and to control rival males. We infer that it was for a long time in the reproductive interest of each sex both to take on and to be influenced by such appearances. But we do not, so to say, agree to these terms of sexual attraction—not because we do not recognize ourselves in them, but because what we recognize is less than fully human. If gender is the humanizing of sex, then feminine and masculine must be fully personal attractions. But since gender also reflects the sexing of humanity, it must be possible to find an affiliation between our gender attractions and our animal signals of sex-related aptitude.

The idea of *refinement* brings a scale-of-nature continuum into the realm of human value. Gender can be thought of as a "finer" nature, and gender appreciation as a "finer" feeling for human nature. But the refinement metaphor can be turned in different ways. It makes one think of a working of given materials into more precise and intelligible forms, an inclusive realization, yet also suggests a purification process, the separation of a valuable core from dross. The metaphor thus perfectly captures an uncertainty at the heart of gender: Can we really be sexual *and* human?

It is no accident that the first waves of modern gender theory appeared in a century much concerned with refinement. When Kant composed his discourse on those "finer feelings" that "fit the soul for virtuous impulses," the *Observations on the Feeling of the Beautiful and the Sublime* (1764), he could assume the meaningfulness and aptness of relating finer feeling to the abstract qualities "beautiful" and "sublime," for these qualities had already been defined and discussed by Burke and other British writers.[1] (The possibility of linking "beautiful" and "sublime" to the genders more systematically than Burke had done may have been suggested to Kant by Rousseau's gender generalizations in book 5 of *Emile* [1762]; and Kant was certainly inspired by the larger Rousseauvian ideal of culture as cultivation or sublimation of natural human endowments.)[2] The finer feelings, in Kant's view, are those that tend toward steadiness and universality so that they can be called "principles" in contrast to "impulses" (60, 65). They are thus reason-like and worthy to be affirmed on that basis, at the same time that they are acknowledged as facts of our empirical nature. By concentrating on such feelings we can construct something like an a priori aesthetics and normative psychology: we know what, in principle, the human subject is crucially moved by.

Grace and law, sweetness and right, love and respect—we always knew how we were supposed to be thrilled, and that there was a difference, sometimes a conflict, between the two ideal channels of valuation. Kant puts a humanist face on this ancient duality. The ultimate object of finer feeling, he says, is the "beauty and dignity of human nature" (60). We note that although humanity as such possesses both forms of worth, lines of sex-related specialization are plain to see. The human aesthetic is actually a summation of two gender aesthetics, and the gender components are referred in turn to established poles of aesthetic value in general, the "beautiful" and the "sublime."

The beautiful is everything that delights, charms, and makes us feel lively and gay—the happiest versions, one might say, of our ordinary selves. The sublime, on the other hand, is everything we pleasantly feel to exceed our ordinary scale. The "terrifying sublime," as in a tempest or mountain crag, provokes fear as well as pleasure; the "noble sublime," a quiet wonder (47). Kant suggests that the "beautiful" and the "noble sublime" are respectively the "proper reference points" from which to judge women and men (77). Not that women are exclusively talented for the beautiful and men for the noble. Neither type wholly lacks the qualities of the other. Nevertheless, all of a person's merits should unite in such a way as to enhance the leading quality of her or his own type. The two types are equally human, for their leading qualities are qualifications of common human powers or virtues. For example: "The fair sex has just as much understanding as the male, but it is a *beautiful understanding,* whereas ours should be a *deep understanding*" (78). "*Neatness,* which of course well becomes any person, in the fair sex belongs among the virtues of the first rank and can hardly be pushed too high among them, although in a man it sometimes rises to excess and then becomes trifling" (84).

Clearly Kant is speaking of the types that we call genders. There are really two separable claims here: that genders are constituted by valuable qualities, and that genders coincide with "the sexes." The second claim can be amended without prejudice to the first. Acknowledging that sex is a reference point for the meaning of gender, and also (in all likelihood) one of gender's causes, we can also acknowledge that a woman (say) need not be feminine and a man may be, or that an individual may be both masculine and feminine. Thus we can interpret Kant's assertion that the sexes must be educated and evaluated according to these different value criteria as applying not to women and men per se but to people insofar as they are feminine and masculine. For example, insofar as I am feminine, all my qualities would support my affinity for beauty and receive in return the twist of an overarching orientation to the beautiful. I would be more perfectly feminine the more strongly and harmoniously I could center on the beautiful. With this revision, the ground is taken out from under Kant's most offensive pronouncements ("A woman who has a head full of Greek . . . might as well even have a beard" [78]).

Turning back to the first claim, we can ask how well Kant is able to account for masculine and feminine beings' experience of each other by ordering all qualities valued in humans to the beautiful and the noble sublime. It cannot be denied that his remarks are in line with familiar gender stereotypes, which revives the question, *Are* genders stereotypes? One could reply in the affirmative and attribute any incongruities between the stereotypes and our experience of individuals to the fact that women and men are more than simply feminine and masculine. Or—without denying that women and men are more than simply feminine and masculine—one could persist in distinguishing ideally revelatory generic-nature conceptions from repressive "stereotypes." On the latter view, a gender stereotype would be a degenerate form of a more open and nuanced conception. Thus what is at issue when we ask how well Kant accounts for gender attractions is human adequacy as well as logical coherence.

At least it must be said that Kant covers a fair amount of ground in perceptive fashion. He shows a reference to beauty in merriness, charm, facility, *refinement itself* ("Women . . . refine even the masculine sex" [77–78]), grace, sympathy, neatness, and cleanliness, and a certain amount of excusable vanity—everything "lovable." Related to the noble sublime are the virtues of earnestness, profundity, fortitude, generosity, magnanimity, and self-restraint—everything "admirable." Surely there are strong tendencies for women and men to be judged differently and to have different aspirations along just these boundary lines, not only in Kant's society but in our own. And it seems that Kant is both accurate and appropriately broad when he claims that, according to gender prescription, the feminine faculty most worth developing is "sense" or sensitivity—the crucial faculty for monitoring and adjusting human affairs for the sake of the beautiful—while masculine beings are called upon to excel in formal rationality and erudition, as befits those specially charged to master relations with the hidden and distant.

What ultimately is the force, for us, of this gender aesthetic? We want to know which of three conclusions we are entitled to draw:

1. The strong thesis that human attractions cannot be fully appreciated or consistently thought about except in the beauty and sublimity constellations, pinned in turn to the sexes. (Kant is hitting an a priori nail on the head.)
2. A weaker thesis—for instance, that human attractions are experienced more richly, or become more legible in reflection, if they are ordered in a scheme like the one Kant suggests, although different schemes are not precluded. (Kant is on to something.)
3. The null thesis that the grouping of human attractions in relation to aesthetic ideals or sexual reference points is arbitrary—the "heterogenous collection" of which Sandra Bem spoke[3]—and therefore must be understood to be motivated by considerations other than pure aesthetic form or sexual fact. (Kant is a mouthpiece of conservative gender ideology.)

To justify any one of these conclusions, we must be able to identify principles by which valuations of humans would or would not belong with each other. As a first step, let us reflect on the general form of valuing.

The structure of valuing

Valuing in the broadest sense includes everything we would call a pro-attitude, but in the stricter sense a valuation must have two sorts of objectivity: first, a structural constancy in the valuing intention that allows us to contemplate it and discuss it, and, second, an interintentional extension, or in other words a conditioning of its performance by responsive awareness of other valuing subjects and by all the politico-moral issues that belong to life-in-relationship.

The intentional structure of valuing

To value a thing is to feel that one lives well, in fact or in principle, in relation to the thing. The most general expression one can always give for the wellness of life is that it involves, either actually or potentially, the expansion of one's being. And of course it is the feasibility and flourishing of intentional life that is at stake. Valuation is an issue of intentional hygiene.

To intend affirmingly, to value, means to aim at something in such a way as virtually to qualify one's position relative to it: either to approach closer to it or to tarry in its presence. This is done for the sake of two corresponding goods. The distinctive (if not sole) good of closeness or contact with a thing is to qualify one's own existence, to let the form or force of the thing determine one's own form or force in a happy way. The distinctive good of tarrying in the presence of a thing is to have one's theater of action formed so that a happy array of possible self-expressions and impingements on self is given. (Evidently much depends on how "self" and "one's own" are defined and experienced.) Complex combinations of these two basic moves are possible with regard to any object or set of objects; the purpose of an aesthetic, or of criticism generally, is to maximize the yield of happiness by encouraging certain combinations and discouraging others, always taking for granted some basic reference points of satisfaction.

The question is how such complex valuations can be put together.

Congruence and contiguity. The most obvious primary kinds of harmonious relationship between valuations are congruence and contiguity. Consider the Kantian set of valued feminine qualities: "beauty, fineness, sensitivity." These belong together because the feeling of plenitude in beauty, of needing-to-ask-no-more, largely coincides with the feeling of recognizing the perfection of fineness, of a nothing-more-could-be-done, which in turn overlaps with one's feeling (about a "sensitive" person) that nothing is being missed. We could also say that there is contiguity between these valuations in the sense that an intender spontaneously shifts from one straight to another. It is common to call the beautiful fine and the fine beautiful.

There can be no disputing the existence of congruence. If I have the same general feeling of nothing-more-ness with respect to what I call beautiful, fine, and sensitive, then I do; it is a fact, neither an option nor a constraint. The genuinely controversial question is which of a variety of overlapping congruences should receive the most attention. Claims of contiguity are similarly controversial when they are taken as regulating the movement of intention. Is there an a priori reason why we attend to certain congruences of goodness and make certain moves between our valuations? We could suppose a Platonic universe of definite forms of intentional possibility, this scheme dictating the connections among valuations. But a Platonic interpretation exaggerates psychological facility into necessity—which would, in the present case, lend false necessity to the genders. Our free, that is, spontaneously polymorphic intention is never bound to assume any particular one of these forms; moreover, the possibilities of intention crisscross each other so very thickly (our symbolic action continually thickening the intentional fabric) that no single arrangement is ever the only one available. For example, while we can smoothly connect the sense of beauty to the profound calm of feeling oneself in the presence of perfection, we can as readily link the beautiful to the sublime, as one feels pulled out of oneself, drawn into a larger arena than one's own action fills, by a beautiful being's attractive power over one. Or one feels transcended by perfection, conscious of a gap in grades of being, aware of oneself as incomplete, vulnerable. Or again, the not-missing-anything of valued sensitivity can be felt in the next moment not as a calming stability but as a disruptive acuteness, the sort of curious attention that leads to critique and adventure. Which congruences we feel and connections we make seems to depend on what is going on in our life.

We can think of counterexamples to any alleged a priori order of valuation—and of course the ethnographic literature teems with striking variations precisely in this realm—but it does not follow that our own valuing has no basic tendency to conform to a pattern. We may follow such patterns very reliably. For example, I and most of my readers are far more likely to associate the quality we call "sensitivity" with stability rather than with adventure.

Connateness. Another reason why a valuation might belong with certain others is that it shares with them a common root in some more basic valuation type. If all valuations in the set were versions of a common underlying valuation, they would echo and reinforce each other in being performed, rather in the way that digging ditches and playing basketball (though neither congruous nor contiguous activities) reinforce each other by exercising arm muscles. Suppose, for example, that the basic move of approaching an object to partake of its qualities is common to the emotionally dissimilar postures of ecstatic surrender and connoisseurship. The word *beauty* might be used to designate the very general relation between valuer and object that holds these two sorts of experience together. Valuations in this case are connate.

Kant himself favored the idea (foreshadowed in our initial analysis of valuing) that there are two basic valuational moves, at least with respect to persons: attraction and repulsion. In his *Metaphysics of Morals* he writes: "We are considering a moral (intelligible) world where, by analogy with the physical world, *attraction* and *repulsion* bind together rational beings (on earth). The principle of *mutual love* admonishes men constantly to *come nearer* to each other; that of the *respect* which they owe each other, to keep themselves at a *distance* from one another."[4] Affirmations of relatively off-putting qualities like earnestness and fortitude can plausibly be classed as species of Kant's distance-keeping "repulsion." It is true that a person can also be loved warmly for such qualities. Still, in our everyday emotional traffic they do not play the part of leading attractors; instead, their most notable large-scale role is to provide a conventional way of valuing the members of an otherwise threatening and not at all warmly attractive class, namely, the power wielders. (Who receives this valuation depends on who belongs to this class.)

Conquisiteness. If valuations can belong together by virtue of a common foundational element, they can also fall together by lying on the same line toward or away from a point of reference, that is, in the same direction of change. In this case we can call them conquisite, that is, sought or found together.

Quite different valuations can be found en route to the omega-point of perfection. Justice and love, for instance, have been thought of as equally essential components of divine valuing, and yet at the same time a deep tension between the two has been recognized. (We shall have occasion to consider how masculine and feminine values are conquisitely united in the androgyny ideal.) But valuational schemes that are too inclusive become conceptually problematic, as indeed we run into difficulties thinking of a loving Creator who accepts a world history like the one we see.

A price of incoherence is also paid when valuations are grouped by shared difference or opposition to a point of departure. From an order-affirming posture, for example, every valuation of wildness, freedom, novelty, or even strong attraction is a basic shift. Or if we start with the problem of pain, then sweetness, structure, and oblivion are all solutions to it; whereas if we start by affirming life energy, then sweetness, structure, and oblivion can all become antitheses to it. Nietzsche's "Dionysian" aesthetic complex could be formed in this way relative to the "Apollonian" valuation of civilized order, or the Apollonian goods could arise as antitheses to a Dionysian experience.[5] So too with Burke's pleasure-based "beautiful" and pain-based "sublime," to the extent that pleasure and pain, even when "positively" conceived, are still relative to each other.[6]

All valuation patterns are conquisitions in that we become aware of them by looking for them. Even the *arché* of connateness was a *telos* that we sought in our desire to move from a state of relative bewilderment about valuations to an analytically powerful grasp of simpler order. This would suggest that the truth of any valuation pattern will come out most clearly if we can give an account of the nature of the quest that leads us to it.

Our seeking and finding of valuations seems very free in abstract reflection. Forms of goodness can be arrayed in discourse any way we choose, so that what looks like opposition in one perspective turns into alliance in another. Practically speaking, however, we always find ourselves already caught up in particular affirmations, so that value oppositions, though ideally relative, become practically absolute. I cannot but view the wild, the new, and the unusually forceful as all belonging to *the other realm* if I am installed in a regime of harmonious proportion and stability. I cannot but think of God as both perfectly just and perfectly loving if I now burn with shame at my own lovelessness. (So it is, too, that the conception of gender B can be aligned in relation to the actuality of gender A; but if gender B's qualities are held together *only* by this principle, only as "Not-A," then they will never form an intelligible whole. Some other principle of relation must be in effect if gender B has structural integrity.) [7]

Reciprocity. The final main principle of order among valuations is more important than any other in Kant's account. By reciprocity, one valued quality promises a reward that can be attained only by moving from it to another, or joining it with another, either because the felt self and environment are set in motion by a dynamic inherent in their own configurations—as, for instance, the unstable "terrifying sublime" tends to resolve into either horror or splendor—or because a self, configured one way, waits for its flourishing upon an altered environment (or a certain environment offers room for a more flourishing self). The complementarity of gender values is an example of this kind of order. Kant wants to exhibit reciprocity between the beautiful and the noble sublime.

> In matrimonial life the united pair should, as it were, constitute a single moral person, which is animated and governed by the understanding of the man and the taste of the wife. For not only can one credit more insight founded on experience to the former, and more freedom and accuracy in sensation to the latter; but also, the more sublime a disposition is, the more inclined it is to place the greatest purpose of its exertions in the contentment of a beloved object, and likewise the more beautiful it is, the more it seeks to requite these exertions by complaisance (95–96).

The generosity of the sublime person points our attention toward a recipient of all this beneficence, affirmatively to a fit recipient, so constituted that its receiving suits its own excellence. On the other hand, the lovingness of Kant's sublime husband, so deeply engaged in appreciation of a particular beauty, could be felt to be detrimental to the impartiality and independence that are supposed to belong to the same disposition. (We recognize this valuational instability in the classic problem of the "uxorious husband.") As for impartiality and independence, which we admire from an inviolable distance, they seem to repel rather than to encourage complementation. It is more evident that beauty, inherently absorptive, is incomplete unless it can draw in an admirer, who in turn must possess a certain valuable adventurousness or self-forgetfulness; thus we can project a form of complementarity from the feminine side. Or if we began by positing admirable daring as central to masculinity, we would be led to seek elsewhere (since the one who dares is self-forgetful) the selfhood that is worth running risks for. But whether Kant's version of the sublime individual will realize "generosity" in such a way as to enter into the masculine–feminine complementarity seems, in principle, optional.

*

Everywhere we turn, then, we find that intention has options and cannot be pinned down, a priori, to a certain regimen. But the work of a culture is precisely to establish intentional stability by deciding whole classes of these options for us. Thus it is always possible to diverge from (say) Kant's portrait of the valuational complexes of feminine beauty and masculine sublimity, but one *would not* disagree with Kant if one were in fact a fellow member of his culture and he were a competent spokesperson for it. We do value in agreement with him just to the extent that we are still defined by the cultural stipulations he is expressing. Consciously, we may go either with or against the grain, but we always follow already-set gradients of valuation, even when we are earnestly trying to reshape ourselves. Much of this topography, of course, is the same for us now as it was for Kant and his readers. The deeper we look into its structure, the truer it is to say that although we can conceive alternatives to it, we cannot really feel them.

The interintentional structure of valuing

Kantian marriage is ultimately a reciprocity between persons, not just valuations. But once we concern ourselves with relations among valuers—as we unmistakably do when valuers themselves are the objects of valuing—we move in a different frame of reference than when we were mapping possible relations in an intrasubjective intentional economy. Actually, whenever we speak of "valuing" in a stricter sense distinguished from "liking," we have already placed ourselves in the interintentional frame of reference; valuing in this sense intends a relationship among affirming subjects. Now we will address this dimension explicitly.

When I value X, I affirm X for Anyone. Claiming that X is good or beautiful, I report on the positive response to X that you would have if you were perceiving it from my position, with my preparation. That is not to say that your reactions to things are supposed to be identical to mine. On the contrary: the peculiarly public satisfaction given by X lies on top of private satisfactions in their variety, and my feeling of this different, extra, public goodness is the specific quality of valuing associated with its implicit judgment that a response is sharable. We were on the lookout for such public affirmability, our value detectors turned on, when we crept through the forests of beauty and sublimity. Had our results been negative, the major premise of critical rejection would still have been this form of valuing.

Valuing X does not necessarily involve a conscious affirmation of the intentional community assumed in the valuing act, and yet it seems that a valuing of the very form of valuing, hence of one's fellow valuers, must be implicit in every valuation; otherwise we could not account for the "rise" from liking X to valuing X. If I like or personally prefer valuing to mere liking, then that is a peculiar liking already conditioned by my responsiveness to other intenders, already more than a private preference (if spiritual beings like ourselves have any such things as a purely private preference). There is room for speculation about the psychology of our fundamental responsiveness to each other, no doubt, but the chief point about it is just that, however it happens psychically, it superordinates itself in the order of meaning to all other dispositions and issues. My awareness of other intenders puts me in the position of needing to seek right relationship with them. Because they are other (qua other intenders) than anything I can grasp, the question of what counts as right-enough conduct with respect to them is permanently open and always defines the context in which other meanings register, always determines what other meanings finally mean. Thus relationship "value," unlike any other goodness, can never be determined or weighed except relatively, that is, in its superiority. If this superiority is not recognized, interintentional relationship itself (as distinct from any subject–object relation) is not yet acknowledged.[8]

The primordial and supreme valuing of communal valuing as such, along with the next-to-primordial and next-to-supreme valuing of the concrete forms in which such community can be realized, is one of the basic meanings of "humanity." Thus we are bound to ask how gender inflects the valuing of valuing and fellow valuers.

When I value valuing, I position myself with respect to another

intender to realize the happiness that belongs to interintentional relationship. Some sort of teamwork is posited. The other intending teams
with mine in various ways—it may echo mine, or elaborate on mine
in a certain direction, or contribute a quite different but complementary quality of its own—but in all cases the event of the intentional
togetherness is the foundation of the flourishing involved, and the
sense of this, triumphant or trusting, is the foundational pro-feeling in
the valuing.

To value a particular valuing is to value a particular relationship,
and vice versa. A gender system is a system of relationships of a particular kind—centrally, for us, a relationship of one kind between masculine and feminine beings (which Kant epitomizes in the marriage
ideal of his *Observations*), of another kind among masculine beings,
and of yet another kind among feminine beings. (We do not forget that
there are, in addition, significant subtypes within these main types of
relationship as well as significant "noncentral" relationships like those
between gays and straights.) A gender system is therefore a scheme of
valuing valuing in which we enjoy the experience of particular kinds of
interintentional teamwork or at least orient ourselves to the prospect
of such teamwork. The sharing of sovereignty among valuers means
that one understands one's fellows in an interintentional scheme not
merely as role players but as jointly responsible representatives of the
whole. Thus a failure of the other to act consistently with the requirements of the scheme is more than an occasion of cognitive dissonance.
It is a betrayal of trust. We don't feel this betrayal when we adopt a detached social-scientific perspective in which disloyal valuing becomes
"deviant behavior." But betrayal or faith-keeping is the inside of the
interintentional reality, and therein the stakes of gendered conduct are
determined in a commanding way.

The others represent the whole team, including me; I represent
the whole team and each of them. My identity is staked to this interintentional project to the extent that my existence goes into this sort of
valuing and relationship. I like, approve of, and prefer the version of
myself that belongs to the team. Thus a fellow intender's betrayal not
only lets down the larger enterprise, it wounds my selfhood—which
indeed is the sharp point of all real betrayal. How I am liable to be
wounded depends on how, according to my position in the scheme,
I am invested. "I work hard, but *she* isn't impressed or satisfied and
he treats me as though I were a weakling and a fool." We talk of self-
image and self-esteem problems, and of our frustrations in trying to

"play the game," but "self-image" and "game" are fragments taken out of the interintentional enterprise, not independently real. The heart of the matter is that we find ourselves facing the problems and opportunities of humanity, our definitive way of flourishing, in the format of a gender system. That again accounts for a kind of already-established validity in gender-related orders of goodness.

But validity does not guarantee trouble-free valuing. One has to wonder: What schemes of relationship would most nearly be *perfectly* trustworthy? The two ideal approaches to the problem, the way of love and the way of respect, both aim to rectify our valuations by bringing them into superior valuational frames of reference.

The Platonic ascent from beautiful individuals to human (masculine) beauty to Beauty-itself is well known from Diotima's discourse in the *Symposium* (210–12). The key idea here is to discover a more trustworthy object of valuation in valuing relationships, more constant and more purely rewarding. Beauty-itself belongs to the category of pure meaning and so is not subject to generation, change, or perishing. By holding an aim on pure meaning, one brings eternity into the physical realm. Plato explains in the *Phaedrus* how to subordinate the carnal appetite for imperfect earthly togetherness to the demands of reason and pure beauty (253–57). "Neither human wisdom nor divine inspiration can confer upon man any greater blessing" than success in Platonic love.[9]

Another sort of categorical ascent was invoked by the woman who said to Ortega, "I insist that you talk to me as if I were a human being." She asks that he respond to her not as a female or feminine nature but as the intentional commander of a female body and feminine attributes, which is to say, as a being in the superordinate categories of subject and person. Trustworthy relationship depends on connecting with the pure partners to relationship, the intenders-as-such as distinct from their extension and the individual persons-as-such as distinct from their merely generic characters of body or soul. Kant tries to make this sort of connection when he centers sexual morality on marriage in his *Lectures on Ethics*:

> The desire which a man has for a woman is not directed towards her because she is a human being, but because she is a woman; that she is a human being is of no concern to the man; only her sex is the object of his desires. Human nature is thus subordinate. . . .
> The sole condition on which we are free to make use of our

sexual desire depends upon the right to dispose over the person as a whole. . . . If I have the right over the whole person, I have also the right over the part and so I have the right to use that person's *organa sexualia* for the satisfaction of sexual desire. But how am I to obtain these rights over the whole person? Only by giving that person the same rights over the whole of myself. This happens only in marriage.[10]

Notice that gender becomes invisible in this account. No qualities intervene between "sex" and "humanity." And yet we had no suspicion that the Kantian wife and husband of the *Observations* were "subordinating human nature" in their sex-specialized attunements to each other, which presumably gave them some reason to marry. Perhaps the logic of the drive toward the "human" in the later *Lectures on Ethics* would assign gender attractions to the side of sexual desire and exploitation.

Gender drops out of the picture when the American lady chides Ortega and when Kant moralizes about sex because the primary concern in these cases is with the problem of *respect,* that is, of securing the standing of partners in relationship as intentional extenders of a center, as agents. But if the problem were one of *love*—if it had to do with the standing of persons as intentional centers of extension, as owners of apprehensible and actually or potentially pleasing forms—then gender attractions would unavoidably be drawn in, even if they were (as for Plato) ultimately superseded. If "Treat me like a human being" were a request for love instead of respect, a request aimed perhaps at a too-detached, overly "correct" person instead of a gender-bound gentleman, then the humanity appealed to would include everything presented by the person to the world, hence the human body and qualities associated with it.

Love affirms how the person is realized rather than the sheer prerogative of self-realization. In fact, it may assert the lover's own prerogative of sponsoring wonderful new realizations of the beloved. In this sense, it grounds a trustworthy valuing partnership on the generosity and resourcefulness of the lover. But love is never merely delight in a pleasing object as such, not even if the object is another person's style of valuing. It is a disposition to delight in pleasing form *as* owned by an intender and in an intender *as* displayed in pleasing forms, such as in sensitive or earnest valuing. Thus personal love, like respect, always affirms relationship-as-such (which makes it a superordinate valuing) even while it also affirms independently identifiable properties that persons might or might not really have and that might or might not really be valuable (which makes it changeful and corrigible, unless the property affirmed is Platonic Beauty).[11]

It may be thought that love is too much a private and nonrational affirmation to count as valuing in the stricter sense with the superordinate standing created by interintentional reach. Certainly the special conviction carried by love's inordinate subjective force should not be identified outright with the validity of ideally sharable valuations. But the fact that the objects of love are so variable, according to what individual lovers are capable of perceiving, imagining, and delighting in, should not distract us from two equally important considerations. The first is the general validity of the basic form of love. An affirmable scheme of relationships must make lovableness and loving possible, since without love human beings cannot flourish. The feeling of righteousness we have when we are in love is not entirely spurious. The second point is that individual love experiences, "wild" as they sometimes feel, do not really occur wildly but are guided by conventional schemes of belief and attitude such as religio-moral teachings and the gender system. The gender system sets up a masculine valuer to love another masculine valuer in one way and a feminine valuer in another way, according to the attractions of the sexes. Sexual attractions provide a basis on which human beings can be lovable in determinate, somewhat reliable ways (and consequently it will be interesting to probe, bend, and break these conventions in literature and in life). The "beauty and dignity of human nature," or feminine beauty and masculine dignity separately, are generally intelligible formats in which individual instances of lovableness and loving, in all their variability, are achieved.

The gender system seems to interfere with good fellowship in various ways; as with grammatical gender, we often run into it as a way of going wrong. This prompts us to ask whether the system actually promotes lovableness and loving better than gender-free frameworks might do. Positive gender thinking, well represented in this respect by Kant's *Observations*, implicitly asserts that it does. Here is what it has to say for itself if challenged on this point. Human fulfillment must include love, but love is a broad-spectrum disposition. At one extreme it takes the beloved for an utterly unique and free personal subject, investing hope and creativity in the love relationship in conformity with spiritual requirements—we might call this the theomorphic pole

of love—while at the opposite extreme it takes the beloved as a naturally fitting occasion of satisfying a determinately given, type-oriented,
hunger-like need—which we might call the zoomorphic pole. Now
the "refinement" of love is best conceived as a reward-maximizing formation and management of all of these feelings rather than as a strip-
ping away of the lower for the sake of purifying the higher. Gender
is precisely a mediating conception that makes it possible to interpret
attraction without either degrading humanity by making it a function of sex drives or attenuating human attractiveness by abstracting
from the sweetness and power of the feeling that attaches to a kind
of body. A gender aesthetic enables Spenser to mount a ladder from
carnal excellences:

> Her lips like cherries charming men to bite,
> Her breast like to a bowl of cream uncrudded,
> Her paps like lilies budded,
> Her snowy neck like to a marble tower,
> And all her body like a palace fair . . .

to related perfections of character:

> There dwells sweet love and constant chastity
> Unspotted faith and comely womanhood,
> Regard of honour and mild modesty,
> There virtue reigns as Queen in royal throne,
> And giveth laws alone.[12]

　　Although beauty is not irreconcilable with masculine virtue (think
of Michelangelo's *David*!), often it is expressly denied in masculine figures to bring out other attractions by contrast. The fleshly frame of the
sublime being is more transparent, more evidently pierced from inside
by will, more straitly harnessed to purpose. Still, there are conventionally acknowledged physical charms to match masculine virtue, many of
which appear in George Eliot's introduction of Adam Bede:

> Such a [sonorous] voice could only come from a broad chest,
> and the broad chest belonged to a large-boned, muscular man
> nearly six feet high, with a back so flat and a head so well poised
> that when he drew himself up to take a more distant survey of
> his work, he had the air of a soldier standing at ease. The sleeve

rolled up above the elbow showed an arm that was likely to win the prize for feats of strength; yet the long supple hand, with its broad finger-tips, looked ready for works of skill. . . . The face was large and roughly hewn, and when in repose had no other beauty than such as belongs to an expression of good-humoured honest intelligence.[13]

But why must bodily attraction run so consistently to female and male types? Mightn't we let each body be attractive in its own surprising way? One ideal of sexual liberation would abolish the gender pattern to enable fuller appreciation of carnal individuality. The gender system is a sexual impairment, on this view, because it excludes so many possibilities of feeling and satisfaction.[14] A plausible way of meeting this objection is to blame the unhappy restriction on the Western order of sexual decorum rather than on the gender principle as such and to note that while the gender principle relates finer feelings to female and male sex types, it neither prohibits different classifications and correlations nor dictates the placement of lovers or beloveds within the gender scheme of attractions. It does offer a way of humanizing generic sex types that are assumed to be objects of spontaneous interest insofar as "sexual orientations" really do govern sexual attraction. (Apart from the encouragements of the gender system, it seems that the exigency of reproduction makes sensitivity to sex type a highly probable feature of our physically inherited constitution.)

In any case, we do not have to choose between valuing the general and valuing the particular. Since valuing is not, in practice, a single intentional episode, like shooting an arrow at a target, but a dense, continually flowing stream, it can be conceived as ranging over a spectrum; thus the frame of reference in which fellow valuers are valued might be the Kantian Kingdom of Ends founded on reason, or the supremely particular prospect of carnal relation, or both, oscillating or ambiguously superimposed. Probably valuing a fellow valuer *always* actualizes *all* such possibilities, sounds all the notes on the scale, however much the relative prominence of certain notes might vary and however hard we have to work to retain balance along the way ("Treat me like a person"). Such is the presumption of gender, which unites the more universal attractiveness of a human subject as such with the more concretely determined attractiveness of the sexed body type—not to the exclusion of individual attractions—and likewise unites the more disinterested and theomorphic modes of valuation with the individually interested and passionate. One sounds such chords whenever one says, with the normal appreciative force, "X is feminine" or "Y is masculine"; to set up this intriguing resonance is one of the main points of gender valuing.

The same complexity usually comes with the question, Do you love me? For one wants to be loved "as a person," as a locus of ideal beauty and dignity (and indeed as an object of full-blown romantic obsession one is apprehended in just this way, as the abstractness of much romantic discourse shows), but one wants to be loved also as everything else one is, including one's carnal attributes and motives. Answering this desire, too, romantic love offers itself as the format of the greatest possible love fulfillment, more inclusive than Platonic love. (The Platonic retort is that sex is bound to muddle the different levels of attraction and so must fail on the crucial issue of valuational ranking. Must it?) In line with the promises of romantic love, Kant's gender story in the *Observations* comes to climax in a marriage of sex-linked appreciations—which may or may not remain an implicit possibility in the grim marriage contract of the *Lectures on Ethics*.

By virtue of its valuational inclusiveness, the gender principle also addresses a problem in the grounding of moral valuation. One's first thought about Kant's *Observations* may well be that he is responding to uncertainty and discomfort in the gender system by linking gender norms to moral ideals through the "finer feelings."[15] The genders would not seem arbitrary or oppressive or prone to breakdown if they could be shown to anchor in the two great principles of perfect community, love (the feeling for the beautiful) and respect (the feeling for the noble sublime). But we can also turn Kant's line of thinking back around and see it as a response to uncertainty about a rationalistic moral ideal that hangs in the air without solid connections to empirical human nature. The "finer feelings," in this perspective, show a way from the more abstractly attractive moral ideal to the more concretely attractive human gender qualities and beyond, even unto our flesh. A continuum of fineness is established along which valuations can move, without blockage, from the beauty and dignity of human nature all the way "down" to sexual desires and trepidations, and back "up" again.

*

Awkwardly enough, I do not think we can entirely rule out either the strong thesis of an a priori gender-value order or the null thesis that any gender-value scheme is arbitrary. The two most telling considerations in favor of the strong thesis are the relativity of valuing to culture (provided we humbly bear in mind that our own culture forms our valuing foundation and horizon) and the probability that gender systems express and elaborate physically based dispositional endowments generally found in the sexes. (Cross-cultural evidence is not inconsistent with this view—for instance, the virtually universal male concern for "prestige" is explicated in other cultures in concepts different from those employed by Kant, yet Kant's theory of masculine dignity is recognizably continuous with the others.) [16] In favor of the null thesis, however, we can cite both the more abstract point that various schemes of valuing humans in relation to sex are conceivable and the more concrete point that discomforts in our gender system prove our valuing to be conflicted and our valuational horizon to be open.

Partly for positive reasons already given along the way, partly to hold the strong-thesis and null-thesis possibilities dialectically in play, I urge this form of the weaker thesis: an aesthetic like Kant's is an indispensable aid to the full recognition of gender reality, although the extent to which the form disclosed by a gender aesthetic actually constrains our valuing is not exactly determinable. We know only that the constraint is neither absolute nor illusory.

A puzzle: How can a valuer value a different way of valuing?

Kant sometimes speaks in the *Observations* as though men's nobility and women's beauty are simultaneously what men and women have special feeling for, respectively, and what any and all observers specially appreciate in them, respectively. For example, he says it is beautiful in a woman both to love merriment in others and to be merry (77, 81). It stands to reason that one should value other people's valuing more than anything else about them, provided one values them as persons, and that one would most value valuing like one's own. It seems as though one would be involved in a self-contradiction if one valued a different valuing than one's own. Certainly the rational valuers of Kant's ethical Kingdom of Ends are constrained to value their own and others' valuing on identical grounds. There should be an analogous attunement in all same-gender relations. But how, by this logic, can feminine and masculine subjects (whatever their sex) value each other's valuing? Cross-gender attraction, the affective axis of gender complementarity, appears to be in jeopardy.

Kant sees the problem and gets around it by making this claim:

"Woman has a superior feeling for the beautiful, so far as it pertains to herself; but for the noble, so far as it is encountered in the male sex. Man on the other hand has a decided feeling for the noble, which belongs to his qualities, but for the beautiful, so far as it is to be found in woman" (93). Perhaps this is the tale told by the appearances. But how can valuing work that way?

Kant gives another indication that it isn't necessary for valuers mainly to value the same qualities that they mainly exemplify when he says that persons of sanguine temperament, and indeed the entire populations of Italy and France, are marked by a dominant feeling for the beautiful (67, 87). Presumably one could be a sanguine or Italian or French person of nondefective masculinity. Presumably one could be Immanuel Kant, a sublime moralist, and write appreciatively of feminine excellences. Our challenge is to discover how this is possible.

One sort of solution would be to decouple valuing from attractiveness. Persons could be thought of as having beautiful or dignified surfaces that are valued as such by anyone, perhaps differently according to temperament or culture. To *have* one of these surfaces is to be feminine or masculine, but to *value* one of them is to be sanguine or melancholy, French or German. And why not value a surface different from your own? But there are two equally fatal objections to this answer. First, to separate a person's "surface" from his or her intending is surely a degradation of humanity on the terms Kant has set forth in his sexual morality. One cannot be said to be attracted to a person if one is attracted only to an abstracted surface. Or the surface may be imposed on the other; as Kant observes, feelings of attraction rest "not so much on the nature of the external things that arouse them as upon each person's disposition to be moved by these to pleasure" (45). This suggests, as a second objection, that to separate one's liking for an appearance from one's more fundamental valuations is degrading to oneself. Shouldn't my disposition to be moved to pleasure be integrally related to my purposes and my practical style? Or is *liking* a relatively trivial, peripheral, or unaccountable intention compared with the moral willing that we know to be Kant's paramount concern? (Although Kant has bestowed a sort of dignity on these likings by calling them "finer feelings," he cannot keep from distinguishing the merely "pretty" nonmoral charm of a lady's features from a "properly beautiful" charm that "beautifully" expresses a respect-earning moral *sublimity* [87–88].)

Assuming that a person's valuing is indeed central to his or her attractiveness, let us try to understand the possibility of valuing a different valuing, making use of the conception we have already formed of valuing relationship. To the extent that we make headway toward solving this Kantian problem formally, we will prepare ourselves to see how it is possible for Kant himself to value the feminine and how that accounts for the equal-but-unequal status of the feminine in his gender vision.

Let X and Y be differently gendered valuers who value each other. Since to value valuing is always to affirm someone as a member and representative of an interintentional team, X in valuing Y has to admit that Y belongs to and represents the team as a complement to X; X must also take responsibility for being Y's complement and representative, in spite of Y's difference. In this case, the happiness attained through affirming X's participation in a larger life would transcend X's gender quality rather than expand it. One affirms something opaque because one is capable of enjoying the spaciousness of an intentional world with alien inhabitants. One knows that the larger world is enjoyable not *in spite of* X (as when I put up with something repulsive for the sake of a principle of toleration that gives me room to pursue my own happiness) but *because of* X, and yet not with full insight into X.

How is it that one has this capacity? Is there a generic human Z valuing—say, of personal expression as such and fellowship as such—on the basis of which one can feel the inadequacy of gender specializations if they try to stand on their own? (There may be truth in this, but it points us away from cross-gender valuing.) Could it be that the character of every X contains Y qualities that stay hidden in the regime of the X gender but still provide the necessary receptivity or motivation for affirming the Y gender? Or is it that X and Y like each other as foils, realizing that their capacities are exercised to best advantage when set in contrast (that is, when the feminine has the challenging noble to attract, and the noble has the challenging feminine to administer)? This suggests the possibility of X and Y valuing their cross-gender relations as expressive of their own leading qualities. Affirming the other-than-noble can be seen as noble, and affirming the other-than-beautiful can be seen as beautiful. It is noble of the Kantian husband to indulge his wife (up to a point); he says of his marriage—by way of enunciating an especially sublime principle, a most strenuous obligation—"it takes all kinds." Meanwhile, it is especially charming of the wife to put up with her husband's plain ways; she gracefully concedes a diversity of kinds. One is blindly noble, the other blindly charming. (Their blind appreciation may, of course, thin into pragmatic toleration, and then degrade into misunderstanding and distrust.) Nobility and charm are realized within these limitations, but insofar as they allow themselves to be checked nobly and gracefully, they excel.

A second dimension wherein there is room to be inclined toward the alien gender in spite of oneself lies in the distance between ideal judgment and personal attraction—that is, in a split between the valuer's modes of valuing. That which I cannot lucidly approve of, I may yet be moved by. Kant says quaintly that a "single sly glance" from a woman sets a man "more in confusion than the most difficult problem of science" (79). (Wollstonecraft, the champion of virtue's "one eternal standard," will cite Pope's lines with scorn: "Yet ne'er so sure our passion to create, / As when she touch'd the brink of all we hate.") [17] Feminine attraction reaches a masculine subject from the blind side of sexual susceptibility or other dispositional aspects not featured in the project of nobility. It happens in the other direction, too. "In pain you shall bring forth children, yet your desire shall be for your husband" (Gen. 3:16)—gender teaming does not make good sense, for at certain points one not only doesn't understand it, one suffers from it palpably. And yet this sort of attraction, though nonrational, need not be disvaluable; it is a wild music sweeter than words, again an affair of relatively blind, admittedly dangerous yet life-enriching valuing. Kant sees a natural providence in this: "the motives of the sexual inclination work according to the hint of nature, still more to ennoble the one and to beautify the qualities of the other" (95). Each gender forms a blindly appreciative audience of the other, stimulating its development.

While none of these interintentional structures will necessarily obtain in relations between men and women, all of them are admitted by the concept of gender or sex-inflected humanity, which means that any of them *may* play an important part in gender attraction at a given moment. The attraction may actually come about in one or more of these ways or, while arising for whatever underlying reason, it may be interpreted by the subject in one of these ways—the interpretation having its own effect on the course of relationship.

Now we can better understand the part played by Kant's own valuational masculinity in his interpretation of gender attraction. The aesthetic parity of "beautiful" and "sublime" that is the main premise of the *Observations*, the ruling formula of "the beauty and dignity of human nature," and the fair apportioning of temperamental and cultural sensitivities all seem to balance the feminine and masculine aspects of human worth. Kant's discourse often sounds like salon conversation among ladies and gentlemen; he seems to be negotiating a view of gender relations that will be acceptable all round. If we picture him in this setting, we can easily account for his ability to appreciate the feminine while remaining masculine. He clearly thinks it is *noble* to honor the feminine: "We [men] could make a claim on the title of the *noble sex,* if it were not required of a noble disposition to decline honorific titles and rather to bestow than to receive them" (76). In his "single sly glance" remark, he admits that he is liable to be moved by an attraction without comprehending it.

If, however, the masculine valuer were to insist on being judiciously rather than blindly noble, if "he" wanted full disclosure of worth rather than a bushwhacking by charm, then "he" would withdraw from these salon conditions, or at least name other conditions to which they are subordinate. And that is exactly what Kant does, not only in his other books (where, as we know, a rigorously sublime ethic is articulated), but in numerous gestures within the *Observations*. He knows that discoursing about the genders implicitly grants them parity, yet he represents the move into such discourse as a kind of straying, or possibly a stooping: "The field of observation of [such] peculiarities of human nature extends very wide, and still conceals a rich source for discoveries that are just as pleasurable as they are instructive. For the present I shall cast my gaze upon only a few places that seem particularly exceptional in this area, and even upon these more with the eye of an observer than of a philosopher" (45). This is the intellectual style that suits ladies, he remarks later: "easy examples" concerning "sense" and "feelings" (79–81) are the best means of developing the feminine mind. That the very project of gender theory is feminine and, as such, alien to Kant's superordinate valuation is marked by his characterization of the "distinction that nature has chosen to make between the two sorts of human being" as "charming" (77). It is also suggested in a harsher way by his claim that feminine virtues of sympathy and complaisance are only "adoptive," not "genuine" (61), and that what is at issue in his gender theory is not "what of itself deserves" affirmation but "what is actually felt" (83). A crucial footnote shows the ambivalent position Kant has put himself in by offering a gender theory: "Above, in a strict judgment this [feminine virtue] was called adoptive virtue; here, where on account of the character of the sex it deserves a favorable justification, it is generally called a beautiful virtue" (81). Apparently Kant is so far charmed by the fair sex that, at least while he remains in that salon into which he has strayed, he is willing to speak of a "deserved justification" in his appraisal of the feminine. But he never lets us forget for long that there is a superior frame of reference in which this justification loses force. (Notice that Kant's rhetorical moves are pointedly reversed by Wollstonecraft in her *Vindication*, where earnestness, rigor, and what of itself deserves approval are insisted upon. Wollstonecraft and Kant both believe in a disjunction between rational and emotional frames of reference.) [18]

Even within the charmed circle of the Kantian gender theory there is a masculine bias. Simply as defined, the sublime surpasses the beautiful. Ultimate reality and value would have to be apprehended in sublimity rather than beauty. One cannot say much in appreciation of the beautiful without patronizing it, since its domain is the surface of life, mere appearances and transitory effects. Kant's noble sublime is not needy for its complement in the way that the beautiful is; in its self-sufficiency it seems more like a definition of human excellence than of a gender. This is a reflection within his gender portrait of the condescension involved in a masculine thinker's taking up the question of gender.

No doubt the masculine gets defined as superior to the feminine because Kant assumes the superiority of the virtue he takes to be embodied by males. This is an axiom. He judges beautiful virtue inferior just because it may lead one to act against the requirements of noble virtue (58), but he does not show why we should not mistrust noble virtue for steering us differently from beautiful virtue. Burke had given a more interesting account of the logic of this subordination in his *Philosophical Enquiry into the Origin of Our Ideas of the Sublime and the Beautiful*:

> Those virtues which cause admiration, and are of the sublimer kind, produce terror rather than love. Such as fortitude, justice, wisdom, and the like. Never was any man amiable by force of these qualities. Those which engage our hearts, which impress us with a sense of loveliness, are the softer virtues; easiness of temper, compassion, kindness and liberality; though certainly those latter are of less immediate and momentous concern to society, and of less dignity. But it is for that reason that they are so amiable. The great virtues turn principally on dangers, punishments, and troubles, and are exercised rather in preventing the worst mischiefs, than in dispensing favours; and are therefore not lovely,

though highly venerable. The subordinate turn on reliefs, gratifications, and indulgences; and are therefore more lovely, though
inferior in dignity.[19]

At least Burke opens the door to argument about how to measure
the "momentousness" of the various human concerns. He also lets us
glimpse a less fine feeling underlying the civilized sentiments described
by Kant, namely the sense that males more than females are causes of
terror and pain.[20]

But to return to the more formal question: Given the materials
provided by Kant, can we decide that the salon, not the masculine
philosopher's study, is the superior frame of reference for valuation?
Can we then interpret Kant's absolutizing of the noble sublime as a
function of his masculine relativity? It is sometimes claimed that any
gender aesthetic like Kant's must inevitably privilege one gender over
another, that its real purpose is to rank human attractions (the Asymmetry Thesis). Can this objection be met by pointing out that the
gender theoretician always climbs up to a comprehensive perspective
on the ladder of one or another particular gender? Is it only due to the
fact of historic male dominance in the academy that a masculine gender
theory like Kant's so often reaches us unaccompanied by a balancing
feminine theory?

We are not yet ready to draw a conclusion about this. But it is an
important step to recognize that we have a choice of frames of reference and that how to order them is an open question and a point of
instability in gendered life. We must also ask how a feminine valuation
of the genders would balance the masculine. Would it absolutize feminine valuing, playing counterpoint, or would it stress relativity and
complementarity over absolutizing, playing harmony?

Another question is how adequately Kant or the culture for which
he speaks represents the potential of a masculine apprehension of gender. Part of the problem lies in the qualities he emphasizes. Does a
masculine valuer have to choose beauty as the center of femininity
rather than qualities grounded in the undoubtedly crucial maternal
aspect of female life—say, sympathy and patience?[21] Couldn't Kant
have chosen a more balanced and mutually responsive pair of reference
points, like sympathy for the feminine and strength for the masculine?[22] Better still, what if he had avoided the pitfalls of oversimplifi-
cation by working out a pair of richer ensembles of associated values,
neither one defined or appreciated in such a way that it could be as-

signed a lower ultimate rank than the other except by an obviously arbitrary preference?

The other part of the problem, more fundamental, is Kant's imperfect admission of bias and blindness. We can judge that the *Observations* cry out to be balanced by feminine correction, but Kant cannot. He speaks of incapacity on the feminine side—"I hardly believe that the fair sex is capable of principles" (81)—but never says, for instance, "I hardly believe that the noble sex is capable of doing anything graciously." That is because his basic assumption is not that gender *divides* humanity but that "the charming distinction" *adds* something to a humanity that already stands on two feet in its male version (as Adam might be thought to stand on his own before Eve). Kant can be complacent in his judgments of "genuine virtue," "deep understanding," and so forth because the gender principle has not thrown him off center. Is it incorrigibly masculine to hold the center in this fashion? Not if we can imagine a much more flexible and ironic version of the *Observations*, still with strong affiliations to a formalistic ethics. I think we can, although I do not dare to claim that such a theory can be made acceptable to everyone, or perfectly acceptable to anyone.

But even if this sort of gender theory is bound always to have questionable content, we are still not free to dismiss the general normative–aesthetic form of representing gender if genders do actually give normative direction to our sex-related human attractions. Clearly they do; therefore, we should expect the genders to make appeals to our "finer" sensibility, offering us a deal that we will not *want* to refuse. Contrary to the impression given by much literature on sex-typing, we do not maintain a gender aesthetic for the sake of order and predictability only. In fact, gender is felt (for better or worse) in its impact on life's intrinsic goodness. Consequently, anyone would make a great mistake who did not construe genders as Kant did, as organizations of valuable human qualities—whatever else one thought about them. A purely functional theory of gender that represents only its social effects cannot substitute for an aesthetic theory.

If we embarrass ourselves when we make explicit the aesthetic norms that influence our sex-related dealings with each other, so much the better. We have become conscious of a need for change.

*

The notion of a continuum of feeling and attraction, from "coarser" to "finer," implies that the significance of any channel of valuing, including a gender, is felt incompletely as long as any part of the scale of human value is bracketed off. Thus Kant found it impossible to break "moral" away from "aesthetic" gender value cleanly, for in order to talk about human pleasingness in the full sense, as distinct from strictly physical qualities like "prettiness," he was forced to qualify beauty itself as a "moral" or "character" quality (87). He would hasten to explain that "moral" in this case refers only to a morally congruous empirical disposition rather than to moral willing proper; still, a connection is admitted.

Another slope by which we reach moral valuation is the valuing of valuing relationship as such, which is implicit in all "higher" valuing as distinct from private liking. The quest for the perfect form of such relationship has to be, at least in part, moral.

Since we cannot adequately contemplate the attractiveness of persons without regarding them as moral agents, we will shift now to consideration of genders as structures of moral valuation.

The gendering of ethics: Gilligan

Kant's portrait of beautiful and noble virtue in the third part of his *Observations on the Beautiful and the Sublime* suggested a gender division in the realm of moral value, although he would not let it count as such. Beautiful virtue turned out to be pseudovirtue, or at best "adoptive" virtue, that is, a quality that the moralist is happy to find in empirical humanity but cannot recognize as a manifestation of the authentic moral will. The question left hanging in our reading of Kant was whether his de-gendered critical ethics amounts to an assertion of moral masculinism.

Since Kant we have seen Romantic exaltations of the feminine; the flourishing of a "separate spheres" doctrine of feminine and masculine moral vocations; several waves of feminist criticism of the "feminine sphere" (in the women's suffrage movement and then in the milestone writings of Simone de Beauvoir, Betty Friedan, and Shulamith Firestone); and lately a renewed attempt, in the work of Carol Gilligan, Nel Noddings, and Sara Ruddick among others, to appreciate female-associated moral valuing as distinct from, and at least equal to, masculine moral valuing.[23] This work consciously responds to the dilemma we saw in Kant's thought: either one marks the feminine off from the masculine and thereby lands it in a valuational ghetto, or one erases gender marks and thereby allows masculinism to prevail incognito as the consequence of male social dominance.[24] The newer moral theory tries to avoid both horns of the dilemma by combining a critical awareness of the cultural flexibility and political riskiness of gender norms with the positive thought that there are sex-related ways to excel as human beings, failure to recognize which can be oppressive.

Carol Gilligan's 1982 report on her studies in women's and men's moral development, *In a Different Voice*, and her subsequent writings have a very clear (though partly antagonistic) relationship to Kantian gender theory.[25] Her perspective arises in resistance to an implication in Lawrence Kohlberg's work that women tend to make less progress than men do toward moral maturity—an implication that depends on conceiving moral value in Kantian fashion as the degree of formal universality and autonomy in practical judgments. She disputes the authority of Kantian ethics as a sole standard of moral maturity. In returning to positive gender thinking, however, she takes us back to the ground traveled by Kant in his *Observations*.

Relying mostly on interviews with girls, boys, women, and men about moral problems, Gilligan discerns two complementary styles of moral reasoning or "voices": an "ethic of care" (or "responsibility," or "love") more prominent in females, and an "ethic of rights" (or "justice") more prominent in males.[26] She denies that these voices are bound by gender (2), but her denial seems to equate "gender" with "sex"; on our interpretation of gender it is impossible not to read her characterizations of the moral voices as a gender theory. Her claim that both voices can play a part in any individual's moral life does not run afoul of the concept of gender, and her observation that people tend to rely on just one of the perspectives in a given situation, for the sake of clarity and justifiability in moral reasoning, rightly acknowledges the normative authority possessed by genders.[27]

Gilligan's two ethics do not exactly reproduce Kant's visions of the genders, but they overlap. The female-associated ethic of care is primarily oriented to protecting and enhancing actual persons and relationships. In its most mature form, it "reflects a cumulative knowledge of human relationships [and] evolves around a central insight, that self and other are interdependent" (74). (Kant had said: "The content of woman's great science . . . is humankind. . . . Her philosophy is not to reason, but to sense" [*Observations* 79].) Gilligan does not deny reason to women, of course, but she speaks of their "psychological logic of relationships" in contrast to the "formal logic of fairness" that flourishes among men (*Voice* 73). Her "ethic of rights" is the principled rationality that Kant assigned to the masculine, with the difference that she shows its moral weak side, its failure to attend directly to the wellness of real relationships and how people are liable to get hurt.

Since we rely on morality to mediate between persons of all kinds, requiring it to be a function of common humanity before we let it be a function of anything else, the notion of gendered morality is disturbing. Kohlberg's own answer to Gilligan, though accommodating to a degree, is a reassertion of the fundamental unity of morality.

> We believe that Gilligan's distinction between a morality of care and a morality of justice is a distinction held in the minds of all human beings, be they male or female. . . . In our view, however, these two senses of the word *moral* do not represent two different moral orientations existing at the same level of generality. We see justice as both rational *and* implying an attitude of empathy. It is for this reason that we make the following proposal: that is, that there is a dimension along which various moral dilemmas and orientations of special obligation can be placed. Personal moral dilemmas and orientations of special obligation . . . represent one end of this dimension, and the standard hypothetical justice orientations represent the other end.[28]

Insofar as this position continues to determine the meaning of the particular case according to a general rule of justice, it looks from Gilligan's perspective like a masculine transformation of the feminine theme. On the other hand, feminine empathy and special attachments can be understood to be implied as complementary to the justice ethic (as justice would in turn be complementary to care). On this interpretation, we arrive at an adequately encompassing human morality by addition of genders together rather than by subsumption of one gender by another. The disagreement between Gilligan and Kohlberg would finally turn on the difference between the more inclusive and more exclusive meanings of the word *justice*, or on how the concepts of justice and morality are related.

A more significant issue is raised by Kohlberg's claim that the justice and care orientations are situation-linked rather than sex-linked. (He cites studies suggesting that moral orientation varies according to the kind of problem a subject or group is faced with.)[29] The answer here seems to be simply that sex *is,* partly, a situation: to be a member of a sex in a given society is to be challenged morally in certain distinctive ways on a continuing basis, and the character formation of gender is a product of this situation.[30] If it turns out (as one would expect) that the situations in which all human beings tend to adopt a caring orientation more resemble women's general situation in our society than men's—and the data should be scrutinized with this question in mind—then the chief ethical issue will become the relative moral importance of woman- and man-associated situations. (Note that if there is a real duality of basic moral situations, or a duality of aspects of moral situations, then no ethical argument rooted in just one of them will be competent to determine their relative importance. Only if one manages to incorporate and balance that duality in one's own existence and valuing will one be able to think one's way toward a balanced estimate of the two.)

Adopted as the touchstones of a gender theory, moral orientations should comprehend or link with all of the qualities of gender. The qualities that appear in Gilligan's account are feminine affiliativeness, empathy, and nurturance contrasted with masculine assertion of a separate self, achievement ambition, and aggressiveness; affinity for the private, domestic realm contrasted with affinity for the public realm;[31] and, in words borrowed from Joan Didion, "a sense of living one's deepest life underwater, that dark involvement with blood and birth and death" (71) contrasted with the lack of such experience. We hear nothing of feminine charm, gaiety, or cleanliness—connections with these qualities could be established or not, I suspect, as one chose, and similarly for the masculine counterparts, whatever they are.

Gilligan makes a point of rejecting the supposed feminine propensity for altruistic self-sacrifice. (The pre-Victorian Kant had credited men with a greater capacity for sacrifice.) She finds that with the development of the ethic of care women outgrow their sense that moral authenticity requires denial of self. By the very working of their "psychological logic," women come to see that they themselves are appropriate objects of concern along with others, that indeed healthy relationships presuppose a healthy self. However, this development in the feminine ethic is mediated by "recognition of the justice of the rights approach" (132). That is to say, an adult moral character can be seen as a synthetic achievement to which both the feminine and masculine moral styles contribute—even though maturity still carries feminine or masculine identity.

Evidently Gilligan conceives genders as constituents of the human, or resources to be appropriated for full humanity, rather than as fragments of the human. The link she forges between gender and sex shows this as well: "Rather than viewing her anatomy as destined to leave her with a scar of inferiority (Freud, 1931), one can see instead how it gives rise to experiences which illuminate a reality common to both of the sexes: the fact that in life you never see it all, that things unseen undergo change through time . . . and that the boundaries between self and other are less clear than they sometimes seem" (172). The claim is that there is no woman's truth that is not a human truth, yet that there is a distinctive female-derived revelation of human truth. Thus human existence is thought to be the real ground of the genders, its truths differentially revealed. At the same time, there is an ideal humanity implicit in Gilligan's notion of the "adult"—not the gender-free humanity of the common rational nature posited in liberal views, but instead a gender-full humanity with permanently distinct feminine and masculine constituents, one or the other always regnant because of the cognitive and justificatory clarity it provides. Here there is a parallel with Kant's conception, according to which a person of either sex must bring both gender qualities together in such a way as to enhance her or his primary gender character. (An equally close but significantly different parallel, however, would be the view expressed in Schleiermacher's *Christmas Eve* dialogue that "in the development of their spiritual nature, although it must be the same in both, men and women have their different ways—to the end that here too they may become one by sharing knowledge of each other.") [32]

Gilligan agrees with Kant that moral valuations fall into two sets because there are two basic valuations, distance keeping and closeness seeking, which are responsive to the two basic threats of oppression and abandonment.[33] More explicitly than Kant (in the *Observations*), she goes beyond the distinction between two kinds of object relation to a distinction between two ways in which selfhood can be set up, one keyed to autonomy and the other to interdependence. Masculine and feminine selves love differently and respect differently. Neither of these divisions implies that moral concerns on the order of friendship, family, business, or politics fall into two separate sets—say, "private" versus "public," or "natural" versus "civil." What is implied is that we always find ourselves framing these concerns in one or (more complexly) both of two perspectives. We can and should talk of "justice" in the family and "care" in international policy.[34]

Reciprocity among valuations is important for Gilligan as it was for Kant, and she suggests a more advanced answer to our earlier question about the reciprocal valuing of the differently motivated valuers X and Y. Although she does not take up the question of masculine and feminine attractiveness, she does relate moral style to the construction and maintenance of selfhood, and the question of what the gendered self wants and fears for itself is a crucial piece of our puzzle.[35] Various sorts of observation and testing suggest that the masculine self wants a secure individual identity and is threatened by affiliation; for example, masculine imagery in daydreaming and storytelling tends to be violent and explosive. Strength is highly valued, and strength means getting along by oneself and not having to impose on others. The feminine self, on the other hand, wants to be secure in relationship and is threatened by separation. Sensitivity is highly valued and hurting someone else is the chief sin. How then can feminine and masculine subjects value each other, if—and this is worse than merely being tuned to different wavelengths—they actively threaten each other? Relatedness and individuatedness seem antipathetic. But the truth is that the feminine and masculine modes *need* each other, not only for the sake of rounding out the whole of human nature, but for the development of each on its own path. A more maturely feminine subject is one who has learned to let self count as an object of care equally with others; masculine maturity, in turn, has learned the truth of interdependence. The genders do not converge on a single post-gendered humanity, but they refract through each other so that each comes to more adequately represent the whole of human possibility. The tension between the two is the basis of a dialogue (174).

With this conception of the development of self, we are led to interpret the attractiveness of the other gender at least partly as the allure of one's own enriched gender identity. X is not exactly blind in valuing Y and the larger human reality to which X and Y jointly belong; rather, X sees a prospective development of X's own gender wherein present dangers will be reduced and present capacities will be exercised to better effect. Y holds the key to that higher grade of X's happiness. (X is regarded here as the sort of "enlightened," other-regarding self who, according to normative moral psychology, experiences happiness in virtue.) The move to maturity actually removes blindness inasmuch as the later X, the X that *has* appreciated Y, is aware of a wider range of valuation consistent with its own gender.[36] (X would also attain virtue by this means, insofar as the valuations have anything to do with conduct. X is, in ideal terms, a more welcome fellow subject.) The Kantian "straying" into a frame of reference where the feminine is valued is thus a step toward moral maturity, even if Kant was not able to judge it so. His formula for moral sense, the "feeling for the beauty and dignity of human nature," can be taken as an androgynous composite filling Gilligan's recipe for a mature gendered view, even if in the Kantian critical ethics dignity supersedes beauty, willing supersedes feeling, and the valuations of beauty and care have to be sought in the so-called duties of benevolence.[37]

Gilligan's gender ethic sets up a triple barrier against the relative devaluing of either the female- or male-associated. It takes gender division seriously enough to rule out any neutral basis for esteeming one of the forms of valuing more than the other; it takes gender complementarity seriously enough to deny that either form of valuing can stand alone as an adequate moral perspective; and it disallows the segregation of gender qualities by sex. If certain admirable qualities belong to the masculine affinity for relatively abstract justice, that is to say that *anyone* can be morally masculine insofar as upholding abstract justice is a salient feature in their moral experience; it is not to say that only men can be just. Thus neither feminine worth nor the worth of females can be outflanked, as it were, by moral appraisal.

If genders are not seen as reaching all the way to the foundation of humanity in a valuational sense, then one of them will always be exposed to derogation. A theory like Gilligan's secures this depth. The only other way to prevent gender oppression would be to abolish gender (if that were possible) so that any insistence on a single supreme moral principle or end would not make the perspective of one gender absolute at the expense of the other.

*

Gender ethics and gender aesthetics require and complete each other. The aesthetic task Kant took up in the *Observations* cannot be neglected by moral reflection because the gendered experience of which Gilligan speaks includes and is pervasively affected by desire and attraction. For example, the ethic of rights is really associated with the attractions of the masculine sort of independence and disinterestedness, and these qualifications have their real point of reference in male freedom from pregnancy, which is a metaphor for anyone's life to the extent that pregnancy does not impinge on it.[38]

Kant went on to deny any such link, detaching moral motivation from "feelings," no matter how "fine," so that he could speak instead of "reason becoming practical"; he kept the special feeling of "respect" as the mysterious aesthetic trace left by the direct self-assertion of reason.[39] *Practical* love and respect are indeed named as twin moral principles in his *Metaphysics of Morals*, but, among the emotions, respect is the one and only junction of our sensuous nature with the practical requirements of reason.

In Kant's moral logic, the anthropological duality of gender modulates into a spirit–flesh dualism. The root of moral duty, he writes in the *Critique of Practical Reason*, "is nothing else than personality, i.e., the freedom and independence from the mechanism of nature . . . so that the person as belonging to the world of sense is subject to his own personality so far as he belongs to the intelligible world. For it is then not to be wondered at that man, as belonging to two worlds, must regard his own being in relation to his second and higher vocation with reverence and the laws of this vocation with the deepest respect."[40] It is not surprising, in a masculinist culture, that when masculinity comes to be described in a text like Kant's *Observations* it carries a reverence-evoking dignity that makes it the worldly image of personality-as-such. We can easily imagine a Kantian argument for the subordination of women to their husbands formed on lines similar to Paul's in I Corinthians. (Neither is it psychologically surprising that the more ego-anxious gender would define "personhood" primarily in terms of freedom and independence.)

I noted earlier that any valuational scheme rests on a system of trust among valuers. Going by the *Observations*, it appears that for Kant there are three different prospects of trust: the perfect concordance of rational beings willing rationally, the lucky concordance of people when they are moved by "finer feelings" somewhat analogous to rational principles, and the zero trustworthiness of sensuous inclination. Gender would be a system of trust at the middle level. Luckily (or by some providence), gender institutions like marriage bring about human good with some regularity.

In Gilligan's view, gender relations are more than fortuitously good; they are essential means of human self-realization. The fundamental reason for this is that Gilligan's anthropology is not dualistic. Instead of the Kantian poles "person" and "nature," she assumes a continuum of maturation—the notion of maturity carrying both psychological and moral meaning—along which people turn to greater and greater account the endowment of their physical natures and the situations in which they are placed, making a métier of everything about themselves rather than of reason or any other power alone. Part of maturing, the morally crucial part, is bringing individual intentions into accord with interintentionally tenable forms; Gilligan's gendered subjects achieve this by learning from and responding to differently gendered subjects, that is, in worldly sociality, not by Kant's strict catechism of reason.[41]

When we were earlier faced with an analogous alternative between pure Platonic love and inclusive Romantic love, we saw that from the side of purity it can be judged a good bargain to estrange ourselves from the dangerous aspects of human life in the flesh. Surely Plato and Kant are right to hold that the gender system of relationship is not perfectly trustworthy—that we are ultimately lucky (or well provided for) if it works for moral maturity rather than degeneration, and that we can never rid it of degeneracies and betrayals. A fair view of gendered valuation must take its pathological forms into account, not just its approvable ideals. In order that a gender-value scheme be accepted with appropriate diffidence (according to the weak thesis recommended at the end of the last section), it is necessary that we touch some of the real discomforts in our gender system.

Pornography and other pathologies of gender valuation

"The idea of the masculine and the feminine originated in the sadomasochistic imagination," writes Susan Griffin in *Pornography and Silence* (1981).[42] For Griffin, pornography is a most important clue to the nature of gender culture. At the heart of pornographic fantasy is the angry domination of objectified flesh, typically if not always male domination of female flesh. The truth thus revealed about gender culture is that an "elevated" and domineering masculinity is set up in relation to a fascinating and complaisant femininity for the sake of playing out a sadomasochistic drama of revenge—revenge against the mother whom we could not control as infants and against fleshly existence in general insofar as we still cannot control it.

While pornography can bear a wide range of meanings, depending on social conditions and the disposition of the subject, we will take the undoubtedly very real and objectionable aspect of pornography to which Griffin points as a touchstone for this stage of our inquiry.[43] (The category "erotica" is available to receive sex representations insofar as they are not fair targets of our usage of "pornography.")

If we go back and look through these spectacles at the ideal marriage of Kant's *Observations*, we can see a pornographic dream or nightmare in it. *"The more sublime a disposition is, the more inclined it is to place the greatest purpose of its exertions in the contentment of a beloved object, and likewise the more beautiful it is, the more it seeks to requite these exertions by complaisance"*—but the greatest purpose of the exertions of the pornographic hero is precisely to force on his "beloved object" the "contentment" of receiving his sexual explosion, and the pornographic heroine (if we may call her such) requites these exertions with an unreal, obsessive enthusiasm.

The gender complementarity that graces Kantian marriage is only one side of the coin; the darker side is that the genders are alienated from each other. Once the genders were defined by their contrasting valuational attunements, Kant could only allow them to appreciate each other blindly, "according to the hint of nature," for the sake of promoting their separate perfections (*Observations* 95). Now we should follow Kant a step further in that passage: "If all comes to the extreme, the man, confident in his merits, will be able to say: 'Even if you do not love me, I will constrain you to esteem me,' and the woman, secure in the might of her charms, will answer: 'Even if you do not inwardly admire me, I will still constrain you to love me'" (95). Kant would say that this constraining to esteem and to love reflects the irreducible goodness of the genders. Masculinity and femininity cannot merely insist on their own types of goodness, or on an arrangement that incorporates their own types, but have to bow to each other no matter what. This "coming to the extreme," however, can also be read as a deterioration of marriage into a subhuman relationship—the spouses becoming less than whole persons to each other—or else as an unmasking of marriage's pornographic face. The masculine being who must be obeyed no matter how disgustingly "he" behaves is the omnipotent dominator in pornographic drama; the feminine being who fascinates no matter how "she" is degraded is the essential pornographic sex object.

Is the pornographic drama a breakdown of marriage? A poisonous caricature of it? Or is the marriage ideal, at bottom, a deceptive refinement of pornographic drama?

In the perspective of positive gender thinking, masculinity and femininity are fully human forms of good, their partnership a greater good. Any good can be perverted: the strong can become the domineering, the beautiful can become the inert, and teamwork can become exploitive and oppressive. Yet good remains apprehensible in the midst of perversion. While the heroes and heroines of pornography exemplify the gender qualities in a twisted way, they yet point to natural human needs and modes of excellence. The proof of the goodness and humanity of Kantian marriage, for instance, would be that wife and husband can enjoy each other, be enlivened by each other, and form between them a greater "single moral person" because each party is able both to love and to respect the other, notwithstanding their gender contrast. When the gender system operates successfully, it renders the duality of attraction and distance keeping fruitful; when the system breaks down, it gives the duality a sinister character.

From Griffin's critical perspective, however, it can be asserted with some plausibility that *we do not know "masculinity" and "femininity" except in a sadomasochistic intrigue created by sexual alienation and male domination.* The darkness at the back of Kantian marriage leaks through when we ponder the implications of his admission that in the "extreme" form of the sexual encounter the man claims all and only respect and the woman claims all and only charm. Here the goodness that we think we perceive in gender qualities is already twisted away from a transgender humanity that we are estranged from. Twisted too is our sense of what is normal and desirable in the way of bringing people together or keeping them separate.

Although the positive and critical perspectives compete, they do not cancel each other out. Within Kantian marriage one can use Griffin's view as a heuristic in attending to the requirements of humanity. Meanwhile, one can take bearings from the poles of Kant's gender aesthetic in ascertaining the unwarped contours of human goodness, so far as sex shapes goodness, for a more lucid critique of pornography. Whether our normative gender aesthetic is surpassable, whether we can form a language of human attractions that is not gendered, has to be reckoned an open question, since, by general (if inconsistent) admission, we are now gendered.

Pornography, the "depiction of the whore," represents the degradation or "extreme" of gender relations from the masculine side. What about its feminine counterpart? Would it be something other than a picturing? The graphic character of pornography is consistent with the greater male susceptibility to arousal at the sight of members of the opposite sex. (This "sight," of course, might be conjured up literarily.) But females, by contrast, do not gain proportionally as much reproductive advantage just by connecting with young, good-looking or lusty-acting mates. If there is a physically based female emotional bias in sexual matters, perhaps it reflects the circumstance that female reproductive interests have generally been best served, over evolutionary history, by mating with "good providers." Moreover, what constitutes good provision depends on variable circumstances and social arrangements, so that it cannot be disclosed so well in a sight but must be told in a story. Thus if there is a feminine view of masculine beings that warps them by absolutizing their female-relative significance or that writes them into a script of specifically feminine anger and revenge, we would expect males to appear as pure instruments in stories of female advancement, taking the forms of instrumental advantage that count for the most in a given society. The male is required to be a great hunter and fighter, in the politically and technically simplest conditions; a prince or king, in a status-governed society; a millionaire, in capitalist society; or somebody "brilliant," in the artistic or academic worlds.

Yes, Sleeping Beauty is just lying there, but what is the man who comes to her except—a prince? If the evil masculine principle underlying pornography is rape (toned down to the kiss that Sleeping Beauty is waiting helplessly to receive), then the corresponding feminine evil is a kind of manipulation. We can call it *heterocracy* since it is a project of ruling through another. In the lurid extreme the heterocrat will be Lady Macbeth, treating her husband as a vessel of her own ruthless ambition, or the "golddigger," whose real best friends are diamonds. She is heartless, and that is the revenge she takes for the power advantages of men. Just as the rapist or pornographer negates the putatively charming beauty of females by degrading it, remaining all the while fascinated by it, so the heterocrat turns the admirable male into a contemptible dupe and yet continues to be bound by the male-associated attractions of domineering power. This is an "everlasting irony" in her own soul.[44] (Our feelings about this proposition must deeply color our judgments about "matriarchy.")[45] The pornographer is in a rage about flesh, bodily extension as such, which "he" tries to tear free from the personal center so that "he" will no longer be frustrated by uncertainty about the will of the beloved; the heterocrat, meanwhile, wants to realize will and personal accomplishment as such in abstraction from anyone's flesh (and thus from the love of any individual), fundamentally because "she" has to live outside "her" own body and body type to exercise power.

Did the pornographer and the heterocrat somehow collaborate

on the story of Sleeping Beauty? Does such a story become popular because it expresses the trustless hates and ambitions of the genders under a silky veil of happy-ever-after? We could look at it quite otherwise: we could see the lovely girl and the prince as icons of the gender attractions, their human thinness innocent within the charmed circle of the tale (much as Kant believes his gender types to be morally acceptable and symmetrical within the delimited realm of "feeling"). In truth the story has something for everyone, for the happy as well as the restless.

Is she a heterocrat at heart who wants a Kantian husband, even as he might be a pornographer who loves a Kantian bride? This doubly unsavory perspective lets us notice how "charm" can be a feminine weapon, not merely an object of male interest, and "dignity" can be an asset to be controlled by the feminine, not merely a male privilege of lordliness. But Kantian marriage is like the story of Sleeping Beauty in accommodating both inhuman and human intentions, which could even be mixed in one individual. The Kantian husband may be eager to place his status and wealth at the service of his wife both because he nobly exerts himself to content his beloved and because he senses that if he is not instrumentally serviceable to her she will not feel rewarded by the relationship. The complaisance of the Kantian wife may cater at some level to her husband's desire to dominate female flesh. "May"? No sooner do we broach these possibilities than we realize that we are sounding familiar notes in the chord of actual gender relations. Positive gender thinking may have played them down, but it wasn't ignorant of them.

*

There is a purely aesthetic aspect of the pathologies we are discussing: sex objects and power proxies are less attractive than real women and men because they are not centers of interest in themselves but only mirrors in which certain strong and unhappy feelings get reflected. Denied the chance to reveal their own qualities, they cannot enrich their beholders' lives. Even to say that much, however, is to raise a moral issue. The pathologies of gender aesthetic are moral problems because they impair the awareness and affirmation of humanity. They tear down trust.

The ideal concordance of moral fellowship is jeopardized by other gender slants as well. Two of these are simple to state, if not to cure: they are the pathologies of projection. The virtue assigned to one gender may contain nothing more than the projected preoccupation of the other, as for instance the ideals of feminine chastity and modesty clearly reflect male anxiety about sex and reproduction.[46] In this case gender complementarity is reduced to a one-principle system, an identity articulated as a pseudoharmony instead of a real harmony. Alternatively, one gender's vices may be projected onto the other's virtues, twisting gender complementariness into opposition. For example, the vicious opposites of manliness, in many cultures, are "indolence, self-doubt, squeamishness, hesitancy, the impulse to withdraw or surrender, the 'sleepiness' of quietude"[47]—and we are reminded of Sleeping Beauty. It is possible to form a warped appreciation of feminine virtue by putting a decorous face on these masculine vices, that is, *saying* that feminine merit consists of (let us say) gaiety, intuitiveness, and sensitivity, but really *meaning* by these terms indolence, self-doubt, and squeamishness. Or one could credit masculine virtues of initiative, daring, and directness while really perceiving these qualities as femininely unacceptable selfishness, inattentiveness, and crudeness. To the extent that the features of action that are describable as virtuous ("enterprising") coincide with features describable as vicious ("selfish"), there will always be substantial grounds for generalizing unappreciatively about the character of a gender and thereby losing sight of its portion of moral goodness.[48]

Yet another gender-related moral distortion is harder to pin down. There is a fear, sometimes expressed in criticisms of Gilligan and other proponents of feminine ethics, that any conception of feminine moral valuing will legitimate the old "separate sphere" notion of an inferior and subordinate women's ethic—an "ethic of care" suitable only for a circumscribed domestic role.[49] Now an ethic of restricted application might or might not be an ethic of inferior validity. Suppose two practical spheres A and B, each including activities that are necessary for the realization of full humanity and sufficient for the realization of some major part of it. If the structure of action and relationships differs profoundly between A and B, so that an ethical scheme appropriate to one cannot be justified in the other, then ethical subordination of one to the other is out of the question. But if there is an asymmetrical practical relation between A and B—if, for instance, agents primarily located in A have a strong interest in acting in B, while agents primarily in B have a much lesser interest in acting in A—then the residents of A will be at a great disadvantage.[50] Their practical equipment, including their morality, will be useless when they act or attempt to act in A.

Women have often been in this position. For example, lip service may have been paid in the "separate spheres" era to the importance of the home and to an unimpeachable feminine morality presiding over it, but in practice, men could usually be confident that domestic affairs would be satisfactorily taken care of without their participation, while women could be much less confident that economic and political developments directed by men would be beneficial to them. Thus women had a disproportionate interest in asserting themselves in the public realm or in the management of family affairs as these relate to the public realm but were considered to lack the moral passport necessary to enter it.

Feminine ethicists like Nel Noddings and Sara Ruddick try to resolve this problem by demonstrating the adequacy of women-associated modes of moral valuing in dealing with a wide range of problems. If maternal care, for instance, can effectively be generalized to shed indispensable moral light on international relations, then it is less to be feared that the "carer" moral identity will perpetuate women's practical disadvantage.

More important than these rather schematic considerations, however, is the sense one might get, in contemplating the traditionally feminine virtues, that they belong to a degenerate form of morality. Male-biased measurement of women's moral development made women appear to be retarded or infantile in comparison with men. Shouldn't everyone, if possible, follow the traditional male itinerary of maturation and go forth from the enclosed family circle to a life of "participation, responsibility, and role-taking in the secondary institutions of society such as work and government," therein developing a more universalistic and autonomous mode of moral reasoning?[51] Or does this attitude betray an uncritical and unwarranted acceptance of the priority of male-associated morality?

The best way to get a grip on the question is to unfold the concept of morality in such a way that its inner structure can be compared with the clue of gender-divided valuation. Morality does in fact always incorporate two chief elements. Lacking *other-regard,* one's pursuit of a good life, however rigorously conducted, will always be judged "prudential" as distinct from "moral." In the absence of a felt and formulable *obligation,* one's actions, however responsive they are to others, will count as "impulsive" or "natural" rather than "moral." (I point out in passing that "Other" and "obligation" share a meaning: to encounter an Other is to be subjected to a claim, while in turn obligations have categorical force only because they relate us to unencompassable Others.) We obtain the elementary degenerations of morality if either of these elements is lost while some semblance of the other is preserved. To maintain a framework of obligations without genuine other-regard is the hallmark of *legalism;* to respond warmly to others without the discipline of principles is called *sentimentalism*.

The peril of an "ethic of care" is that it might pin women not only to a restricted social role but to a morally inferior sentimentalism. It should be evident, however, that the "ethic of justice" is no less morally dangerous. Bureaucratic devils like Adolf Eichmann can give themselves justifications in the language of formal obligation, and all sorts of criminals can claim "autonomy."[52] Of course, true justice and autonomy are incompatible with genocide and selfish crime because they do not allow the moral standing of one's fellow beings to be impaired by arbitrary definition; but we can equally well say that true care is never whimsical or heedless of the claims of absent parties and future situations.

Sentimentalism is actually a disorder of feeling as well as of thought, and legalism is a disorder of thought as well as of feeling. To spell out these problems in relation to gender is to see more clearly what is needed to correct them.

Sentimentalists are relatively thoughtless and undiscriminating, and (partly for this reason) they are unreliable in their very feeling. The feminine sentimentalist has a bias for those in "her" home because "she" is like a mother. The masculine sentimentalist feels selectively for "his" comrades, those to whom "he" is tied by work and play activities. To rectify these versions of moral other-regard, it is necessary to generalize the relationships of mother and comrade so that they become in-principle obligations with respect to anyone.

Legalists are insensitive, and (partly for this reason) they are irrational in defining the source and application of principles. The masculine legalist insists on standards that make sense to "him" because "he" is like a Father—that is, it is as though "he" has the personal responsibility and authority to define rules mediating between an outside world whose requirements "he" understands and an inside world of personal lives and relationships that must be brought into conformity with those objective norms. The feminine legalist claims less authority for "herself," is more likely to subordinate "herself" to the rule interpretations of a personal associate, but is therefore freer to choose "her" authority. (It could be a god; it could be an astrologer.) Now legalism is often nothing more than a strategy for simplifying one's decision making, not a specifically moral posture at all; when it is a moral posture, however, it is an errant form of distance keeping with respect to others. The corrective is empathy. Only by paying warmer attention to others will the legalist become aware of the moral distortion in following rules for the sake of rule regularity instead of for the sake of one's fellows.

That sentimentalists need to learn to generalize and follow principles implies that they can profit from legalists' advice. But how to generalize, or where to seek principles, remains a question, and the two sorts of legalist would give different advice on this point. Likewise the two sorts of sentimentalist would recommend different empathies to the legalist. Although all these characters have been portrayed as examples of moral error, still their valuations all become necessary ingredients of an adequate moral posture when we combine them to overcome their weaknesses. To be responsible *for* the well-being of others (and for oneself among others), hands-on, as prompted both by the concerns that arise immediately in our various practical relations and by a sense of a formal order governing everyone's conduct; and to be responsible *to* others (and to oneself among others), hands-off, in acknowledgment of personal and impersonal sorts of authority and sensitive to others' actual wants, is the whole complex recipe of the moral life.

Androgyny and perplexity

The ultimate purpose of theorizing about structures and modes of valuation is to make a better way of life generally available. Are the aesthetic and moral powers of each gender accessible, in principle, to every individual? Is "androgyny" an attainable ideal, or even an intelligible one? While it is true that the concept of androgyny begs the fundamental gender question by accepting femininity and masculinity as ingredients of personhood,[53] and while the androgynous combination of gender qualities cannot of itself rectify imbalances in their valuation,[54] we cannot avoid taking up the question of androgyny if genders are allowed positive standing.

To be alienated from any human excellence is intolerable, an occasion of grief and envy.[55] Like the cut-in-half hermaphrodites of Aristophanes' myth in the *Symposium*, we long for some manner of wholeness, and this longing sets us against any conception of gender that would make some experience unavailable. (The same longing drives Kant's gender exemplars to form the "single moral person" of marriage.) We must have been profoundly encouraged when our study of the structure of valuing showed us that valuations are not nailed into fixed gender sets but can, in principle, be combined in any number of ways. In order not to fall into perplexity, however, we need to see the valuational possibilities precisely as ways, that is, as nonarbitrarily connected ensembles. (We say of a marvelously disturbing novel that it teaches us new ways to feel.) Genders offer themselves as such ways. Now the androgyny ideal posits freedom with respect to the genders, but at the same time it relies on them, letting them serve as reference points, which seems contradictory.

Separation is inherent in gendering in another way that appears to be even more deeply inconsistent with androgyny. Belonging to a gender means possessing not only a different character but an already-granted permission to feel, think, act, and appear in ways that everyone does not or could not. Affirming masculinity, for example, enables a community to grant the license "Boys will be boys"; they will allow males to be annoyingly boisterous, to a degree. Or the permission is more in the nature of a freedom-from: girls don't have to act tough. It belongs to the category of the human to assert commonality among all humans, to humanely limit the boisterousness of boys and humanely require girls to be strong. Thus the ideal of androgyny seems to contradict itself by simultaneously affirming genders and robbing them of their point.[56]

Kant is unmistakably rooted in the traditional view of sex difference, but his reflections are part of the beginning of a great change in how the logic of our problem is understood. Even though Kant constantly associates femininity with women and masculinity with men, he makes possible the separation of the genders from the sexes by defining the former in purely aesthetic terms; and even though he rigidly prescribes two value constellations, he starts us thinking about new possibilities for combining valuations. By our own time it has become routine to speak (without horror) of femininity in men and masculinity in women and of mixtures of femininity and masculinity. With this evolution in the understanding of gender comes a lessening of the tension internal to the androgyny ideal. For example, if boys do not monopolize the possibility of boyishness, neither will they monopolize the license that accompanies recognition of the relative autonomy of the masculine style. The traditional sense that it is good for some to be like that, but it wouldn't do for everyone to be like that, now translates: it is sometimes good for one to be like that, but it wouldn't do for one always to be like that.

In Gilligan's theory, and in actual people, we find not the ultimate androgyny by which every individual would fully and equally live out all the gender capacities of humanity but rather a pattern in which females and males tend primarily to dwell in femininity and masculinity, respectively, without being sealed off from their complements. They are like Aristophanes' hermaphrodites bulging largely to one side or another but never halved. They may acknowledge their relatively specialized ways of being human—appreciatively, ruefully—or, going further, they may consecrate the exclusiveness of gender with personal commitment, adopting their genders as métiers. But gender exclusiveness is interpreted according to the measure of the human, the ratio of inclusiveness, so that the coloring of gender is not allowed to alter the drawn outline of the picture, humanity, which must be seen by everyone the same. "Androgyny" is possible in the sense that the picture can be colored differently in different parts or at different times, and with any number of shades on a spectrum.

When we take the category of the human as fundamental and interpret genders as human qualifications, we are not thinking the converse, that is, we are not positing a fundamental gendering of our understanding(s) of humanity; we cannot be, for this would place us not on the common ground of "gender theory" but *in* genders, their difference giving rise to divergence in valuations. Yet it is of the nature of genders that we are in them and that they make this difference.

The gender difference that we live in is disguised by our valuational theories of gender for the reason that whenever we name a goodness or a valuation we appropriate a generally intelligible notion and, even in assigning it to a gender, proclaim it for humanity and thereby reestablish it as common moral or aesthetic coin. To speak publicly of an "ethic of care" is to make care incumbent on everyone. To speak of masculine strength or feminine sympathy is to identify qualities that may be required of anyone, when the situation requires, or admired in anyone, if the qualities appear in the right setting. Masculine beings may have boorishness more easily forgiven them, and feminine beings emotionalism, but as boorish and overemotional, respectively, they are inferior. On the other hand, experience and imagination show that the feminine being who meets a demand for strength can feminize it; "her" realization of strength can be harmonious with the other elements of the feminine ensemble. (Weakness as such could be essential only to a debased femininity; to read essential weakness into femininity is to insult it or despair of it.) And the sympathy of the masculine being will be masculine.

As an ensemble of commonly appreciable and realizable forms of goodness, androgyny stands on one side of the gender reality, the side of humanized gender. On the other side, where everything human, including humanity as such, is gendered, there is a residue of meaning that cannot appear in common rules of acting or commonly intelligible language. Gender in this sense cannot be shown under concepts because it is the sort of thing that *steers conceiving*. The notions by which we might have thought we had captured the content of genders are, when looked at carefully, quite indeterminate, even though they line up nicely in formal oppositions.[57] (There might have been a more determinate meaning in *saying* them than we now find in their abstracted, generally available sense.) Qualities like "strength" and "sympathy" in actual gendered living always elude or confound theoretical definitions, which finally (along with jokes, songs, and the rest of our lore) do no more than locate them in a general way. If we can speak of androgyny at all on *this* side of the gender reality, we can only mean an alternating or mysterious mingling of some of the currents by which our capacities of valuation are borne. There is something odd in theorizing about these "modes of valuation" as though we apprehended them in full clarity. To the extent that they do alternate and mingle, we are deeply liable to perplexity; indeed, it seems that our greatest known perplexities of feeling and judging have their roots here. Perhaps our amazement in the presence of a "drag" performer—an amazement that goes deeper than our laughter or disgust—is the strongest emotional connection we have with this perplexity, a giddy realization that it is somehow central to human life.[58]

The deepest possible explanation of valuational perplexity is a metaphysical model, like Kant's attraction–repulsion theory, that shows why incommensurable realizations of goodness are to be expected from the most fundamental nature of things. Here the question becomes marvelously intelligible, and yet the answer is disappointingly thin. What do attraction- and distance-dependent forms of goodness concretely mean in our existence? Much nearer to life is Gilligan's claim that abandonment and oppression are the two fundamental evils.

These are specifically personal evils. But the various meanings that abandonment and oppression bear for different sorts of people are not accounted for. Finally, approaching still more concrete data, we form conceptions of human kinds like gender; but now it is a prominent part of our insight that our insight is limited.

Gender character and "true self"

The self has walked before us now in the guise of the intender and, more specifically, the valuer. But it is possible to raise doubts about the independent reality and centering power of the individual considered as a psychical or spiritual entity. What we call "self" could amount only to an appearance created by linguistic or other social processes, or by physical processes, or even by a cosmic will. In any of those scenarios "self" would be, in an important sense, unreal; on the other hand, even if we accepted the metaphysical thesis of the unreality of the self, we would go on acting as if we were, individually, the authors of intention and officers of valuation, because acting that way is precisely what the appearance of "self" is. And in any case the question of self has more to do with plotting the curve for a series of intentions than with a substrate of intention. Selfhood as such is a pattern of intending a-forming; coherent ways of intending (like genders) are building blocks for such patterns, and decisions about their assembly; embodied selfhood is an ostensible locus to which questions about such patterns can be aimed.

We have been mainly concerned about gender in relation to the category of humanity, but the alarm about stereotyping told us that the self has its own worry: Will gender let the self be itself? Must I strip away my femininity and masculinity to claim my "true self" and show it to the world—or, alternatively, to understand how femininity or masculinity can be "mine"?

We must learn the use of the concept of "true self." What exactly do I need a true self for? How does it matter—how does it most matter—what I mean by "I"? What is most seriously *worrisome* here is the double jeopardy that Gilligan spoke of, the basic self-relative evils of oppression and abandonment. To fail to know or be my true self is to be exposed to greater risk in these two ways. What is not the primary problem, then, is finding a uniquely or lastingly or provably true picture or account of myself. Perplexity about gender identity is not intolerable in itself. For all I know, indefinitely many self-representations will turn out to be helpful in avoiding or overcoming the evils that make the question of self most exigent; I may even be led to accept a pluralist ontology of selfhood.[59] I do, however, require just those limits on self-representations that will preserve my self as *my* self, distinguishing me from free-floating models of selfhood such as the greatest possible self in general (to describe which is to do a kind of theology). My own greatest possible future self is still tied to my distinctive causal conditions and experiences in the past.

Alienation from my true self would be oppressive because it would prevent me from realizing some part of my potential. True self is a norm of unhindered access to my power and style resources. If these resources are blocked off, I have a prudential problem in that I am handicapped in my pursuit of happiness, and I also have a moral problem in that I am prevented from becoming fully responsible. My moral status remains unresolved as long as my decisive self-interpreting intentions are not engaged in life and displayed in it.

A worse oppression to fear is that for failure to grasp my true self I will not be able to hold my life together in good order. There may be pillars missing underneath my house. In the work of Gilligan and other developmental psychologists, the problem of self-tenability appears in intimate connection with moral responsiveness. One cannot stably maintain one's way of intending if one cannot connect with others to realize tenable interintentional forms. The moral challenge here has to do not only with one's moment-by-moment dealings with others as they might call on "true self" for trust or commitment or creativity; it is also a matter of having a moral career, that is, being able to draw together one's own actions past, present, and future so that they cohere in a satisfactory life story.[60]

Notice that quite different forms of stability and tenability could come into play in a person's life. The self-referential rigidity of the masculine subject has been strongly contrasted with a more diffuse and flexible feminine subjectivity, both in traditional gender thinking and in contemporary feminist criticism.[61] Supposing one adopts Freud's conceptions of ego and id, one need not agree with his program of appropriating the latter with the former; one might want a more open or friendly relationship between conscious and unconscious elements in one's life.[62] In sum, the concern for self must not be tied to one version of selfhood, and criteria of integrity must be interpreted broadly, all the way out to the limits of the meaningfulness of speaking of selves.

The uncertainty of interintentional connection threatens abandonment as much as oppression. If I fail to affiliate with others, I cannot exist as a personal self, a centered centerer and centerer of centers. Since the personal condition is essential to me, my true self holds the key to my membership in community; if I am ultimately untouched by the ties that hold me in community or if I cannot commit myself deeply to communal enterprise, then I am lost. Here true self functions as a norm of authentic belonging. I may belong in a male-associated manner, say, as one who can be counted on to "get the job done," or in a feminine way, as one trusted to "be there" for support and sustenance. I am the bearer of virtues according to my way of belonging. But the virtues must form bridges between my intending and the intending of others. To participate in community, *I* must *really* be (somehow, to some extent, in principle) brave, chaste, just, sympathetic, earnest, or tactful.

Now we know that gender is alienating in a number of ways. It imposes on individuals a typical "second nature" that they are expected to act up to even though they are not originally responsible for it. By dividing humanity, gender makes some capacities of the human less accessible than others for each individual. It delivers gendered subjects into the hands of a foreign valuational power by inclining them toward different forms of goodness than they most lucidly value, as they are attracted to differently gendered subjects and want to be attractive to them. They can be fully justified only in a court that brings strange laws to bear, and fully understood only in a partly incomprehensible perspective.

Precisely in taking the self away from itself, however, gender works as a key to discovering powers of the self and as an enabling structure for expanding and strengthening the self. The nearer self that feels shackled by gender to foreign sorts of intention, the self that can see and judge itself, is not the whole self—there is more to it, whether in the present moment or as a career potential. Femininity and masculinity give me patterns firmer than my apparent feelings, and programs more ambitious than my private plans. That they put me at the disposal of other subjects is only another way of saying that they make the interintentional connections that are necessary for personal existence. The genders position me so that I can meet the others, and through such meeting the ultimate expansion of self into community occurs. Thus the genders are solutions to the problems of oppression and abandonment, and, as such, solidary with "true self."

Such is the ideal. The facts, it might be objected, look different. Gender norms actually block the discovery of self and weaken its development because they cut the wealth of human possibility down to fit into two small boxes. The masculine and feminine profiles are inevitably oversimple, in relation to human possibility, because they serve the end of large-scale social regulation. (If a social order perpetuates itself by herding males into factories and armies while females are kept in private homes to perform reproductive labor, will it not also teach conceptions of masculine and feminine virtue that reflect and reinforce its labor assignments?) Defined as polar opposites, or treated that way even if more sophisticated definitions mitigate their opposition, it seems that the genders must work more to break up interintentional connections than to establish them.

Let us formalize the issue in a way that will bring those who think of or experience gender as rewarding into a common frame of reference with those who think of or experience gender as frustrating. First conceive humanity as One, either as a common human nature or as the totality of human possibilities. A human kind like gender is a first division of this One into a *small* number—say, Two. Beyond the Two are indefinitely numerous human possibilities, both collective and individual, including all "selves"—the Many. Any member of the Many belongs also to the One, in its first sense, while if you add up the Many you get the One in its second sense. Now the problem has to do with how the Two mediate between the One and the Many. According to the critique of gender, the Two are bottlenecks that *restrict* recognition of humanity on the one hand and the individual's true selfhood on the other. But according to the gender idealist, the Two are channels that *open up* a perception of humanity as larger than the individual and of the individual as larger than herself or himself. If gender is a restriction, then it must be the case that gender leads our attention from more to less, from Bill and Bob and Betty to "masculine," their individuality filtered out. If gender is an opening up, then it must lead us from less to more, in this instance from "masculine" to Bill and Bob and Betty, their individuality more richly appreciated in the context of a generic perception. (For them, gender must lead to an acting up to a richer form of life rather than an acting down to a stereotype.) But the enrichment could only occur on two closely related conditions: first,

that the generic perception is warranted in the first place (which implies that there is a kind of restriction we cannot get away from in our
quest for the richest revelations of persons) and, second, that Bill and
Bob and Betty's generic nature can in fact be perceived and conceived
together with their individual differentiae and their flexibility.

Satisfaction of the first condition seems necessary to satisfy the
second, since gender vision could not be true if the color of gender
lenses were false, but it isn't sufficient. The extra question in the second
condition is, How can a generic-nature conception be a window onto
individual identity? If I look through pink and blue lenses, how can I
see anything but pink and blue?

Masculinity is *not* a window onto the souls of Bill and Bob and
Betty if we make it an a priori description of them. We can see this if we
apply the masculine virtue of bravery to our three putatively masculine
individuals (when and insofar as they are masculine). "Bill is brave"—
well, say he is. "Bob is brave"—but Bob is not brave in exactly the
way that Bill is. Some dangers that Bill would rather face, Bob would
rather avoid. "Betty is brave"—but she faces a very different set of dangers. It is true that the men are treated as equally and interchangeably
brave when their society drafts them into its army. That is one way
in which a gender norm befalls them. But even an ordinary war story
will explore the differences in how individual platoon members deal
with fear. When we want insight into individuals, we use gender not
as an answer but as a starting point for asking questions about them.
If Bill confronts me in an adult male body, I wonder, relatively early in
my approach to him, about certain features like bravery. It is possible
that I do not want to detect individual inflections of bravery, or qualities other than bravery; I might be an army officer interested only in
overall induction statistics, or I might never have read the *Iliad* or *War
and Peace* (or *Jane Eyre* or *Their Eyes Were Watching God* or *The Doll-
maker*) to explore the psychology of bravery, or I might simply be dull.
Gender norms do make my dullness, my ignorance, and my functional
specializations more comfortable. They help keep me separated from
much of what there is in people. But when I try to find what there is in
people—if I try to write a good novel or play, or if I try to be a good
manager, or if I simply pay attention to personal relationships—then
these norms come back into the picture irresistibly, except in a more
experimental mode, with an increasingly fine grain, and filled full of
holes through which unique and unforeseen qualities can appear.

The color metaphor has another implication: gender answers are like filters that define color by subtraction (with monochrome results), while gender questions are like lamps that define color by illuminative addition (ending in a rainbow).

Whether it is intelligent to employ genders as starting points for knowing individuals depends finally on whether the original gender conception, the thought of Two, is arbitrary or well founded. We will pay further attention to this question in the final two chapters.

Gendered selfhood and the asymmetry problem in *High Noon*

Selfhood is not real in an instant, or knowable from a snapshot; it is always deployed in action. "Character" is dramatic and narrative. Our hunger for story is not really separate from our hunger to know true selfhood. Now the opposition between gender-as-answer and gender-as-question carries into the narrative perspective on selfhood, as well, for the standardized gender stories by which a society disciplines the consciousness of its members can be viewed as repressive at the same time that exploratory gender stories can be embraced as revelatory and even as morally indispensable devices of self-clarification.[63]

The great majority of stories familiar to us are gender stories in an obvious way. (We know a priori that *all* stories are gender stories in part, obviously or not, if humanity is always gendered.) As they disclose possibilities of selfhood, the gender stories present us with questions as well as answers relating to gender, just as they can serve as vehicles of gender trust and gender cynicism alike. Which aspect predominates in a given reading of a given story, the question–opening or the answer–closing, depends more on the readers' program than on anything in the story. For example, Paul (in 1 Cor. 11) does not linger over the lines of the Adam and Eve story to tease implications out of it; its significance for him is that he can assign it a single determinate meaning that will contribute to an argument for a general practical rule. But if we look at the same story guided by Phyllis Trible's interpretation, it becomes provocatively indeterminate.[64] Trible also wants us to draw a certain conclusion from the story (quite different from Paul's), but her experimental and sensitive approach allows a wealth of meanings to occur to us.

We have to look at stories to see an adequate display of selfhood; we also have to see how gender stories tend to come out to understand how various harms might be inherent in gender relations. It is easy enough to show sublimity and beauty and care and justice on a chart with plus signs all round. But how will the bearers of the different kinds of goodness fare when they are thrown into a gender plot?

I choose a movie as a point of reference for our study of gender plot because movies are where the most commanding gender icons of our time have appeared. I choose a "Western" because, as everyone knows, the conventions of the Western allow for a very bold carica-ture of gender character, centrally the masculinity of gunslinging males but also, by implication, the feminine elements from which the West is separated. Here, if anywhere, we would expect to find an asymmetry in the status of the genders as part of the very backbone of the plot. But the most interesting Westerns place the principles of the West in question, test them, and sometimes dismantle them, either by showing their internal frailty or by bringing them into relation with a differ-ent frame of reference. (This is often done by magnifying the role of women in the story.) The leverage these movies have on our feeling is very great because of the simple intensity of the fictional elements that they manipulate.

High Noon is one of the most interesting of Westerns in its aspect as a wonderfully (or frightfully) powerful gender essay.[65] As it appeared one year before I did, it somehow represents the world in which I was conceived.

Let us first take stock of what we know about the mythic Ameri-can West before any particular Western begins. The West is a "wide-open space" governed by "the law of the gun": half a tragic Hobbesian experiment in unregulated ambition and conflict, half a playground on which we observe the height of male boisterousness. The restraints of civilization are felt, to be sure, in several ways, as farmers and towns-people struggle to create a settled order, Easterners wander into the scene with their Eastern ideas, and the wild Westerners themselves grope for a code to live by. But the main purpose we have in visiting the mythic West is to experience freedom from civilization. To connect with us and to become an interesting problem, this freedom must be made to rub against civilized order in some way.

The West is not "Nature." The desolate landscape of the Ameri-can West provides the backdrop for a life that is unnaturally explosive, on the one hand (for guns are hardly natural), and sterile, on the other. The quintessential masculine freedom of the Westerner is "his" having nothing to do with procreation. Women and children in the West are mostly secluded in remote farms or carried by crawling wagon trains across the vast expanses over which adult males range at whim. (The nonprocreative women of the saloons and brothels are somewhat more broadly distributed.) The West can almost be defined as the maximized space of everything other than marriage and procreation.[66] When procreation does intrude on a Western story (as when a baby is born on the stagecoach journey of *Stagecoach*), it can be extraordinarily interesting, even eerie.[67] This has to happen now and then to make us feel that the West is adjacent to us; but essentially it is not, cannot be, where we are. Deprived of the futurity of procreation, the West is an unnaturally desperate place. Men roam freely in it, expressing and enforcing themselves with incomparable intensity, and yet they do so under a shadow of a deeper sort of extinction that gunfighting and the other visible dangers of the West only symbolize. Cowboy masculinity is stripped of paternity so that it can exist away from marriage, on its own, as a powerful but necessarily incomplete maleness. For that reason the Western plot often presents itself as a prelude to a different kind of life, especially married life, awaiting the heroes who survive—as if the Dangerous Male who is the true Westerner has to survive himself to reach the success of paternity.

Will Kane (Gary Cooper), the hero of *High Noon*, already stands on the boundary between the masculine freedom of the West and the saner life of civilized responsibility in his position as Hadleyville's marshal. A Western lawman is always, of necessity, drawn from the dangerous males, but his violence is redirected, now with skill and scruple instead of passion, against the wilder destroyers for the benefit of those who wish to live in peace. Kane, we are often reminded, made Hadleyville livable for decent folk, a place where children can be raised. Before Kane was marshal, women were afraid to go on the streets in daylight. On the other hand, a considerable male element enjoyed the town more when it was "wide open," and these people hold a grudge against Kane. This is one of the ways in which the voice of irresponsible masculinity is heard.

Now Kane is going to take the next step toward civilization. He is resigning the marshal's job to marry Amy Fowler (Grace Kelly), a Quaker, with whom he will settle down to run a store. We hear about the wedding even before we see Will and Amy, for the movie's theme song plays over an opening image of a gunman in the wilderness.

Do not forsake me, o my darling
On this our wedding day

Do not forsake me, o my darling
Wait, wait along

The unidentified man looks self-sufficient, serene and tough, alone in the positive Western sense, a free and powerful agent; but the song speaks of aloneness in a new negative meaning introduced by the issue of marriage. Soon enough we learn exactly what the man and his comrades have to do with the song. They belong to a gang that Will Kane once sent to prison. Now they have been turned loose again to menace everyone, and specifically to take revenge on Kane. (We seem to hear an argument *en passant* for capital punishment: were it not for political meddling, the incorrigibly harmful Frank Miller would have hung.) When Miller arrives on the noon train, the complete gang will come to kill Kane. Will and Amy learn of the threat only a minute after taking their wedding vows. Contrary to everyone's advice to get out of harm's way, Kane decides that he has to stay to face the threat. This is his masculine integrity—not to run from danger, not to betray the trust conferred in his badge (to which he now has an equivocal relation, since he has just resigned). But at the same time he is going against Amy's integrity, her principled nonviolence, for a moment earlier he had sworn he would do his best to live up to the marriage, and this, at least she assumed, was part of the bargain.

Amy shows her commitment to principle by telling Will that if he does not come away with her to avoid conflict with Miller's gang, she will leave on the noon train without him. She is not so much afraid as intolerant of violence. Her threatened separation from Will is highly unattractive, if we judge her on the premise that a woman ought always to stand by her man—but we could as well ask Will to stand by his pacifist woman (or just to *go through with his marriage* and not dally on the gun playground). Still, we excuse Will for insisting on what seems right to him, and he is perhaps all the more ruggedly appealing for being unable to justify himself in words.

As the prime truth-teller and pain-bearer of the tale, Will possesses great credibility, so that the moral surface of the story, from one angle, looks like a lesson to Amy that violence is necessary to contain violence. She does indeed jump off the train when she hears the first shots from town and return to kill one of Will's foes. But the moral scales are balanced by several factors. First, Amy has her own credibility. We learn that she came to her pacifist resolve by seeing her father and brother die violently—so she too has suffered, albeit off-screen. Second, her "unnatural" abandonment of her new husband is, in the

context we are given, an act of great courage.[68] So brave is she that
she goes to see Helen Ramirez, the rich Mexican woman with whom
Will had formerly been involved, to seek insight into Will's motivation.
Third, when Will enters the town's church looking for deputies (and
we learn that Will is not a churchgoing man, which goes along with

his lack of articulateness about principle), the preacher declares himself unable to say whether Miller's gang should be resisted by violence.

Will Kane is poised, then, between two morally valid postures. They are not really balanced for him, however, because Amy's pacifism is not the only counterpoint to masculine honor. Honor is also shadowed by fear. We are allowed to see fear tempt Will when he goes into a stable to think about jumping on a horse and leaving town. His former deputy, Harve Pell, comes in to try to make him leave, and Will has to fight and subdue Harve (representing his morally weaker self) to stay on course for the gunfight with Miller. He also has to prove that he still has the physical capacity, in his older age, to answer the call of duty. It is as though he is receiving a backward initiation into manhood—although at the same time Will is so maturely realized an individual that we can test our conception of manhood against *him*.[69] As he remains a masculine being, Will is not *free* to avoid violence on the grounds that all violence is evil. It is an axiom for him that running away from problems, cowardice or inconsistency, is the greater evil, because he could never avoid violence and know that he was not doing it out of ignoble fear, or because he had become too weak to play the part of the ideal man.

> The noonday train will bring Frank Miller
> If I'm a man I must be brave
> And I must face that deadly killer
> Or lie a coward, a craven coward
> Or lie a coward in my grave

Of course Amy, in contrast, does not feel free to uphold integrity by engaging in violence, and when she does finally kill a man it is to help to save Will, not to be a rock of resoluteness or an officer of the law. Still it must be said that she obeys our gender system in taking the step from being Amy Fowler (she of Quaker principle) to being Amy Kane. Her position changes in a way that Will's does not. Yet it is possible to admire her for changing, while insofar as we are anxious to have a marshal protect us, we hope and appreciate that Will does *not* change. We count on a valuing rigidity in him, and we ourselves assemble his ideal character more rigidly, in a more anxious conquisition, while we want flexibility in her and compose her more opportunistically according to the story's changing demands.[70]

Femininity in *High Noon* is divided between Amy and Helen Ramirez in something like the way masculinity is divided between the lawman and the outlaws. Helen belongs to Will's past life, and for that reason she understands his determination to stand up to Miller in a way that Amy cannot. But Helen cannot understand Amy's principle that transcends her own "stand by your man" ethic. She is forsaking Kane, even more surely than Amy is, for the pertinent reason that Kane is no longer her man. That the weaker Harve is now Helen's lover encourages us to think that Will outgrew her—that is, outgrew his own prepaternal masculinity. We learn that Helen was once involved with Frank Miller; Will took Frank's place with her after sending Frank to jail, which makes Will and Frank symmetrical in their tie to Helen as well as in their use of guns. What this means for Helen is that she has acknowledged and accepted the wild side of masculinity more fully than Amy has. As a matter of fact, she stands to be directly harmed by it: Harve suggests that she might not look so pretty when the returning Frank takes revenge on her for her liaison with Kane. (Although Amy is unaware of it, she too is threatened by the dangerous males. One of them spots her at the train station and says, "*That* wasn't here five years ago." "So what?" says another. "Nothing—*yet*.")

Do not think that Amy is a babe in the woods. She deliberately chooses not to acknowledge the frame of reference in which the coming gunfight makes sense. When Kane stands alone in the town's streets, she and Helen ride by in a wagon on their way to catch the noon train. Helen looks at Kane, but Amy will not. At the station, when Miller gets off the train, Helen's eyes meet his, but Amy is looking elsewhere. After Amy has gone back to help Kane, though, and has been taken hostage by Miller, she turns and scratches Miller's eyes to enable Kane to shoot him. Thus she maintains a sort of consistency in her intolerance of what Miller represents. This would be beyond the pragmatism of Helen Ramirez.

The masculine principle in *High Noon* is not violence as such but something much more general, namely, determination or decision, selection among possibilities that cannot coexist. Lethal gunplay is the vivid image of this decision. It resolves the question, Which of these contestants is going to live? Which way will the town go? (Thus contest is assumed, along with disjunction—A *or* B—and the extent to which contests and disjunctions are really necessary is the extent to which masculine practice is warranted.) The complementary feminine principle is permission, the opening up or preservation of possibilities. (This is premised on the underlying possibility of conjunction, A *and* B.) Men as well as women adhere to the principle of permission in *High Noon*—notably the city official who wants Kane to leave

Hadleyville so that the conflict with Miller will occur elsewhere and not give the town a bad reputation with investors—but in Helen, for whom (as a Mexican) the town could never have been home, and Amy, for whom violence is unacceptable, the avoidance of conflict is honorable, whereas in the men this avoidance shows corruption.

The balance between the two principles in *High Noon* is constantly restored by the arguments that are made against Kane fighting Miller, but the story as a whole is focused on the masculine issue of determination just as surely as the character of central interest is Kane. No one can escape from the fact that something terrible is going to happen at noon. Everyone is mindful of the ticking clock. Noon will be like the Day of Judgment: Malachi 4 is being read in the church when Kane enters ("For, behold the day cometh, that shall burn as an oven; and all the proud, yea, and all that do wickedly, shall be stubble: and the day that cometh shall burn them up"),[71] and when the clock strikes noon Kane releases the town drunk from his cell, like a resurrected skeleton.

Amy Fowler/Kane is caught up in the problematic of determination, too, because at noon she must decide whether to be a pacifist or a loyal wife. And it seems that just as she earlier upheld a masculinely consistent position unsympathetic to Kane's plight, in the end she (like so many other movie heroines) makes the masculinely tough decision to resort to arms, *but to express authentic feminine supportiveness*. That is, her feminine selfhood seems to resolve itself by bowing to the masculine, acting as the masculine requires. I submit, however, that *High Noon* lets her embody the feminine principle of conjunction in a more profound way. There is no suggestion that she has "learned her lesson" about the necessity for righteous uses of violence. She has not surrendered her principle; rather, she has preserved the other good in her life, the husband to whom she swore loyalty. She and Will are both in moral shock after the gunfight with the Miller gang: he because he has realized the worthlessness of his "tin star" relationship to the hypocritical townspeople, and she because she has participated directly in evil. But that they have survived and are reunited is her doing. She engineers the conjunction between Will's integrity and her own; thus, her own is the more inclusive.

> Do not forsake me o my darling
> You made that promise when we wed . . .
> Although you're grieving
> I can't be leaving
> Until I shoot Frank Miller dead

The song asks Amy's indulgence of Will, which she finally gives. That Will is indulged implies that his plea of "can't" is a mark of immaturity. His inability to imagine a future life in which he has not dealt with Frank Miller, his inflexibility in relation to Amy's expectations, is a kind of weakness as well as a kind of strength. She overcomes her own version of that weakness, and his as well; thanks to her finally inclusive gesture (which is certainly not pliancy) he is permitted to be masculine without destroying marriage. Thanks to marriage, there is a spiritual home for him after the hollowness of his relationship to Hadleyville, and thus the questionableness of marshal-masculinity, is revealed.

*

The question we wanted to pursue was, What is revealed about selfhood when it is played out, on one side or the other, in a gender plot?

A story strengthens our feeling for the gendered forms of selfhood by putting samples of them to appropriate tests. The self-sufficient, justice-valuing masculine ego of Will Kane is threatened in *High Noon* by universal abandonment and hypocrisy; the affiliative, caring feminine self is challenged, especially in Amy but also in Helen, by uncertainty about what affiliation and care can mean in circumstances of violence. The masculine decisive self is given the supremely difficult decisions, whether or not to face death, and whether to be loyal when the loyalty of others fails; the feminine permissive self is asked to permit the impermissible, killing. Both sorts of agency could fall into an inhuman extreme, but Will's stern demands on himself are balanced by a gentle refusal to judge the townspeople who fail to help him, and Amy's strategy of conjunction can be carried out in the end only by decisive, aggressive acts. That is how they can remain attractive to us.

We especially want to know how feminine and masculine goodness stand in relation to each other in the working-out of a gender plot. Because of the ancient, painfully familiar story of female victimization—we might call it the Dido story, in honor of the Carthaginian queen of the *Aeneid* who is allowed to be strong only as an obstacle to the hero's destiny and is reduced in the end to poignant suicide—we perhaps feel that we have to read Amy Fowler/Kane's last acts as a moral self-immolation, an expiation for her flawed masculine pretention to uphold principle, or at least a displacement of her feminine agency to one side so that the pure masculine can be dominant.

I confess that I first took *High Noon* this way. I revered Will and nearly hated Amy until she was shown (as it seemed) the masculine

light. My excuse is that anyone would be likely to take a Western in
this way, inasmuch as the centrality of the masculine, and so a gender
asymmetry privileging the masculine, is a convention of the genre. As
I initially observed, however, an interesting Western transcends such
conventions. That is true in any genre. So the question becomes, What
makes for interest in a story and how is this related to the rectification
of gender relations—whether in Trible's interpretation of Genesis 2–3
or in my own later interpretation of *High Noon*? And how would the
balancing of gender relations in a story be related to the humanizing
of gender relations in real life?

The makers of *High Noon* have carefully built up the principal
feminine characters so that they have virtually every strength that Will
Kane can lack and still be a credible masculine protagonist. Amy is
an articulate and bold idealist; Helen is worldly-wise, accomplished in
love, and a rich and competent businesswoman. Amy is like a flaming
arrow shot into Hadleyville from a more civilized or spiritual world
beyond, while Helen is the chief power *of* Hadleyville, the owner of its
main facilities. Each character (or so I have argued) is allowed to play
out her hand without either compromising her identity or losing our
sympathy—which is remarkable, considering that a large part of their
action is the forsaking of good Will Kane.

Meanwhile, Will Kane's masculine integrity is criticized relentlessly. His wife disapproves of him acting the "hero." The fleeing judge
tells Kane that noble effort is wasted on a squalid place like Hadleyville.
The crippled former marshal tells Kane that a lawman gets no real reward for putting his life on the line. For the most part, these challenges
are aimed at Kane's relationship to the town; as a man unto himself,
he comes in for unqualified admiration from Helen (who keeps telling
Harve that Kane is a real man) and even from the pro-outlaw bartender
(who admits that Kane has "guts"). But now we cannot but ask, What
are guts for? What is the final cause of masculinity, if not precisely that
protection of the community of which Kane's badge is the emblem, but
which has now been rendered absurd by the revelation of Hadleyville's
moral emptiness? Kane triumphs, in the end, by facing the Miller gang
as he believed he was obliged to do; yet his last act is to cast his tin star
in the dust. Thus we have as much reason to say that his critics were
right all along as to say that his own integrity was confirmed. Courage in the service of no community is a doubtful thing, and when this
point sinks in we find that masculine selfhood has been circumscribed
and made relative to larger issues of interpersonal order.

Why has *High Noon* been designed this way? Is the movie trying to make points of pop sociology, showing American anxieties about violence and civic virtue, or psychology, illustrating arguments like Erikson's that selfhood takes culturally available forms and depends on social support?[72] In these perspectives, *High Noon* is bound to seem lame. But the movie is gripping. Therefore its design must serve dramatic purposes effectively. The femininity bearers have been built up for the sake of contrast and to introduce greater tension and uncertainty in the story. The story is strong, in narrative and dramatic terms, to the extent that its elements are strong, that is, capable of affecting the action and of affecting our minds, and also to the extent that the relations among its elements have their own detectable effects. Imagine a more routine Western in which the gist of the action is that good gunmen shoot it out with bad gunmen to prevent the rape of innocent women. There is, undeniably, a ritual force to this sort of story. It provides a vehicle for living through strong feelings, like a favorite thrill ride. But ultimately it becomes a bore unless new tensions are introduced. Underneath the shallow "conflict" of a routine story we know exactly where we are, and in that depth we are asleep, unstirred, unengaged.

Which is the stronger version of the story of Adam and Eve? The traditional religious version, which says that a secondary and weak female was created for the man's sake (*just like the females that we see*) and that sin conquered the human race by striking at us in this soft underbelly? Or the version one sees through Trible's reading, which puts Eve as the latest of God's works at the pinnacle of creation (*a female possibility*), there to fall through that hubris that so characteristically afflicts bold leaders? The first version is a resentful finger pointing, like Adam's in Genesis 3:12; the second is a species of that especially strong kind of story we call tragedy.

The more interesting stories, like Genesis 2–3 and *High Noon*, provide demonstrable support for the stronger readings that find gendered selves symmetrically and complexly deployed. That we find such taller islands in a vast archipelago of conventionally masculinist narratives makes it very easy to read them sleepily, in the easier way—just as we are liable to read each other by stereotypes that reflect male dominance in our social arrangements. But something in our storytelling *wants* to be interesting and wants thereby to redeem us, to construe our feelable conflicts and harmonies as a question linking our past and our self-knowledge to a humanely open future. Caught up in that question, any of the forms of selfhood will appear more as a working position in relation to ultimate issues than as the manifestation of some ultimate fixed nature.

Human nature as a set of gendered métiers

The gender attractions of nobility and beauty, the gendered moral orientations to rights and to care, the gender paragon-personalities of Will Kane and Amy Fowler—none of these belong to human nature in the sense that they form an unavoidable starting point for our life or an inescapable consistency in it. Human life can be differently envisioned. And yet there would be something unnatural about refusing to measure ourselves by such standards if we were not in possession of standards as good or better. We would be wasting our potentialities.

But how could we know that alternative standards were as good as these or better? If we are paying attention to strength, a character able to make a vivid, consequential, and durable showing in the world is preferred to a more puny one. By the criterion of inclusiveness, a character that incorporates a rich and flexible array of strengths is better than a more specialized one. As far as these standards take us, the androgyny ideal reigns supreme. Will Kane should develop a theology of love, and Amy Fowler should work up a fast draw. But we have taken no account yet of the issue of optimality in the use of human resources. It usually passes in our gender plots as too obvious for comment that if Will Kanes and Amy Fowlers gave equal attention to martial skills, the contributions of Kanes in violent situations would significantly outweigh those of Fowlers. There is a complementary assumption about the greater value of women's service in warning of hurt and tending it. Kane and Fowler's characters are adapted to what can be accomplished by their bodies in their world, generally speaking. *We* give them their slant: we would rather a male defend us from the dangerous males of the world, and we would rather a member of the mothering class be the central presence in caring for us. The division-of-labor rationale is pushed as far as it can be without making the male and female seem inhuman.

Character counts for more than body in a division-of-labor scheme. If a tough spirit who warms to Will Kane as a model of excellence happens to be female, then an enlightened society would rather have her as marshal than a more timid male. It would be a waste of her masculine resources not to employ her so. But if we asked her instead of Will Kane to be the masculine hero of *High Noon,* we would create a story about an interesting and possibly admirable individual, yet not a gender archetype. The male Kane (Gary Cooper playing Kane) confronts us with an impressive specimen of the male center of meaning for "masculine" virtue. His body is the image of toughness. The métier of marshal is a cultural ideal of one of the best possible uses of the male body; but while a female marshal implies a cultural ideal of flexibility and, more positively, a principle of individual self-determination, she implies nothing about a distinctive female excellence. (It is nevertheless a point of capital importance if she demonstrates that women need not live more timidly than men just because they are smaller on average.)

The noble, just Will and the beautiful, caring Amy fit very well into the sex-differentiated fields of possibility that their society offers them. The more we stress the functional rationale for their specializations, the more their gendering resembles class division. This leads us to suspect that the problem of class-system legitimation that we alluded to earlier would most powerfully be addressed by visions of class-specific attractions and virtues, especially as these could be exhibited in "class plots"; and one need not look far in our literature to find wise patricians, hardy miners, faithful body servants, cheerful milkmaids, and so forth. And it also prompts us to lift our eyes from Will and Amy to the situation in which they live—where armed, irresponsible males threaten from all directions, and dependent, vulnerable women are tending home fires—to examine critically this larger order that makes Will and Amy look like optimized uses of maleness and femaleness. The question about best use of human resources pushes back onto everything that could be different in human life; thus, once we have appreciated the métier significance of genders, our next step is to think about larger patterns of putatively wholesome harmony and the place of gender schemes within them.

Chapter 6

Gender and Duality

The goal of this chapter is to understand the basic logical and ontological reasons why our thinking sometimes takes the form of dichotomy and to see the relevance of these reasons to gender thinking. One indication that an important part of the cogency of gender thinking lies in the formal duality of the gender scheme is Simone de Beauvoir's powerful attack on the gender system, which premises the identification of masculinity and femininity with the logical positions Same and Other. What is vicious in the Western gender system, according to this line of criticism, derives ultimately from improper attributions of Sameness and Otherness, or from fixations on one or the other sort of identity. But a gender theorist might wish to argue that sex-related dualizing is inevitable—which seems indeed to be the thesis of certain well-known psychologies and sociologies—while an apologist for gender might argue that sex-related dualizing has benign forms. Either way, we are confronting the idea that gender schemes are humanly natural because, like sex itself in the realm of reproduction, they *harmonize* people.

How can we judge these conflicting visions of duality? First, we have to get past a roadblock found in much contemporary writing on gender, namely, a routine, superficial denunciation of dichotomies that takes their whole truth to be that they are (1) arbitrarily imposed and (2) hierarchical and oppressive. To expose the inadequacy of this thought, it is necessary to achieve a general view of all the most important warrants for dualizing and to show how these warrants do and do not obtain in sex-related interpersonal experience. The latter project takes us on a critical tour through the great gender-duality theories of Hegel, Levinas, some Christian theologians, Freud, Lévi-Strauss, and Marx and Engels.

This chapter is hard going, particularly at the start. For the writer, at least, it was a Himalayan climb. If some of the pictures from the expedition seem to show more blank sky than landscape, still the poorest of them would be worth passing along if it added in any way to our insight into a pervasive and controlling pattern in our experience. But I submit that the conceptual materials made available in the first section of the chapter do not merely open up *some* new insights into the gender-duality theories; they are actually *decisive* in forming our final assessment of these theories.

The problem: how to think

If stereotyping is a disease of thought, an impaired awareness of real particularities caused by a demand for simple models, then we might fear a still deadlier syndrome in dichotomizing, the paring down of cognitive possibilities in some given field to a wonderfully simple Two. The only thing worse would be the night in which all cows are black, the undiscriminating thought of One.

And yet dichotomizing would not be so common if it so obviously enfeebled the mind. Under some circumstances, for some purposes, it must at least appear to be advantageous.

"There are two kinds of people in this world," begins a dichotomous thought. We cannot judge its intelligence until we see how it finishes and know who is saying it, and how, and why. A poet goes on: "The people who lift and the people who lean."[1] Surely, in the sort of gesture a poem or aphorism is, there is nothing stupid about capturing a feature of human affairs in a simplified way; the great purpose of these formulations is to condense a wealth of meaning into a symbol we can hold before us, feeling in it the complexity of the signified together with the distinctness of the signifier. But if we were told that the two kinds of people in the world are "Aryan" and "non-Aryan," we could not interpret so generously. That statement would enlighten us only about the limits of the mind it represents.

One consideration is the degree of richness to be found in the dichotomizing mind, but this has to be related ultimately to whether the real world divides in the proposed way, and if it does, how this division relates to the world's other characteristics. Now a suitable definition can make it true that people are either Aryans or non-Aryans, truer, in fact, than that they are either lifters or leaners. Genetic standards could be set up precisely to create an artificially clear disjunction. But the racial statement becomes less true the more we want to make of it, for its duality does not map well onto the political or cultural or psychic facts of our world; whereas the poetic statement, by contrast, wakes us up to all sorts of lifting and leaning significances that our actions do actually have. And my suggestion that dualizing propositions are of two sorts, one relatively stupid and one relatively intelligent, means to be intelligent in the same way, that is, by opening up an issue or a choice that confronts us in much of our thinking, of which we might otherwise be unconscious.

There is an analogy between the duality of gender thinking and sex thinking (as developed from the sex–gender distinction) and the duality of intelligent and stupid dichotomizing. "People are masculine or feminine" ideally has a sort of purport resembling that of "People are lifters or leaners," while "People are male or female" is more like "People are Aryan or non-Aryan" to the extent that it is a less perceptive, less discriminating judgment. More precisely: a gender conception becomes stupid and practically harmful in the measure that it collapses gender into sex and treats it as an outward, rigid, conventionally clear distinction that substitutes for paying close attention to people, while it becomes intelligent and beneficial in the measure that it guides attention to people's characters flexibly and revealingly.

That analogy stated, it must also be said that the male–female duality is more inherently interesting, consequential, and symmetrical than the Aryan–non-Aryan duality. The latter has little practical relevance unless Aryanist fanatics insist on it, and then works more to exalt Aryans than to reveal anything. The male–female duality does indeed get magnified and unbalanced by the insistence of sexual ideology, but basically it is of a much less arbitrary type. It is more like the duality between edible and poisonous mushrooms. Both mushroom and sex distinctions reckon with a formidable causation that will affect us no matter what we think: death from eating some mushrooms and not others, reproduction with some sexual combinations and not others. That all three of these dualities are "socially constructed" and belied by refractory particulars does not erase this difference in their foundedness.

Gender thinking is tied to our perception of sex types as centers of meaning; it is definable, in fact, as the way in which the real duality of physical types entailed by the sexual mode of reproduction shows up in our appreciations of persons. But gender thinking as we have thus far studied it, while persistently dualistic, has offered no argument that there must be two and only two basic sex-linked character types. Sublimity and beauty, rights and care, pornography and heterocracy might all have been fortuitously dual arrays. Why not, say, nine complexly complementary genders with important aesthetic and moral aspects—three predominantly male-associated, three female, and three bisexual? Is there something about the character formation process that guarantees duality in gender and so warrants dichotomous strategies of thinking about gender? Or is it true—as has become virtually an axiom among gender critics today—that what guarantees duality is a project of domination, as for instance Aryans are advantaged by that nakedly domineering distinction between Aryans and non-Aryans?

Some gender theories try to show a deep, nonarbitrary warrant for gender dichotomizing. For example, Freudian theories trace a continuation of the duality of sex into the formation of individual psyches. Correlated with sex duality, on these views, is a necessarily dual system of psychologically determinative ways of managing desire. Other theories attend to the reduplication of sex duality in social structure; their claim is that necessarily dual structures of social life as we know it are derived from, or premise themselves upon, the male–female difference. Both sorts of theory bear on the truth-value and intelligence of gender thinking, for they make arguments for the real pervasiveness and relevance of sex duality in human life, connecting them (whether positively or critically) with fundamental *intentional* dualities. Therefore they demand our attention. But if we are to assess them with insight, if we are to avoid the twin mistakes of falling under the spell of stupid dichotomizing or failing to recognize an intelligent or otherwise approvable dichotomizing, we must first explore the range of warrants and styles of Two-thinking in general.

Structures of duality

(I am about to say that dualities are of *two* kinds. Why? Probably because examination so often begins by detecting a difference, a contrast. But when does examination *end* in a perception of duality? What sorts of question require the answer Two?)

Two basic sorts of duality show up in our language. First, there are dichotomous terms expressing the relations of things within a perceptual field or representation, and these are ordinarily understandable without any overt reference to the subjects who are referring to the field—terms like *same/different, greater/lesser, to/from, in/out, over/under,* and so on. As long as we know which field is being referred to, we do not need to know who is saying something like "The red car is *on* the bridge and the blue car is *off* it." On the other hand, there are terms like *here/there, this/that,* and *yes/no* that cannot be understood without seeing how subjects are relating themselves to a field. *Here* and *There* mean nothing on a world map unless a subject puts a finger on them, taking her or his own position on the map. The meanings of *Yes* and *No* cannot be found within a field because they express judgments *about* its content (*Yes* in response to "Is the red car on the bridge?" means not merely "The red car is on the bridge" but "*I do* see it there"). I propose to call the first sort of dichotomy semantic, the second existential. A semantic duality divides a perceived or represented manifold into two areas by drawing a boundary in it. Its milieu is extension. An existential duality registers the separateness of having an experience from not having an experience and of Here from There; its milieu is the life of an intender, that is, the activity of centering extension and extending a center.

Existential duality must be regarded as the more fundamental of the two dualities for two chief reasons. First, semantic duality differs from the existential not by virtue of a positive qualification of its own but only by abstracting from the existential Here/There and Yes/No questions; in itself, the semantic field is just a There without the Here and is neither experienced nor unexperienced. Second, what makes semantic distinctions usable and interesting is that virtual Hereness and Thereness are imported into them—for instance, one virtually positions oneself Here on "this" bridge or in "this" car when perceiving the car "on" or "off" the bridge. (This is the basis of a subject's identifying with things or categories: the Here orientation is shifted between frames of reference.) As Parmenides saw the inseparability of thinking and being, and Berkeley the correlation of perception and the object, so we can see that the dualities from which semantic distinctions are compounded will not signify anything unless we read our own centerednesses into them.

Existential duality is radically asymmetrical, and one might see in it the root of all inequality; we can make sure of symmetry only by representing it in semantic duality. On the other hand, symmetry only matters, only counts as equality or fairness in the senses that we most care about, if we apprehend the semantic projection of it as manifesting the composition of a Here, an *us,* wherein it must take on the meaning of a kind of solidarity—equality as cobelonging.

The logical properties of the two sorts of duality will constantly be mixing. Not only will the properties of existential duality get imported into semantic dualities: since our theorizing about existential duality construes it as a semantic duality (as, within this discourse, Here and There divide a map of possible positions), we will be liable to attach properties of semantic duality to the existential, including even the existential indifference of its pervasive Thereness. An illustration from our gender discussions is ready to hand. Anyone who sets out to speak neutrally of feminine and masculine qualities can array them as sets of equal size and value, as equal as left and right halves of a whole. At the same time, no one is simply neutral; every speaker is actually gender-positioned and thus confronts one gender as nearer and the other as farther, one as the Same and the other as the Other, one as the token of all humanity and the other as humanity's problematic margin. Yet it is further the case that every speaker is engaged somehow in constructing a collective human Here within which a solidarity of genders would be felt. The complexities of Here–There relationship will have to be taken into account, therefore, in judging the adequacy of any gender thinking.

Since it is crucial to understand the logical shape of the different basic duality types, let us take a closer look at each, attending first to the founding one.

Existential duality

To be a living subject (whether as an individual or as a group) is to be central, occupying a Here, and thus to look and move outward from inside and to judge outside events as they might or might not impinge inward. If subjectivity did not exist, all forces and changes in the extended universe would simply pass across it without *registering* anywhere, that is, without being held together. Subjectivity's holding-together *is* Hereness. Without the separation of the subject's Here from the rest of the universe, the subject would not exist; therefore, duality in this case is fully necessary, which is to say that it is impossible to withdraw from. Existential duality is in fact the root of all necessity and seriousness in dualizing. *A question that requires the answer Two is a question in which my existence—whether and where I exist—is at stake.* (Thus there must be two basic kinds of duality because one is implicit in my existence and the other is not.)

The mood of subjectivity—whether it is disposed more to secure itself or more to expand its reach—makes an important difference in how the duality of inside and outside, Here and There, is represented. In an anxious, separating mood the Here–There duality is represented by such oppositions as purity versus corruption and will versus fortune. But in a more secure or ambitious affiliative mood we think not of opposition between inside and outside but instead of a correlation between the microcosm of the subject's inner order and the macrocosm of the larger world order, which often involves an enlarging and complexifying of inner order. See how this is illustrated by Jessica Benjamin's description of a psychologically happy sort of gender identification:

> Toddler boys and girls are struggling equally to maintain identification with both sexes, to keep both parents available as objects of attachment and recognition. Optimally the identification with both parents allows the child to assimilate much of what belongs to the other—identification is not yet limited by identity. In this phase, gender identification is much less rigid than the oedipal organization that comes after it: cross-sex identification can co-exist with same-sex identification; sexual identifications have not yet hardened into polarities.
>
> . . . Individuals ideally should integrate and express both male and female aspects of selfhood (as culturally defined). This integration already takes place in the constant alternation of identifications in early childhood and can subsequently become a basis for understanding the other as well as the self. When this cross-over is permitted at the appropriate time, individuals do not grow up confused about their gender identity; rather, they can be flexible in their expression of it. In the individual's mind the gendered self-representation coexists with a genderless or even opposite-gendered self-representation. Thus a person could alternately experience herself as "I, a woman; I, a genderless subject; I, like-a-man." A person who can maintain this flexibility can accept all parts of herself, and of the other. . . . In other words, the core sense of belonging to one sex or the other is not compromised

by cross-sex identifications and behaviors. The wish to be and do what the other sex does is not pathological, nor necessarily a denial of one's own identity.[2]

Or, with reference to the "cultural" level, a call from Iris Marion Young:

> The dissolution of cultural imperialism . . . requires a cultural revolution which also entails a revolution in subjectivity. Rather than seeking a wholeness of the self, we who are the subjects of this plural and complex society should affirm the otherness within ourselves, acknowledging that as subjects we are heterogeneous and multiple in our affiliations and desires.[3]

Anxiety makes us want mutual exclusiveness, even (as Emile Durkheim remarked of the sacred–profane distinction) "a sort of logical chasm" between Here and There, forbidding "the two corresponding things to be confounded, or even merely to be put in contact with each other";[4] but if we are ambitious to connect the Here with the There we will figure coincidences and analogies that have the effect almost of nullifying boundaries. When the Here stands off from the There, continuity between the dualized realms will be lacking, and the There will be "negatively infinitized" to contain a chaos of everything real or unreal that is not Here (for instance, Woman imagined by men as Whore or Witch, or Meaning treated by philosophers as an unencompassable proliferation of senses and references in every case). But when the Here reaches toward the There, continuity will be requisite, and the There will be positively infinitized or divinized (Woman as Holy Mother, or God as the center of a system of analogies of being).[5]

The Here is not necessarily the positive reference point in Here–There duality. If Here is an intolerable present and There is an affirmable future, then we will address the future in the apocalyptic, revolutionary mood—in which case negative value is infinitized in the Here, positive value in the There—or else in the continuity-preserving reformist mood. If we ruled out this possibility by saying that Here-identification is always with the good or better pole of a duality, we would only veil the anguish of knowing ourselves mired in personal and political problems.

The great dual principles of decision and permission express the separating and uniting moods, respectively, and draw force from them, but they are not strictly bound to them. One can act decisively (like a benignly disciplining "good father") for the sake of union and permissively (like a "good mother" letting go) for the sake of separation. Yet we always know which mood is manifesting itself when we see "permissiveness" and "exclusiveness" projected as *evils,* because that is how one sounds the alarm about a drift opposite to one's own.

(It is important to use prevolitional terms like *disposition* and *mood* to characterize the original setting up of Here–There duality. This setup is presupposed not only in organizing cognition but also in every experience of a specifically volitional or practical duality, such as the duality between the present state of affairs and a prospective changed state of affairs; the alternative of acting or not acting in a certain way; or the duality, classically expressed in Aristotle's theory of virtue and vice, between More and Less on some continuum of effort or self-qualification. Practical dualities split Here–There relations at the core of the Here, determining what comes forth from the Here, yet they can never detach Here from There, for volition is always volition with respect to a world and practice is always practice in a world. In sheer unextended Here there can be no duality. Thus practical dualities are best seen as specifications of existential duality rather than as a separate kind.)

Notwithstanding the pin-pointiness of Here, it is, in actual life, always plural. My personal Here coexists or even merges with *our* Here, for various sorts of We's, together making a complex Here within which the moods or qualities of Here–There relation can vary. To understand my consciousness at a given moment you might need to know that my religious tradition holds a cheerful view of the place of humanity in the universe, my society is currently in a panic about the threatening impurities of crime and drugs, on top of all this I address the world expansively and soaringly because I am newly in love, and at the moment I am participating in a Here of conversation with the mail carrier.

In the microcosm–macrocosm correlation, any qualification of the Here can be transported to the There, and vice versa; and a qualification carried one way can then be carried back, and carried back again. If, for example, I apprehend the cosmos as qualified by intelligence (in correlation with my own intelligence), I can then understand my own intelligence as a part of this larger fabric. These continuities between Here and There do not erase Here–There duality; the explanatory force and the reassurance of the correlation depend on remaining aware of it.

For our purposes, the most important of all complexities is the case of duality within a Here. The Here of the human community contains, among other dualities, that of female and male, so that a full correlation of the human microcosm with the transhuman macrocosm would involve a carrying over of sexual duality into a sexlike cosmic duality, a Yin–Yang pattern, which in turn would be carried back into interpretation of human affairs. Further, the confident carrying over of female and male to the macrocosm might or might not be infected with a panicky mood born in the microcosmic human group, say in the male Here with respect to the female There, so that (strangely enough) the female principle in the universe could become alien and threatening even though a basic attitude of security vis-à-vis the universe was first requisite for perceiving it there. The security would temper the panic, the panic subvert the security.

The point about correlation with a macrocosm applies to any greater order taken to be our inescapable environment or governor, whether that order be physical or mythical or logical or psychological. In the absence of reference to a transcendent sacred realm, polarities that were microcosmic can effectively redefine the microcosm–macrocosm relation. Modern revivals of the culture–nature distinction illustrate this shift.

Semantic duality

Semantic duality divides in two some universe or There-world—not necessarily *the* universe. Thinking about picking up something to write with, the universe of your decision may comprise only a pen and a pencil; the point is that for the given purpose these two items fill your field of view. (Gender identity theories stress the importance of the fact that as children form an apprehension of self their field of view is filled by the female–male alternative represented by their parents, their siblings, and their own bodies.)

For what reasons, if any, would a universe have to be seen as dual?

Initially it seems that nothing prevents any map from having three or more parts instead of two. For many purposes it is in fact useful to divide the world into more than two parts, and in such cases it would seem stupid or manic to insist on bipartition—for example, to maintain that just two human races or ethnic groups exist. But often we are not concerned strictly with marking and ordering differences and relationships that exist *within* the There-world but instead to insert a Here into the There-world in a certain way. This is the motive of orientation. For political and cultural reasons, for instance, a state is established, and with it a division of the world's population into those who have the state's citizenship and those who do not. For (say) Americans, the world thus divides into "Americans" and "foreigners." Now the proposition that humans are either "American" or "foreign" is painfully stupid, taken as a disinterested description, for it fudges all sorts of differences among non-Americans and among Americans, and also masks commonalities between Americans and others. But that is judging it as a grid placed on the map instead of as a way of addressing the map. Taken as an index of the political project of maintaining an American state, that is, of constructing a particular communal Here, the proposition is inevitable and serious. In criticizing the uglier manifestations of us versus them thinking we should bear in mind that the purpose of political association is precisely to enjoy the benefits of an us-condition and the orientation that goes with it.

An elementary requirement for orientation is that the subject be able to pay attention to differences. Bipartition is the simplest and most easily managed of differentiations. It is, from every starting point, the beginning of the noticing of difference insofar as this involves a turning of the subject from one set to another (which may or may not involve what is called "negation" in the Hegelian tradition) or follows a path of binary yes–no reactions to data. Illustrating the second case, a computer program sorts a population by some such series of bipartition as white/*non-white* (thus) black/*non-black* (thus) Asian/*non-Asian* and so forth. By bringing different bipartitions to bear, specific objects can be picked out of an indefinitely rich field—as in Twenty Questions. But this constraint on how differentiation can proceed does point finally to the locatedness of the differentiator, who always works from a Here toward a There. Likewise the "from" and "to" vectors of turning assume a Here and There. Sets A and B may be equally "There," but the intentional radii subject-to-A and subject-to-B exchange Hereness and Thereness as the subject turns from A to B.

Bipartition as an empirical occurrence we call splitting. A rock or a cell splits in two. But under what conditions must the results of such a breakup be dual? Geometrically we know that a field of dimension n will be split by a realization of dimension $n - 1$ (as a plane divides three-dimensional space, a line divides a plane, and a point divides a line). The products of the split *must* be dual because of the removal of the nth dimension in the $n - 1$ partition, and they *cannot* be dual if the partition is n-dimensional, if only because of the partition's thickness.[6]

Empirical splitting comes under this form once we realize that the moment of an actual event of splitting is a realization of dimension $n - 1$ in n, where n is four-dimensional space–time. It is not just that a rock or a cell splitting into more than two pieces at once is unlikely; it is that the complexity of more than one separation occurring is ruled out by the removal of the time dimension in the dividing moment. (We can conceive of instantaneous tripartition like we can conceive of balancing the Earth on an infinitesimal point, but neither event can occur in a moment that is a moment *of time,* that is, in the $n - 1$ relationship with n.) Only the subject, however, causes the removal of the nth dimension. The moment, the plane, the line, and the point are all the subject's imaginary constructions of an unextended position between separated realities.

Semantic dualities are guaranteed with the insertion of a subject into a world because the dimensionless center-point of subjectivity splits all continua. Right and left, front and back, up and down, and future and past are all expressions of my betweenness, that is, my position as a Here-position, an orientation, rather than as a plotted point in a There-world. The vertical plane that separates my right and left, for example, is a generalization of my betweenness in a horizontal continuum, the sum of all midpoints on horizontal lines, covering a whole class of steering alternatives of the same type. Thanks to my unextendedness, I can realize any $(n - 1)$-dimensional splitter: I am the drain down which all subtracted dimensions disappear.

It follows from the general point about dimensions that to split the human realm descriptively it is necessary to use a less-than-human divider. Whether it is femaleness, maleness, blondness, blood type O, IQ 100, or even Christianness or Jewishness, such a criterion will be certain to divide humans into just two sets only if a dimension of humanity is abstracted from it. Restore humanity and the partition loses its definiteness. (For instance, interpreting Christianity as a human condition leads a theologian to introduce the fuzzily bounded category of "anonymous Christianity" for persons who inhabit this condition without a formal profession of Christian belief.)[7] Since gender mediates between the subhuman variable of sex and the human variable of character, the duality that is obtained by applying a sex criterion cannot be clearly and definitely repeated at the level of gender, as we have by now seen in numerous ways.

The same considerations apply to combining, the inverse of splitting. If we think of it occurring at a point in time, a combining always involves just two parties. More than an empirical illustration of this principle, sexual reproduction is a powerful symbol for it. The event of conception cannot be conceived in a space–time moment as a coming together of more than two elements. Likewise in subjective experience one can be joined only by one other at a time. (The "other" may in this case be a rich manifold of personal Others united in a collective here—for instance, all my fellow Jews joining me in the moment that I convert to Judaism—but I cannot simultaneously experience my unions with these individuals as individual.) Moreover—and here is the pathos, the element of futility, in joining up with other persons—the surfaces that make contact must be of one dimension less than the beings who combine. (The Judaism I specifiably share with other Jews is thinner than the Judaisms we respectively embody.)

Another deep dualizing necessity is found in comparing. Comparing rests on back-and-forth turning or alternating, for X's similarities and differences with respect to Y and Z cannot be brought into focus together—that would require flopping over in different directions, across two frontiers, at the same time. Consider an apparent counterexample. If bowl of porridge 1 is too hot, bowl 2 is too cold, and bowl 3 is just right, then it seems that 3's in-betweenness with respect to 1 and 2 is taken in by a single comparative perception. But is "in-betweenness" an immediately apprehensible complex comparison or rather a summation of one-to-one comparisons? It *is* an immediately apprehensible relation, and it implies certain comparisons, but it is not a comparison. To put the same point differently, a choicemaker cannot directly resolve an alternative of more than two parts: "This or this or this?" The complex has to be broken down into a series of "This or this?" alternatives, or else the Thises have to be grouped to yield a pair (as bowls 1 and 2 form the extreme-temperature group in comparison with moderate-temperature bowl 3). A spectrum looks like a multiple-contrast gestalt, but the only true comparative inspection that can take it all in at once would be one that aimed at a single binary alternative such as (for the light spectrum) lighter versus darker. Notice that attending to one alternative as This necessarily construes the other alternative as That; the This–That relation flops over when the other becomes This in turn. The growth of self-knowledge, including its gender-identification component, is largely a comparative process and therefore is dualizing in this way.

Yet another important structure of duality is signaled by the phrase "as opposed to." Oppositeness is maximized contrast in a given continuum. The oppositions between left and right, up and down, and forward and backward take advantage of all 180 degrees of possible variance in each of the three spatial dimensions. But opposition in the sense of opposedness or over-againstness means that opposed things address each other *from* maximally variant directions in a continuum. (If the main point of opposedness is just the facing each other or collision of two beings, then there is no need to measure their angles of approach—for practical purposes, they might as well be coming from exactly opposite directions, although only exact oppositeness formally requires them to be two.) Opposedness is necessarily dual when experienced by a subject who feels caught between forces, whether torn by them or balanced by them; a theory of psychic conflict that postulates just two great psychic forces is founded on such an experience.[8] Or the experience of balanced opposedness may be invoked by a norm of "creative tension," as between the projects of recognizing Others and obtaining recognition for the Self.[9] For either oppositeness or opposedness, the continuum is established from a particular point of reference, that is, a Here positioned between the opposites. One such Here is intersexual or intergender collaboration, wherein the slightest friction, in the character of opposedness, evokes a projection of opposite and therefore dual perspectives.

The mood and position of the subject are important qualifiers of opposition. Contrast is enlivening for the venturesome, threatening for the defensive. Over-againstness is a tragedy for those who feel, who grieve that conflict is *here* in the form of discomposing pain, and a comedy for those who think, who glory that conflict is *there* in the form of "incongruity."

The metaphysical consolidation of dualities

Speculative thinking takes flight by leaping from oppositions in particular continua like high and low, cold and warm, or dark and light to super-oppositions in a metaphysical continuum-of-continua: Yin and Yang in Chinese thought, for example, or, in Greek speculation, rarefaction and condensation as opposed principles of change in the Anaximenian world substance of air, or the Love and Strife principles of Empedocles. These metaphysical oppositions have great explanatory power, since all phenomenal variety can be derived from the interaction of two opposed principles if the principles are sufficiently abstract, and they have great orienting force, since they ground all our betweennesses on one, or consolidate them all into one. If we can locate ourselves in one fundamental betweenness, then we are in the best possible position not only to know where we are but to bring the inescapable forces of life into reconciliation, either as a stable equilibrium or as a creative synthesis.[10]

With a hierarchical metaphysical duality like Aristotle's form–matter duality, which rests on a single decisive continuum of value (pure form as perfectly good and pure matter as worthless), we do not really leave the "between" position—for the discernment of opposition always occurs there—but we project ourselves out of it insofar as we identify with one of the contraries. The other contrary becomes, so to say, doubly There, not just one referent among others taking its turn as There but a There-in-principle, not just one pole of an opposition but a to-be-opposed. Our task is to secure ourselves against it rather than to balance it with a complement. But this intense There-ing could be a way of realizing opposition preparatory to a less defensive (and thus less essentially hierarchical) apprehension of it.

What did not become fully clear in Western thinking until Hegel is how the basic principles of speculative comprehension—the structures of opposition and synthesis as such, "negation" and "supersession" as he called them—belong together with the existential center of Hereness, "self" or "spirit." Hegel showed the dependence of semantic distinctions on existential duality by exhibiting human knowledge and practice as the building of an ever-richer Here. Empedocles' cosmic forces of Love and Strife became the Here-ing and There-ing of the subject *for* whom the cosmos exists, a subject challenged by the vast cosmos to become commensurately great. Hegel teaches us to recognize the one primordial and necessary duality as that of Self and Other and to see it, as far as the project of comprehension is concerned, as an aspect of a unification process. The ultimate condition of the subject, for Hegel, is to be between all things—not in the manner of being torn between alternatives, "turned this way and that," alienated along continua of otherness, but rather as the center of all, possessing everything along continua of identification, turning always toward itself.

We shall see presently what shape a gender theory can take when it is derived from metaphysical duality. But let us first take stock of our findings to this point.

Probing the grounds of semantic duality has led us repeatedly to the Here–There orientation of existential duality. Without some form of Hereness, nothing forces duality on semantic structure. (It follows that forcing *nonduality* on the world is a way of expressing existential indifference, denying that one has a Here, or, at the other extreme, a way of expressing "the dream of the innumerable," "the desire to invent incalculable choreographies."[11] Whenever we find a semantic division treated as unalterably dual, then, we can be sure that we are dealing with a projection of an existential duality, and we know that the seriousness of the subjective enterprise of maintaining a center is involved. "Projection" in this case should not be regarded as necessarily fallacious or dishonest, for shuttling back and forth between neutral and personally engaged views, and interweaving the two perspectives, is the very stuff of communicative life. No less essential to communication, however, is the questioning of all projections and interweavings.

Metaphysical gender-duality theories: Hegel and Levinas

Hegel's gender theory is more profoundly a priori than the theory of Kant's *Observations on the Feeling of the Beautiful and the Sublime* that we studied in Chapter 5. Kant had built on data of empirical psychology, albeit in a tidying sort of way. For Hegel, the genders arise from the primary self-division of "ethical substantiality" for the sake of the vitality of its "concrete [that is, differentiated] unity."

> Thus one sex is the form of spirit that splits away from itself [*das sich Entzweiende*] to exist *for itself* in personal self-subsistence and the knowledge and volition of free universality, i.e., the self-consciousness of conceptual thought and the volition of the objective final end. The other sex is spirit maintaining itself in unity as knowledge and volition of the substantive, but . . . in the form of concrete individuality and feeling. In relation to externality, the former is powerful and active, the latter passive and subjective. It follows that man has his actual substantive life in the state, in learning, and so forth, as well as in labor and struggle with the external world and with himself, so that it is only out of his self-splitting that he fights his way to self-subsistent unity with himself. . . . Woman, on the other hand, has her substantive destiny in the family, and to be imbued with family piety is her ethical frame of mind.[12]

With one adjustment, Hegel's gender norms map fairly well onto the models of masculine and feminine selfhood that we encountered in Gilligan's moral psychology. That is, by removing the social restriction of women to a domestic sphere, we would allow "feeling" and the orientation to "concrete individuality" and familylike harmony to play as large a role in human affairs as autonomy, the orientation to the universal, and fighting. Hegel's account thus shares the descriptive plausibility of Gilligan's, at a high level of generality. But he is not concerned to support it empirically; he primarily wants to make a point about stages of spiritual development, and the genders (and the subordination of women, too) appear to him as handy illustrations. The "daylight" of public life and self-conscious conceptual thought lies *beyond* the intimate communion of family life, in human terms; family life is not *enough* for human spirit, although it is an essential part of its trajectory.[13] Spirit is destined to construct a larger Here than the family and the feminine represent.

The Hegelian gender duality turns out to be inhumanely asymmetrical because the metaphysical principle of difference that governs it is one of progress through stages—the subject of that progressive history a single Spirit. Only one true Here is allowed. But what if, on the contrary, more than one irreducible Here were admitted? And what if it turned out further that relations between a plurality of Heres can never be appropriated by one of them to form a history of progressively more valid stages? A pluralist, suprahistorical metaphysical alternative to Hegel, with a correspondingly different linkage to gender duality, is offered in this century by Emmanuel Levinas. Levinas opposes the Hegelian cancellation of Otherness in order to indicate how moral relations transcend all projects of comprehension.[14] The Otherness of one's fellow humans qua moral claimants is absolute—their superordinate status is as to-be-heeded rather than as to-be-known—and so too the genders are guaranteed a priori significance as they are identified with aspects of fellow humans' Otherness.

The Levinasian counterparts to Hegel's two portions of "ethical substantiality" are two basic modalities of moral relationship, responsibility *to* the Other and responsibility *for* the Other.[15] In the first instance the Other confronts me with masculine "dignity," from a "dimension of height," as the one to whom I am bound to make apology for myself; while in the second instance the Other recedes from my solicitous "caress" with feminine "modesty." The Other is strong in the first aspect, frail in the second; the first sort of face is irresistibly frank, the second vulnerably nude. Thus a sort of feminine receptivity to the sublime is made a metaphor for coming under moral claim, while the male's sight of the female becomes a metaphor for moral solicitude.

In his remarks on feminine modesty, Levinas sketches a masculine philosophy of erotic relations at the same time that he elucidates a universal dimension of moral experience. This coincidence of themes points again to the continuum of human attractions that was implied by Kant's gender aesthetic: benevolent neighbor love and carnal love are not independent of each other.

The question must arise, of course, whether we can stand for males to continue to look at females as vulnerable and secret, given all the evil that accompanies this look. We can also ask whether it is safe for females or indeed for anyone to take an utterly submissive attitude with respect to any human being, even in the character of moral claimant. These questions would not be settled by a demonstration that males are constitutionally more liable to be aroused by the sight of the female, or (more dubiously) that females are in some way constitutionally pliant with respect to the male. Such tendencies cannot determine the whole meaning of encounters with human females and males, nor can they prevent us from designing social relations to form that meaning in desirable ways.

Granting that the Other's authority and vulnerability are permanent poles of moral experience, is it necessary that men be linked to the first and women to the second? Apparently not. As a matter of fact, Levinas's thoughts about the feminine nudity and vulnerability of the Other are powerfully (and more typically) stated without gender restriction.[16] His metaphysic is not weakened internally if it is cut free from sex connection. Because all moral subjects are placed between the reference points of the authority and vulnerability of the Other, and because neither aspect of Otherness can be subordinated to the other aspect, Levinas's metaphysical scheme does not rely on a particular social gender order to the degree that Hegel's scheme does. Take away the masculinist cultural background of Hegel's account of spirit and the supersession of personal affiliation by fought-for public status suddenly seems anything but inevitable.

*

In the two metaphysical schemes under review, masculine and feminine gain their content from dualities of spiritual form—the conceptual and externally active principle opposed to the intuitive, passive, and private principle, in Hegel, and the moral exigencies of sovereignty and vulnerability, in Levinas. Neither position makes a connection with features of physical sex, although both allude implicitly to the practical subordination and seclusion of women in Western society. The arbitrariness of these views with respect to physical sex does not entail that they lack cogency as gender theories, however, for it is possible that culturally realized versions of masculinity and femininity have been constructed from the promptings of a metaphysical logic rather than read off from sex in a more naive way. Why, indeed, would we have gender conceptions that only raggedly fit our experience of people unless they derive from an independently powerful logic? How could it be worth Gilligan's while to defend a conception of different moral "voices," with admitted weakness in the sex correlation of the voices, unless a logic of moral maturity (which she herself calls a "dialectic of human development") requires that the two voices be heard?[17] But why, on the other hand, would the poles of moral experience coincide with the sexes, unless maleness and femaleness showed aptitude for their spiritual roles—males by virtue of their adaptation to fighting, females by virtue of their adaptation to bearing and nursing children?

It seems that a gender-duality scheme must always have one foot planted in perception of maleness and femaleness—an empirical and semantic duality—and the other in an intentional structure that divides ways of maintaining Here–There relation. Since men's and women's lives are very probably structured by such a logic to some extent in any society, the appeal of a gender-duality theory to a logic rather than to an accumulation of empirical observations is not wrongheaded in itself. What is at stake in a gender-duality theory and in a gender system too is not simply perspicuity in rounding up There-world facts but *how to be a person,* and not only as a subject but also as an object of personal attention. We have to judge the logic as a formula for personhood; we have to ascertain whether the anatomy of intentional possibility is well captured by it and whether we can accept the life it holds out for us. (Clearly, the gender balancing of Gilligan yields a more approvable intentional duality than Hegel gives us; one could respond that the Hegelian structure reflects real constraints while the Gilligan scheme is wishful, but in fact Hegel's assignment of spiritual stages to the sexes is much more weakly defended than Gilligan's.) At the same time, we have to test the fit of the logic with the facts of sex to judge the propriety of putting it forward as a *gender* theory.

The chief weakness of the metaphysical gender-duality theories is that they cannot tell us how to join metaphysical structure to empirical reality. This difficulty is supposed to vanish once we realize that our empirical reality is always mediated by metaphysical structures of meaning. Nevertheless, the course of true interpretation never runs smooth; the world has all sorts of unexpected bumps and twists in it that turn out to be of great practical importance, especially when they have some bearing on the characters of human individuals. Sex is such a twist, and so is the social order of relations between the sexes. The metaphysical interpretation of gender makes us aware, however, that we face a dilemma between the empiricist and rationalist modes of justification, the two ways of respecting the Other: acknowledging the Other's perceptible particularities according to the requirements of the Other's own centering over There, or maximizing the Other's intelligibility according to the requirements of my or our own centering Here. The metaphysical resolutions of the dilemma cannot be entirely right because they rationalistically sublimate, whether in totalizing (Hegel) or pluralizing (Levinas) fashion, the Other's own worldly self-centering. But they cannot be ignored, either. Gender thinking must contain a moment of metaphysical interpretation for the sake of carrying through reflection on the intelligibility of the dualities in our experience; and insofar as we are always subject to the intelligibility requirement in thinking, no matter how "empiricist" the approaches we adopt, our descriptions of experience can never be free of metaphysical contamination.

Now we can turn to "empiricist" gender-duality theories. Actually what is required is a series of turns, because empiricisms are of different kinds, according to different modalities and fields of experience.

Theological gender-duality theories: The Shakers and Paul

The visible order of *male* and *female,* by which all animated creation exists, proves the existence of the order, in the invisible world, from which our existence is primarily derived . . . an Eternal *Parentage;* the Eternal Two, as distinctly Two, as *Power* and *Wisdom* are Two; and as the Father and Mother are two.
—*Shaker* Testimony of Christ's Second Appearing[18]

Following a Western religious tradition, we can call "theology" any discourse that is explicitly concerned with setting forth an *existentially* unsurpassable microcosm–macrocosm relation—that is, a relation between a Here including all the important powers of self and a There including all the important powers with which the self must deal. Theologizing is distinguishable from metaphysical thinking (although it incorporates metaphysics) in that it does not merely project or stipulate all-important powers but finds itself (somehow) faced with a supreme power and acknowledges and responds to it as such. Theology is thinking and discourse carried out in the religious situation of encounter with the divine; it is the empiricism of this extraordinary experience. (We must admit that the divine can be understood as a nonduality in which illusory Here–There opposition is dissolved; this would be the ambiguous limit-case of "theology.") Theology is definable, then, as the would-be supreme eloquence of existential duality in the religious situation. Now, in addition to the invisible support that a religious attitude gives to the fixing of an anthropological center of meaning for our major ideas of duality, we know we will also find overtly theological dualities written into sex. The question is, By what argument or evidence can a theological duality be established and correlated with human sex duality?

Theological dualizing has two fundamental bases. One is the nature of divinity itself; the other is the relation between the divine and the human, or between the holy and the mundane in general. Accordingly, a theological gender theory will rest on a conception of the divine as gendered or on a conception of the holy–mundane relation as genderlike.

The passage given above from the Shaker Bible represents the first possibility. Portraying the divine as Father Power and Mother Wisdom may challenge formal monotheism in one way, yet it reflects a sense of duality that is repeatedly expressed in monotheist faith, that troubles Israel throughout its scriptures, and that shows up at the beginning of the simple table prayer, "God is great, God is good." It is a duality knitted of oppositions in the experience of the *tremendum et fascinans:* in realizing one's own fundamental separateness from the greatest power, one faces the question whether friendly relation with this power is possible or not, and in realizing one's fundamental attraction to the best principle of wisdom or love, one faces the question whether or not this principle holds ultimate sway. For monotheism, these oppositions typically appear as the *problem* of reconciling the divine power with the divine wisdom and benevolence in light of the world's imperfections. But they can also be stated as a divine richness of dual identity.

The Shaker statement relates the twin glories of power and wisdom to the creator–creature relationship between divinity and the world. The correspondence between the male–female order of richness and generation within the world, on the one hand, and the divine duality, on the other, is too suggestive to ignore. It is the very nature of creaturely dependence on the divine, and not creaturely presumption, that requires us to trace the basic structures of our life into the divine order from which we are derived. Thus we are not free *not* to link our sex duality to the divine duality. As one Shaker interpreter puts it, "To speak of God as Father–Mother is to look up through our human experience to the One we *begin* to recognize as in Union with us the way we actually are."[19] Just as the name "Father" is as it were forced to the lips of traditional Christians by their Jesus-modeled attitude of confiding dependence on God, so a fuller realization of the structure of human dependency—of the fact that every child has a natural mother and a father, and spiritual mothers and fathers in the Shaker community—mandates the fuller name "Father–Mother."[20]

What is abstract or arbitrary about this version of a Father–Mother theology is its assignment of gender *content*. Assuming that both representations of duality, one of power and wisdom and the other of sexed progenitors, are well founded, there is yet no specifically theological warrant for identifying power with males and wisdom with females. In principle, power might as well be feminine—as we might be most inspired by the awesome power of female fecundity—and wisdom might as well be masculine. To admit this, however, is to drain the names "Father" and "Mother" of most of their meaning. Of course the circumstance that makes gender assignments nonarbitrary *for us* is a particular experience of males and females in the human world. If, for example, the kinds of wisdom that females are more called upon to exercise in our world is a great issue for us, then we are not free not to identify the divine Motherhood with divine Wisdom. But a change in our world would entail a change in thinking about the divine Parents. From this it follows, not that divine gendering is nonsensical, but that the content of divine genders cannot be carried over *in one particular way* to human genders as their interpretive support and guarantee. Religious experience may furnish reason to respect a power–wisdom duality in human affairs, and even to map this duality in some fashion onto the genders insofar as power–wisdom and male–female partnerships are jointly necessary to sustain life; but definitions of human power and wisdom, and the distribution of these qualities by sex, remain theologically undetermined.

The point about gender content should not distract from the momentous formal implication of gender *symmetry* to which Shaker thinking points.[21] A witness to two equally irreducible divine genders, regardless of their content, supports a symmetrical valuation of the human genders, at least ideologically, and also continually provokes an interpretive checking back and forth between the human scene and the experienced divine in this respect.

The first letter of Paul to the Corinthians brings the second possibility before us, wherein the point of departure for gender theory is the nature of the divine–human relationship. On this initially thornier path we will finally discover a more substantial theological interpretation of sex duality.

Paul's key statement of principle is that "the head of every man is Christ, the head of a woman is her husband, and the head of Christ is God" (1 Cor. 11:3; cf. Eph. 5:21–33). "Headship" is integral to the conception of God. The divine has precedence over humans and all other mundane beings, as the alpha-point of their creation and the omega-point from which they are regulated; humans cannot interpret themselves from themselves (giving precedence to something mundane) but can understand themselves rightly only if they acknowledge that they are derived from creation and aimed toward salvation. The "greatness" or worshipfulness of the divine implies this precedence (although precedence is not the same thing as greatness). Thus when religious subjects locate themselves in an existential duality of greater and lesser, they not only commit themselves to a judgment of ontological or moral inequality—as might be expressed, in de-existentialized language, as the duality of the absolute and the conditioned—they also enter an order of first-and-second, a rule of interpreting one thing in light of another or guiding one thing by another. Paul makes it as clear as he can that he does not think men and women are of unequal ultimate worth ("Nevertheless, in the Lord woman is not independent of man nor man of woman; for as woman was made from man, so man is now born of woman. And all things are from God" [1 Cor. 11:11–12]). It would be plain idolatry to assign to men vis-à-vis women the status of the absolute vis-à-vis the conditioned. But the chain of "headship" running from God to the mediator Christ and from Christ to the rest of humanity has another link in the man–woman relation, a link Paul finds already established in the Genesis 2 story of a two-step creation of humanity.[22] Paul worries that in their enthusiasm for sexual equality the Corinthians will obscure a decisive anthropological reference point for the relation of humanity to Christ and God, the social precedence of men with respect to women. Male–female social asymmetry becomes a theological center of meaning.[23]

One can say from a strictly theological point of view that Paul's reasoning is suspect. In spite of his protestations of ultimate sexual equality, his sanction of male superiority implicitly idolizes men, putting the creature in the place of the Creator. Furthermore, the use of this particular center of meaning for theology means that thought about the nature of divine precedence will be biased in favor of the kind of precedence ("lordship") that men have over women in patriarchal society.[24] A needed control is missing from this thinking.

*

Human sexual duality itself is not only a theological trap but a warning of traps and a resource for escaping them. Employing human femaleness as a clue to the divine–human relation, for example, one notices that divine activity, whether creative or redemptive, must have a maternal aspect: creatures and their occasions are born from a fundamental matrix of possibility, and if thought of as belonging to the divine in this way will also be thought of as eschatologically destined for some sort of boundary-transcending reattachment to it or reentry into it. The notion of a divine gestation and nurturing of the world balances the more familiar image of a fatherlike regulator. Here the religious duality written into sex is not that of the absolute "sacred" and the conditional "profane," or even that of initiative and response, but instead one of divine immanence and transcendence. A dialectical relation then springs up between human parenthood's centering of theistic meaning in naming God "Mother–Father," on the one hand, and the God-idea's centering of anthropological meaning in turn, so that a supposed likeness of humanity to God must be rendered androgynously.

Unlike the duality of divine power and wisdom, the duality of divine immanence and transcendence connects unavoidably to the two sexes qua modes of parenthood. More than that, transcendence and immanence only become meaningful terms of an existential duality (as opposed to an abstract semantic duality) if they are referred to maternity and paternity as centers of meaning. In turn, human maternity and paternity become symmetrically exalted, secured in value in relation to each other, in their parallel referral to the divine. (Because of their turn toward the celibate realm of Christ's Kingdom, the Shakers forbear from investing themselves in the reference to this center of gender meaning.) When dualizing disorders appear in the relations between men and women, such as the restriction of women to the "immanence" of the "natural" that Beauvoir described, they can be fundamentally rectified only by theological clarification of the misused or misunderstood principles.[25]

There will be no specifically theological cogency in affiliating human maternity with divine immanence or human paternity with divine transcendence unless these Here- and There-relations with the divine are *realized* and not merely posited. Just here, however, we have to reckon with a crucial ambiguity in the religious foundation of theology, and that is the coincidence of the category of the Divine in mature religious experience with the category of the Parent in infantile experience. As we already saw in considering the Shaker passage, God and Parent are both indispensable creators-and-sustainers, from which it follows that both are reference points of ultimate concern. Thus Freud could not but portray infancy as an inherently religious mode of being to the extent that bliss and lostness are nakedly at issue in it (and then, circularly, interpret religion as infantile).[26] Our observation and knowledge of motherhood and fatherhood join with our feelings about them (feelings of unparalleled magnitude carried forward from infancy) to give them a privileged place in our constructed human Here. But if Mother and Father are God-names of infinite emotional resonance, uniquely adequate for registering the pains and joys of a creature–creator or lostness–foundness relation, then religious encounter cannot be realized in separation from the psychological funding of our earliest life. No more can the psychological interpretation of human feeling be detached from theology's lucid, articulate view of what frustration and bliss consist of. Theological and psychological warrants are mutually entwined.

Social-scientific gender-duality theories: Freud and Lévi-Strauss

There are unmistakable real dualities in mundane human experience—earth where we stand and heaven where we cannot reach, light where we can see and dark where we are blind, life in us and non-life around us—and one of these is the reproducing pair, woman and man. A reproductive system involving more than two sexes is thinkable, but improbably complex. We see the recombinative principle of sex realized everywhere in one-to-two splittings and two-to-one combinings: in meiosis and fertilization, at the level of chromosomes, and in differentiated sex characteristics and reproductive behavior (including family formation) at the level of the organism. Two circumstances follow. First, every viable human group must bring female and male together with some regularity, which practically entails that systematic arrangements will be made for this purpose, probably centering on some form of "marriage" and "family."[27] Second, every human child will be born into relation with a female and a male and thus confronted with a riddle: though I am a product of two kinds, I belong to one kind. (If the essence of sexual reproduction is variability by synthesis, one might say that a trend in nature is consummated in a child's using its consciousness to solve the equation of its new identity using the values of its parents' identities.) These two features of the sexual system are the worldly reference points of all gender dualizing.

Now let us examine the child's situation in light of the theory that made childhood the key to human self-interpretation.

Psychic duality

Freudian accounts specially commend themselves to us because they take sex and gender to lie at the heart of the problematic of selfhood. We will get the most advantage by constructing a model of this general type of gender account, and then, with reference to the model, evaluating psychoanalytic gender dualizing generically.

The principles of Freudian gender theory are these:

1. The prime datum, the substance of every new human life as it comes into the world and joins the others, is Desire, so that human experience is structured from the beginning as a dialectic of gratification and frustration and the subject is structured as a strategy for attaining the one and avoiding or compensating for the other.

2. Desire is bodily, not only in the sense that gratification and frustration have somatic experience as content but even more importantly in the sense that the original schemas for desire are determined by bodily form (oral, anal, genital).

3. The earliest structuring of experience and subjectivity is de-

cisive for a human being's whole life. Just as the basic links of neural function are forged in the first couple of years of physical development, so a ground plan for Desire is established in the rewards and disappointments of infancy. (Clinical psychoanalytic experience furnishes important grounds for believing this, but the very idea of a subject's career in time implies that every new situation is entered and understood on the basis of an orientation established in the past; and it seems that proportionally a huge part of a subject's necessary orientation, emotional or otherwise, must be established very early to get her or his career going.)

4. The life of Desire is an experience of fulfilling or frustrating relations with others, "objects" targeted by Desire, of which the earliest and most important is the main human presence in the infant's life, the primary caretaker(s). (I refrain from saying "mother" now to leave open the question raised by Chodorow and Dinnerstein whether fathers could equally share early child care with mothers and thus equally assume the mother's kind of emotional importance for the child.)

But now there are three complications:

5. The adults with whom the child is most concerned differ by sex, which has crucial implications for what gratification is and how it is achieved. Desire is pluriform. There is an "Oedipal" drama in which the child takes one or more roles in relation to each parent according to her or his own sex-type.

6. A further lesson for the child in "object relations," or rather a pair of lessons, are that objects have careers of their own independent of the child's desire and that the pursuit of fulfillment in relation to an object must often be indirect—deferring, substituting. In a sense, the object (distant, separate) exists only in its absence, as what wish or word point away to, and thus the "subject" exists only in aiming at an absence.

7. Since the fundamental desires are unchangeable and the primordial losses irrecoverable, the subject splits from itself in repressing awareness of them. There develops, for instance, a calculating "I" with which one consciously identifies distinct from an unconscious "it" behind the scene. The psychic Here becomes problematic, therefore, and whether psychic reunification and wholeness are within human reach is a deeply open question.

8. The child's experience is made up of fantasy as well as percep-

tion. Hence points 6 and 7 apply to relations with real objects in one way and to relations with imaginary objects in another.

9. The capacity systematically to defer and substitute for desired gratifications, if not to renounce them outright, is a precondition of attaining full membership in a communicating community, that is, in "culture." Language, the signifier system, is indeed the prime example of substitution. (Thus if gender identity formation is part of the very process of acquiring this capacity, our humanity and our gendering would be inseparable. And if repression and ego-splitting are inherent in these processes, then both gender and acculturation are neuroses, albeit "normal" ones.)

Now see how these principles play their parts in the classic Freudian account, as summarized by Juliet Mitchell:

> The little boy and the little girl initially share the same sexual history which [Freud] terms "masculine." They start by desiring their first object: the mother. In fantasy this means having the phallus which is the object of the mother's desire (the phallic phase). This position is forbidden (the castration complex) and the differentiation of the sexes occurs. The castration complex ends the boy's Oedipus complex (his love for his mother) and inaugurates for the girl the one that is specifically hers: she will transfer her object love to her father who seems to have the phallus and identify with her mother who, to the girl's fury, has not. Henceforth the girl will desire to have the phallus and the boy will struggle to represent it. . . . For both sexes, this is the insoluble desire of their lives.[28]

In the beginning is Desire aiming at the Other, here the Mother. (The bliss of union with the mother is irregular from the start, happiness alternating with unhappiness; still, it takes the infant some time to organize its feelings to develop what we would call anger about that object independence.) As the gap between self and other is felt, there are two realizations of what the self–other relation calls for: first, that the other is best predictable if treated as an other Desire, and second, that there is a way in which the child can cater to her Desire. However, the fantasized formula for successful relations with Mother runs into a barrier. Girls and boys are prevented, in different ways, from giving Mother what she wants, which means that girls and boys alike are alienated from their own Desire. It began when they adopted something they could not directly own as the vehicle for their Desire and met the castration threat. "Femininity" and "masculinity" crystallize as relations to the phallus that are opposite in one way (since males are posited as owning it, even if under a problematizing constraint, while females are posited as lacking it) but alike in instituting an alienation from self and subjection to a rule. Gendered interactional qualities like the aggression and authority of the masculine and the receptivity and compliance of the feminine, *along with* the social structures that rest on these sex-correlated personal qualities, all are psychically founded on the divided relation to the Mother and the phallus, the definitive first-order (blissful end) and second-order (omnipotent means) objects of Desire.

There is enormous room for variation or debate in such an account. What is the real character of Desire at various points in its life? ("Sexual"?) To what extent is it an innate constant in human nature and to what extent the product of socialization? [29] What are the actual or possible attractions and repulsions, satisfactions and frustrations, at different stages of life? Which has more governing force, psychologically: the primordial Desire, the conscious or unconscious formations that get built up out of Desire's adventures, or a preexisting structure like language? What exactly can children be aware of, and how, and when? How are imaginary, perceptual, and language-mediated "objects" related? But disagreement on these points very often stays on the playing field bounded by the premises set forth above.

Dualizing comes into this picture in several different ways. The subject splits from the object as the child learns its separateness from its sources of gratification. The subject splits from itself in separating an imaginary whole and capable self from its experienced incapacity;[30] in being able to aim *at* but also, via "identification," virtually *from* another subject; and in ambivalence (a splitting of valuation) and repression. The instrumentality of Desire splits according to the duality of physical sex. Even if everyone's Desire does not revolve around possession of the penis, it certainly does center on body-shaped possibilities of sexual gratification in several forms: somatic pleasure, the power to please someone else, and the power to engender children. All these possibilities divide by sex. The binary interpersonal roles of nurturance and discipline (the Yes and No of the Other) are taken up by every parent, and under still-prevalent social and familial conditions the mother will very often be found specializing one way, the father the other, especially when they are jointly present to their child.

Gender comes to be understood in this perspective as a dual

formation of Desire guided by maternal and paternal mediation of children's entry into the human world. "Maternal" and "paternal" are structural features of the interpersonal world inhabited by a child's Desire—respectively a Yes shadowed by a No (a bliss you can't completely count on) and a No with a nimbus of Yes (a discipline you can be loyal to)—rather than sexual facts in a naturalistic sense. The structure is read into the sexual facts and gives them their full significance. Some writers argue that the intentional structure could be freed from sex linkage if child-care patterns were changed.[31] But while we are in this system, at any rate, the fundamental principle of gender duality and complementarity is the psychic duality between subject and object of Desire mapped onto sex difference. As the subject becomes a conscious member of society, she or he steps into one of the two sex–gender camps, "genitally organized," and takes up the mission of representing one of the polarities of Desire—disciplined male subjecthood or darkly promising female objecthood—the dual structure now reinforced by all the social exigencies that express themselves through sex. Gender duality is Desire's proposed solution to every subject's incompleteness, a recovery of the lost primordial wholeness of union with the nurturer. Desire's solution is parallel to the solution sex provides for every subject's mortality. That subjective completion is impossible takes nothing away from the force and tenacity of the aim.

The dualizing structure of *turning* from one to an other appears in Desire's adventurous search for an Other-than-anything-yet-possessed that might complete the self (for which reason alone it is necessary to posit the "mysteriousness" of the supposedly complementary gender). And there is another turn in the specifically moral venturing of other-regard, that is, the turn from self to Other. The gender scheme provides a map for checking whether the turn is made, a map on which every individual can locate the other that counts (by convention) as truly Other. Same-sex preference may be made to bear the stigma of narcissism, a disagreeable, morally dangerous, and "regressive" self-absorption; for the heterosexist imagination, the turn to the other sex represents moral sanity and good citizenship. (But if the heterosexist imagination is fundamentally neurotic, then sanity would be achieved by annulling the order to "turn" away from primal bisexuality and autoeroticism.)[32]

The two most cogent vindications of same-sex preference are instructive, for both appeal in their own way to the moral imperative of the turn from self; both argue for a more perfect turn. A popular ancient argument contrasted the aesthetically and morally sensitive male love of males with the merely natural, animalistic love that can attach to females.[33] According to the rationale supplied by Plato in the *Phae-drus* and *Symposium*, love of male beauty and virtue aims finally at the definitive fulfillment of the soul, a transcendent Beauty–Goodness–Truth. To turn toward sexual relations for their own sake—and it is assumed that sexual relations with women would generally be more sex-absorbed than such relations with men, given women's relative lack of spiritual attractions—is to turn back from the true soul venture, away from the true Other. Even if the spiritual quality of women and men were equal, the turn toward men would signify as a turn away from the relation that is compromised by its involvement with the blindness of natural appetite. A second argument, one that enjoys more contemporary favor, claims that the morally important turn, the more perfect departure from self-absorption, is attention to another self as such rather than to generic qualities of a sex. At bottom, this is an argument against any sexual orientation whatever, or at least against attaching importance to sex type. Heterosexuals and homosexuals alike could claim that their sexual orientations are incidental or merely instrumental to their establishment of love relations with persons most decisively distinguished by their individual attractions. The maps of the human territory are not authoritative, on this reasoning; the Other appears only when love occurs. (Another way to erase the sex line is to order desire to *every* person's well-being, as in the commandment of neighbor love.)

To conceive homosexuality as a "perversion" is to construe it not as a failure to turn, an abortion of difference, but instead as a *second* turn relocating one's There (the Other), different from the conventional difference, too different. A new duality is created of normal and abnormal Here–There relations. We are not bound to understand other-sex and same-sex preferences as "normal" and "abnormal" respectively, but the two orientations do refer to each other in that the turns constitutive of each are correlated opposites; therefore we should expect the turns to comment on each other with some antipathy to the extent that they are really lived out. Either of the orientations can accuse the other of "heterophobically" resisting the very possibility of difference in desires, if it wishes to conceal its own commitment while (perhaps justifiably) taking offense at the committedness of the other side.[34]

Within the heterosexual female–male duality we find the other sort of opposition in sexual attitudes: the two heterosexual classes make turns that are formally the same but opposite in their bases and objects. One way to theorize it is to say that those who lack the means of pleasing the Mother but can identify with her stand opposite to those who cannot identify with the Mother but represent the means of pleasing her. Jacques Lacan says that from the position of the one who represents the signifier of Desire, the phallus, "the woman becomes, or is produced, precisely as what he is not, that is, sexual difference, and on the other, as what he has to renounce, that is, *jouissance* [bound-less joy]."[35] This way of marking "woman" must produce a radically asymmetrical gender scheme. That the Lacanian "woman" is a fantasy object is small consolation, for gendered life *is* fantastic.

Would the two sexes understand heterosexual duality in the same way, or should we look for duality in the understanding of the sex–gender scheme as well as in gender itself? Certainly we expect gen-dering to reach into the understanding of gender; but because human subjects speak a common language and inhabit a common system of conduct, we should not expect to observe a neat division between feminine and masculine theories. What we will find is different people exploiting and inflecting in their own ways theories that have become common human property from the moment they were put forward.

Good contemporary materials exist to illustrate this. We shall con-sider the different gender-theoretical responses of Julia Kristeva and Luce Irigaray to Lacan's "phallocentric" account. As Juliet Mitchell and Jacqueline Rose note, the main line of rebuttal to the phallocentric Freudian definition of "woman" as the negative opposite of "man"— namely, as one who lacks the phallus and who does not fully become the disciplined subject of language and reason or even an intelligible subject of Desire—has been to assert that women have "something of their own."[36] The female *proprium* would include the equipment of the female body, a distinctively female sexuality, a different itinerary of psychic development, the unique experience of maternity, and conse-quently (for some or all of these reasons) a different but fully valid way of feeling, judging, and acting. This positive definition of the feminine implies either a symmetrical appreciation of the genders or an asym-metrical view granting privilege to the feminine instead of the mascu-line. One response to Freud–Lacan would be to accept the reading of the feminine as the radical Other of a phallocentric regime, and then to valorize that difference principle positively—thus Kristeva. Another response would be to construct femininity not merely in antithesis to the masculine (even if the antithesis cannot be entirely escaped) but from the ground of female reality up, escaping the masculine version of gender complementarity—thus Irigaray and *écriture feminine*. The two approaches are complementary in principle.[37]

Kristeva has argued that feminine difference properly functions as a critique of masculine illusion and therewith of "everything finite, definite, structured, loaded with meaning, in the existing state of society."[38] This positivizing of negativity "obeys ethical exigencies" and thus parallels the ethically oriented critique of cognitive or symbolic totality that was earlier advanced by Theodor Adorno and Levinas.[39] The negativity here is only idea deep: the negative principle is just a marker in the symbolic system for a reality that transcends it, a reality that in relation to our thinking would better be called overflowingly positive.[40] In any case, Kristeva not only affirms what Lacan denies, a real fulfillment of Desire located outside the ascesis of symbols first in the pre-Oedipal relation with the Mother and possibly attainable afterward in somatic experience; she also affirms a nonalienating immersion in language, a "semiotic" plenitude different from "symbolic" signification, and in so doing she rejects the root mistake of taking one theory of language (the masculine "symbolic") as language's whole truth.[41] But just insofar as the Lacanian account of the linguistic subject's situation is correct, she accepts the negativity of the feminine as linked with unintelligibility and *jouissance*. Confronting Freudian–Lacanian culture with its Other, she simultaneously inflects its category of the Other with her own positive interpretation and poses an alternative to that categorization.

Irigaray develops a "logic" that is an alternative to the Freud–Lacan "logic of mastery" by which psychoanalytic theory perpetuates male domination of women.[42] Like Kristeva, she ironically agrees that Woman is a "mystery" within masculinist culture, but she wants the previously unspeakable specificity of women to come into language, and she tries to enact this, albeit at first (of necessity) "only in riddles, hints, allusions, parables . . . until the ear tunes into another music."[43] Female sexuality rests on a pleasure "more in touch than in sight," a continuous self-touching, in fact, that does not need the helps demanded for male pleasure. Feminine character, for which Irigaray uses female erotic sensitivity as an extended metaphor, is diverse and diffuse:[44] "Woman always remains several, but she is kept from dispersion because the other is already within her and is autoerotically familiar to her. . . . Woman derives pleasure from what is *so near that she cannot have it, nor have herself.* She herself enters into a ceaseless exchange of herself with the other without any possibility of identifying either. This puts into question all prevailing economies."[45] Irigaray carries out a turn from the Same–Other dualizing of sex in the Freud–Lacan scheme to a different experience of otherness, yielding a differently organized duality. The feminine Here that she is turning *to* semantically and *from* existentially—where she already is, to which she wants to lead discourse—as a Here that is avowedly "several," yet not "dispersed," contains within itself a dividing and turning that in the regime of the dominating Same can occur only as estrangement and conflict. As the terms of duality itself are redefined in this thinking, we cannot assume that the Irigarayan feminine opposes the masculine in the same way that masculine gender thinking takes the feminine to be its opposite.

For all that, the Irigarayan feminine cannot be presented otherwise than as *the* alternative to phallocentrism.

The category of "the Other," or difference, forms the common horizon of masculine and feminine essays in gender theory. From the Here of patriarchal culture, the first turns out to an enigmatic There that is always being lost or repelled; the second turns in exodus to a There with which it identifies, yet trying to preserve the fluidity of the disruption—making the There Here *as* There, and the Here There even while still Here.

*

It is no reproach to say that the Freudian type of gender theory reads an intentional duality into the duality of sex, for a gender-duality theory's purpose is precisely to expose such a conjunction of intentional and sexual dualities in the actual gender system, along with any constraints that perpetuate it—including metaphysical ones. I will argue now, however, that the greatest of all such constraints is simply the logic of this sort of theorizing.

A remarkable feature of Freudian thinking, which belongs in one way or another to all theorizing about ourselves, is that in creating a new analytical representation of the position that we are pretheoretically *in,* the theory at once poses an alternative to our original position, our "natural attitude," and places us in yet a third position as the thinkers of the theory. Our Here, in other words, becomes very complicated, the project of maintaining it becomes very difficult, and our options are freighted with this difficulty.

Position 1. In the natural gender attitude, I locate myself on one side of a semantic duality between masculinity and femininity, which thus takes on Here–There seriousness centering on the side of my gender identity.

Position 2. As the object of psychoanalytic theory, "I" am revealed to be the deposit left by events in the life of an originally undifferentiated Desire—an ungendered Desire that, moreover, continues to assert itself in "my" life and in fact remains "my" ultimate source of emotional energy and orientation. So my Here is not squarely located in a gender identity, after all, but is in part poised *between* the options of gratification offered by sexed/gendered humanity—female and male, feminine and masculine now looming as the two sides of a continuum that "I" split at that point in "me" where Desire confronts the world. I can turn in either direction. That the subject is divided between splitting this continuum (in Position 2) and standing on one side of it (in Position 1) *only deepens* the felt necessity of gender duality (in either position).

Position 3. Finally, in my position as a theorizer, I am not targeted on certain sexed embodiments (as belongs to my status as a subject of Desire) but instead face sexual orientations as alternatives in a field of view of human possibilities. I realize, of course, that my theoretical position rests on and must express my other two positionings willy-nilly, but it seems nevertheless that from the theoretical vantage point I am relatively free to turn from one human type to another, and another, and another, since I am somehow hovering above them instead of being caught between them. In this relative de-existentializing of the gender scene, I attain the very freedom with respect to objects that Desire deeply wants (in Position 2), but of course only at the price of neutralizing Desire. (Thus there is a contradiction in any attempt to win the bliss that the unconscious asks for by the mediation of psychoanalytic insight.) But now, ironically, new dualities arise, because as a theoretical thinker I split *intellectual* continua. The theorizer is free to imagine a variety of human character types but *not* to escape polarities like active–receptive, attraction–repulsion, form–energy, and so forth;

to think conceptually just is to find oneself between these opposites. So the freedom gained by escaping the bondage of Desire to the sex duality is taken away by the new dualistic constraints of theoretical interpretation. I can represent complexity in human relationships to sex, but only by dualistic iterations that reinscribe gender duality. For example, Jung knows that a thought–feeling opposition runs through human experience and across genders; he records this by postulating an affective anima in men and a logical animus in women.[46] The anima of men is, inevitably, "feminine," as women's animus is "masculine." How indeed could Jung have escaped the gender format so long as he was thinking about humanity in relation to sex? For gender *is* the human relation to sex, both as a psychic formation and as a principle.

Aesthetic or moral gender thinking creates an analogous complex of positions added to the natural gender attitude. By reflecting on ourselves in these valuational perspectives, we first focus on ranges of goodness as such, desirable and approvable in themselves—beauty and sublimity, care and justice—and then we arrive at gender métiers by relating the dualities we face on practical continua ("Do I act more this way or less?") to sex duality.

The radical alternative to these styles of thinking is not some sort of dialectical mediation, which always preserves the terms of duality; it is to pay no attention to sex duality, to let sex define neither Here nor There, so that when dualities crop up in the development of our thinking they will not write themselves into sex to capture the souls of women and men. We have seen that one of Freudian theory's definitive assertions is that regard for sex is a fundamental part of the structure of Desire becoming human. But this is based on the observation that the Mother-and-Father family compels such regard. Why *is* there a Mother-and-Father family of the kind that produces gendered persons? Why is the Mother the unique center of pre-Oedipal bliss and bonding? Why is the Father the archon of discipline and gateway to public life? To say that mothers have breast-fed and fathers have hunted is to go some way toward providing a historical explanation, but what is the status for us now of a psychic scheme based on a much-altered and further alterable division of labor between the sexes?

Such questions go beyond the scope of psychoanalytic theory; they become questions about social structure. Psychoanalytic theory leads us to ask them, though, and in that way effects a junction with social theory.

Social duality

Our chief model for theorizing a relation of sex to dual social structure will be the approach of Claude Lévi-Strauss.[47] Of course we will want to keep an eye on Karl Marx and Friedrich Engels as well. The most important lessons we learn will apply to structuralist and socialist theories alike.

Something like the scheming of Desire is a central desideratum of social theory, as it was also for psychoanalysis, but at issue in this case are the logistical demands of a structurally durable society. It became apparent in our preceding discussion that social structure is a condition of gender duality in that the family crucible for psychic gender identity formation is itself formed by a certain differentiation of maternal and paternal functions. One might question the relevance of social pattern to "gender" proper and prefer to speak in this context of "sex role"; yet social stipulations of sex role do reach into the dimension of gender to the extent that they call for and produce not merely behaviors but characters. We will observe them in this light.

Social theory must begin with some axioms of social existence. To have a continuing career, human groups must organize their practices and shape the consciousness of their members so as to ensure that they reproduce themselves, produce their material necessities, and protect themselves from all attacks and internal disruptions that would be fatal.

A sex-class system is the answer to the first requirement. That is to say, minimally, that "women" and "men" must be marked as such and allowed or compelled to generate a sufficient number of acculturable children and that there will be some institution, some version of "marriage," to provide a stable format for breeding. But it is not to say that either of the sex classes must be dominant or that sex-classing or marriage have any relevance for aspects of life other than breeding. And yet the minimal constraint that belongs to this limited-purpose classing and institutionalizing is ready to be strengthened and elaborated when other social requirements overlap with that of breeding. For example, the need to divide labor efficiently between hunting and gathering adds new meaning and deeper constraint to the sex classes, if the men are in a better position to hunt. The sex classes then become work classes as well. Or if a stable allocation of rights and duties within the group requires a home-based administration that women are better able to provide, then the sex–work classes become political classes. (This is the prehistoric matriarchal scenario for which Engels argued.) Or if an unequal capacity for violence distinguishes the sex classes, then they become political classes in another way, as the coercers and the coerced.[48] By the same token, marriage becomes an economic and political institution.

Of these different kinds of classing, none except sex are essentially dual. They *become* dual in being grounded on sex. Primitive economics becomes "hunting" and "gathering," modern economics splits between "the workplace" and "home"; leadership congeals in male "rulers" in the state or statelike organizations like the patriarchal family, while females come to epitomize that-which-is-to-be-ruled; and there are similar sex associations with "art" (vs. "craft") and other departments of culture. It has been a central socialist argument that the dualities in human affairs are caused by the institution of private property, of which the latter-day antagonism of the capitalist and working classes is only the climactic form. But Marx and Engels observed that the first form of property is given with the "natural" division of labor in the primitive human family insofar as it involves a "latent slavery" of wife and children to husband.[49] Property's first presupposition is sex duality. The reproductive value of the coercible sex is the first important resource for an owner to dispose of.

If sex duality makes ownership in the sense of disposing over women possible, we must ask, Why would it be socially necessary to realize this possibility? We cannot read capitalism into different conditions and construe every husband as an entrepreneur, every family as a sweatshop. But in premodern cultures there is, according to Lévi-Strauss, a crucial social structure—one he identifies with the principle of sociality itself—that is only realizable if women can be exchanged between one group and another. In this arrangement, women are "owned" by a group in the sense that owning is assumed by *giving;* and to see how sexual duality gives rise to the duality of giver class and gift class, we need to appreciate the logic of kinship systems.

In simple-technology societies, the kinship principle of organization goes a long way toward coping with all the group's practical problems. It is the *principle* of classing rather than natural kinship per se that is crucial. Human beings are inspired by natural facts of kinship (as they understand them) in representing this principle to themselves, and by and large it is read into the natural facts, but the operation of the principle is ultimately constrained by the community's survival needs rather than by particular relations of consanguinity. In theory, a kinship system could organize individuals in a fashion that was utterly arbitrary genetically and that still managed to renew the generations regularly, say, by tabooing sexual relations only within the class of persons who see a hawk before seeing a crow after their puberty initiation. (To be sure, genetic relatedness seems a more readily workable criterion of kinship than others we can imagine; but some societies do have other criteria.) And these kin groupings could be advantageous enough for economic and military activities, and conducive enough to internal peace, to persist for these reasons as well. One may assume that cultural evolution, not genetic, is decisive in accounting for such customs, even though the population as a whole cannot go on without perpetuating its gene pool.

If the ultimate social imperative is continuation of the community, the proximal imperative is sociality itself, or practical togetherness. There must be peaceful relations between group members—not merely absence of conflict but active cooperation and reciprocity. Now a kinship system looks at first more like a *splitting* of the community that would open it to dangerous oppositions. How could it serve as an instrument of sociality? The answer is that a kinship system is not just a splitting but, like sexual reproduction itself, a splitting and combining. Cooperation is initiated, maintained, and repaired by means of gift giving, and stabilized by mutual dependence. (Lévi-Strauss suggests that the sexual division of labor, whence comes so much of the content of gender norms, is a parallel "device to institute a reciprocal state of dependency between the sexes.")[50] For gift giving and mutual dependence to occur on a large enough scale to assure the well-being of the communal unit of survival, the splitting of kinship classification opens up interior space in which new combinations and thus renewals of mutuality are possible.

The incest taboo assures the splitting, while some system for forming subgroups and subgroup relations assures the combining. The reproducing or "biological" family is the likeliest element to be employed in subgrouping. But no matter how membership in subgroups is determined, their formation requires some mechanism for placing people in them. For the subgroups to be involved repeatedly in the process of forming subgroups, for them to be prevented from setting themselves up as indivisible social worlds unto themselves (enemies of the community, as Hegel also saw them), and for them to relate to each other group to group, it is necessary that persons be in some sense awarded or assigned by one group to another. Persons are the most important gifts in a gift-exchange network, and "marriage" is the form of a long-lasting or permanent givenness. "It is always a system of exchange that we find at the origin of rules of marriage."[51]

The binary pair of functions that translates sex duality into social duality is, thus, that of gift and giver. Sexual anatomy tells everyone that an individual belongs to one or the other class. It is a nearly irresistible criterion, even apart from its relevance to reproduction and the potential stability of the breeding unit, because it is the one binary mark that anyone can see right from the individual's birth. Wherever men are strong enough to hold the role of gift giver—which is to say, virtually everywhere—women are the gift-people. (Note further that members of the childbearing sex are better suited biologically to the role of "the valuable," the "precious gift," than members of the fertilizing sex, who individually are so much more expendable. Even so, an economic or other sort of scale could yield a different indication of value, depending on the situation.)

The kinship system will demand psychic differentiation according to the sexes' different destinies. Hence, as Gayle Rubin writes:

> The precision of the fit between Freud and Lévi-Strauss is striking. Kinship systems require a division of the sexes. The Oedipal phase divides the sexes. Kinship systems include sets of rules governing sexuality. The Oedipal crisis is the assimilation of these rules and taboos. Compulsory heterosexuality is the product of kinship. The Oedipal phase constitutes heterosexual desire. Kinship rests on a radical difference between the rights of men and women. The Oedipal complex confers male rights upon the boy, and forces the girl to accommodate herself to lesser rights.[52]

While kinship systems form the political and economic backbone of small, simple-technology societies, it might seem as though the politicoeconomic order of societies like ours depends not at all, or only exceptionally, on exchange of persons between families. But that appearance could be deceptive. If the family is always an important potential threat to larger identifications and allegiances, and if exogamy remains for that reason a prime condition of sociality, then kinship-system sexual duality should still be regarded as fundamental to civilized life. And in fact we do still think of "family" as fundamental. We can abstractly conceive of living conditions in which consanguineous groupings have no such threatening autonomy, where the affiliations with society are the only ones felt or valued; seemingly we are closer to such conditions in this century than ever before. But that we can really imagine so profound a psychic change as a removal of family attachment, and that, supposing we can imagine it, we could presently want it, are doubtful propositions.

Our attitude toward our own kinship system becomes awkward as we grow morally horrified by the main mechanism of an exogamous kinship system, the *giving* of members of one sex class. A woman today may resist the giving-of-women by keeping her "maiden name" in marriage, but this gesture, though symbolically powerful, is belied on two sides. Her maiden name is in all likelihood her father's name—which means that it continues to record the giving of her foremothers to her forefathers—and her own children's last names must carry either her husband's or her father's name forward. Her name independence is misleading, then, because her procreativity has still been appropriated by the male line. Radical resistance to the customary giving of women would consist of simply staying out of heterosexual marriage, but that option is by its very nature open only to exceptional persons and could not be a group norm—not, at least, without a different technique of reproduction.

Another possibility is open to us, however, if it is true (or when it becomes true) that patriarchy is practically obsolete in general. A revision of custom that would equalize the kinship status of the sexes and not significantly disturb the practical relations among nuclear families would be to create a new name for every marriage. We do not really need patrilineal or matrilineal markers to keep track of our relatives and observe an incest taboo; yet we may have more use for a name linking marrieds to each other and to their children. (Or if not, then all family naming can be stopped. But notice how great a difference there is emotionally between correcting sexual asymmetry by an apotheosis of the nuclear family and doing it by an erasure of familiality.) If exogamy can continue on this basis, coexisting with family attachments, then sociality does not depend, after all, on a politico-economic duality based on the sex classes.

*

The "natural division of labor" in the family is no longer binding. Although current arrangements perpetuate inequalities, it is possible to structure economic activity in such a way that breeding does not entail significant economic asymmetry between the sexes (except as values intrinsic to the activity of childbearing are concerned). If we continue to think in terms of sex-linked social dualities, therefore, the great constraint on us must (as we saw also with psychic duality) lie in the nature of our theorizing about society.

The traditionally more remote male role in reproduction has no doubt fostered a masculine sense of Hereness in "production" (Marx) or "culture" (Lévi-Strauss) conceived in opposition to "natural" processes. For Marx, the distinguishing feature of human life is that it is self-"produced," and indeed the production–nature opposition is embraced by feminist arguments for which the key to overcoming the oppression of women is dissolving the illusion that any human arrangement is unchangeably "natural." But since real sex difference implies that one sex class engages in an important activity, childbearing, that does not readily fit the "production" conception of human self-fulfillment, we perpetuate a sex-linked duality in our theory of human practice when we rely on that category.[53] So too the "cultural" ideal of full humanity, which we encountered earlier in Hegel's gender scheme, implies a transcendence of "biological" family life, which it has to posit as the to-be-transcended. Although women and men are equally involved in the biological generation of children, women are more involved in "biological" life insofar as they are, physically, together with their babies through birth and closely tied to them for a while after. This is just the woman–man difference. And so the culture–nature duality is planted in sex duality, women distinguished often by a unique mediating role between culture and nature rather than by a strict identification with nature.[54] If culture is then elaborated in binary oppositions, repeating the first opposition that set it up, so much the better.

The turn away from reproduction that constitutes these social dualities is not performed in just one way. From the nonmaternal Here, childbearing can be hushed up, dreaded, and disciplined, or it can be romantically celebrated, positively infinitized in value. Feminine turns *to* reproduction from the zones of life that have been separated from it ("the workplace," "the academy," "government," etc.) can balance the masculine turns within the total human Here, if women have as much foothold in the nonreproducing spheres as men have in the family. When procreation is Here it is neither chaos nor cosmos; rather, it is defining of Self (and the Here-word for it is *parenting*). But in any case, as long as our attention is caught by natural maternity, our practical sphere is bound to be structured by turns to and from it, and dualities in our interpretative schemas will mirror the turns.

The mirrorings of interpretation are affected by another factor as well, a further turn that brings our abstract thoughts back to ourselves. We cannot stop thinking until our major ideas acquire anthropological value. Ultimately, it must be the crucial ideal of a friendly macrocosm–microcosm relation (a religious attitude and principle) that makes us seek a *center of meaning* in human bodily life for such abstract dualities as attraction–repulsion or activity–receptivity, or for social dualities like public–private. Three great factual dualities in bodily life—living–dead, young–old, and female–male—are centers that stand waiting to receive all sorts of connections, both intelligent and unintelligent.

Human nature as a harmony of the sexes and genders

It would not be reasonable to conclude, either from what we have seen of the psychic and social dualizing of humanity or from our reflection on religious dualizing, that our own gender scheme is "logical" in the sense that it precludes alternatives. It seems that every aspect of the scheme we inhabit has conceivable alternatives. But should we admit ourselves to be pinned down at one point, the necessity of *some* form of dualizing? Is there some sense in which gender duality is "natural"?

Lévi-Strauss's claim that sex-classing accomplishes a socially essential "reciprocal state of dependency" implies that gender dualizing is humanly natural, if *nature* means that which satisfies conditions of harmonious adjustment. The adjustment in question is of humans to themselves. Because humanity is a social reality, it has to be balanced within itself; the category of complementarity is bound to be invoked in the self-interpretation of beings who form, so to say, their own environment. But here we must be careful about the relation between the natural and the necessary. It is plain that a set of utterly autonomous and self-sufficient individuals would not make up a society and, for that reason, would have a life decisively different from the human life we know; therefore, it is humanly necessary that forms of reciprocal dependence exist. Consequently it is natural to find reciprocal dependency realized in various ways in actual societies—and I mean not merely that we would expect ethnographic research to turn up such things as gender schemes, but that these schemes really express the human social necessity and render people humanly social by embed-

ding them in this expression. That is not to say, however, that any particular scheme must exist. Nor is it to say that a more highly elaborated
system of reciprocal dependency, as according to Durkheim's ideal of
an "organic" social synthesis of maximally specialized individual vocations, is necessarily better than a less differentiated system.[55]

Reciprocal dependency may take any number of forms, but duality
is a preferred principle for elaborating such forms because of the nature
of the problem of balancing. We have the most direct and sure feel for
the stability of a balancing system when we can weigh its forces in our
two hands, when *too much here* means *too little there*. I suppose I have
to admit that there can be a balancing of three because my own fairly
stable national government is designed on a principle of legislative,
executive, and judicial powers balancing. But this three is a system of
overlapping twos; when imbalance threatens, the virtue of the third
is that it can prevent the first or the second from overwhelming the
others.

Now we can take a further step with the idea of harmonious
adjustment. The humanly natural would also include any adjustment
that enables different aspects of human life to be held together in a
stable whole. Gender, the holding-together of character and sex, has
been natural all along in this sense. The relating of all our schemes
of self-interpretation to each other is similarly natural. Do we then
call "unnatural" any skepticism about gender scheming or programs of
microcosmic and macrocosmic dualizing? No, because the thoughts
of common humanity and of an open human frontier also require to
be held together with sex and the other given features of our life.
Totally unsympathetic criticism of gender dualizing would, however,
snap part of the linkage in human nature. By this conception of the
natural, a total renunciation of humanity's harmonizing project (or of
the differentiations of the human that set it up) would be "perverse."
Not abhorrent or illicit, necessarily, but definably perverse.

Does male–female duality have to be central in our construction
of human harmonies? Must a thinker be perverse who totally disregards it, or who proposes abolishing it? On the other hand, don't the
Impairment and Asymmetry Theses point to the possibility that gender duality is itself unnatural because it is more alienating (in its essential incompatibility with full individual humanity and justice) than
harmonizing? Do we now see, in this light, that the worst perversity
lies in constructing an illusion of sexual symmetry to cover a hideously
unnatural condition?

To appreciate the meaning of human harmony in relation to sex and gender, we must recall that gender duality is not an inanimate thing like a partitioned box but instead becomes real as people make *turns* in a sex-mapped situation.

The center of our psychological and sociological deliberations has been the breeding pair. I come onto the scene of the procreative relation first as a child, turning in one way toward my problematic self and in another toward the powers and privileges of adults. The adults belong to two sex types, one the same as mine, one different. I actualize elements of "reciprocal dependency" by comporting myself as a child in relation to grown-ups and as a gender-assuming subject who somehow realizes that only one sexual possibility, not both, can be mine. (This original renunciation of comprehensive humanity could be the psychic anchor of the social principle of "reciprocal dependency" in general.) [56] Then the entry of adults into the procreative relation involves a turn to "the Other" in multiple dimensions: the gratification or completeness projected by Desire, the other intending, the other sex. We need to perceive how these turns are made as well as their Here–There references. The particular Here–There relation instituted in each case of gender identifying, or for each party to the procreative transaction, gets interpreted according to several parameters: each party's existentially dualizing address of the other, with its mood; the semantic sex–gender duality posited by the common culture, colored according to whose Heres lend their perspective to its formulation, and in what moods; and, most importantly, the two parties' relative success or failure in being sensitive to each other's perspectives and in realizing through empathy and trust a common human Here.

(We must realize which turns are *not* made. In one conceivable culture, a reciprocal deference of genders is enshrined in a grammatical rule: males use "she" and females "he" for the indefinite third-person singular pronoun. But this beautiful practice is not our own. Another culture, nearer our own, uses linguistic markers of sex in a balanced fashion, so that neither sex bears alone the charm or onus of being the one to which we turn *aside*. For instance, an "actor" is anyone who acts, an "actoress" is a woman who acts, and an "actoret" is a man who acts. But the marking we do is unbalanced.)

The problem of asymmetry in gender value has to be taken up in these terms. Sherry Ortner and Harriet Whitehead observe that "in every known society, men and women compose two differentially

valued terms of a value set, men being, as *men*, higher."[57] They conclude that gender schemes are in themselves prestige structures (which
often fuse outright with other prestige-related scales that Westerners
would distinguish, like age or occupation) and that they reflect concerns more characteristic of males than of females. Across cultures
we find men typically positioned to compete for degrees of "public"
status (prestige) and women typically excluded from that competition,
assigned for better or worse to the subsocial, subpublic "biological
family." We could say that on this theory the Here-base of gender
scheming is that of the male, or more precisely males in relations of
rivalry and mutual esteem with each other and of centrality in relation
to women. The point is confirmed by the fact that it is much more
common for women to be categorized in their mother–sister–wife–
daughter relations to men than for men to be similarly categorized.[58]
And of course this asymmetry must shape the content of children's gender identifications, since children cannot perceive their parents otherwise than as how they are acting toward each other and as how everyone else acts toward them.

    In their millenia-long turn from the procreative family, males have
created realms of "production" and "culture," "politics" and "art," "philosophy" and "religion" in their currently dominant senses (although
they could not have done this without the collaboration of females).
No one who sets out to study "culture" can refuse to recognize the
masculinism and the self-proclaiming sublimity of these realms. But
the official restriction of women to lower-valued realms has meant not
only that they have been prevented from gaining male-associated prestige; more seriously, it has meant that a position was denied them in
which it would be possible to turn *from* "production" and so forth
to procreation—or, putting it in Beauvoir's language (though partly
against her reasoning), to make of reproduction a "project" with which
a free being can identify.[59] Males have long had their turning-from base
in the family. Not until women have what we credit as "careers," however, can there be a fully complementary valuing of mothering or other
family-linked activities. (What *can* happen is that Woman and Family
can be hypocritically pedestalized by men who actually prize their own
freedom from the domestic sphere more highly than anything in it.) It
is easy for a critic to confuse this feminine valuation with some sort of
backsliding to the oppressed position, and for a woman to be confused
about it herself—unsure of the relation between what she wants and

what men want for her—but the two positions are essentially different.

Is anyone who turns toward procreation returning to the scene of the original gender crime of male domination? But can human beings ever refrain from making this turn in some fashion?

Our answer will turn on our interest in affirming a human relationship to sexual reproduction. A person's sex could only be of zero consequence to the other persons with whom she or he deals if interpersonal dealings were generally severed from reproduction—that is to say, if we all turned *away* from reproduction. Such a turn could only be effected, it seems, by spiriting sex cells off to laboratories and would involve a near-total repression of awareness of the significance of the human sexual anatomies in any human-nature perspective: they would become a meaningless endowment, they would play no acknowledged part in the consistency of our life, they would be removed as points of reference for vocations, and they would not be terms in any harmonizing equation. In short, they would have nothing to do with what we are. We catch sight of this major change in the meaning of "sex" in a gender-abolitionist scenario like Rubin's: "We are not only oppressed *as* women, we are oppressed by having to *be* women or men as the case may be. . . . The feminist movement must dream of . . . the elimination of obligatory sexualities and sex roles. The dream I find most compelling is one of an androgynous and genderless (though not sexless) society, in which one's sexual anatomy is irrelevant to who one is, what one does, and with whom one makes love."[60] If sexual anatomy is irrelevant, "sex" becomes a universal capacity for certain kinds of pleasure. But the lack of differentiation in this "sex" means precisely that it lacks any common form with the sex in "sexual reproduction." (For the same reason, it is difficult to think of "infantile sexuality" as sexual.) I do not think that this de-dualized sexual sensibility would entail a separation of the feelings one has about being a child of parents and being a parent of children from one's pursuit and enjoyment of erotic happiness; it seems that the child–parent relationship is bound always to be present in some form and to have pervasive emotional ramifications in our lives. The difference would be that the "sex" of sexual reproduction, one of living humanity's basic physical endowments of harmonious differentiation and interdependency, would have been rendered invisible.

To get clear on whether or how we could affirm a de-dualized sexuality, therefore, we will have to see how profoundly we are now

committed to sexual reproduction as an explicit format for human fulfillment. This is the question to which all roads have been leading, and
we shall tackle it in the next chapter.

Here, meanwhile, is a summary analysis of the relations between
gender thinking and One-, Two-, and Many-Thinking.

1. Questions that require the answer "One" have to do with getting objective identification right—that is, ascertaining to what or
from what one may make a turn—and with ideals of inclusiveness.
Hence each gender is conceived to have a central meaning and a center
of meaning, and a chaotic, negatively infinitized field of meaning cannot be a gender at all. In turn, humanity must be unsplit if we mean by
it an inclusive realization of experience or power, and human nature
is ideally one set of harmonious relations among human qualities and
principles—which implies, not that gender division is unacceptable,
but that some principle of androgyny or complementarity is required
to form a single human Here out of reciprocating turns.

2. A question that requires the answer "Two" concerns whether
and with what fundamental orientation a subject exists. Hence gender thinking, which (like religious thinking) revolves around issues of
subjective location, is characteristically dualistic, and for the sake of
ideal human unity (point 1) we are moved to align gender conceptions
with the terms of basic intentional dualities. That is not to deny that
genders have a complex texture of subtypes and individual variations
or that the dual gender system is deeply unsettled by alternative sexual
orientations.

3. A question that requires the answer "More than one" is, How
is social life constituted? Hence no society exists without some sort
of interdependency; the social *vision* of interdependency is some sort
of class scheme. The existential duality of a social subject's life will coincide in part with such a scheme, so (by points 1 and 2) gender duality
is likely to appear as a fundamental social class duality.

4. The two chief questions that require the answer "Many" are
the empiricist What is there? and the critical What else can there be?
when these questions are cut loose from any concrete claim on the subject.

Hence dualistic gender thinking is at odds with existentially indifferent empiricism and existentially free criticism alike. But then so is all
thinking that would try to say what humans are. Human-nature thinking is self-identifying, existentially bound thinking. More at home in

an interplay of the One and the Two, the envisioning of a Here and a There and of an encounter between them, it says "Many" only when manifestations of generic and individual natures force it to, and then as a way of opening up to *them*—not as a way of opening up to anything at all.

Chapter 7

Gender and Procreation

If gender is the humanizing of sexedness, then the best reason we could have to affirm the gender principle or some optimal realization of gender would be that we want or need to affirm sexedness. The companion point is that if gender is intolerable, then we had better explicitly negate our sexedness, just as some of the most lucid radical critics of gender (Ti-Grace Atkinson, Shulamith Firestone, Monique Wittig) have recommended. But negating our sexedness would require us either to abandon the whole enterprise of procreation or to devise a different means of pursuing it. The first alternative is unthinkable, except with other-worldly premises. As for the second alternative, we can imagine various new reproductive strategies, each having distinctive advantages and drawbacks; all, however, share the overridingly important feature that they require so fundamental a change in the shape of our lives that they cross the border of the human. In other words, they go outside the domain of philosophical anthropology.

So much the worse for philosophical anthropology, you may say, if some of the main lines of human life as we know it cannot be accepted—give us science fiction, and utopian politics!

We do need science fiction and utopian politics. But insofar as we *are* human, insofar as we draw the meanings of life (also the meanings of fantasy and speculation) from the wells of basic human experiences like those relating to procreation, we need to recognize how we are involved in meaning these meanings. And so the attention of philosophical anthropology must be aimed toward such strangely neglected matters as what it is to be a child and what it is to be a parent; how female parenting (as such) and male parenting (as such) differ; and how the general *standing* of the feminine and the masculine depends on characteristics of mothering and fathering.

In the last part of this chapter we face an immediately urgent problem caused by the mothering–fathering difference. As our social order is now constituted, women and men do not have equivalent choices with respect to their participation in procreation, and the burdens of procreation are unfairly distributed. Insofar as our morality and politics govern our social order, then, the redemption of gender becomes a moral and political task. But gender difference infects our approaches to this task, as we can see by examining arguments for and against elective abortion. A free-abortion policy is justifiable, for there is a compelling moral objection to forcing an unhappy childbirth, but it is still not an adequate solution to the problem of gender injustice because there is also a compelling moral objection to abortion in most cases. Are there any policies that could break the practical link between sex difference and morally unacceptable consequences? I suggest one: universal reversible defertilization.

The relevance of procreation to gender and human nature

Procreation is the bringing of new human beings into the world. Although thought about procreation turns insistently toward the part of it that begins in conception and culminates in childbirth, in fact the generation of new human beings is not complete at birth but requires much subsequent "child rearing" or "parenting"; and even though we mark stages beyond which new human beings are considered independent in certain ways and no longer new, or no longer subject to "rearing," the question remains open whether procreation ever ends for any individual.

Mothering and fathering each have both sex and gender meanings. In the first instance, they refer to the human reproductive roles that are female and male by the very definition of the sexes—gestating and delivering in the one case, impregnating in the other;[1] in the

second instance, they refer to parental behavior that is generally apprehended in females and males or expected of them or judged fitting for
them. In the following discussion I will try to focus on what is intrinsic
to sexed parenting and to be wary, albeit mindful, of familiar elaborations of its meanings. For instance, I will not construe fathering as
everything that Sara Ruddick (with excellent justification) says it is:

> Although men can be mothers, in most of the cultures I con-
> sider most male parents are Fathers and most Fathers are men.
> Whether men or women, Fathers are not, in my terms, simply
> the male counterpart to mothers. Fathers, historically, are meant
> to provide material support for child care and to defend mothers
> and their children from external threat. They are supposed to rep-
> resent the "world"—its language, culture, work, and rule—and
> to be the arbiters of the child's acceptability in the world they
> represent. . . . Fatherhood is more a role determined by cultural
> demands than a kind of work determined by children's needs.[2]

Ruddick's Fatherhood takes in much of the conventional male behavioral assignment, or "sex role," and the central meaning of masculinity;
it has not been held closely to the biologically male basis of procreation.
(The disjunction drawn here between cultural demands and children's
needs should provoke us to take inventory of children's needs and to
ask how fathers might be positioned to meet some of those culture-
related needs by virtue of their relative detachment from childbearing
and nursing.) But since the interesting question is how male procreative activity funds the meaning of the masculine, and what sort of
variability this funding permits, I propose to peer through the window of masculine parenting at fatherhood in a narrower sense. By the
same token, I will not identify motherhood with feminine parenting,
even though a feminine female parent will certainly be *apprehended* as
motherly no matter whether she bore her children or adopted them.
What we want to see is how motherhood in the narrower sense might
shape the meaning of this nonmother's femininity.

Deviating from much current usage, I will not mean by mothering either a norm of ideal parenting or the fact of the primary role in
child care, because I take it that an equalizing of maternal and paternal
contributions to child care is for us a live social option.[3] Mothering by
men would be a matter of men's performing actions that are linked,
not only by convention, to the female body; paradigm cases would be

couvade and giving a baby milk.[4] It must be acknowledged that what women have customarily done affects the female center of meaning for mothering, even affects it a priori in showing what women *can* do, and so justifies in one way a definition of mothering as primary child care; on the other hand, the custom of predominantly female child care is now contested, and our thinking about the custom should not be closed by a definition.[5]

*

Although mothering and fathering are gendered realizations of humanity, procreation is not gender's center of meaning. We observe the sexedness of females and males apart from it. Yet we cannot make ultimate sense of female and male apart from it. If we lacked awareness of procreation, we could not tell why an Eve and an Adam should come onto the scene as female and male, no more than we could explain their teeth if we had never heard of eating. Furthermore, the only reason to *affirm* our specifically sexual duality is that we affirm our procreation scheme. Femaleness and maleness may be good for many things besides engendering children, possibly even more important things (as teeth, by analogy, are good for talking, which is sometimes worth more than eating). A goal other than sexual reproduction, perhaps some sort of psychic or spiritual complementarity, might be regarded as the final cause of sex difference—but we could not expect that goal to dictate the particular forms that make their difference a *sex* difference, in the way that the functional requirements of sexual reproduction do.

A great part of women and men's conduct is related to mothering and fathering. The achievement concerns that so often rule men and the affiliative concerns of women are extensions and supports of fathering (impregnating and being freer to provide) and mothering (gestating and being equipped to nurture), respectively. They are not only that. It would be a mistake to view all human action as a vast exercise in parenting. But it would be no less a mistake to suppose that procreation is a separate phase of life in which women and men suddenly adopt new manners. In many animal species there are indeed drastic changes of behavior in breeding season, but human life is not like that because in consciousness and acculturation we knit together all the meanings that are important to us and thus transcend hormonal seasons.

It has been observed that women are customarily linked all too closely to their maternal function; it has been argued that their iden-

tification with motherhood is their essential impairment and the key
to the social inequality of the sexes. Jeffner Allen writes: "If woman,
in patriarchy, is she who exists as the womb and wife of man, every
woman is by definition a mother: she who produces for the sake of
men. A mother is she whose body is used as a resource to reproduce
men and the world of men. . . . Motherhood is dangerous to women because it continues the structure within which females must be women
and mothers and, conversely, because it denies to females the creation
of a subjectivity and world that is open and free."[6] Taking as symp-
tomatic of our culture a statement by the Soviet Women's Committee
that motherhood is "woman's most important social function," Allen
(a woman) concludes: "I am endangered by motherhood."[7] Now suppose that the Soviet Women's Committee replied that by "woman"
was meant not "any human being who is female" but "a female human
being in the respect that she is female," and that "woman's social function" is not identical with, or exclusive of, or necessarily superior to,
human social functions that women also possess. This retraction of
an impairment implication is plausible, both logically and in the sense
that we can imagine the committee saying it and believing it. In fact,
this is the way Mary Wollstonecraft wanted to have it: "Speaking of
women at large, their first duty is to themselves as rational creatures,
and the next, in point of importance, as citizens, is that, which includes so many, of a mother."[8] Yet it is far more difficult to imagine a
Man's Committee asserting that fatherhood is man's most important
social function—this notwithstanding that the assertion is virtually a
truism, if by "man" we mean male human beings in the respect that
they possess the defining attributes of maleness. So we are alerted to a
real asymmetry in our practice.

The looser identification of males with fatherhood may help explain an amazing unawareness of procreation in philosophical anthropology.[9] One would gather from most philosophical portraits of
humanity that the generation of human beings and their reciprocal
formation in parent–child relations have no more significance than
our breathing air or circulating blood. Plato, whose *Republic* is the
greatest exception to this pattern of neglect, nevertheless understood
philosophy as a reach toward the kind of being that is not subject to
generation, namely, eternal form (which yet belongs to a process of
generation, as the cosmology of the *Timaeus* makes clear). Rationality,
the human being's power of apprehending eternal reality, must also
be timeless in principle. For rationality there is no "old" or "new"—

nothing unexaminably prior and establishing (except eternal reality itself as an object of recollection in the fable of the *Meno* and *Phaedo*), nothing unforeseeable and invigorating (except eternal reality as the erotic object in the fable of the *Phaedrus* and *Symposium*). Rationality acknowledges no creator and no messiah. It brings the past into the present in the form of a "metaphysical" analysis of the already-given; it encapsulates the future in the present in the form of an "ethical" analysis of the yet-to-be-done. Education is conceived as the charging-up of this ideal present for every subject rather than as the forging of relations between generations.

But what is concretely and momentously constant if not the generation of philosophers through procreation? Who ever thought, who hadn't been born? (To have a mother and a father is the universal human endowment.) Who ever reasoned, who didn't help in some fashion to educe reasoning in the young and consequently had to negotiate with new reasoning? (To participate in the succession of the generations is one great strand in the consistency of human life.) How many have ever reflected on embodiment without having within view their own equipment for mothering or fathering? (The default métier of human life.) Whose plan for society could ever bypass the requirement of sexual cooperation? (The fundamental harmony.)

All these considerations can be masked by a theomorphic construal of the human. Pure reason and purely open "human potential" know no parents and no children. The most interesting moment in the struggle to define a transhuman condition comes when the language of procreation is spoken but metaphorically bent—as when Plato directs our quest for renewal toward spiritual begetting (*Symposium* 208), or when Jesus fiercely distinguishes his spiritual parents and siblings from his natural ones (Mark 3:31–35). It is unclear in these cases what survives of the metaphorical vehicle. Plato and Jesus could be negating, not adapting, the structures of sexual reproduction; if that is the case, then the bold attack of our contemporary, Shulamith Firestone, on gestation and "child rearing" can be seen as a candid restatement of an old transanthropology.[10]

Two idealisms can be equally mystifying and false: an affirmation of the structures of procreation that does not acknowledge the dehumanizing effects of the actual forms they have taken, and a theomorphic revision of the human condition in which procreation is kept from playing any part. I do not say that either idealism is necessarily vicious. Maybe as paired partners they can keep each other honest.

But to assess this prospect we must first test our understanding of the anthropomorphically a priori category of procreation.

The structure of procreative activity

Taking up the question of what it is exactly that female and male procreators do, we can get a first orientation by looking at a problem that attaches to the word *reproduction* in Marxian social analysis.

Marx and Engels drew a suggestive distinction between production and reproduction as twin principles of social creation. Their own deepest tendency, however, was to assimilate the latter to the former. They call reproduction "the material production of life itself" or "the production of human beings themselves," thereby cleaving to their main principle that human life is self-produced.[11] To the extent that an important division between kinds of production does loom in their mind, it is the division between the more "natural" everyday renewals of human life—traditionally thought of as women's domestic work, including the bearing and rearing of children—and the more "historical," traditionally masculine activities in which technology and work relations develop in interesting ways.

Is it better to insist on a single all-embracing conception of production for the sake of overcoming the false separation of "natural" and "historical" spheres that has been a linchpin of gender oppression? On this path, we are readier to see how women's work has contributed to the making of the whole human world; and we are more sensitive to the historical specificity and alterability of women's roles. Or is it better, on the contrary, to reject production-monism as a symptom of patriarchal-capitalist thinking and to seek instead new renderings of women's and men's activities that are more sensitive, both descriptively and valuationally, to gender and other human-kinds differences?[12]

The most important clue here is how strange it is to speak of the production of human beings. Lynda Lange remarks, "If children are products, it makes sense to ask who should own and control them, a question which seems to me . . . morally unsavoury."[13] For her, this is a reason not to think of "procreative labor" as production. Alison Jaggar answers that under capitalism it does become natural to think of children as owned, and that we should expect a socialist society to abolish this objectionable aspect of "production" in the realm of procreation just as it would in other realms.[14] But I do not think that Jaggar can deflect Lange's point in this way. For all that capitalism may have favored treating children as property, and for all that some parents evidently do think of their children under this aspect, it is immediately evident to most of us that the ownership model is a distortion of the parent–child relationship and a crime against the humanity of the child—not least because we subscribe to capitalist individualism. Parents typically see themselves as regents; the regency model allows for strong (and possibly dangerous) motivation to control children's lives and yet excludes the conceit of ownership.

A related difficulty lies in the very notion of reproduction as applied to human beings. The object of reproduction is species-life or a family line; but while it is true that species-life and family-life are reproduced as a result of procreation, the proper object of procreation is neither of these things, but rather the new person. We stay closer to this center of meaning by speaking of procreation instead of reproduction.

It is not so strange, or not strange in the same way, to speak of nonprocreative domestic labor as production or reproduction. For the purposes of philosophical anthropology it is better still to interpret domestic labor precisely as "labor," observing the distinctions between labor, work, and action that Hannah Arendt formulated in *The Human Condition*, partly to oppose Marxian production-monism.[15] Domestic labor conforms to Arendt's conception of labor as activity that sustains life without changing or adding to our material culture, distinguished from the freer and more creative activities of work—"the work of our hands, as distinguished from the labor of our bodies" (136)—and also from deed- and history-making action, which uniquely requires speech for its fulfillment.[16] Procreation, however, does not fit the labor model, not even if it is identified with parturient "labor." Unlike cooking, cleaning, and so forth, procreation momentously changes the world: there is something definite to show for it (though not an artifact), something that reshapes the human situation (though not a deed).

The birth of human beings is the basis of the natality metaphor by which Arendt tries to capture the history-creating novelty of all true action.

> To act, in its most general sense, means to take an initiative, to begin. . . . Because they are *initium,* newcomers and beginners by virtue of birth, men take initiative (177).

> The miracle that saves the world, the realm of human affairs, from its normal, "natural" ruin is ultimately the fact of natality, in

which the faculty of action is ontologically rooted. It is, in other
words, the birth of new men and the new beginning, the action
they are capable of by virtue of being born (247).

Arendt grants a certain primacy to action over childbirth—"The new
beginning inherent in birth can make itself felt in the world only because the newcomer possesses the capacity of beginning something
anew, that is, of acting" (9)—and this may have the effect of allowing
procreative activity (which after all is quite unlike the political activity
that Arendt is most interested in) to slide back into the category of
labor. But procreation remains the first cause of action, and although
it is body-bound and belongs to a large-scale natural cycle, we cannot
but view it as the extraordinary beginning of beginnings, the "production"—in a sense more theatrical than industrial—of the advent of
persons. Anyone who pays attention is astounded by the procreative
accomplishment: "Another person!" Another person is not another
clean wash, another supper, or even another crop, but rather a new
road in world history and a new spin on the whole of it.

It is crucial to respect the extraordinary character of procreation if
we are to know what mothering and fathering are. The safest assumption to make is that procreation is an activity nonpareil. What, then,
distinguishes its manner of occurrence? What is unique about its time,
space, and causality? And where will it be necessary, in pursuing these
questions, to record a difference between mothering and fathering?

Procreative time

How an activity requires and shapes time determines how we are
able to pay attention to it and identify with it.

Procreation differs from other forms of labor in beginning at
a certain moment as a discrete venture. This is true whether or not
conception is intended, remains true even if the venture is repeated
ten or fifteen times, and is equally true of mothering and fathering.
Mothering and fathering also end together, by convention, at the point
of a child's majority. The whole period of childhood divides into a
gestation-and-parturition segment that is intrinsically very different
for the mother; a birth-to-weaning segment that is still crucially different for the mother although both females and males, with their unequal natural aptitudes, can "mother," that is, nurse; and a postwean-
ing segment in which any remaining difference between mothering

and fathering is only a prolongation of earlier experiences and arrangements. These three segments are of decreasing significance, therefore, as centers of meaning for the gendering of parenthood.

Outwardly, the nine months of gestation seem to be the same interval for father and mother alike. But for the mother this is increasingly an occupied time marked by an ever more constant and insistent awareness of the child. The father has this experience less directly, only by empathy and by the effect of changes in the mother's shape and habits on his relations with her. Every other human activity, except thought, at least stops for sleep, but even sleep does not remove the mother from the bearing of a child. If early child care is the sole responsibility of one mother, then this exceptional occupation of the mother's life continues in the child's constant need of attention. For the mother, procreation is grounds for incomparably strong feelings of happiness and frustration because there is nowhere to turn away from it. It is nearer than any other worldly activity (except for thought) to encompassing heaven or hell within itself. The mother is stamped by this. The popular notion that women are necessarily and exclusively fulfilled by motherhood is, of course, offensive in one way with respect to nonmothers, and in another way with respect to mothers (of whom it is not true), but it has its grain of truth in the fact that motherhood really does take over mothers' time.

Gestation is for both parents a time of waiting, of deferral and anticipation, but more so for the father, who can have almost no direct contact with the child. It is quite a long wait, like a farmer's for a crop, and those who do it (if they are not distracted by other events in that period of their lives) are affected in their valuing; in desiring a slow-arriving reward, their standard of worth lengthens and their expectations and appreciations become more long term. Possibly the school of gestation prepares the parents to weather the trials of child rearing and to sense redeeming quality in the experience as a whole, but in any case the ideal meaning of parental character includes this capacity for long-term valuing, just as the ideal meaning of the child is to be more than one is, an object of valuations that refer to hidden future developments.

Seen in historiographic perspective, childbirth is a climactic event thickly tangled with the ends of timelines past and the starting points of timelines future. There is the long past investment not only of gestation but, in many cases, of wanting a child, and, before that, of wanting a spouse or simply wanting to love and be loved; there is the long future of parenting, and the child's own life, and the lives of those who will be engendered or otherwise affected by the child. The birth channel in the mother's body, gateway between epochs of personal history, is the site of the climax; her pain and joy in childbirth is its central subjective intensity. Childbirth becomes the most powerful metaphor for any analogous reaping-and-beginning, like winning a political election or sending a completed book into the world.

After birth, the total duration of procreation, ending with the "result" of the grown-up child, is longer than all but the most ambitious life-spanning projects like building up a business or a professional career. It must be life-defining for those who invest care in it. In eulogies for dead people who have parented, the quality of their parenting is invariably held up for contemplation, not only to strengthen the general marriage-and-family sanctions but to give a pertinent and justly proportional description of a parent's life.

The lengthy time spent in parenting is not the whole reason it is life-defining, however, for the child is never strictly a material to be shaped. The child has all along a power of beginning and a futurity independent of the parent's. This open temporal horizon registers in procreation like a distant tug on the rope of everyday parental practice. Hence Emmanuel Levinas observes that the engendering of a child goes "beyond every possible project" and that the unencompassable time of the relation with the child transcends the fatality of the parent's selfhood—not the mortality of the parent but the tedium of *being chained to self*—in a way that the parent's own continuation in existence never could.[17]

The independent personal reality of the child implies that an essential part of procreative activity is conducting a relationship. Time spent in parenting is often labor or work in the usual sense, the getting done of chores, and quantifiable in the way that paid work is ordinarily quantified; but the other side of parenting, living in fellowship with a child, does not fit this model at all. Conversing and doing things with a child is, to be sure, an exertion of a kind, and an allocation of one's time. It involves a special watchfulness and thought. It is not just like spending pleasure time with a peer-friend. But it is *partly* like that, partly spontaneous, nonprofessional, not a chore, and not measurable by clock-time units. To the degree that parenting and related activities like teaching and health care consist of relationship, they are neither alienating nor prestigious in the manner of work; to the degree that the rewards intrinsic to relationship are not realized in these activities, or are insufficient to compensate for their strain, they become horrible in relation to the thwarted normative expectation. (Some of this horror is *typical* in mothering as we know it.) [18] The time of relationship is not a segment of life's timeline but a loading of the whole drift of one's life into each of the moments devoted to being with the other. What is at stake in a relationship is the rightness of one's life-defining orientation—so that love, blossoming in a day or in a decade, is always forever. This rightness is what relationship activity achieves. It is not an alienable "product" (as might be implied by Ann Ferguson's subsumption of relationship activity under "sex/affective production"), even if it is bound to psychological and social effects and is affected in turn by other social dispositions. [19]

A difference appears between the sexes in their possibilities of spending time in procreation, whether the clock-time of procreative work (to which issues of economic justice can be pinned) or the personal life-time of relationship. Procreation can be almost entirely incidental to a man's life. A man can leave his child before it is even conceived, and never return—thus, *never* be with his child. One wants to say in such a case that the father is not really a father; yet it is still "the father" who is less than a full father, the one on whose genetic line natural selection is operating, the one who, like the mother, can always significantly say, "That child *is* me *as* other-than-me." A procreating woman cannot keep all her time free in this fashion, although she can, by giving up her child or hiring a surrogate mother, cut down the time taken by procreation to the point that it becomes similarly incidental to her life. (Here we do not consider the alternative of reducing the time by aborting procreation. Notice, however, that by abortion a woman does not share the male possibility of procreating without an investment of time. She gains a kind of freedom with respect to procreation, but not a freedom of manner of procreation.)

If she is destined to spend more time in procreation, it follows from the relationship dimension of procreative activity, and not just from domestic seclusion or the dirtiness of child-care chores, that the female parent will gain less prestige than others who spend more time setting accomplishments before the public and that she will nonetheless be seen as enjoying an unparalleled opportunity for "happiness." A subordination that is a privilege! No amount of emphasis on the physical and mental demandingness of procreative labor, or on the political significance of personal relationships, will remove this implication. If by "mother" we mean the parent who spends more time parenting, then this is an a priori point about the nature of mothering. I think we do assume this about mothering, because of the division of labor we have grown up with; but procreative time could be allotted differently to remove this inequality without erasing the category of mother, that is, the qualitative distinction between the parent who bears the child and the parent who does not. Childbearing is a peculiarly full time and childbirth is an irreducible climax for the parent who is directly its subject.

Procreative space

The general mark of labor is that it is body-bound; its spatial sphere, therefore, is that of close proximity. The effects of work are more remote. It fabricates physically independent products precisely to satisfy aims that require space-crossing, like the transfer of goods or the sending of messages. A corollary of the work-product's independence of the worker's body is the possibility that work can in a sense be *done* by an instrument other than a human body—whereas machines can only save labor, never do it.[20] Thus the space of work is infinitely large, whether we are considering whence it might be effected or where its products might end up.

Procreation looks like labor rather than work to the extent that it involves a peculiarly intimate proximity during the mother's gestation and much physical contact for a long time afterward. But the labor connection proves tenuous on close inspection. Some aspects of procreation actually explode the labor model by virtue of their extremeness. The part of procreation that is called "labor," parturition, is one of the ultimate corporeally wrought changes in the human world—the other being the death of the hero.[21] Neither childbirth nor the death of the hero are voluntary actions in the normal way. In both cases the agent is imposed on, not merely by the general necessity that labor always answers to, but by a commandeering Other. The agent becomes the site of a necessary event as much as its doer, which makes a caricature of labor. Before childbirth, the object of procreative activity is *nearer* than near, inside the mother's body, while after birth the child's infinitely extended future prospects break open the everyday proximity of cohabitation. (Even as parents swaddle their clinging babies they can wonder who in the world their children will grow up to love, and this is not at all a tangential reverie but belongs to the substance of their parenting.)

The space of parenting is the space between persons, filled, like the space of lovers but unlike the space of friends and colleagues, with a sort of gravity of bodily contact; it is always being closed by washing, feeding, and reassuring embraces. Something remains of the presumption of contactibility between parent and child even in their friendship (or enmity) during the child's adulthood; when the grown-up child gives bodily care to an aged parent, this is a renewal of their original relationship, not simply a reversal.[22] Contact is the verification and symbol of the continuity between parent and child, the child feeling the parent as foundation, the parent feeling the child as vitality and possibility. Those who wish to sanctify some vision of the "home" or the "family sphere" are probably making appreciative reference, consciously or not, to parent–child contact—although many different practical arrangements allow for this contact.

Labor and work are done for the sake of parenting, but in this case the horizons of labor and work are bounded by the mutually attracted carnal reference points of the persons in relation and the potentially infinite space separating their independent spheres of activity. It becomes increasingly feelable, as the child's personhood forms, that a voice on the telephone realizes proximity and the proffering of a morsel realizes distance. Analogies with labor and work break down unmistakably here, and so too the initial difference between the spatialities of mothering and fathering disappears.

Procreative causality

What makes procreation happen? The first cause could be the senior members of two families deciding on an alliance twenty years before its consummation. It could be the hostility of a rapist toward a woman he doesn't know. It could be a single woman's desire for a child, which she can conceive through artificial insemination or by contracting with a so-called surrogate mother. Or it could be a heterosexual married couple's desire to create their own portion of the next generation as a sort of overflow of their love for each other. Of these scenarios, it is the last that has the most direct connection with the familiar idealism of gender and that therefore makes the first claim on our attention.

A sort of overflow? What is the actual connection between eros and fecundity? Impregnation confirms and extends the interpenetrating mutual belonging that sexual intercourse realizes only momentarily: the mother belongs bodily to the father whose seed she hosts, and the father likewise (albeit more abstractly and dismissibly) belongs to the mother to whom his seed has been consigned. The future of the child concretizes the future of the lovers' relationship and extends it into the new dimension of parental collaboration and the lifelong drama of the relationship with the child. In turn, the oceanic bliss of erotic love colors the parents' apprehension of this fruit that (often) comes so spontaneously from sex. The child is part of a greater stream of life to which we may entrust ourselves. (Possibly, as Schopenhauer suggested in his "Metaphysics of Sexual Love," the seriousness of erotic love is rooted in the lovers' unconscious will to determine the composition of the next generation; certainly our awareness of this issue helps explain our extreme interest in love affairs.) [23] When a child is spawned by calculation, or hate, or technical intervention, not as the overflow of love, there is a jarring sense that parents are forcing an event that of its nature lies outside their disposal and requires the special warranty of a generous, self-transcending motivation.[24] Who could be equal to the responsibility of bringing a person into the world?

On the multiparent model, the inordinate parental responsibility for a child is more adequately (if never perfectly) addressed by partnering, which has a logic different from simple combination. The parents' relation is collaborative in a remarkably profound way: collaboration in conducting a *relationship* lays claims on the self that go beyond the shared corporeal claims of labor, the shared technical claims of work, and even the inspirations of joint history-making. Nevertheless, the distinct parental partners can never form a completely united front in dealing with a child but must in some ways alternate in bringing their temperaments and principles into play. Although the parents began procreation by conjoining their sex cells, over time their contributions must often come in sequence. Ideally, alternation is fair to the parents and enriches the child's life. An ethos of alternation would be appropriate for any set of parents, not only for the stereotypical standards-setting male father and emotionally supportive female mother; but the presumption of alternation gives crucial support to a gendered scheme of parenthood inasmuch as it licenses and even promotes difference up to a point. It leads us to see sex difference in parents as an opportunity to diversify the parenting portfolio. Good-mother and good-father norms are instituted to keep the difference fruitful and within safe bounds.

Parents are the causes of procreation as decision makers and agents, but also as material causes. The medium of begetting is neither something external to themselves, as in ordinary forms of labor and work, nor their bodies alone, as in more superficial forms of play, but instead their *substance,* which is *spent* on a child. It is necessary that they spend themselves if the child is to be a being like themselves and not an artifact at their disposal.[25] (What the father spends can be infinitesimal, but the man who withholds this little seed and prefers to generate life by sheer technique, Dr. Frankenstein, is a horribly deficient parent who produces a horribly distorted child.) That parents are transmitters rather than authors of human actuality is as true of their psychic self-giving in parenting as of their first donations of flesh and a mother's direct provision of milk. Thus parents both do and don't do procreation; it is and isn't their project. They have a running joke about taking credit for their children.

A grim corollary of the transmissive-rather-than-active aspect of procreation is that people can be involved in it without conscious choice and even against their will. Women are specially vulnerable in that they find themselves the original site of unintended procreation. Consequently motherhood is tinged, even in happy circumstances, with an involuntariness that is foreign to fatherhood, and our sense of parental graciousness is profoundly different for the mother than for the father. The father is the one who could always choose to be elsewhere, otherwise occupied, so we thank him for being with us. (Alas, he thinks of himself this way; as Marguerite Duras says, "He has a terrible tendency to think he's a hero if he goes out and buys some potatoes.")[26] But the mother is the one who could hate us for what we put her through. What we thank her for is her love. The received meaning of motherhood would be profoundly changed if Adrienne Rich's vision were realized: "Ideally, of course, women would choose not only whether, when, and where to bear children, and the circumstances of labor, but also between biological and artificial reproduction. Ideally, the process of creating another life would be freely and intelligently undertaken, much as a woman might prepare herself physically and mentally for a trip across country by jeep, or an archeological 'dig'; or might choose to do something else altogether."[27] But what sort of grace would I recognize in a mother who freely chose to bear me in her body rather than employ easier artificial means? Why would she have imposed herself on me in that way, in such terrible closeness? Is she trying to magnify my debt to her—to glue us together forever? How would *she* feel if *I* had chosen to come into the world through her instead of by a clean and painless alternative route? None of these questions arise, at least not in reasoning consciousness, when childbearing is the inescapable order of things. The extraordinary burdens of childbearing and the absolute dependence of the fetus on the mother are tolerable precisely because they are not chosen. Or, to put it in the opposite light: if many women made this choice freely, what then would it mean if my mother chose the more distanced way of engendering me? If there were a *good* reason for a woman with choice to choose "natural childbearing"—if, say, the mother–child bond when realized in that way is indeed emotionally rewarding to the greatest degree, as has so often been claimed for it—then how could a woman really be free to choose the artificial alternative? Here is the knot in which the ideal of maternity is tied to suffering.[28]

The two sharpest edges of childbirth pain are cognitive, not sensory, in origin. They lie in the knowledge that a woman's life is actually threatened in childbirth and that a baby may arrive dead or abnormal. Under modern conditions these two uncertainties are greatly reduced, but they cannot be eradicated. The joy of successful delivery is overwhelming, then, for the twin reasons that the baby is safe and that it has stopped being a potential lethal enemy of the mother. Fathers who love mothers experience the relief very intensely in their own way, partly no doubt because they have guiltily relived the ordeal they inflicted on their own mothers; corresponding to this mother-referred aspect of fatherhood is the mother's awareness of fulfilling the trust or hope of the father in bringing forth the child that is also his (or, in the case of a father-counterpart companion, the child that *is to be* also his or hers).

The axis of female procreative experience and thus of female experience as such is the Good Birth, an astonishing event called by all commentators "marvelous," "magical," and so forth, but shadowed always by some degree of danger and fear.[29] Birth is also, perforce, the center of reference of male procreative experience, but in their distance from it men's imaginations have often run to the opposite dramatic center, namely, the Good Death, the hero's death, the ultimate commitment to the right cause, where the shadowing dangers are cowardly inability to face death and captivity to wickedness or folly in dying. The Good Birth and the Good Death are the carnal anchors of the permission and decision principles.

*

What is accomplished by procreation? The cynical answer, "More males for the armies and factories and more females to produce more males and females," states an important if oversimplified truth. The machinery of life requires the continual enlistment of the young; without regeneration, an aging population could not, while it yet lived, keep essential production and services going. One suspects that there would be a terrifying psychic staleness in this dying world as well. So society maintenance is an entirely valid motive for procreation that men and women would share alike, so long as they affirm their human milieu, and also a reason for procreators to be supported by their societies.[30] It is the *chief* motive, in principle, because the personal fulfillment achieved through procreation is dependent on this its objective significance. Children are rewarding to be around because they are tokens of the renewal of everyone's world. Furthermore, the sort of personal immortality that is envisioned in procreation presupposes a continuing human world to sustain one's lineage.

The renewal of the human world is only equivocally a "project" because, as we have seen, when we think of its human results we are bound to say that it happens through people, not that they undertake it or do it. In other words, procreation really is renewal and not mere maintenance: the coming of new persons into the world guarantees a future unlike the past, and our acceptance of this scheme entails a commitment to value the humanly new as well as, correlatively, our own finitude. But in the respect in which procreation is, for all that, an activity that people undertake, it must be counted supreme among the central human projects. One could call it the Project of projects to mark the fact that it furnishes the precondition for all others, that is, a continuing human world in which justice and knowledge and beauty and personal expression may be realized. It is true that procreation would be pointless if human beings did not pursue these other goods, but it is also true that apart from procreation no being with our sort of character would exist to pursue them. Unlike, say, respiration, procreation *addresses* the constitutive human limits of death and need of others and thus counts as an eminent project of reconciliation. And all these considerations must weigh equally on males and females.

In our discussion in Chapter 3 of central human projects we distinguished between the project horizons of opportunity and limitation. Returning to this distinction will help us understand how the great commonality in maternal and paternal motivation, the necessary human interest in sustaining the human world, implies a difference as well. Insofar as the sexes and genders are differently positioned in this world—and if they were not differently positioned, then sex and gender would be beneath our notice—their attitudes toward it must differ. Now, over and behind and beneath any strictly personal business being transacted through it, procreation means what the world means. If the finality of armies and factories really is imposed on procreation, and women are practically alienated from these activities, they must also be alienated to some degree from childbearing and parenting; and when they create a domestic world-within-the-world in compensation, men will be alienated from this alternative world in turn. If a note-worthy product of procreative activity is *lineage,* a corporate identity with a potentially endless extension over time, and women are rendered relatively invisible in the recording of lineage, then women must experience themselves as relatively submerged in the procreative process, and men must be alienated in turn from any woman-sponsored meanings of parent–child relation.[31]

Generationality, potentiation, and determination

The more particular accomplishment of procreation, the one that mainly fills the parents' field of view, is of course the raising of a child. A description of mothering and fathering is not complete if it does not reach into the parents' consciousness of the effect of their actions on their child; but to bring this out we must change our focus from procreative activity to receptivity, that is, the child's side of the child–parent relation. Returning to the scene of the Freudian story, we ask now what is implied by such a thing as a child–parent relation.

Every human life is generational in the broad, objective sense that it has a place in a long and unended sequence of births. It belongs to the generations. The human generations together form a unity both genetic and historical; within it, there are specific family and social lineages to which a life belongs in recognizable ways. I inherit my great-grandmother's eyes, and certain attitudes and manners of my region. I would not know myself if I did not know these connections, and at the same time—such is the unity of the generations—my own life counts toward the ultimate definition of the family, society, and humanity as a whole.

One dimension of generationality that strictly concerns the living is that a human being is virtually always older than some contemporaries and younger than some others. We use the structure of the procreation sequence along one line, the generation, to interpret the age distribution of the population, so that my "seniors" are those who may be age-classed with my parents and grandparents, while my "juniors" are the age-fellows of my children and grandchildren. Until I am old enough to identify with parents, I have no juniors, and when my parent class has disappeared I have no seniors. These consistencies form another warrant for saying that human nature is generational: we are subject to generation not only in having to be born but in having to live within a spread of generations. But the importance of saying this becomes apparent only once we apprehend the content of seniority and juniority relations. Here the child–parent relation is the center and paradigm.

The defining character of children as relationship partners is their dependence. Parents and parent equivalents are constantly pulled to them to meet their practical needs. Less conspicuous because usually less urgent, yet utterly pervasive and fundamental, is the dependence of children on parents for the forming of mind. To be a child is to rely almost totally on seniors for a knowable and interpretable world. The condition of the possibility of Kant's deducing the conditions of the possibility of knowledge was Kant's having learned from his seniors, centrally his parents, to speak and think. We could make the same point about his sense of justice.[32] The world-interpretive powers of his seniors, though not ahistorically immutable, formed a mental instrument that Kant could not decline to make his own; and if we can after all detect historical contingency in Kantian conceptions it is because they were formed on a mental foundation bequeathed to Kant by his elders. The "historical a priori" in both senses—the structure that constrains thought at a given historical moment, and the general necessity of a historical conditioning of thought—is concretely enforced in the parent–child relation. In spite of our tendency to think of this endowment as a free-floating structure, a "heritage" or "objective spirit," and notwithstanding the real structural autonomy of language and other elements of culture, all parents rediscover the fact that the endowment *happens* in their engagement with their children. As we continue to teach each other through life we prolong or extend this in some ways blessed relation. Learners are always children (and one who lacks mental childlikeness cannot learn well); those who mediate learning are always parents (whether or not they are good enough parents to be good teachers).

Childish dependence implies parental power, helpful or oppressive. Parents have authority over children not as their *makers* (as Sir Robert Filmer had maintained, to be perspicuously refuted by John Locke) but as their *disposers*—we should further say, their already-disposed, culturally transmissive disposers.[33] Children's characters are formed in a negotiation between their own spontaneity and parental response, and children's access to the central human projects is through parents who say what is right, what is true, what is to be loved, and what has to be accepted and how. If there is a dimension of choice in trust then it is a bit misleading to say that children trust parents in all this, because children have to grow up mentally before they can do other than accept parental determinations. (Nevertheless, even the most mature and active learning or spiritual formation includes not only trust but this original childish pliancy, which always lives on in our need for parental blessing.) In the continuing limitedness of our alternatives we are all children—of our culture, and of the universe. Utopians and skeptics, proponents of apparently radical alternatives, are in this condition, too, though in the maximally active way; and they are originally installed in it by really being children.

Generationality is a structure at once of age difference and, in its relation to sex, of gender. "Parent" is concretely "mother" and "father," while these are always also "parent," in the way that "human" is "feminine" and "masculine," while these are always also "human"; the only difference is that the centers of meaning are formed by the specifically procreative functions of women and men rather than their continuously observable sexed bodies. The weight of the mother–father distinction is indicated by the features of human generationality just noted. The construction of the collective Here of family and society and the shaping of the child's knowing and valuing are inflected according to this distinction.

What can we determine a priori about the child–mother and child–father relations, setting aside all hypotheses that could be superseded by different parenting arrangements even if they were verifiable in the present order?

In a single-parent or same-sex-parent household, a child may not know this for some time, but in principle all children know that they depend at least for their existence and perhaps also for much else on members of two different human types. The equation that yields the child is female *and* male, a union of the different. And only for the child—not for any particular man or woman, who might pass each other by—does Marx record an existential truth in asserting that "the immediate, natural, and necessary relation of human being to human being is also the *relation* of *man* to *woman*."[34]

The child's dependency therefore runs in two channels, through two dispositions. In a world in which cooperation between women and men had been shrunk to the minimum of secret, indirectly accomplished breeding, children growing up with one sex or the other would experience an incongruity: where (they would wonder) is the fabric in which my existence is rooted? Among us, any child ignorant of one or both of its biological parents entertains a version of this question, and although it is never a trivial question it need not be, in such cases, fateful. But children who were ignorant of male or female parenting in general, or whose exposure to either sort of parenting was significantly attenuated, would be missing data that bear crucially on their apprehension of the genders. They would be underdisposed.

Before saying more about the nature of the data, I want to prevent the misunderstanding that the point I have just made constitutes an objection on the part of positive gender thinking to single or same-sex parenting. I think it does imply a question about single or same-sex parenting, but only one question among others, including questions that anyone would want to pose to two-sex or two-gender parenting. No doubt it is better to grow up in a peaceful and loving environment without a father or mother than to be subjected to destructive strife or oppression with both. No doubt it is unwise to expect one or two primary caregivers, whatever their sexes or genders and however desirable they are individually or as a team, to bestow on a child everything that she or he needs from parenting; the parenting enterprise should be envisioned more widely. But it is equally beyond doubt, in the anthropomorphic perspective of positive gender thinking, that the exclusion of mothering or fathering from a child's life is an impoverishment of it. We can imagine situations in which such an exclusion occurs involuntarily or is justified, as a defensive act, by the poisonousness of the available forms of one of the genders, but (in the positive perspective) we would have to judge the situation unfortunate and the decision desperate.

One part of the child's sexual nexus has been indicated: the biological parents must be male *and* female, so that the child's dependency runs on these two lines. An exclusive *or* now joins this *and*. Children must come to know themselves as embodying one, not both, of the sex types, so that they are of the mother's *or* the father's type, unchangeably. Aristophanes' myth of the hermaphrodites expresses children's incompleteness when measured against the conditions of their own generation. The sex system entails a great decentering, the subjection of children to a system of complementarity—perhaps a "narcissistic wound," or perhaps the first stirring of a sense of vocation—and invites children to see heterosexual marriage as a prime opportunity to achieve completeness through their own action. Admittedly, other considerations may put them off heterosexual marriage, and they may attain an experience of completeness otherwise than by repeating the heterosexual liaison, but that liaison is always, we might say, the first thing to consider, privileged by its proven efficacy and the claim it makes on our gratitude for existence.

When children grow to become fecund parents, they are faced by a significantly different *or*: their child will always be a boy *or* a girl. That parents stand behind a veil of ignorance with respect to the sex of their unborn children and are powerless to change sons for daughters or daughters for sons is an important humanizing factor that militates against devaluation of either sex. It pits their prereflective child-fondness against sex discrimination. (Unhappily, sex discrimination can still operate through abortion and infanticide.)

What do the essential differences between female and male procreative activity come to, for the child's purposes? The child will learn that the father is the one who *could* be totally absent from its life, who is present by choice; and one implication is that the fundamental reassurance desired by the child from the father is regular (not necessarily continuous) appearance to the child to prove that the child is still chosen. (Israel developed a theology of chosenness to express its relation to a fatherly god.) By observation or by hope, the child associates this parental identity with an ethic of scrupulousness, perhaps imitates it, in any case counts on it. This ideally stable form of child–parent affirmative encounter, or spirit, becomes a core constituent of the spirit of masculinity. For the mother, in contrast, it is physically impossible to stay away from the child while gestating, and practically almost impossible to stay away from the child (except by mother substitution) as the provider of milk. She is not, therefore, so much the one who chooses the child as the one who puts up with it, and the reassurance wanted from her is continuous presence or presence on demand. That means that she cannot be allowed five minutes' peace. Her body is important to the child more for the experience of carnal continuity than for other sorts of contact (compare the checking, testing contact of fatherly roughhousing). The maternal ethic to be relied upon, and possibly to be entered into, is one of sympathetic responsiveness. Feminine spirit is then prompted by this form of child–mother meeting.

It is traditional to point out that the paternal negative, the father's freedom and potentially near-total absence from procreation, has a positive implication in the father's prerogative of choosing the child (so that children may experience chosenness) and in "his" greater freedom to represent the larger world to the child and mediate the child's entry into it; and also that the maternal positive has negative "apron strings," continuity with the mother threatening to hold back the development of the child's independence. These views are not simply false, but failure to think them through adequately causes fathering to be seen as superseding mothering. The relative importance of fathering is supposed to increase as the child matures. But it can be shown that the parenting balance is more complex than this and cannot be asymmetrical in principle—even if female and male parents can be valued unequally in a particular culture, family, or situation.

To be a child is to need support. No child is genuinely supported, however, who is imprisoned in dependence, on the one hand, or abandoned, on the other. Thus it belongs to the nature of parental support, whether maternal or paternal, to provide both challenge and affirming continuity. The smothering mother and the distantly exigent father are degradations of maternal and paternal presence. These are, however, the *characteristic* distortions of mothering and fathering, recognizably related to the sex-based parenting specializations. The specializations are grounded in this way: the mother's self-giving solidarity with the child is emotionally and metaphorically potentiated by "her" real experiences of childbearing or nursing, while the freer and more critical aspect of the father's relation to the child likewise draws force from "his" actual separation from those functions. This means not that the mother-as-such *is* a nurturer, as womb or breast equivalent—for the mother-as-such is a *parent,* and parental support includes more than this nurture—but instead that the nurturing side of mothering is especially heavy with significance and relatively more (though not exclusively) trustworthy psychically and socially. (When we judge smother-love to be a deficiency in mothering, we prove that we intend mothering to be parenting; when we feel smother-love to be a betrayal, we show that we had begun by really trusting mothering to be parenting.) By the same logic, the way in which we trust fathers to parent includes a relatively greater trust in their exercise of the more critical parental offices.

Thus even before we get as far as acknowledging that women father and men mother, we see that mothering and fathering each involve a combination of functions, albeit with opposite slants of strength, and that it would be an error (and an insult) to judge either mothers or fathers—let alone women or men—incapable of parenting adequately in the absence of their role complements. If the present analysis grants an advantage to a two-gender parenting ensemble, on the grounds that it allows for stronger representation of both sides of parenting, it also admits a greater danger that one or both gender representatives will specialize too much, resulting in a partial or pervasive degradation of the parenting that a child receives.

A second advantage/danger belongs to the alignment of sex with parental gender. For example, a woman's childbearing or breast-feeding experience is a subjective intensification and symbolic funding of maternal specialization; she has an advantage in this over a male provider of mothering, an advantage sufficiently large that I hold back from calling any man a "male mother." But her physical motherliness could cause her to be less free for the more detached side of parenting, and this effect would be reinforced by social arrangements that "confine" her to childbearing and nursing. It seems, therefore, that her society owes her an encouraging measure of freedom from primary child care *for the sake of her mothering* just as society ideally supports good fathering by enabling men to be more attentive to their children and their pregnant mates. (We know that society most often acts quite otherwise: it anxiously tries to secure the base of mothering precisely by confining women as much as possible to female procreative functions. We can take this as an index of the magnitude of the trust that is trying to form in order to rectify our generationality.)

Perhaps the most worrisome implication of the present analysis is that it appears to ratify a traditional parental time schedule in which fathering takes over from mothering the preeminent role and thereby renders it of lesser value in adult consciousness. An impressive manifestation of this scheduling is the change in the sex ratio among children's teachers as they move from earlier to later schooling. We do not have here a happily symmetrical division of responsibilities. Men only rarely want to work in early education, while women very often aspire to teach in colleges and universities. There is a marked slope of prestige upward to "higher" education, which together with the sex bias in its leadership implicitly elevates fathering over mothering. Why does this sexist pattern obtain?

To appeal to the notion that "prestige" is at all events a masculine affair is to abort the question rather than answer it. Nor will it be a satisfactory answer to assert what is true as far as it goes, that higher education is more prestigious because advanced learners are more mature, from which it follows that their educators are less parental (more "collegial"?)—not if we have been right in thinking that all teaching has a parental aspect.

The question of prestige in education launches us on a detour that will take us to a new set of metaphysical grounds of gender duality, grounds that also offer a new perspective on education.

The weightiest-seeming reason that could be given for the greater prestige and male-affiliation of so-called higher education is that the Good Death is more interesting and creditable than the Good Birth. It is more intellectually and morally absorbing to contemplate the circumstances in which Socrates and Jesus and Nelson died, and their reasons, than to reflect on an event that is outwardly always the same and ideally always happens for the same reason. As education progresses, the balance of emphasis shifts from the enabling basic habits, skills, and information to the "great issues"; we learned to read and write and behave ourselves in groups so that we could one day wrestle with the implications of Socrates' conflict with the polis. True, Christian culture has maintained a terrific interest in the Good Birth of Jesus, but only our knowledge of how Jesus goes on to die picks this baby out from the masses of other babies.

To try to lift out the fundamental structure responsible for the shift of interest to death and to decisiveness in general (battles, treaties, elections), we could say, "Death is always after birth. Death is always in front of us, subject to calculation—it is up to us to determine our position with respect to it—while birth is always behind us, necessarily to be taken as granted, over and done with." But somewhere in the unfolding of this line of thought, a bell goes off warning of bias. Birth always behind us? That is not true for a pregnant woman or, more broadly, anyone with an interest in procreating. Death always after birth? Is the world about to die, then? No, in reality the world is always being renewed. Are "decisive" events the key ingredients of history? No, history is equally constituted by the arising of things and the opening and incubating of possibilities. If one fails to see this side of history, one cannot understand what has been decisive in it. (Did Lincoln's war lead, as he said it would, to "a new birth of freedom"?)

We may back up now and question the privilege of maturity, or actuality as fixed form, in relation to youngness and potentiality. We do live forward, trying to do and be certain things, moving from fields of possibility into possibility-closing determinations. Looking ahead, our attention is always caught by the conclusions or decisive occurrences that terminate most sequences of occurrences. We also look back in time for the births or arisings that set up those achievements; the from-many-to-one structure of determination (>) is only half-graspable without its preceding from-one-to-many structure of potentiation (<). But interest in births is not only a nostalgic reading-backward of the sign of potentiation (which would make it a quasi-determination). In our continuing progress in time, every determination, if it retains significance for us, becomes apprehensible as a new potentiation. The kind of determination it is (and whether it is worth making) depends on the kind of potentiation that it also will be. Neither determination nor potentiation can be called primary with respect to its complement, because each requires interpretation by the other preceding it and again by the other following it. Thus the whole of any sort of history, ideally simplified, could be represented either in this way:

$$\ldots < > < > < > \ldots$$

or, equally well, in this way:

$$\ldots > < > < > < \ldots$$

To represent a primal ground of history, whether as creation or salvation, it would be necessary to cross the signs thus: $\gtrless$. Could it ever be entirely clear what this signifies? Can we understand, for example, a fundamental unity of Form and Receptacle as these principles are deployed in Plato's *Timaeus*? Potentiations and determinations have to be separated from each other to interpret each other. A genderist account of creation would of course be one that assigned one gender to the creative principle, but to do this it would be necessary to place one of the metaphysical signs first, *the complementary one*. For example, a story of a masculine creator presupposes the metaphysical priority of potentiation-asking-for-determination, like Tiamat awaiting her conquest by Marduk, or the face of the waters awaiting the divine spirit of Genesis 1. It seems, then, that the will to make history intelligible tilts us toward some gender bias or other, and not simply because we relish the concrete analogies of mothering and fathering; but, on the other hand, the same will to intelligibility never lets us absolutize one principle in a way that would leave us at peace with our bias, because each principle is always joined to the other, before and after.

The duality of determination and potentiation comes to light in human generationality. In the $> < > <$ or $< > < >$ sequence, we read the determination signs as marriages (preceded by births), the potentiation signs as fecundities (followed by deaths).

We were already following these metaphysical lines of opening and closing when we interpreted intentional life as a dialectic of bodily extending and centering ("The Structure of Embodiment" in Chapter 4). Now we can see better why genders would be affiliated with modes of embodiment—why, for instance, José Ortega y Gasset would say that Woman is " 'substantially' confused" and "her body *is* a soul." [35] The birth function of potentiation is aligned here with the extending of the intentional center. Woman's soul is her body and is confused (for Ortega) because, in the outward, opening-up reach of potentiation, any focus held in the center is subject to blurring or mingling with other forms as the perimeter of the reach expands. In contrast, masculine consciousness is clear and definite because its overriding reach is inward, centering and focusing. It is in making this latter sort of reach that a woman could feel endangered by motherhood and by gender discourses like Ortega's. But as we contemplate the alternative sorts of consciousness (which are always at the same time alternative sorts of embodiment) we are reminded by the logic of determination and potentiation that centering and extending must interpret each other, that assertion and wondering cannot be free of each other, that ascesis (ultimately the Good Death) and commitment to the flesh (ultimately the Good Birth) cannot be free of each other. That this is true as a proposition about the conditions of intelligibility, and not merely as a proposal for social complementarity, ensures that sensitive psychologies will be "androgynous" in some way—that Jung, for instance, will give men their anima and women their animus.

Potentiating and determining modes of intention should be detectable in manners of conversation. In one place C. S. Lewis refers without enthusiasm to women "whose general conversation is almost wholly narrative"—its substance being particular persons and incidents, rather than ideas and arguments.[36] This would commonly be taken as illustrating the traditional feminine affinity for the particular as opposed to the masculine affinity for the universal. I propose, however, that feminine contemplation of the particular is deeply interesting because it opens from the particular onto all the possibilities of life, held in view *as potentiality*—making each person equivalent in one way to every person, your child as interesting as my child or anyone's—while the secret of the masculine interest in the universal is that it throws a rope around sprawling possibilities and ties them down, not to just anyone (which would be arbitrary), but to "historically significant" persons and definite ideas. The interest in the particular or concrete actually expresses a certain universality in the scope of reference, while the quest to define abstract universals reflects a narrowing of attention to mental particulars.

The ascetic corporeality of the Good Death is the purest possible concentration on the Good Idea. It gets the body out of the way (for the women to cry over) so that the Idea may hold the field. But the Good Birth puts a life in the field, the food and referent of thought. The death of Socrates is interesting because it implosively centers the meaning of Socrates' life in his poisoned body; the interest of Mary's giving birth is that it writes the meaning of her life (and another) outward into someone else, which is an effacement of the self-as-determiner insofar as it takes our attention away from the birthing self, yet at the same time an exaltation of the self-as-potentiator.[37] Socrates, as a death, interestingly sums up a career; Jesus, as a birth, interestingly opens for new definition the lives of humanity and God. A good essay written on Socrates—and this would be the more usual college essay—would discuss possible formulations of *the* meaning of his career as defined by his death, while a good interpretation of the birth of Jesus—paradigmatically, Luke 1–2—would amplify its portent without settling a definite fate on it.

In studying history, we find it difficult and often painful to consider the meaning of births. We can never fully know the potential of an actor or situation, and with the knowledge that we do have we must be resigned to the loss of most possibilities (including, usually, the best ones) as events unfold. Beginnings do not leave the same kind of trace as endings; even when we can locate significant beginnings in human births, majorities, weddings, the commencement of reigns, and so forth, our living forward from them more than toward them makes them less graspable. To the limited extent that women's contribution to history can be identified with childbearing, we find here a metaphysical reason for the effacement of women in history—certainly not a sufficient reason, either normatively or explanatorily, but not a negligible reason either. No sooner do we state one such asymmetry, however, than we realize that there must be another one visible from another point of view. In a different sort of history, perhaps the male-associated happenings currently thought of as "decisive" would be harder to grasp and more easily effaced. How many "decisive" events have been sterile in fact? How many events that were both decisive and fruitful deserve less attention than the fruit they bore? The pages of prestigious deeds, opportunities capitalized upon, would yield to evocations of what it was to be alive, to worry and to rejoice, in a more nurture-minded construal of the past.

One might think that no such alternatives of construal can exist in the natural sciences inasmuch as these disciplines are committed to a purely determining view of phenomena for the sake of the practical determinations of experimenting and engineering. But analogous issues do exist wherever there are zones of what we call "indeterminacy," as Evelyn Fox Keller's treatment of the problem of slime mold aggregation beautifully illustrates: dissatisfied with the widespread but unsupported assumption that a "pacemaker cell" must regulate the process, Keller seeks a mathematical expression for the *order of compossibility* in which the slime mold action occurs—a "global, interactive model" providing the two-sided sort of insight that both rules out and rules in possibilities.[38] Most important arguments in evolutionary biology seem to me to be of this form. I will exercise restraint and not say anything about quantum physics.

But to return to our nearer concern: The metaphysical study of potentiation and determination does expose some of the roots of masculinism in the higher studies and a bias toward fathering in the higher teaching. The actual state of affairs is not, however, as one-sided as ideology or sex-ratio statistics might lead one to fear. All good teachers and faculties strike a balance between mothering and fathering, both in the quality of their relations with students (challenging and supporting, being scrupulous and being present on demand) and in their construals of inquiry (aiming at closings and openings of thought). And the balance is needed in kindergarten and university alike. But the success of teachers or faculties in realizing this balance cannot be unrelated to gender alignment. Do not let this analysis of education pass as mere illustration of ideas about mothering and fathering: individual gender sensitivity and faculty sex ratio really are central issues for pedagogy and scholarship.

Only by a collaboration between mothering and fathering—which ultimately assumes an enabling partnership between women and men—can a generationality be formed in which sons and daughters are equally at home and the determinations and potentiations of our existence are equally appreciable.

*

Our detour through the question of the Good Birth and the Good Death has produced yet another gender-duality theory, this one linking the difference between female and male procreative activity to the metaphysically fundamental duality of potentiation and determination. I am attracted by the tint of this conceptual lens, but I realize it must like any other gender-duality theory be held loosely and used as an exploratory heuristic or as a diagnostic of imbalance. For genders not only transcend dichotomous gender definitions, because they are human; they also transcend any assignment to metaphysical poles, because they are real. (Our discourse on gender is not finally controlled by the metaphysical structures we are able to conceive, anyway, but by spirits.)

Gender and issues of procreative choice

Maternal involuntariness is an ethical and political problem. Under still-prevailing social arrangements, mothers are hindered more than fathers in fulfilling their responsibilities to themselves and their children alike. Clearly their physical bond to their children is being taken advantage of. A mother cannot get away from her child without doing what looks like violence to the child. (Paternal neglect is a less obvious sort of violence, partly because it is refracted through the mother, who must try to compensate for the father's absence by her own work.) The bondage of mothers is variously shaped by their communities' policies governing marriage, birth control, abortion, sterilization, maternity, child care, divorce, and inheritance, and globally by the whole gender system that spiritually sustains the formulated rules.

The most elementary unfairness in a gender system would be an inequality here at the effective core of gender's center of meaning, the procreative core of sex. It is a question not just of the burden carried by women within the procreative enterprise but of their freedom to become involved in procreation or not. On the first point, one can say that the issue of fair distribution of the procreative burden is addressed, however imperfectly, by the Good-Provider norm of fatherhood: there is a demand on the father to do *everything* for the children's well-being other than what the mother is bound to do. This "everything" might be too little, or—if the father takes over the child from the mother, posing as a higher officer of culture—too much. At least it represents a possibility of a kind of balance. But as for the second point, there is a decisive imbalance in Western tradition that norms of parenthood have done nothing to ameliorate. While women are expected to become mothers and their lives are considered defective if they do not, men are generally allowed much greater liberty with respect to conceiving children.[39] Of course men are endowed with greater liberty insofar as they are far less vulnerable than women to being forced to participate in conception. But we can imagine a cultural interpretation of this state of affairs quite different from the one we have, one that would see the interesting male challenge as finding a mate and the prestigious female accomplishment as leading a life separated from procreation.

The explicit policies that most directly affect the freedom of women generically with respect to procreation in our society have to do with contraception and abortion. The latter is now the most intractably controversial, but the former has important, relatively unappreciated implications for the meaning of gender.

Contraception

By separating sexual intercourse from procreation, contraceptive practices (like same-sex relations) symbolically remove individuals from their generationality. This is perhaps the spiritual nerve of natural-law objections to all forms of nonprocreative sexual activity. The principle explicitly defended by Aquinas is that reason, reflecting divine order, must rule our sexual behavior;[40] but what is reason watching out for here? Not to see whether sperm and egg cells are wasted (for they abound), nor whether the population level is about to decrease dangerously (which it rarely does, except in relation to questionable economic and political purposes). Rather, there is a threat to an ideal continuity between the identity of children in the respect that they are products of conception and the identity of adults in the respect that they are sexually active. There is an apparent impiety, a

dishonoring of human nature, in disconnecting these two identities—
as though the sexually active but nonprocreative adults were presuming to set themselves up as radically independent beings outside the
generational life stream. Part of the threat is gender specific. If sexual
activity is not part of a process that also includes women becoming
mothers and men becoming fathers, then the core of gender's center of
meaning is suppressed (in one way), so that, in principle, gender van-
ishes (in one way) from the sexual encounter; but since gender is our
humanizing interpretation of sex, the sexual encounter becomes objec-
tionably abstract, "hedonistic," in relation not only to social utility but
to the Self–Other gradient that sex was supposed to incarnate.[41]

In reality, the gender and generational meanings of sexual intercourse are not so easily erased, although they are veiled when we speak
vaguely of the "unitive" function of sex. Emotionally, a sexual encounter is most often like being united with a parent (your daddy, your
mama) and a child (your baby) at the same time. Thus generationality, with its gender inflections, shapes the meaning of sex acts willy-
nilly, because we are in fact generational beings, whatever our proximal intentions may be. It is true, nevertheless, that nonprocreative
sexual agents are spending spiritual capital that has been produced by
procreation. The generational meanings that make sexual activity feel
uniquely important arise in part from the matrix of mothering and
fathering. It would be the substitution of other means of procreation
for mothering and fathering, not nonprocreative sex, that threatened
this funding; but nonprocreative sex whispers (to ears *outside* intercourse) that we can get along without mothering and fathering.

One can argue that separating the emotional generationality of
sexual expression as such from the practical generationality of actual
procreation is dangerous because the rule of parental partnership—
mutual respect and long-term fidelity—is needed to humanize sexual
partnership. This too can be seen as an issue of continuity between
the child's indebtedness for existence to the combination of female *and*
male and the adult repetition of that combination in which mates assume the dignity of the parental position, for each other as well as for
the world. Some such logic of dignity must inform Pope Paul VI's
warning that artificial birth control opens a "wide and easy road . . .
towards conjugal infidelity and the general lowering of morality": "The
man, growing used to the employment of anti-conceptive practices,
may finally lose respect for the woman and, no longer caring for her
physical and psychological equilibrium, may come to the point of con-

sidering her as a mere instrument of selfish enjoyment and no longer as his respected and beloved companion."[42] Here the man seems to be able to look through the woman, in a fashion, if she does not figure as his procreative collaborator and as the mother of his children, sharing the dignity of his own mother. Now, even if we have established that the generational meaning of sex is present apart from the intention of procreating, we cannot deny that relationships do degrade into instrumentalism (including the instrumentalism of treating one's partner as a mere means of producing children). But why is it that the woman's more than the man's dignity is thought to be in jeopardy? Even on the premise that men are more liable than women to instrumentalize their sex partners, why are we bound to take with special seriousness any imperfections in women's hold on men's respect? The reason for the slant in our concern is that women become mothers and mothers are crucially different from fathers. And the logic of this slant comes more fully into the light in arguments relating to abortion.

Abortion

We have two compelling reasons to study the abortion debate. First, we should expect a gender theory to prove its worth by throwing light on any sex-related conceptual problem. Second, part of adjudicating the Asymmetry Thesis on gender is finding out whether an acceptable policy can be formulated to balance the procreative burdens of the sexes.

The ethico-political community faces a dilemma once it takes an interest in life in the womb. If elective abortion is permissible, then "innocent" unborn life is denied a protection that is granted to persons already born; a right to life is violated. But if elective abortion is not permissible, then mothers are harmfully and unfairly imposed on by the community, and unhappy births and lives are forced; right choosing is suppressed. To argue for one of the horns of the dilemma is to try to show that one of these concerns outweighs the other. Now while it is, to be sure, appropriate and necessary to interpret abortion arguments as ideological weapons in a struggle for control of procreation, what is presently of greater interest is the nature of the reasoning in each, or the way in which each tries to be right, good, or sufficient.

A valuable perspective on the abortion debate comes to us ready-made in Gilligan's work on moral psychology (see Chapter 5). The right-to-life position very well illustrates the masculine modality of moral concern in that it isolates the zygote, embryo, or fetus as the bearer of an abstract universal right. The mother's relation to the unborn child counts for nothing, unless her life is threatened so that her own possession of the right to life comes into play. On the other side, emphasis on a "right to choose" can be misleading, for, as Gilligan's interviews illustrate, the moral core of the decision to obtain an abortion is less typically an assertion of individual liberty and more typically an expression of feminine moral concern for the well-being of particular individuals and relationships. The morally bound character of decision making about abortion is not a reason to dismiss the right-to-choose formulation, however, for without the legal right of choice people cannot meaningfully make decisions in this or any other manner. Moreover, the right of choice secures the human freedom of women to engage in "rights" reasoning. Thus the outrage felt on the right-to-choose side with respect to the right-to-life argument is both that it unfemininely disregards the unique responsibility of mothers for children and that it violates mothers' masculine standing as choosers, treating them as mere reproductive utilities without a meaningful destiny of their own at stake. A corresponding ironic tangle in the thinking of right-to-life proponents is that they exhibit masculine reverence for the freedom of an individual's life from anyone else's disposition and yet also invoke a feminine horror with respect to a mother's rejection of her child.

Fundamental to the "rights" logic of arguments against elective abortion is the Good Death perspective; that is, elective abortions are subjected to Good Death tests and found wanting. Fundamental to the "responsibility" or "care" thinking that would sometimes choose abortion is the Good Birth perspective: some pregnancies are found to fail Good Birth tests. The abortion debate turns out to be more difficult to resolve than we would have suspected simply from noting the rivalry between "rights" and "responsibility" perspectives, because the very *possibilities* of applying the Good Birth and Good Death perspectives here *exclude* each other by that very nine-months' thickness of gestation that incorrigibly separates the sexes. The subject of birth reckoning is other than the not-yet-born child in the womb, while the subject of death reckoning in this case is other than an already-born child. We see this problem as though through a glass darkly in all the arguments that have been offered for and against the "personhood" of the zygote, embryo, or fetus.

For a full understanding of the dilemma it will be necessary to study the arguments. Readers who already recognize the moral antinomy in the abortion question may want to skip ahead to the solution I propose in the last section of the chapter. But anyone who does not believe that an antinomy exists, who believes that valid thinking is found only on one side or the other of the debate, should examine the evidence presented in the next two sections.

The Good Death argument. I will first give what I think is the best version of a right-to-life, Good Death argument for a moral (*not legal*) constraint on abortion. This version does differ from others that I have seen in several ways, most significantly in the grounds that it adduces for the wrongness of homicide; my purpose is not to be novel, however, but rather to make as clear as possible the strength of a well-known moral position that maximizes Good Death scrupulousness.

The argument (1) begins by establishing the conditions of justifiable homicide; (2) shows that the destruction of a zygote, embryo, or fetus is homicide; (3) shows that homicide is not justifiable in this case, except on the standard ground of self-defense; and (4) elucidates the homicidal intention in choosing abortion.

1. Death cannot be disapproved absolutely, since it is naturally inevitable, but we can and must disallow bad deaths, avoidable deaths, deaths caused by destructive intention rather than natural necessity. Voluntarily destroying a human contradicts and undermines a social peace on which we all depend and a spiritual togetherness from and toward which we all live. The human right to life expresses the requirement that each member of the community accept the existence of every other. But even though there is a fundamental evil in intentionally destroying human beings, sometimes killing *must* occur and therefore *can* occur in a justifiable way. As diamonds can be cut only by other diamonds, so one person's right to life can be overridden only by someone else's. I am entitled to kill to save my own life; by delegation of responsibility and authority, the military and judicial systems are permitted to kill to protect the lives of everyone in a formally constituted community. The fundamental outrage of homicide, that someone, "playing God," decides that someone else shall not exist, is qualified in self-defense killing by the forcing of this decision upon the one who does kill by the one who would have killed. Would-be killers precipitate death; self-defense killers do not decide that someone will die but instead which of the persons who could die would die more justly. They play God involuntarily.[43]

2. Does abortion of a zygote, embryo, or fetus cause the nonexistence of "someone else," a "member of the community," a "person"? Arguments in the negative rest on two related distinctions, one between biological humanity and morally considerate humanity or personhood, the other between potential and actual human life. Neither of these moves, as usually made, is reasonable.

It is claimed that while unborn lives are biologically human, the meaning of "human" is equivocated in applying homicide rules to them inasmuch as the morally relevant form of "humanity" is much richer than the biological. Unborn lives fail to satisfy criteria of morally considerate human personhood like self-consciousness and the ability to reason, initiate action, and communicate.[44] But moral consideration of the unborn rests not on a perception of their humanlikeness, or even on any sort of present encounter with them, but rather on the expectation of their future humanity and of future encounters with them. This expectation is held by the human community, not by the unborn themselves, and so is in force even though the subpersonal unborn cannot be reckoned owners of their lives and futures in the same sense in which conscious beings own their lives and futures.[45] A zygote is not a person, certainly, but it is the first stage in the life-career of a being who typically is a person later on. (We cannot trace the career of this being back to sex cells before conception because, first, no single sex cell can become an individual, and second, a sperm–egg pair cannot be regarded before fertilization as an entity and thus cannot be a subject of becoming-a-human.)[46] Destruction of the zygote is homicide because the existence of the human person the zygote would have become, had it survived, is decided against.

At this point, a distinction is sometimes drawn between potential and actual life. The unborn life, since not *yet* human, is classed as potential rather than actual human life and therefore allowed the value of a resource but not the status Subject-of-a-Right. But this argument fudges the meaning of potentiality. It construes the zygote as a material that might or might not be used in the formation of a human being (which is roughly true of a sex cell), whereas the zygote is in fact becoming a human being, and for this reason carries the moral weight not merely of a quantum of life that is valuable insofar as someone might own it, but rather of a future owner of life. (A zygote that we knew was destined to become only a mole, or to be spontaneously aborted, would be in a different category.)[47] That the specific identity of an unborn life is prospectively continuous with the specific identity of a future conscious being means that the human community is preemptively deprived of one of its members by the destruction of a zygote just as, say, a rose hybridizer would be deprived of a unique new rose by the destruction of a certain germinating seed. That the rose was only prospective at the time of its destruction does not remove the consequence of particular, more-than-quantitative loss; that the person was prospective does not alter the fact that a particular place-holder has been subtracted from the human community.

The zygote might be deemed "potentially" human also in the sense that its becoming human is contingent on the collaboration of its mother through gestation. If the mother withdraws her collaboration, it may be argued, then no human being is the casualty of the ensuing destruction, because the prospect of becoming a human being belongs only to a zygote's life together with its mother's life, not to the zygote alone. The plausibility of this argument depends on finding a deep difference between gestation and other sorts of nurture on which children are totally dependent after birth. But the fact that one woman can gestate a child conceived in another's womb proves that gestation is indeed a nurturing of one entity (which is to say, a provision for that entity's future) by another and not a single life process. If the predecessor body of a newborn child were not the fetus itself but the fetus-and-mother, then childbirth would have to be seen as a sort of fission in which a mother-and-child being splits into a mother and a child. (And surrogate mothering would involve two fissions.) That interpretation seems even more unfair to mothers than to children. It is more plausible to think of childbirth as a fission of the fetus–placenta ensemble, but if we define the unborn life in those terms then it is the fetus–placenta ensemble that is the casualty of abortion; then we have as much or as little warrant to claim that the fetus–placenta has moral considerateness distinct from the mother's body as was the case with the fetus alone.

Granting the intimate and fundamental contribution of the mother to unborn life, abortion is still homicidal because of its effect. If we want to plumb the significance of the mother's unique responsibility for life in the womb, we had better shift to the question of justifiability.

3. Elective abortion would be justifiable or permissible homicide either because unborn life is to such a degree *continuous* with the

mother's life that it comes, like the parts of her own body, under her sovereign disposition or because the unborn life's interest is *discontinuous* with the mother's, so that she cannot be required to serve it.

Suppose first, then, for the sake of argument, that pregnancy consisted only of an internal budding in the mother, like the growth of a polyp, and that humanoid appearance and heart and brain function came into existence suddenly at birth. In a polyp removed before birth we would not find any properties more impressive morally than those possessed by a boil. But even in this circumstance we would know that the polyp's developmental program is not that of a boil and that the future consequences for the human world of removing it are greatly different from the consequences of removing a boil. Therefore, the action of removing it cannot be classed with actions like removing boils. That the destruction takes place during this undistinguished larval period makes it innocuous only in a superficial see-no-evil perspective; in the same way, it would be an only superficially good death if we suddenly destroyed a humanly inhabited planet while all its population slept, having made sure that no one else would ever notice the loss.

Alternatively, we might allow moral considerateness to the fetus for any of a number of reasons and yet deny that our obligation to the fetus can override our obligation to respect the will and physical integrity of its mother. *"There is room for only one person with full and equal rights inside a single human skin,"* writes Mary Ann Warren, responding in moral horror to invasions of women's bodies and lives by fetal-rights enforcers.[48] Warren's valid point is that one being's rights cannot require us to sacrifice another being's rights of at least equal exigency—in this case, the right of a woman to be treated as a person, not as an instrumentality. But it is possible to hold that a woman's rights as it were screen a fetus's rights, for practical purposes, in the unique circumstance of gestation, without pronouncing the fetus's rights inferior to hers in principle. We could (and should) forbid practical imposition on pregnant women while still proposing to them an ideal moral constraint. And thus we are returned to the moral problem.

Swinging now to the other extreme, we may suppose the unborn life to be a fully formed person (like the famous unconscious violinist who needs to use someone else's kidneys in Judith Jarvis Thomson's scenario of involuntary life-support) to ask whether mothers have a duty to give bodily support to the lives of others.[49] When, in this instance, we dismiss the presumption that either a mother's choice or her sharing of her substance makes her responsible for unborn life, it be-

gins to seem unfair to blame an aborting mother for subtracting someone from the human community, for she is primarily acting to preserve
her own basic bodily autonomy rather than to interfere with someone
else's life course. But two contrary considerations are telling. First, no
such thing as a child can exist without limiting adult autonomy because
children are essentially dependent, most profoundly so in their earliest
life. (Thomson's figure of the adult violinist, which she says is meant
to concede personhood to unborn life, actually represses the feature of
essential dependence.) Second, children's specific dependency in gestation is an ordinary, usual condition of anyone's living a human life.
If it is an imposition on the mother, it is at least not an exceptional
one like the shock of waking up one morning connected to a violinist.
That life *always* begins in this way means that elective abortion unfairly
discriminates against its victim. Analogous fairness requirements are
associated with a universal entitlement to education. Perhaps a school
system could not be blamed for failing to educate children with unusual handicaps if it lacked funds for the necessary special equipment;
but surely it would be culpable if it failed to provide the ordinary and
usual means of instruction, such as teachers and textbooks, to every
child in its jurisdiction. How then can it be fair to deny a human life
the universally necessary means of coming into the world?

It will be objected that we do not have an established social responsibility for birth, a birth system like the analogy's school system.
Precisely because the practical responsibility for birth and child care is
imposed almost entirely on mothers, it is they who must decide, with
each pregnancy, what can be afforded or what is fair.[50] The first part
of the answer to this objection must be that the existing allocation
of parental responsibility is certainly unfair to mothers and in need of
correction. But we must go on to note that if so much responsibility
is given them, they severally compose the de facto birth system—for
there cannot fail to be a working arrangement for births—and it must
be their responsibility to enforce fairness requirements. If everyone depends on mothers for life, it can no more be fair for one mother to
turn away one life than it would be fair for one teacher to turn away
one student in a world where (let us say) all and only red-haired people
were expected to be teachers, and students could get an education only
from the red-haired people in their neighborhoods.

If lives must be subtracted from the human community for individual or social self-defense, there must be a due process for their removal, a process not controlled by private considerations. Unforced

"playing God" is impermissible. Like capital punishment and unlike most other kinds of legal killing, abortion is performed deliberately, not under the duress of some immediate threat to life, so the demand for due process is appropriate. But the unborn pre-person, unlike the convicted felon, cannot be understood as having done something to forfeit its right to life. How then could due process decide against it? An overpopulation problem could conceivably render all new children threats to a society's survival, and then abortions might be performed for the same reason that people are thrown out of lifeboats; but if this were done, it would have to be done fairly, as by the sort of lottery that achieves justice in a lifeboat. In our own circumstances, the sort of harm that babies can involuntarily inflict on their mothers and on society is not of the sort that justifies killing; if it were, many an unwanted relative or drug addict could be gotten rid of.

4. Distinctions among intentions in homicidal acts are morally and legally important (as between murder and manslaughter), even though the nature of an action's consequence has its own separate importance. Therefore, we should look carefully at the intention to abort.

"I do not want to have *a* baby" expresses a contraceptive intention. "I do not want to have *this* baby" expresses an abortifacient intention. The distinction may not be clear, subjectively, to the unwilling mother (or to others who take part in the decision); she probably bears no ill will toward the particular life in her womb, except that she probably would rather it had never existed there. Still, it does exist, and while she does not imagine it to be a person, she does take an attitude with respect to the person it will (or would) be at birth: homicidally, she wants that person not to exist. That is the reason for choosing abortion. If she waits until the fetus is brought to term, it will then be too late to destroy it, because it will then be clearly wrong. She is not yet faced with a person, and so she cannot have a murderer's state of mind; but she is faced with the prospect of a person and therefore knows that her decision determines whether or not a person shall exist. Her more-or-less conscious sense of playing God makes it a soul-searching decision. It feels like a forced decision too, because the consequences of bearing an unwanted or inauspicious child are so dreadful, and that feeling provides subjective justification according to the "Which death?" logic of self-defense thinking.

It appears that although the intention to abort is not murderous, it is inherently divided and uneasy, since the desire to prevent the existence of a person acknowledges that personhood at the same time that it denies it. Therefore it cannot be an innocent intention. The existence of this homicidal intention is, generally speaking, an artifact of women's unhappy and unacceptable social position—they are not free in conceiving and they are deprived of partnering in child care. But arguing that abortion is nonhomicidal, either objectively or subjectively, cannot give us a morally acceptable solution to the problem.

*

Some elements of the preceding argument, and its main tenor overall, will stink in feminine nostrils. (I can tell this with my own feminine nostril.) The argument is decisively abstract in several respects. It treats the mother as a utility by which new lives come into the world, and that is an outrage to her, not merely as a person but as a mother. The asymmetry between the female and male parts of procreation is not allowed to count for anything. The circumstances of the particular births and prospective new lives have no significance, unless they activate the purely formal self-defense rule; such an argument, as is often said, cares nothing about "quality of life." Worst of all, the ideological smoke screen thrown up by the argument's abstraction has reactionary force: it assures the continuing subjection of women to their disproportionate procreative duty and, as a necessary consequence, their powerlessness to change the arrangements that oppress them.

No one may decline to take these problems seriously. Nevertheless, I submit that our moral thinking about procreation cannot do without the masculine perspective expressed by the right-to-life argument, a perspective founded on a certain detachment from pregnancy that *frees* us to realize the significance of conception, the unborn life's kind of potentiality, and its illimitable moral weight.[51] No one who understands this argument can ignore it in good conscience. The cogency of the view of the unborn pre-person as the bearer of a right to life licenses the abstract invasion of the woman's body and the setting aside of quality-of-life issues, for it is an essential moral gesture to say, "Let there be justice for all, though the heavens fall." No doubt a pragmatic justification can be given for crediting this gesture—for one thing, a legal system cannot exist without its support—but originally it credits itself: we find in it one of the basic affirmations of other persons as spiritual fellows and thus one of the origins of moral existence.

There is another.

The Good Birth argument. The "right to choose," we have already noted, is a misleading principle in the present context. To show that the autonomy of the abortion chooser has moral priority is not yet directly to show why anyone should choose abortion. The heart of our problem is that women (and also men) sometimes believe that abortion is their best choice, that it is not just indifferently permissible but *right* in some way. We must therefore pay attention to the moral thinking that motivates elective abortion.

The primary object of contemplation for the one who chooses abortion is not the act of abortion, and the lead question is not whether the death it causes is morally acceptable. Rather, the abortion chooser looks ahead to the prospective birth of the child and asks whether the birth and all its consequences are morally affirmable. "What kind of life would the child have?" "What would this do to my family?" "What would this do to my life?" In other words, Can I accept what the birth means?

Good Birth arguments in favor of elective abortions have several typical ingredients that may or may not be found together. They (1) consider the implications of a birth for the lives of everyone who would be related to it, (2) apply criteria of beneficence, and (3) appeal to a concrete need of self-defense.

1. While the right-to-life argument abstracts unborn life from all its human connections, willing as it is to let the heavens fall, a Good Birth argument insists on taking all effects into account, rejecting abstraction's violence against the particularities that engage compassion.[52] Fully actual persons make a fuller claim on care; one sees in them what there is to spoil or lose; hence a birth that does serious harm to living persons is unacceptable. Besides measuring the threat of harm to herself, the woman considering abortion feels the impact of birth along the lines of relationship in which she stands to the father, her family, her friends, and social and economic institutions. Among the harms to be reckoned with are results of disturbances in these relationships. The prospective birth is a new object thrown into this web, possibly a bullet that would tear it apart.

The sheer complexity of considering everyone who would be affected by a birth has the negative result of deflecting the application of general rules. Gilligan reports that Sarah, one of her abortion decision interviewees, "sees no resolution that does not leave conflict, no way of acting that does not exclude" and "no formula for whom to exclude."[53]

2. Sarah says, "I would not be doing myself or the child or the world any kind of favor having this child" (92). A good birth must at least do *someone* a favor, preferably everyone. To bring a human life into the world without expressing love in the act is impermissible because

it only achieves, at best, a distorted version of interpersonal affirmation, the respect-for-life half of relationship without the concern-for-life half; in this it is like "respecting" the life and autonomy of sufferers by leaving them alone in their pain. The abstract respect for the unborn shown by the right-to-life argument must not be confused with love.

To decide whether having a baby would be beneficent, it is necessary to make utilitarian calculations, and in doing so one overrides other general moral rules with the principle of maximal utility. Admittedly, the meaning of "utility" and "benefit" is logically dependent, in part, on moral rules that must be independently definable, which is a weakness of utilitarian metaethics;[54] but this does not constitute an objection to the utilitarian weighing of benefits in a concrete situation, where what counts (and what can be positively measured) is the meaning of consequences to particular parties. It is conceivable, for example, that one father's hope for a child, another's feelings of inadequacy, and another's objection to abortion on right-to-life grounds would be equally weighty in the calculations of love so far as they concern fathers.

Betty, another subject in Gilligan's abortion study, says that she finally decided not to have the baby so that she would be able to go back to school. Looking only at her conclusion, one would think that she had violated the rule to maximize benefit by preferring her own interest to anyone else's. But her train of thought shows that the issue is not so simple: "When I first got pregnant, I wasn't sure what I was going to do, and when I first found out, I thought to myself, 'This time it was my fault, and I have to keep the baby.' But then, I stopped drinking and stopped getting high because I didn't want to hurt the baby. And then, after a couple of weeks, I thought about it again, and I said, 'No, I can't have it, because I have to go back to school'" (112). The decision to go back to school is in Betty's own interest only on a morally advanced conception of her interest. By taking herself seriously as a prospective mother, a new field of need comes into her view; the self that feels the need for education is more responsible and constructive and will become still more so as a result of education. The moral advance is rooted in the character of her reasoning process, which moves from the heteronomous thought that she has to keep the baby because "this time it was her fault" to the autonomous thought that she does not want to do harm. (Another advance sometimes seen in abortion thinking is from fantasy to moral realism.)[55] Once Betty takes responsibility for avoiding harm, she realizes that a precondition of promoting a good life for children is helping herself. The abortion is one step backward that prepares for two or more steps forward. She would not be a good mother if she did not lay the foundations for the best possible life for her children.

(We can see, incidentally, that Betty's shift of perspective implies more than one individual's maturation. It represents a social event, an assumption of responsibility by women generally. The woman who says, "I have to keep the baby because it's my fault" is a prisoner of patriarchal regulation. Even if one thinks that she should decide to keep the baby, one cannot wish her to do it for that reason, nor may one prescribe to her in a way that amounts to maintaining that imprisonment.)

3. Women choose abortion not only for constructive purposes but simply to prevent what would feel like their own destruction. Ellen says, "I think it is a matter of choosing which [course of action] I know I can survive through" (89). Cast in this light, the argument might be thought to lack moral respectability. While it appeals to the self-defense rationale for killing, the definition and necessity of defense are here subjective, psychological, and ideally discretionary. The victim of a fatal bullet cannot be asked to get up and make something of life, but the mother of an unwanted child can be. And yet to disregard a prospective mother's requirements for livable existence—which ultimately must be measured not by degree of "adversity" or "suffering" as such but instead by the quality of her inclusion in the spiritual community—is to attack the foundations of moral life. Moral decisions cannot be made over her spiritually dead selfhood. Shakespeare's Caesarean-delivered Macduff, not of woman born, carries a tragic ghastliness with him: a dead mother's birth cannot be called a good birth, for all that we can console ourselves for her death with the life of her issue.

*

Thus forms our antinomy. The right-to-life argument ideally expresses a perfection of *respect* because it prohibits taking advantage of human life in its position of greatest vulnerability—tiny, silent, and invisible. The right-to-choose argument ideally secures the possibility of *love*. How can we be loving if we cannot stop a bad birth?

Formally, the divergence of emphases is easy to resolve. We should be both respectful and loving, regardless of sex, and we are obliged to arrange our lives so as to maximize and balance the fulfillments of both intentions. But we still have to reckon with a structural division of a different (though related) kind in the moral landscape, the fact that the maternal moral perspective centers on a point nine months later than the point at which the decisive paternal moral interest is awakened.

Birth is invisible in the right-to-life argument (just as it is not an event in the father's body). Indeed, it is of the essence of this argument that it prevents our being distracted by the circumstances of birth so that we can focus our moral attention on the individual human career that abortion would preemptively destroy. Any person's career is inevitably traced back to conception, the point at which a genetically fully funded individual first exists and a single developmental process starts. But the Good Birth perspective locates us elsewhere. Now we *cannot* any longer take the zygote-, embryo-, or fetus-centered perspective, for we are subject to a moral exigency arising from the impact of new life on the human world. This impact is traceable only from the event of birth. When we envision the moral situation from the vantage point of birth, life before birth becomes invisible.

The moral antinomy of abortion is one manifestation of a general tension in the procreative partnership of the sexes. The father, alienated from his seed, uncertainly and inessentially awaits the mother's delivery; the mother, alienated from her own body in pregnancy by the invasion of another life, effaced in a birth event the main significance of which is the fact that the other life has now entered the world, watches uncertainly for help from her mate and her community. The two parents' positions can be made equal before conception and after birth, but for nine months their perspectives are wrenched apart. A gender scheme mediates this contradiction but cannot dissolve it, since the contradiction is part of sex itself, gender's center of meaning. The maternal–feminine and paternal–masculine character types adapt to each sex's need to make the best of the procreative situation from its own position and to give practically necessary reassurances to the other sex. Abortion arguments arise and move against this cloudy spiritual horizon. While much can be made of the problem posed for intersex trust by the father's uncertainty regarding the facts of paternity, we should not overlook the destabilizing effect of this sex-based moral divergence.[56]

Both the arising of a human life in conception and the entry of a human life into the world at birth are binding points of moral reference. That is why each of the arguments we have examined is valid, yet insufficient. But we are obliged to put ourselves, if we can, in a position in which it is possible to make fully valid choices expressive of love and respect alike. Is it possible?

The solution: freedom of conception. The easy and plainly un-satisfactory solutions of our problem are to abolish the significance of the nine months: either to fix our birthdays at our conceptions and regard the gestating mother as a human hospital for care of the very young or to reject the claim of independent moral considerateness for unborn life and treat gestation as a female bodily process no different in its ethico-political status than, say, menstruation. These two theses simply deny their antitheses and so do not advance us. Nor do we solve the problem of principle by making a compromise choice of the approximate midpoint of gestation, fetal "quickening" or viability, as the boundary between the jurisdictions of the two moral arguments (although I believe that this is the prevalent intuitive solution in our society, supported by legal precedent).

The fullest solution imaginable is to rearrange the circumstances of procreation so that our problem does not arise. One possibility is to take gestation out of the womb altogether, substituting artificial means for the biological core of mothering. Or we could learn how to implant or develop wombs in male bodies and thus give all human beings the choice and responsibility of childbearing. Perhaps gender injustice will drive us to one of these expedients, either of which would annul the specific significance of sex difference and thereby lead to the disappearance of gender and therewith a decisive transformation of human life.

But there is a way to keep our problem from arising that does not do away with sex difference and so can be harmonized with the affirmation of gender. That is to prevent unwanted pregnancies *consis-tently* and otherwise to assure, so far as it lies in the power of everyone besides the mother, that no impending birth is a bad birth. Under modern conditions, the only sufficiently effective means of preventing unwanted pregnancies is to render every prepubescent child infertile by a safely reversible operation. (We do not presently possess such an operation, but it is not at all fantastic to suppose that one can be devel-oped.) It would of course be everyone's right to reverse the adjustment to enable conceiving by choice, and it would be everyone's responsi-bility to revert to infertility when the intention to conceive is no longer present. Conception could result only from intercourse between two people who had made this choice.

Various supporting innovations would be required if we did possess the medical technique and wanted to use it in this way. One foresees that state offices would keep track of fertility and perhaps issue everyone a dated card attesting to her or his status, to be revised with every operation. If the operation were compulsory, or even if it were at the discretion of parents or youths, constitutional protection of the right to conceive would be indispensable. A government could be allowed to limit fecundity only on a compelling showing of social need and only with popular approval; the implementing policies would have to be constitutionally forbidden to discriminate against classes of persons in any way. Backup fertilization techniques would be required in case reversal turned out to be impossible in certain cases.

I am sure that the reader can think of other practical difficulties—and also imagine means of solving them. The important point is that the difficult and disturbing change would be worth it. The evil of bringing the government and the medical establishment more deeply into our procreative life does give pause, but it is surely outweighed by the now-tolerated evils of female vulnerability to procreative imposition and the vast destruction of unborn life. Who will dispute the proposition that freedom to conceive is a more wholesome form of procreative freedom than freedom to abort?

Freedom in conception furnishes one part of the procreative discretion that eludes women *as a class* in the present regime of haphazardly available contraception and morally problematic abortion—but only a part. There is also a need for new social arrangements like expanded and restructured parental leaves from employment, publicly sponsored child care, and, of more fundamental importance, an ethos of fair distribution of procreative burdens between mothers and fathers. Without these supports, women will continue to pay an unfair price for their involvement in procreation, which must perpetuate their private-sphere seclusion.

The removal of pregnancy consequences does not automatically prevent men from expressing and reinforcing their social dominance by imposing themselves sexually on women. Possibly the contraception-based "sexual revolution" begun in the 1960s has harmed the fundamental interests of women by allowing men to take less responsibility for procreation. In any case, we see that the sexual revolution has not caused sexism or genderism to disappear. But it is not unreasonable to think that the procreative freedom of women has not been established fully enough or long enough to cause the changes in economic structure and social psychology that are needed to sustain an affirmable procreative ethos. The sexual revolution looks at first more like a holiday cruise from the old world than the building of a new one, and yet new forms of economic and family life are actually shaping below decks.

*

Grounds for optimism cannot, of course, be considered a definite solution. Even with ideal technologies and arrangements, gestation must remain a source of problems in gender relations. The mother's involuntary tie to the child's life is what defines her position, just as relative alienation and freedom from childbearing define the position of the father. Even though mother and father are equally hostage to the child in their quality of *parents* who must *care,* and also equally free from the child as autonomous adults for whom sexual relations have nonprocreative meaning, their common parenthood and autonomy is inflected by their difference. As long as human individuals are subjected to different generic expectations—as long as two would-be collaborators in procreation who are female and male must accept differently shaped responsibilities that are understood and dealt with according to the general experiences of the two sexes—injustices and rebellions must arise. Gender cannot exist without this sore spot.

Conclusion

Realizing Sex

"In principle," as men like to say . . .

—*Mary O'Brien*

The genders have often been conceived as psychic exfoliations of sex—as though the feminine and masculine intentional styles and their variants are directly stamped by female and male body structures and hormonal balances, and as though physical interactions among sexed bodies transfer directly into the interintentional realm. This thought is probably not entirely false, but it misses the mark. Its ineptitude is betrayed in one way by all our information about gender's cultural and historical variability and in another by our insight into the distinction between gender and sex; yet we remain dialectically captive to it when we draw the superficial conclusion that gender configurations are arbitrary and without ideal normative relevance to ourselves.

The more important truth about the genders (and about the other publicly intelligible human kinds, mutatis mutandis) is that they "express" sex not so much by transcribing sex into character but rather by making representations *about* sex—about the significance of our endowment of sexual difference, about sex-linked regularities in everyday practice, about what constitutes an individual's best use of sexual resources, and about the best adjustment of the sexes to each other and to other important differences. Genders are *theses* on sex, one could say, and like all theses (as distinct from factual reports or manifestations of someone's state of mind) they speak to their object as an open question; they are always contestable, and the beliefs they represent are posited as corrigible. The gender principle keeps a critical distance from actual genderings. Gender theories, then, whether positive or critical, must be understood as elaborations of the gesture that has already been busy creating (and watching over) sex-linked character norms. "Feminine sympathy," for example, is a spiritual position taken with respect to the female capacity for childbearing and also (by way of compensating or complementing) to the male displacement from mothering and specialization in fighting, among many other factors. "Feminine sympathy" is both an answer and a question, both a complementary affirmation and a critical alternative, vis-à-vis "masculine strength" and "manliness" in general. To be acculturated in a gender scheme is to be taught an understanding of issues of this sort. Such is their unresolvable complexity that a great part of our cultural effort seems always to be devoted to grappling with them.

One might suspect that the reason we put so much work into gender norming is that we are caught in a trap: we invent simple stereotypes to keep a firm cognitive and practical grip on the world, but teeming individual variations constantly give our stereotypes the lie. In this scenario, if the stereotypes turn out to vary after all by context, they are convicted of incoherence; or if they evolve, it is proved that they are contingent and arbitrary. What this reading misses is the internal sophistication of gender norming. To recognize that gender thinking is a thesis-formation process is to realize that the texture of real individuals and circumstances is constantly being woven into gender—for gender is about all this. The doings of women and men form gender's center of meaning in this sense too. The center is moving.

Critical gender thinking is obviously like positive gender thinking in the respect that it produces theses on sex difference. But the link between the two goes farther. We have taken the principal fruits of critical gender thinking to be the Arbitrariness, Impairment, and Asymmetry Theses on gender; but positive gender thinking *already* contributes theses on the limitations and inequalities that are or can be brought into human life on the basis of sex difference and acknowledges the discretion that is involved in doing so. For example, to engage in "manly" or nobly strong conduct, even unreflectively, is to assume a position on the asymmetry between the sexes' capacities for violence. Because manliness is a human attribute, not strictly a male one, the limitation of sex is negated at the same time that it is affirmed in the derivation of gender from sex. Furthermore, norms of masculine strength and feminine sympathy are shaped in such a way as implicitly to warn against the impairment of people getting hurt, physically or emotionally, for lack of appropriate exercise of sex-linked capacities. Thus positive and critical gender thinking are opposed not as naive affirmation to critical negation but as rival forms of humanism—tending to anthropo-morphism and theomorphism, respectively—with rival formulations of concerns about harm and injustice.

We assigned ourselves the task of adjudicating the critical theses on gender. But since a gender scheme already embodies an adjudi-cation of the possibilities of comporting ourselves in relation to sex difference, we cannot stand on logically separate ground in evaluat-ing gender. Not only is our thinking inflected by gender insofar as we are gendered subjects; we are also members of the gender-thinking network insofar as we make judgments on the significance of sex dif-ference, for we intend the object that gender intends. An adjudication of sex difference (even when this is performed only *en passant* while coming to a judgment about gender) *is* a kind of gender scheme, just as a gender scheme is always some sort of adjudication of sex differ-ence. It might be a vestigial gender scheme of calculated normative neutrality with respect to sex, retained only for the last days before gender is wiped away and sex neutrality becomes a matter of course. Or it might be a gender-affirming scheme that believes it has a sufficiently humane solution to the issues raised for human life by sex. Validity is both granted and withheld in either case: the gender affirmer is at least implicitly skeptical of the critic's way of affirming humanity even as the critic is skeptical of positive gender norms.

To answer a charge of arbitrariness, impairment, and asymme-try, a gender scheme presents itself as a cogent *realization* of fullness and equality in the sex-character relationship. (A critically oriented gender scheme might present itself as the realization of traditional gender's *incredibility*.)[1] As an event in the realizer's mind, realization is an epistemic consummation: "I realize that P" not only leaves me no further room for meaningful doubt about P but solidifies my self-understanding in relation with P and thereby binds me to P. (Insofar as the realizer's self-understanding is instrumental to understanding P, all realizations must be qualified, consciously or not, by the realizer's character, and by human-kinds inflections of that character. Trusting the relativity of realized truth to character and to human kinds, we call it insight; distrusting it, we call it bias.) A gender scheme offers resolution in all the main senses of realizing.

1. Perfecting one's *imaginative* apprehension of a being or situation so that one owns in feeling the important possibilities of living with or in it.
2. Achieving an *intellectual* mastery of the forms of thinking rele-

vant to a being or situation, knowing their place in an integrated system of thought.
3. Finding for a given being or situation a *spiritual* position in which it is possible to go forward in fellowship with other intenders.
4. Actualizing all such relations in *practice*.

Let us then compare the fullness and equality claims of the two kinds of gender thinking in these dimensions of imaginative, intellectual, spiritual, and practical realizing. Let us at the same time freshly consider in these perspectives the place of human-kinds theorizing in our self-realization.

Realized imaginatively

Positive gender thinking affirms the sexes in the sense that it imagines human life endowed, funded, given extra opportunities to signify, and secured by the sexed body. It envisions the abundance of a sexual variety of ways to engage in every possible human sentiment, judgment, or action. But of course it also insists on constraint in sexedness, which for the critical imagination is stifling.

The purely imaginative issue is exposed by this argument from G. K. Chesterton:

> Art is limitation. . . . If you draw a giraffe, you must draw him with a long neck. If, in your bold creative way, you hold yourself free to draw a giraffe with a short neck, you will really find that you are not free to draw a giraffe. The moment you step into the world of facts, you step into the world of limits. . . . This is certainly the case with all artistic creation, which is in some ways the most decisive example of pure will. The artist loves his limitations: they constitute the *thing* he is doing.[2]

Positive gender thinking is a kind of anthropomorphism that loves to be limited by femaleness and maleness, in the way that Chestertonian artists love to be limited by the defining characteristics of their materials and subjects. But the limit lovers do not hold the imaginative field to themselves. There are artists who are more interested in ambiguous or transgressive definitions; they would rather tease the imagination with sprays of mixed scent than feed it dumplings, and similarly there is a more open and ambiguous way of constructing an imaginatively rewarding form of humanity, more permitting than determining. The theomorphic concentration on "reason" or "personhood" or utopian "joy" can indeed starve the imagination by departing from human definiteness, but there is a sort of definitely indefinite human image to be drawn from concrete human variability—one that blurs the sex boundaries, for example, to allow a continuum of "sexuality" to be seen—and we often find critical gender thinking sustained by this way of imagining, nourished by apprehensions of real bodies but not by the female–male difference.

The test of imaginative fullness is the life lived in relation with imagined things. One imaginative scheme is clearly preferable to another if it enables me to encounter beings in such a way as to maximize both their power and my own. We faced this issue earlier in our discussions of stereotyping.[3] It is impossible to vindicate a priori either the limiting or opening *principle* of imagining, for neither principle can be excluded; we can only compare two ways of *life,* and for practical purposes that comes down to a comparison between our present life and an alternative to it that in some ways is more definite or more open. Positive and critical gender thinking, as imaginative exercises, are constantly pushing in these respective directions. We lend ourselves to them according to our sense at each moment of which way growth in power lies.

Would imaginative fairness to several things consist of imagining each with equal definiteness, or rather of allotting to each a different imaginative tendency? Is there a "fair" division of imaginative labor between phallic definiteness and feminine elusiveness, for instance, underlying Lacanian discourse, or produced by it? Are the sex-associated imaginative claims balanced in my experience? In yours? Is your equilibrium different than mine, and if so, is there a culturally effected balance between us? We would feel such balance as an underlying peace, ease, and stability. The gender symmetry problem will be imaginatively resolved in the direction of such stability—but of course dispositions of thought, spirit, and practice must also affect the prospects of stability.

The purely imaginative function of a human-kinds theory is to teach us where and how to look for the texture of human diversity. If it succeeds, it enables us to discern commonalities and distinctions in the phenomena all at the same time, so that we are liberated from falsely exclusive oppositions.

Realized intellectually

This book is preeminently an exercise in intellectual realizing (although it would be a poor thing if it did not cater to the imagination and invoke higher spirits as well). Gender thinking of all sorts having long been hampered by inadequate conceptualization of the relation between character and sex, we have now taken the time to compile a reasonably detailed World Map of the possibilities of defining and reasoning about gender. The most important point established by the map is that, while both positive and critical gender thinking can base themselves on fundamental errors—respectively, the error of deterministically confounding gender with sex and the error of presuming to withdraw entirely from the normative claims of gender spirits—neither kind of gender thinking is bound to be fundamentally erroneous. There is an intelligible affirmation that respects the metaphorical character of gender, and there is also a feasible skepticism acknowledging that our normative maneuvers are made, for the time being, in a gender-contoured field.

The fullest intellectual realization of human sexedness would be the one that most perfectly integrates it into our thinking by noting every sort of linkage and formal parallel between structures in sex experience and in our other experiences. A basic and no doubt inevitable gesture in this direction is the mutual aligning of fundamental dualities (Chapter 6). At the extreme end of this path we would come to the superimposition of an ultimate Yin and Yang duality on all other important dualities in such a way that they could no longer inflect each other—in such a way, for example, that we could no longer conceive a difference between masculine determination and feminine determination, or between masculine determination and masculine potentiation, because "masculinity" and "determining" had collapsed into one Yang-meaning. At the opposite extreme is a sort of global empiricist thesis that forbids us to find durable structure anywhere in our experience. Between these thought-impoverishing extremes there are alternatives that jockey with one another in pursuit of greater relative satisfaction—trying to construct a system of maximum intelligibility in which the mind is not left finally clutching its own operations only.

It seems that the maximum of intellectual satisfaction cannot be found in any one mediation of generality and particularity, for any one conception can be enlightening in one context but obfuscating in another. For example, I believe it is enlightening to identify Will and

Frank with a determination principle and Amy and Helen with a permission principle in *High Noon*, but it would be stupid to divide a curriculum into "determining" courses for boys and "permitting" courses for girls. The empiricist perspective is crucially helpful in studying the history of forms of sexuality but does not enable us either to feel the magnetism of gender norms as they now operate or to align them with other ideals. It is hard not to conclude that the supreme achievement of intellectual realizing, regarding gender or any other intrinsically contestable conception, is bound to be some system of complementarity in which disparate intellectual strategies are nonreductively combined. The integration or holding together here would be of a collection of thoughts over time instead of a single grasp.

The complementarity principle implies for the present study a combination of positive and critical gender thinking. We have already seen how an interplay between gender inclination and the affirmation of common humanity is contemplated by positive gender thinking, which sees the potential for trouble in this arrangement but also allows for blendings of the two orientations and smooth transitions between them. But the alternation between positive and critical perspectives would not permit such smooth transitions. Here day follows night and night day.

By leading us through repeated days and nights of opposed kinds of gender thinking, human-kinds theory trains us in an intellectual procedure of alternation of perspectives. With regard to the fundamental attitudes toward gender, the alternation requirement is dualistically insistent: what there is to reckon with is not just *an* other view or *some* other views but *the* other view. One lives with *the* other as with a mate.

Within a world of affirmed gender there is an ideal ethos of intergender alternation, as for instance between aesthetics of the rugged sublime and the sensitive beautiful, or between maternal and paternal styles of parenting; positive gender thinking learns to go back and forth between these reference points, correcting for bias toward one gender or the other. This is the realm of discourse to which Kant contributed his *Observations on the Feeling of the Beautiful and Sublime*. But another, logically deeper division was opened up by Kant's contemporary, Mary Wollstonecraft, beginning a more difficult alternation. It is possible to read Wollstonecraft's remarks on reason and virtue as a plea only for the common humanity that binds the genders together *within* the traditional gender scheme; yet her analysis of gender is sufficiently objective and corrosive that we can recognize in it a form of the critical perspective on gender that has become central in contemporary social science and feminism. Now discourse on gender requires checking back and forth between the affirmation and the denial of the gender-norm premise, and therefore, more fundamentally, between two modes of thought about humanity, two idealisms, that the gender-thinking contrast has helped us define: the anthropomorphic and the theomorphic.

The alternating perspectives do not simply succeed each other, like two insulated fantasies adding up only to a two-part fantasy. Instead, each pulls the other into its own orbit of intelligibility, casting the other as a biased answer to its own question. As we remember this, as we are claimed always by both questions—one having to do more with our limits, the other mostly about our transcending potential— we cannot settle down to asking just one of them. Our best approximation to intellectual satisfaction is to keep shifting between them.

Realized spiritually

In addition to the intellectual problem of comprehending possible interpretations of human diversity, we have the task of discovering what can be accepted and affirmed in them. Affirmation of a gender scheme (or of the erasure of gender) finally depends on conditions other than intelligibility. It is a question of right-enough relationship with fellow intenders who are in this connection neither objects of knowledge nor alter-ego extensions of one's own subjectivity but rather sources of unconditional requirements for respect and love. A gender scheme is a spirit insofar as it functions as a meeting place for interintentional affirmation—an armature of trust, a working technique of justification.

Spirit is for good reason an honorific term, yet spirits are not equally good, and some are bad. Fascism is a spirit. Significantly, though, fascism is a borderline case because it subsumes the individual will into the collective to such a degree that it covers over the not-to-be-comprehended otherness of the Other intender out of which the unclosable question of rightness in relationship arises. Fascism has spiritual structure—for it does commend to its members a right-enough way to live with each other as fellow intenders and draws moral force from their sense of this—but its main tendency is to realize something that is not spiritual at all, namely, the triumphant flourishing of an expanded ego that is incarnate in the nation and the Leader. It is sadly predictable that the life of this ego will be one of nasty obsessions, paranoid and domineering, but the root of the spiritual failure is simply the insistence on the principle of Self.

The problem of spiritual realization can be defined, then, as the problem of finding a framework for interintentional comportment that holds open the question of right relationship with respect to every intender, and in a way that is maximally fruitful—that is, builds up trust and mutual service as extensively as possible so that the question each person poses to every other can become more articulate and individualized. In the historic proposal of Paul, the "body of Christ" was conceived as an ideal spiritual framework in which members would be acknowledged to possess individual gifts "differing by grace" and would nonjudgmentally love each other.[4] Later prophets have written of a new social body whose substance would be "liberation." With particular reference to gender, Simone de Beauvoir (like Friedrich Engels before her) looks to a future liberation from present social constraints in which women and men will be able to open up the space of spirit in a fruitful way thanks to their sexual difference: "To emancipate woman is to refuse to confine her to the relations she bears to man, not to deny them to her; let her have her independent existence and she will continue none the less to exist for him *also:* mutually recognizing each other as subject, each will yet remain for the other an *other*. The reciprocity of their relations will not do away with the miracles—desire, possession, love, dream, adventure—worked by the division of human beings into two separate categories."[5] The strikingly questionable feature of Beauvoir's solution is her mapping of the spiritually positive sense of otherness onto sex difference, with its heterosexist implications. Must I not think it reductive and antispiritual to force my responsiveness to my fellow intenders into the grid of a natural fact like sex type? Are we really any distance from fascism if we let ourselves get written into a script with only two exalted characters, the Female (or Feminine) and the Male (or Masculine)?

What does it mean that we who owe our existence to human conception and birth are already written into a script in which Mother and Father are chief characters? It means that one "miracle" not mentioned by Beauvoir, the miracle of life beginning and renewed, is indeed complicit with sex difference. To be sure, if my life is really new, I am not fated to make the motions of my parents over again; nevertheless, if my life is related intelligibly and, more to the present point, trustingly to its conditions of origin, the specifically sexual form of interintentional relationship cannot count for nothing with me. This is the gravitational force that pulls "desire," "possession," "love," and "adventure" toward heterosexuality. It is neither omnipotent nor necessarily holy, but if we are not aware of it we will not understand the suasion of Beauvoir's vision.

Considered as an ideally empty form, relationship consists strictly of mutual responsiveness, and we always know that we can work for spiritual realization by warding off infringements of responsiveness. But to know what constitutes an infringement, one must know that the contents of responsiveness are power and need. To be sexed is, in principle, to embody a need for the other sex's contribution to procreation and to have the power to minister to the other sex's need. If we set procreation aside, we can speak of a needy and powerful erotic body or "sexuality" possessed in fundamentally the same way by each human being in relation to every Other. This "sexuality" undoubtedly exists and enters our spiritual equation as a very wide ranging variable. But when we turn back to the procreational dimension of sex, and not merely as biological observers but as assumers of the somewhat unprojectlike procreation project, the spiritual question takes on a different form. That procreation is a *central* human project for the human community (and for every individual who parents in some fashion) means that the openness, trust, and individual articulation that we want to realize among persons all pass through the lens of the sexual reproduction scheme. Such is the logic of Beauvoir's linking of sex difference to Otherness: women and men are bound to look for respect and love from each other in their sex character because of the heterosexual grain of procreative power and need.

Critical gender thinking makes the spiritually radical move of cutting loose from the origins of our actual forms of sexed relationship—always from the de facto origins lying in traditional gender conceptions, and sometimes also from the in-principle origin that lies in procreation. Its explicit or implicit thesis is that trusting continuity with these origins has become more harmful to the prospects of rectifying relationship than breaking off with them would be. Positive gender thinking's explicit or implicit counter-thesis is that relationship cannot flourish if we are separated from our origins. To respect and love effectually, there must be identities to aim at and to promote; but without affirmative acknowledgment of the origins by which identities are funded, aiming and promoting become impossible.

We have heard the revolting ad hominem argument that gays, lesbians, and feminist women are at odds with conventional gender norms only because they have failed in heterosexual attraction. (Imputations of unhappy childhood are equally objectionable, even if they wear a veil of compassion.) But something lurks at the back of this argument besides its evident cruelty and stupidity, something only inadequately hinted at in the diagnosis of gender-identity "insecurity"— a certain piety, a certain humble and scrupulous cognizance, with respect to the sexual origins of goodness in life. While positive gender thinking can be formulated in ways that are not cruel and stupid, in any case it possesses its distinctive spiritual character when it expresses such piety; therefore, part of the spiritual justification of positive gender thinking must lie in the rationale for the piety it speaks for.

Piety is a kind of valuational surrender. It may be defined as an attitude of grateful, unconditional affirmation of a thing, motivated by the realization that one is decisively and illimitably indebted to the thing. In one way piety is uncritical, because it arises in the sensing of a limit to the possibility of criticizing, yet the presumptions of piety necessarily raise questions: What are the real conditions of goodness in our existence? What is entailed in acknowledging them?

Here is an illustration. The greater part of Plato's account of the last days of Socrates (*Euthyphro, Apology, Crito*) is framed as a quest for clarity about the nature of true piety. By the end of the *Crito*, in Socrates' imagined conversation with the laws of Athens, we see that every individual is irremissibly indebted to the polis for the conditions of worthwhile life and that acknowledgment of this debt entails as much as submission to unjust capital punishment. Now this philosopher's piety with regard to truth (figured in the *Apology* as the god of Delphi) is the precondition of his acknowledgment of the polis as an origin of his life's goodness. Indeed, it is piety with regard to truth that elicits the arguments of these dialogues, opening up every position to questioning. But any sort of piety ultimately has regard for truth insofar as it makes or implies a truth claim. Even the bigoted Euthyphro has to justify his version of piety by referring it to supposedly true (and therefore discussable) stories of the actions of the gods. In the respect that piety aims at truth it is always basically questional, *for "truth" just is a question put to belief even when belief is formed in the specially determinative way called "realizing."* The point of the idea of truth is precisely to transcend belief so that we are illimitably obliged to seek out the real; our realizations, meanwhile, provide our foundations for seeking.

The questional aspect of piety will find expression either in philosophy, which engages the question of truth, or in insecurity, which flees from it. Gender theory that grows out of positive gender thinking is the philosophy of gender piety. Gender theory may express insecurity too—as we can also tell that the writer of the Socratic dialogues was queasy about the foundations of the polis—and possibly there is no approach to truth questions that is not at the same time an avoidance of them in some way; yet the philosophical aspect of gender thinking remains distinct in principle from its insecurity-betraying aspect. On the one side is some form of thought, on the other are substitutes for thought.

The truth of a presumption about sex, taken as a spiritual question, is its degree of interintentional validity. This has to be measured as deeply and broadly as possible, and so, not content to acknowledge this or that particular instance of goodness, gender piety takes a kind of *summum bonum* plunge, surrendering to an envisioned harmony of forms of goodness that is surpassingly good. Thereby it affirms that the conditions of one's birth are continuous with the structure of the gender scheme; and its theory articulates the continuity. A "good will" is lent to vindicating the stipulation that feminine–masculine relations will be fruitful just as female–male liaisons have yielded the fruit of our lives.[6]

The will that refuses this gesture in any fundamental way, declining heterosexuality or gender, is disturbing. How can it envision a form of human goodness that is discontinuous with the condition of our birth? How can its appreciation of human life not flow from a knowledgeable gratitude for life? Worse: How can it set itself up as God, holding in its own hands the determination of the forms of goodness, when the true origins of goodness so evidently lie beyond our voluntary control? (Theomorphism as blasphemy.) The allegation that gender critics have weakly failed or perversely refused to be happy in the gender framework is the thoughtless yet significant expression of this logic of piety.

The real reason that critiques of gender compel our attention, however, is that they typically display extraordinary, uncomplacent concern for the conditions of rewarding interintentional life. Surely there is a greater energy of love and respect in Andrea Dworkin's attack on the institution of sexual intercourse than in Kant's pleasant observations on the proper attractions of the sexes.[7] But this energy does not run in a channel of piety. It first of all follows the logic of *horror* by constructing a realization of the requirements of goodness out of an apprehension of their unacceptable, painful warping—for instance, in the inhumanity of heretofore "normal" practices of intercourse. This horror superordinates itself to the horror of blaspheming against gender piety. We live forward: to have an unacceptable future is worse than to be cut off from one's origins. (The critic can, however, identify piously with forerunners who exhibited the strength and intelligence necessary to resist oppression. This becomes a spiritual origin by which critique can define and reassure itself.) Second, critique is fueled by the excitement of opening spiritually superior horizons in a creative transformation of our given living conditions.

Can we say that divine discontent with evil or imperfection is better than creaturely reverence for established good? Surely the pertinent question is not which of these stances to endorse absolutely but which combination of them is best. But what is best in this case cannot be determined only programmatically, "in principle," for the principles remain ambiguous when they float free from practice. Love and respect take on definite values only when they are practically realized in the worldly operation of a gender scheme or alternative.

Realized practically

Perhaps the greatest horror of all strikes us when we glimpse incongruities between the official idealism of positive gender thinking and the deformation of human lives by sexist practices. Modern feminism is gripped by this horror. There can be no doubt that the practical realization of most gender schemes has entailed asymmetry in sex relations and a relative impairment of women, and that our gender-system ideology, particularly since the eighteenth century, has masked this state of affairs with pretenses of fulfillment and equality. In this frame of reference, one would have to say that the adjudication of the critical theses on gender is open and shut. The question that remains alive is whether gender-affirming schemes are salvageable, or whether they are indispensable in constructing an acceptable future; or whether modern gender idealism awaits deliverance from its bondage to hypocrisy.

These questions have to do with the ideological effect of thinking rather than with its logical structure as such. They take us to the limit of philosophy's usefulness. Philosophy, like Moses, brings down principles from heaven to the wilderness of contemplation but cannot guarantee that Joshua's implementation of any of these ideas in fertile Canaan will create the best possible human life. Our discoveries of goodness, though always prompted by formulations of principles already grasped, must always be empirical and piecemeal too, in accordance with the different nature of Joshua's work. It is in this practical work that the adjudication of the worth of gender finally lies. Yet we still wish to know, standing here at the edge of the wilderness, what Moses can tell Joshua about the structure of the practical task.

In a community, streams of intention are gathered to form a complex Here. We saw that a Here is always correlated in some mood or other with a There (Chapter 6); thus a communal Here is an Us facing an It or Them. But another major requirement of the existence of a living Here is that some mode of *centering* be in effect—some carrying in and holding together of signals from the surrounding world to constitute a perspective on it—and some mode of *extending,* too, some difference making in the world to constitute a relation with it (Chapter 4). The human body is the preeminent means of centering and extending in the case of the individual subject's life; in the case of communal life, there must be a counterpart means that can be construed as the "social body." (If society is conceived as the sum of observable, factual characteristics of communal life, then we have already defined it as a sort of body. It is a body that *belongs* to spirits.)

The centering of communal life is the forming of collective mind, which must be accomplished by the social nervous system called culture. Our respect-ideal for this process is fair negotiation, and our love-ideal is symphonic harmonizing. Under either ideal, the basic rules for individual members of the community are *I cannot do this alone* and *My most important opportunity to live better lies in this collaboration.* An ideal that is cogent for me is not for that reason communally acceptable: it must be subjected to negotiation and harmonizing to prove how cogent it can be for the community as well. (For this reason an abortion-ethics argument can be right, yet insufficient.) It is a spiritual inconsistency on our part if we do not recognize the authority of the communal centering process and ultimately trust it. Admittedly, I give my unconditional trust only to an idealized community, and the idealization is mine; yet my very idealizing is done in a communal conversation.

Communal life requires propulsive energy and linkages to extend itself into the world, counterparts to the individual body's efferent nerves and bones and muscles: the will of its members, practical arrangements for activity, "political economy," power. And just as the individual's body is not immediately and perfectly cooperative with conscious intention—so that a combination of skill-developing exercise and prudent restraint are required for the best results in individual activity—so the social body has its own historically specific strengths and limitations that have to be respected in the practical realization of spirits. In showing this respect, it is important not to confuse a theory of the social body's extending capacities with a theory of its centering: Marx's "scientific" interest in explaining all aspects of life on the basis of relations of production does not supersede his "humanist" probing of the evil of alienation, nor can a Gramscian interpretation of cultural norms as "hegemonic forces" substitute for logical or moral or aesthetic evaluation of culture. The practical connections and consequences of a society's extending are certainly dialectically related to its centering, in an infinitely deep mutual qualification, but the extending and the centering are not the same thing, any more than individual behavior is the same thing as individual mind, and they cannot be united (as in an ideal "unity of political theory and practice") any more than thought and action can become identical in the individual.[8] The co-implicating principles of extension and plurality both forbid this.

Like individual bodies, the real extensions of collective intention demand respect for what they enable, most profoundly for grounding identity, that is, the possibility of locating an intention and holding temporally or spatially separated parts of it together.

The analogy of the social body raises a question about the respect that might be owed to existing social forms. Does a radical repudiation of tradition amount to a kind of violence against the community— a self-contradictory act (as Burke argued against the French revolutionaries) that must destroy the life it proposes to improve? Incarnate individuals can never be benefited by actions that completely disregard the bodily integrity on which their identity depends. A gangrenous limb might have to be amputated, but if a brain's condition is fundamentally changed then destruction has occurred, or perhaps creation, but in any case not benefit. Radical therapies like lobotomy have a violent character because rather than relieving afflicted persons they seem to substitute different persons for them. So also radical social revision is violent, indeed suicidal, because it would create a different society (whose?) rather than redeem our own.

Is gender abolitionism violent in this way?

I offer a parallel example that might be very close indeed, depend-

ing on how gender and sexism are related. Suppose slavery were practiced worldwide; suppose a conscientious conservative were debating
with a slavery abolitionist. In the conservative's view, abolition will
destroy the prospect of goodness in life by wrecking the framework in
which we have found it possible to realize stabilities of goodness. In
the radical's view, abolition is necessary to realize a superior goodness
in a different framework that we can be confident of being able to construct. The only point of contact between these two views would be
a concern for *saving:* the radical can hope to reach the conservative by
showing that only abolition will save the imperiled humanity of slaveowner and slave, while the slaveowner can hope to show that only the
slaveowning framework will save the goods that the radical wishes to
promote. It is crucial that hearers of an argument about saving be able
to recognize themselves as the objects of the proposed salvation.

Now, slavery abolitionism wins this argument precisely because
slavery so directly offends against the fundamental thing that one is to
recognize in a human being, that is, the dignity of humanity as such,
or the equal entitlement of every human being to opportunities for
self-cultivation and participation in the defining and enjoying of communal life. Whatever slavery saves, it cannot be saving the enslaved
human beings. Whatever the risks of abolition, at least it poses no
such fundamental threat to the humanity of the present slaveowners.
(And the same point would apply to any human-kinds conception that
amounted to an earmarking of some persons for oppression.)

In the case of gender, however, we are defined by the principle in
such a way that we cannot concretely imagine what humanity would
be, or what democratic individualizing and communalizing would
mean, apart from some realization of it. With respect to slavery, we
could see a less debased humanity in the individuals having free status,
and so we could intelligibly claim that the slaves would be redeemed
if they were enabled to enter that condition. But with respect to gender there is no such reference point: ungendered "human beings" are
creatures of stipulation so different from us that we cannot *insightfully*
posit connections between their careers and our own. If gender abolitionism wants to save a humanity that we do experience and identify
with, then it must show what seems to be impossible to show, an ungendered common humanity, a human life that manages to be born of
mother and father into a sexed body yet have an intentional character
uninflected by sex difference. (But even if ungendered humanity were
possible in principle, our experience so far suggests that representa-

tions of ungendered humanity are dangerously dishonest; gender bias is always smuggled in, and the out-gender finds its attributes defined as inferior or deviant.)

The reformist alternative is to save humanity as we do know it, which will require the redemption of gender from sexist barriers to self-cultivation and communal participation. Political analyses converge on the male exploitation of female reproductive effort as the practical center of sexism, just as philosophical analysis leads to the conclusion that procreative activity is the core of affirmable gender meaning as well as the crucial linkage of human bodies by which a social body is extended over time; it is clear, therefore, that the prime target of reform must be our procreative arrangements. For the sake of individuality and humanity we must let a hundred flowers of parental style blossom, not insisting on simple images of mothering and fathering or on heterosexuality or fecundity as such. But we will be able to trust our blossoming more fully, and comment on its patterns more peacefully, in the measure that practical unfairness and frustration are removed from that family structure through which each of us is introduced to the world. For this sexual limitation that is still the condition of all richness in our life, we need an ethos sensitive to the difference between mothering and fathering—in other words, a gender scheme—that we can claim in our happier moments to be a true marriage of minds.

Notes

Chapter 1

1. Michel Foucault, "Polemics, Politics and Problematizations: An Interview," in Paul Rabinow, ed., *The Foucault Reader* (New York: Pantheon, 1984), p. 388. Consider in this connection Foucault's statement in the introduction to *History of Sexuality*, vol. 2, *The Use of Pleasure* (tr. Robert Hurley [New York: Pantheon, 1985], p. 8), that his inquiry was motivated by a certain sort of curiosity: "not the curiosity that seeks to assimilate what is proper for one to know, but that which enables one to get free of oneself. After all, what would be the value of the passion for knowledge if it resulted only in a certain amount of knowledgeableness and not, in one way or another and to the extent possible, in the knower's straying afield of himself?"

2. Such rhetoric is significantly rare in ancient Hebrew literature, but see the "like women" curses of Isaiah (19:16) and Jeremiah (50:32) upon enemy military threats (compare Jer. 48:41 and 49:22, with a slightly different twist).

3. Homer, *Iliad* 16.5–11, Robert Fitzgerald's translation (New York: Anchor, 1974), except I use the more familiar spelling of the names.

4. It is Achilles' pity that forms the pivot of book 24 and the heart of his heroic maturity, as Catherine Freis has shown me (personal communication). The poetic availability of this female attribute is also shown by second Isaiah's likening of God's compassion for Israel to a woman's for her sucking child (Isa. 49:15).

5. Penelope's reputation is likened to that of a good king (Homer, *Odyssey* 19.107–14), and her longing for Odysseus is like a sailor's for land (23.233–240). See Helene P. Foley, "'Reverse Similes' and Sex Roles in *The*

Odyssey," in John Peradotto and J. P. Sullivan, eds., *Women in the Ancient World* (Albany: State University of New York Press, 1984), pp. 59–78. On the intensifying effect of Homer's similes in general, see Martin Mueller, *The Iliad* (London: Allen and Unwin, 1984), chap. 4. The arresting simile's departure from ordinary reality creates a heightened reality in the fiction.

6. Very interesting in this connection is Juliet Dusinberre's *Shakespeare and the Nature of Women* (London: Macmillan, 1975), pp. 231–71, in which she argues that experimentation with female attributes in Elizabethan and Jacobean drama was all the freer due to the use of boy actors who did not "naturally" own the attributes of their female roles.

7. For instance, Xenophon praises a friend's wife in these terms for her competence in household management (*Oeconomicus* 1OX.1).

8. Proverbs dwells repeatedly on two gendered villains, "the loose woman . . . the adventuress with her smooth words" (7:5) and the "hot-tempered man" who "stirs up strife" (15:18). Note, though, that Proverbs' portrait of the good wife (31:10–31) is pretty comprehensively admirable. She excels in wisdom, kindness, diligence, productivity, strength, and dignity. (All biblical translations are Revised Standard Version.)

9. I follow the translation and interpretation of Phyllis Trible, *God and the Rhetoric of Sexuality* (Philadelphia: Fortress, 1978), chap. 4.

10. One owes to Michel Foucault the ability to see this cultural development clearly, and his attempt to understand it is exemplary—see especially his *History of Sexuality*, vol. 1, tr. Robert Hurley (New York: Random House, 1978).

11. Marcel Proust, *Remembrance of Things Past*, tr. C. K. Scott Moncrieff and Terence Kilmartin (New York: Vintage, 1982), 2:938–39; cf. 637, 643–44. Throughout this earlier section (see especially p. 645) Proust's emphasis is on the *naturalness* of same-sex inclinations seeking their proper objects, and the "error" is ascribed to society. I do not know whether the thought that a person might have "a woman's soul in a man's body" (as Karl Ulrichs claimed of himself in 1862) is to be found before the nineteenth century; David Halperin does not seem to me to give convincing evidence against Arnold Davidson's conclusion that "before the second half of the nineteenth century persons of a determinate anatomical sex could not be thought to be really, that is, psychologically, of the opposite sex" (see Halperin, *One Hundred Years of Homosexuality* [London: Routledge, 1990], pp. 16, 23 n. 39). On different ways of construing Proust's vision of the question of sexuality and gender, see Eve Sedgwick, *Epistemology of the Closet* (Berkeley: University of California Press, 1990), chap. 5.

12. Although I infer this development as a precondition for some of the meaning I find in certain eighteenth-century texts (like Kant's *Observations on the Feeling of the Beautiful and the Sublime*, which will be examined in Chapter 5), it isn't, of course, the whole story: the modern history of gender is an ambiguous interplay of many factors and can at no point be read simply

as a loss or gain in women's status. A good initiation is Linda Nicholson's *Gender and History: The Limits of Social Theory in the Age of the Family* (New York: Columbia University Press, 1986). Nicholson instructively explores the influence of the development of the natural/social dichotomy on class and gender thinking in "The Genealogy of Gender" (unpublished manuscript). On the immediate historical background of Mary Wollstonecraft's thought, see Carolyn W. Korsmeyer, "Reason and Morals in the Early Feminist Movement: Mary Wollstonecraft," in the Norton edition of Mary Wollstonecraft, *A Vindication of the Rights of Woman*, [1792], 2d ed. (New York: Norton, 1988), pp. 285–97; and Moira Ferguson and Janet Todd, *Mary Wollstonecraft* (Boston: Twayne, 1984), pp. 59–72, reprinted in Wollstonecraft, *Vindication of the Rights of Woman*, pp. 317–28. There was a complementary development in the scientific understanding of anatomy. Thomas Laqueur shows that a transition was completed in the eighteenth century from viewing the sexual anatomies as variations of a single human form to viewing them as incommensurably different forms (Laqueur, *Making Sex: Body and Gender from the Greeks to Freud* [Cambridge, Mass.: Harvard University Press, 1991]).

13. Text references are to the edition of *Vindication* cited in note 12.

14. The concept of role was developed by G. H. Mead, Ralph Linton, and Robert Merton, among others. Various sociologists and anthropologists have written on "sex roles," but the notion of "gender," first appearing with systematic force in the 1960s in sexologists' study of the "gender identity" of people who deviate from conventional male masculinity and female femininity, has been taken over as a centerpiece of feminist analysis in the 1970s and 1980s. The first book that I know of with "gender" in its title is Robert Stoller's *Sex and Gender* of 1968 (New York: Science House); the springboard for its feminist uses was Ann Oakley's *Sex, Gender and Society* of 1972 (London: Temple Smith).

15. For a review of twentieth-century psychology of the sexes, see J. G. Morawski, "The Troubled Quest for Masculinity, Femininity, and Androgyny," in Phillip Shaver and Clyde Hendrick, eds., *Sex and Gender* (Newbury Park, Calif.: Sage, 1987), pp. 44–69.

16. Sandra Bem, "Theory and Measurement of Androgyny," *Journal of Personality and Social Psychology* 37 (1979): 1048.

17. Margaret Mead, *Sex and Temperament in Three Primitive Societies* [1935] (New York: William Morrow, 1963), p. 313.

18. Dorothy Dinnerstein, *The Mermaid and the Minotaur: Sexual Arrangements and Human Malaise* (New York: Harper and Row, 1976), p. 15.

19. It isn't always easy to tell whether a gender criticism of this form leaves open the possibility of nonharmful gender or not. Consider, for instance, a remark by Evelyn Fox Keller in *Reflections on Gender and Science* (New Haven, Conn.: Yale University Press, 1985), p. 107: "The cultural definition of male and female as polar opposites, the one premised on difference and the other on similarity, works against the development of dynamic autonomy

for both sexes. It leads to a foreclosure of continuity on the one hand, and of differentiation on the other—both foreclosures equally inimical to the recognition of intersubjectivity." Could there be a "masculine"–"feminine" contrast that wasn't inimical to "dynamic autonomy" and "intersubjectivity"?

20. See, for example, Judith Butler, "Gender Trouble, Feminist Theory, and Psychoanalytic Discourse," in Linda Nicholson, ed., *Feminism/Postmodernism* (New York: Routledge, 1990), pp. 324–40.

21. Sandra Harding, *The Science Question in Feminism* (Ithaca, N.Y.: Cornell University Press, 1986), pp. 54–55.

22. For instance, Mary Bittner Wiseman comments in reading Kant: "Stern *duty* commands because seductive *inclination* challenges reason's sway over men's will: there is duty only because there is inclination. The concept of the masculine is parasitic on that of the feminine; it is an operation on it, an overcoming of it, an overcoming necessary precisely because of the power of the feminine" (Wiseman, "Beautiful Women, Dutiful Men," *American Philosophical Association Newsletter on Philosophy and Feminism* 89:3 [1990]: 74).

23. Sherry B. Ortner and Harriet Whitehead, "Introduction," in Ortner and Whitehead, eds., *Sexual Meanings: The Cultural Construction of Gender and Sexuality* (Cambridge: Cambridge University Press, 1981), p. 19.

Chapter 2

1. I give an account of these categories in *The Concept of the Spiritual* (Philadelphia: Temple University Press, 1988), especially chaps. 2, 3.

2. The "male and female" of Genesis 1:27 is not merely a reminder of the category of animal existence that has already been established before the creation of humans, for although God earlier told the animals to be fruitful, sexual differentiation had never been mentioned; thus the introduction of the terms *male* and *female* coming just after the unprecedented realization of the divine image makes human sexedness seem distinctive. "Divine image" and "male and female" are not separate "levels" of human existence, for this story. The proximity between "divine image" and "male and female" even admits the interpretation that "male and female" specifies the divine reality itself: "They were made in the divine image, *therefore* they are male and female." But I take the prime thought here to be of a mutual qualification of personhood and sex in the meeting ground of human nature. This places our life in a different light than when we concentrate exclusively on a "divine image" of reason, freedom, and creativity; it crucially limits Pico della Mirandola's grand idea that God told Adam, "Thou shalt ordain for thyself the limits of thy nature" (tr. C. G. Wallis, quoted by Stephan Strasser in *Understanding and Explanation* [Pittsburgh: Duquesne University Press, 1985], p. 82).

3. G.W.F. Hegel, *Lectures on the Philosophy of World History: Reason in History*, tr. H.B. Nisbet (Cambridge: Cambridge University Press, 1975),

p. 50. In this connection it is interesting to watch Jean-Paul Sartre move in *Being and Nothingness* between equating "human-reality" with abstract freedom, the for-itself as such, and qualifying the freedom that is "human-reality" with the limits of human facticity (tr. Hazel Barnes [New York: Philosophical Library, 1956], see especially 4.1.2).

4. Is it not astonishing that a well-oriented specialist in philosophical anthropology like Michael Landsmann can make a list of twenty-three basic structures of human nature, ranging from "unspecialization" to symbolic capacity, and never mention male and female? (Landsmann, *Fundamental-Anthropologie* [Bonn: Bouvier, 1984], chap. 9.) Robert Paul Wolff shows the link between our self-investment in the abstract category "person" and the liberal program of maintaining a "public" realm where specifically human characteristics like age and sex count for nothing, in "There's Nobody Here But Us Persons," *Philosophical Forum* 5 (Fall 1973–Winter 1974), pp. 128–44. Sartre examined this thinking in "the democrat" and "the inauthentic Jew" in *Anti-Semite and Jew*, tr. George J. Becker (New York: Schocken, 1948) (translation of *Réflexions sur la question juive* [1946]).

5. Hannah Arendt's assessment is different. In her view, no "human condition" or corresponding "human activities and capabilities" are "essential characteristics of human existence in the sense that without them this existence would no longer be human. The most radical change in the human condition we can imagine would be an emigration of men from the earth to some other planet. Such an event, no longer totally impossible, would imply that man would have to live under man-made conditions, radically different from those the earth offers him. . . . Yet even these hypothetical wanderers from the earth would still be human; but the only statement we could make regarding their 'nature' is that they still are conditioned beings" (Arendt, *The Human Condition* [Chicago: University of Chicago Press, 1958], p. 10). But if we insist that the emigrants are human, we think of an array of continuing "conditions" more specific than the fact of being conditioned, like having to breathe, eat, speak, and mate; to the extent that these conditions are altered, the emigrants really do metamorphose into another sort of being.

6. I do not mean that S's whole nature governs everything about it in the sense that S's whole story is exhausted by "S is P" predications, as Leibniz posited for his monads. I mean that there is no better reference for knowing S than the sum of knowable manifestations of S, including that portion of the determination of events that is attributable just to S.

7. Ralph Waldo Emerson, "Nature," in *The Complete Essays and Other Writings* (New York: Modern Library, 1950), p. 5.

8. Immanuel Kant, *Groundwork of the Metaphysic of Morals*, tr. H. J. Paton (New York: Harper and Row, 1964), p. 89 (Akademie 421). In the *Critique of Practical Reason* he calls the natural-law principle a "type" of the moral law needed for common-sense moral reasoning (Akademie 69–70).

9. Kant sometimes ignores this principle. In his famous refusal to lie

to a murderer ("On a Supposed Right to Lie from Altruistic Motives"), he seems to get carried away with the thrill of obeying ideal laws regardless of consequences. But he yields to the principle in another way when he says in the "Dialectic of Pure Practical Reason" that we have to postulate an ultimate apportioning of happiness to virtue if we are to stay morally sane (Kant, *Critique of Practical Reason*, bk. 2).

10. Thomas Aquinas, *Summa Theologica* I–II, 91, 2.

11. Immanuel Kant, *Critique of Judgment*, tr. Werner Pluhar (Indianapolis, Ind.: Hackett, 1987), p. 318 (Akademie 431).

12. Edmund Burke, *Reflections on the Revolution in France*, with Thomas Paine's *The Rights of Man* (New York: Anchor, 1962), p. 62.

13. John Stuart Mill, "Nature," in *Collected Works*, vol. 10 (Toronto: University of Toronto Press, 1969), p. 386. Compare Wollstonecraft: "Firmly persuaded that no evil exists in the world that God did not design to take place, I build my belief on the perfection of God. Rousseau exerts himself to prove that all *was* right originally: a crowd of authors that all *is* now right: and I, that all will *be* right" (Wollstonecraft, *Vindication of the Rights of Woman*, p. 15).

14. Emerson, "Nature," p. 41.

15. To cite just one among a number of good discussions of the male bias in Western philosophical anthropology, see Genevieve Lloyd, *The Man of Reason: "Male" and "Female" in Western Philosophy* (Minneapolis: University of Minnesota Press, 1984).

16. Joanna Russ, *The Female Man* (Boston: Beacon Press, 1975).

17. Adrienne Rich, *Of Woman Born*, 2d ed. (New York: Norton, 1986), p. 33.

Chapter 3

1. José Ortega y Gasset, *Man and People*, tr. Willard Trask (New York: Norton, 1957), pp. 128–29. Consider also Joseph de Maistre's remark that "there is no such thing as man in the world. During my life I have seen Frenchmen, Italians, Russians, and so on; thanks to Montesquieu, I even know that one can be a Persian; but I must say, as for man, I have never come across him anywhere" (Ortega y Gasset, *Works*, tr. Jack Lively [London: Allen and Unwin, 1965], p. 80; quoted in Christopher Berry, *Human Nature* [Atlantic Highlands, N.J.: Humanities, 1986], p. 72). This becomes a truism. Even Sartre can say, in criticism of "the democrat's" blindness to concrete dimensions of human identity, that "*the man* does not exist; there are Jews, Protestants, Catholics; there are Frenchmen, Englishmen, Germans; there are whites, blacks, yellows" (Sartre, *Anti-Semite and Jew*, tr. George J. Becker [New York: Schocken, 1948], pp. 144–45).

2. Criteria other than sex (e.g., animate/inanimate) can be the basis of the same kind of agreement system, wherefore such systems can also be called "genders"; but the sex-related systems were the first to receive this name (*Oxford English Dictionary*, s.v. "gender").

3. Muhammad Ibrahim, *Grammatical Gender: Its Origin and Development* (The Hague: Mouton, 1973), pp. 24–25. The absence of gender does not mean that a language has no way of reflecting a difference like that between masculine and feminine (see Patrizia Violi, "Les origines du genre grammatical," *Langages* 21 [March 1987]: 22–23). For that matter, there are other ways of expressing and recognizing difference than in language.

4. It can work the other way: there is evidence of thought's deriving gender distinctions from the language system rather than the reverse (see Ibrahim, *Grammatical Gender*, pp. 33–34, 92–103). For example, when a gendered language borrows words from a foreign tongue, the gender of the new word is more likely to be determined by the gender of the native words its sound resembles than by the kind of thing it is a word for. Violi argues that even in cases like this speakers are responding to an order of real differentiation that is prior to language (24).

5. An example: if one wants to say that a professor (masculine noun *le professeur*), who happens to be a woman, is learned (masculine *erudit*, feminine *erudite*), one cannot say either *le professeur est erudit* (for the natural subject is female) or *le professeur est erudite* (for the noun is masculine). One has to separate the human being from the noun: *Elle est erudite, le professeur*. (Adapted from an example given by John Lyons and cited by Violi, "Origines du genre grammatical," p. 24n.)

6. There is a kind of confirmation of this hypothesis in Annette Schmidt's study of how the Dyirbal noun-classification system breaks down as the Australian Dyirbal speakers become Europeanized. Succeeding generations speak ever simpler forms of their ancestral language, until Dyirbal categorization reduces to *bayi* for human males and nonhuman animates, *balan* for human females, and *bala* for everything else (Schmidt, *Young People's Dyirbal* [Cambridge: Cambridge University Press, 1985]). I agree with George Lakoff's suggestion that such categories correspond to "domains of experience" and would go along with his wager that human males and females are most central in these domains (Lakoff, *Women, Fire, and Dangerous Things: What Categories Reveal About the Mind* [Chicago: University of Chicago Press, 1987], pp. 92–102).

7. The article, rather than the pronoun—qualifier of subjects rather than, directly, the subject—could conceivably be the unifying agent in this sense. So could other parts of speech.

8. Martin Buber, *I and Thou* [1923], tr. Walter Kaufmann (New York: Scribner's, 1970).

9. See Ivan Illich, *Gender* (New York: Pantheon, 1982), for a host of

such examples and references to pertinent anthropological literature.

10. No one definition of sex serves all purposes. I choose egg production here, rather than everyday phenomenological criteria, to foreshadow the relevance of procreation to our ideal thinking about gender. Even for the purpose of keeping track of reproductive functions, however, "egg" and "sperm" do not, by themselves, define the whole of the female and male relations to offspring. Are not "female" and "male" reversed, for example, in the rare arrangement found in sea horses, where the males exercise the female type of parental investment by taking fertilized eggs into a placental connection with themselves, while the freer females "show aggressive courtship and willingness to mate with any male"? (Donald Symons, *The Evolution of Human Sexuality* [Oxford: Oxford University Press, 1979], p. 24.)

11. For a demonstration of the gender basis of sex conceptions, see, for example, Thomas Laqueur's *Making Sex: Body and Gender from the Greeks to Freud* (Cambridge, Mass.: Harvard University Press, 1990).

12. See note 17 below. Roger Scruton's probing study of the concept of gender, which points toward some of the conclusions I draw in Chapters 4 and 5 below, is handicapped by a failure to distinguish gender from sex identity, so that the possibility of men realizing femininity and women masculinity, which is not only allowed but often highlighted by ordinary gender thinking, never gets serious attention (Scruton, *Sexual Desire: A Moral Philosophy of the Erotic* [New York: Free Press, 1986], chap. 9).

13. The interaction between gender and sexual orientation is discussed in the last section of this chapter. Sexual orientation is singled out for this discussion because, as the other sex-based human kind, it is (with gender) partly *constituted* by the interaction. But if the other human-kind interactions with gender are more contingent, they are not less important in practice. Consider this black woman's classic portrayal of the effect of race and class (and perhaps temperament) on sex/gender centering: "That man over there says that women need to be helped into carriages, and lifted over ditches, and to have the best place everywhere. Nobody ever helps me into carriages, or over mud-puddles, or gives me any best place! And ain't I a woman? Look at me! I have ploughed and planted, and gathered into barns, and no man could head me! And ain't I a woman? I could work as much and eat as much as a man—when I could get it—and bear the lash as well! And ain't I a woman? I have borne thirteen children, and seen them most all sold off to slavery, and when I cried out with my mother's grief, none but Jesus heard me! And ain't I a woman?" (Sojourner Truth, Akron Convention of the Women's Suffrage Movement, 1851; quoted in Miriam Schneir, ed., *Feminism: The Essential Historical Writings* [New York: Vintage, 1972], pp. 93–95.)

14. Judith Butler, *Gender Trouble: Feminism and the Subversion of Identity* (London: Routledge, 1990), p. 6. One root of such arbitrariness is the Cartesian division of consciousness from body (as pointed out by Moira Gatens, "A

Critique of the Sex/Gender Distinction," *Intervention* [February 1983]; cited by Val Plumwood in her excellent review of the conceptual issues, "Do We Need a Sex/Gender Distinction?" *Radical Philosophy* 51 [Spring 1989]: 5).

15. Butler, *Gender Trouble*, p. 110.

16. Margaret Mead, *Sex and Temperament in Three Primitive Societies* [1935] (New York: William Morrow, 1963), see especially pt. 4.

17. Sylvia J. Yanagisako and Jane F. Collier, "The Mode of Reproduction in Anthropology," in Deborah Rhode, ed., *Theoretical Perspectives on Sex Difference* (New Haven, Conn.: Yale University Press, 1990), p. 139. Moreover, one has to assume the particular meanings that sex has in a culture— that women "bear" children (140)—to understand gender in that culture. I do not dispute the authors' contention that "our understanding of 'biological sex differences' is also socially constructed" (140).

18. Actually, we are often caught in a dilemma between false generalizing about specific human kinds and false generalizing about "humanity" of the sort that is most tellingly exposed by reminders about human-kind characteristics. For a systematic unraveling of the latter sort of error, see Elizabeth Minnich, *Transforming Knowledge* (Philadelphia: Temple University Press, 1990), especially pp. 47–81.

19. For this reason "gender" does not belong in a discussion of the place of putative "essences" in science (as in John Dupré, "Sex, Gender, and Essence," *Midwest Studies in Philosophy* 11 (1986): 441–57. Jacques Derrida rightly links sexual relations to the notion of *gift* and shows (albeit with exaggeration) that gifts are distinguished from exchanges by the incalculability of their destinations (Derrida, "Women in the Beehive: A Seminar with Jacques Derrida," in Alice Jardine and Paul Smith, eds., *Men in Feminism* [New York: Methuen, 1987], pp. 198–99).

20. Lakoff has defined an asymmetry of cognitive order associated with stereotyping: what is known of prototypes will be generalized to nontypical cases, but not conversely; what is valuable in nonideal cases will be assumed to be true of ideal cases, but not conversely (Lakoff, *Women, Fire, and Dangerous Things*, p. 87).

21. I adopt this thought from Sartre's *Anti-Semite and Jew*.

22. The conceptual distinction between gender and stereotypical sex role is crucial for interpreting research findings that "global sex stereotypes are rarely activated for self-perception or self-description purposes" but are most likely to have force when little or nothing is known about persons besides their sex (Anne Locksley and Mary Ellen Colten, citing R. Nisbett and H. Zukier, in "Psychological Androgyny: A Case of Mistaken Identity?" *Journal of Personality and Social Psychology* 37 [1979]: 1022). Sex stereotypes may be viewed as the reified extremes of gender graspability.

23. I leave aside the problem that much sex division involves the addition of a special feminine marker to a male-identified basic meaning, so that

we arrive at "actress," for instance, as a modification of "actor" (rather as Eve was taken out of Adam), not as an equally original meaning.

24. Robert L. Simon introduces the issues relating to sex equality in sports and makes a persuasive case for sex pluralism (i.e., for equal respect for sexed persons permitting sex-differentiated sporting opportunities) in *Fair Play: Sports, Values, and Society* (Boulder, Colo.: Westview, 1991), chap. 6.

25. Robert Stoller's summary of his clinical study should be carefully considered: "[I] dispute the implication [of the fact that social ascription, not chromosomes, determines gender] that this fundamental aspect of character structure—gender identity—can shift easily. The evidence is the reverse. When a male has no question from birth onward that he is a male, he will always think he is a male; when a female has no question from birth onward that she is a female, she will always think she is a female. When a person has no question from birth onward that he is either both male and female or is neither male nor female, he will always think he belongs to a different sort of gender from anyone else in the world. He will then be able to shift rather well from an uncertain role to the role of either of the two usual genders, if assisted in such a shift. This capacity to shift gender role is as much an unalterable part of the patient's identity as is the inability to shift in normals" (Stoller, *Sex and Gender* [New York: Aronson, 1974], 1:37). We may distinguish between "sex identity" (which Stoller calls "gender identity") as a matter of thinking one is a man or woman, "gender identity" as a matter of thinking of oneself as masculine or feminine, and "gender personality" as a matter of being masculine or feminine (cf. Nancy Chodorow, "Family Structure and Feminine Personality," in her *Feminism and Psychoanalytic Theory* [New Haven, Conn.: Yale University Press, 1990], p. 50). Thinking one is a man, for example, means expecting to fit into all the social positions that are allocated to men, and being mainly ready to act according to social norms for men; one *could* live this "man's life" femininely, but strain would be created in proportion to the degree to which one thought of oneself as feminine or manifested femininity, since the reference experiential quality for being-a-man is masculinity.

26. Ortega y Gasset, *Man and People*, p. 129.

27. A report of Roger Brown's original "basic-level categories" proposal and Eleanor Rosch's elaboration of it is given by Lakoff, *Women, Fire, and Dangerous Things*, pp. 31–32, 46–47.

28. For a possible-worlds analysis of a systematic difference in linguistic reference that would correspond to a difference in female and male outlooks, see Merrill B. Hintikka and Jaakko Hintikka, "How Can Language Be Sexist?" in Sandra Harding and Merrill B. Hintikka, eds., *Discovering Reality: Feminist Perspectives on Epistemology, Metaphysics, Methodology, and Philosophy of Science* (Dordrecht, Neth.: Reidel, 1983), pp. 139–48. The difference is between a feminine orientation to context dependency and a masculine orientation to persisting discrete individuality in cross-world identification.

29. Illich, *Gender*, pp. 70–76, 116n.

30. Joseph Addison mused on the "alienated" aspect of a gender's identity insofar as it is disposed over by the other gender: "The great Point of Honour in Men is Courage, and in Women Chastity. . . . I can give no Reason for fixing the Point of Honour to these two Qualities; unless it be that each Sex sets the greatest Value on the Qualification which renders them the most amiable in the Eyes of the contrary Sex. Had Men chosen for themselves, without Regard to the Opinions of the fair Sex, I should believe the Choice would have fallen on Wisdom or Virtue; or had Women determined their own Point of Honour, it is probable that Wit or Good-Nature would have carried it against Chastity" (Addison, *Spectator*, no. 99 [1711]).

31. Luce Irigaray sometimes talks like this. "Sexual difference is probably that issue in our own age which could be our salvation on an intellectual level" (Irigaray, *Ethique de la différence sexuelle* [Paris: Minuit, 1984], p. 13; tr. Séan Hand, in Toril Moi, ed., *French Feminist Thought* [Oxford: Basil Blackwell, 1987], p. 118). See also her editor's introduction to *Langages* 21/85 (March 1987): 5, where she asserts that the sexes regenerate each other, quite apart from reproduction, and that our culture's forgetting this has impoverished our sexuality. The issue of salvation is further elucidated in a review of Elisabeth Schüssler Fiorenza's work on early Christianity, where Irigaray suggests that "the cultural marriage between the sexes" is "the liveliest and most creative engagement of human culture," at least in the long term, because the "sexual mix . . . seems to me to safeguard those human limitations that allow room for a notion of the divine not defined as the result of a narcissistic and imperialistic inflation of sameness" (idem, "Equal to Whom?" tr. R. L. Mazzola, *differences* 1 [Summer 1989]: 73–74). In *A Room of One's Own* (New York: Harcourt Brace Jovanovich, 1929), p. 108, Virginia Woolf asserts that true creativity requires a collaboration between the female and male aspects of an artist's mind.

32. Dorothy Dinnerstein, *The Mermaid and the Minotaur: Sexual Arrangements and Human Malaise* (New York: Harper and Row, 1976), p. 91.

33. Karl Barth, *Church Dogmatics*, III/4 [1951], tr. A. T. Mackay et al. (Edinburgh: T. and T. Clark, 1961), p. 168.

34. Here I apply to the relation between the genders Walter Ong's point about the "asymmetrical opposition" in dialectical relationships generally (Ong, *Fighting for Life: Contest, Sexuality, and Consciousness* [Ithaca, N.Y.: Cornell University Press, 1981], p. 32). The point is that dialectical responses are never purely affirming or negating but always contain a "but," a realignment of the axis of joint movement.

35. In the eighteenth century, see especially Immanuel Kant's *Observations on the Feeling of the Beautiful and the Sublime* [1764], tr. J. T. Goldthwait (Berkeley: University of California Press, 1960), sec. 3, which knits together lines of thinking found in Burke's *Philosophical Inquiry into the Origin of Our*

Ideas of the Sublime and the Beautiful [1757] and bk. 5 of Rousseau's *Emile* [1762]. Luce Irigaray's *Speculum of the Other Woman*, tr. G. C. Gill (Ithaca, N.Y.: Cornell University Press, 1985), is an important example of *écriture féminine*. Noteworthy presentations of feminine ethics include Carol Gilligan, *In a Different Voice: Psychological Theory and Moral Development* (Cambridge, Mass.: Harvard University Press, 1982); Nel Noddings, *Caring* (Berkeley: University of California Press, 1984); and Sara Ruddick, *Maternal Thinking: Toward a Politics of Peace* (Boston: Beacon Press, 1989).

36. In the tradition of psychoanalytic theory, Dinnerstein (*Mermaid and the Minotaur*) has very sensitively described and analyzed our "emotional investment" in gendering. It is crucial, however, that we not mistake the normative solicitation of gender for our emotional attachment to it as such. Normatively speaking, we are always at liberty to change our emotional attachments, however difficult the change promises to be; but a norm qua norming is precisely what we are not at liberty to change, except as licensed by a higher norm. Therefore, we must formally distinguish the sensing of validity in gender as a norm from emotional commitment to it, even while we admit that our validity sense is psychically located in emotion—specifically, that range of emotion wherein we respond positively to others as other.

37. This seems to be more conspicuously true for men-as-masculine than for women-as-feminine. It is commonly observed, or theorized, that boys find identity by struggling to establish a different kind of humanity than the mother's. The richest reflection I have found on the significance of this struggle is Ong's *Fighting for Life*. But women are also expected to measure up to standards of "womanliness," so it is misleading to use a model of sharp contrast between some who have to try to be X and others who are simply aware of being Y. See also Symons, *Evolution of Human Sexuality*, chap. 5.

38. With these last six feelings I reproduce J. D. Boucher's list of cross-cultural "psychological universals" (Boucher, "Culture and Emotion," in A. J. Marsella et al., eds., *Perspectives on Cross-Cultural Psychology* [New York: Academic Press, 1979], p. 175; cited by Berry, *Human Nature*, p. 82).

39. In the course of laying bare the inadequacies of racialist thinking, Jacques Barzun notes that benign generalizations made by Madame de Stael about Germans and by Stendhal about Spaniards and Italians were, *at first,* effective in enlarging French appreciation of these other cultures. But then these heuristic sallies took root as popular superstitions, blocking rather than aiding intercultural understanding (Barzun, *Race: A Study in Modern Superstition* [New York: Harcourt, Brace, 1937], pp. 112–21). The moral of this story does not apply only to human-kinds conceptions. Conceptions of humanity and of individual personalities had better be strategic and provisional, too, because they are attended by similar danger.

40. The doctrine of "The Kreutzer Sonata" was worked up into an anti-feminine gender theory by Otto Weininger in *Sex and Character* (London:

William Heinemann, 1906) and reflected anew, this time as a feminist caution, by Andrea Dworkin in *Intercourse* (New York: Free Press, 1987).

41. Dinnerstein, *Mermaid and the Minotaur*, chap. 2.

42. Aristotle, *Nicomachean Ethics* 1178a, tr. Terence Irwin (Indianapolis, Ind.: Hackett, 1985), p. 286.

43. For James's view, see the first lecture in *A Pluralistic Universe* (Cambridge, Mass.: Harvard University Press, 1977), "The Types of Philosophic Thinking." Among the most enlightening feminist critiques of the Western intellectual framework are Susan Griffin, *Woman and Nature* (New York: Harper and Row, 1978); and Evelyn Fox Keller, *Reflections on Gender and Science* (New Haven, Conn.: Yale University Press, 1985).

44. Margaret Mead, *Sex and Temperament*. Mead considers implications of sex for character in *Male and Female* [1949] (New York: Mentor, 1955); see especially pp. 283–85.

45. Mead, *Sex and Temperament*, pp. 80–81.

46. Alison Jaggar takes an analogous way out of the nature–nurture debate on gender by propounding a "dialectical conception of sex and gender such that sex neither uniquely determines gender, as the biological determinists hold, nor is irrelevant to gender, as liberals and environmentalists believe. Instead, sex and gender create each other" (Jaggar, "Human Biology in Feminist Theory: Sexual Equality Reconsidered," in C. C. Gould, ed., *Beyond Domination* [Totowa, N.J.: Rowman and Allanheld, 1983], p. 39). I say "analogous" because her concern is with understanding how the sex and gender categories come to have the content that they do, whereas my point derives from my analysis of the ordinary thought of gender.

47. As Sartre points out for Jews (*Anti-Semite and Jew*) and Beauvoir for women (*The Second Sex*), there may be an "overdetermination" of the subculture members' identity by the larger culture, creating a real *situation* that they involuntarily share and must adapt to. Their self-recognizing traditions must then be, at least in part, reactions to the identity the larger culture posits for them.

48. See Abigail Rosenthal's moral analysis of types of genocide, including cultural destruction, in *A Good Look at Evil* (Philadelphia: Temple University Press, 1987), pt. 3.

49. See J. G. Herder, *Ideas for a Universal History of Mankind*, bks. 9 and 10; Adolf Hitler, *Mein Kampf*, vol. 1, chap. 11, and vol. 2, chap. 2. According to Tzvetan Todorov, race difference came to mean cultural difference for many nineteenth-century thinkers: "Gobineau believed that races could be distinguished by differences in blood, but he was the only one to hold this belief. All the other racialist thinkers realized that too much mixing among populations had already gone on for it to be possible to speak of purity of blood. They did not give up the notion of race for all that, but rather transformed a physical category into a cultural one: for example, Joseph Renan speaks

of 'linguistic races,' Taine of 'historical races,' and Le Bon of 'psychological races.' The word 'race' thus became virtually synonymous with what we ourselves call 'culture,' and nineteenth-century racialism subsists today in the idea of cultural difference" (Todorov, "'Race,' Writing, and Culture," tr. Loulou Mack, in H. L. Gates, ed., *"Race," Writing, and Difference* [Chicago: University of Chicago Press, 1986], p. 373). But it seems to me that talk of race has always gestured somehow toward a physical mechanism of inheritance as the basis of cultural form, even when it has not evinced any definite ideas or commitments regarding "blood" or phenotype.

50. The relation between race and breeding is suppressed in much contemporary writing on race. This is no doubt a justified reaction to the fiascoes of anthropological race theory, but the backlash perspective is nonetheless strangely unseeing. Noting that races have been called "families," Anthony Appiah gets as far as asking whether a supposed special moral status of family relations could properly be generalized to the whole racial community. Though I would not argue for parity between the cases, I do suppose that if there were a special moral responsibility inherent in the procreational relationships in the family then there must be some echo of this in the procreational network that a race is. But the only feature of moral interest Appiah sees in the family is not procreational responsibility at all but "intimacy," which, he points out, must be lacking in so large a group as a whole race. See his "Racisms" in D. T. Goldberg, ed., *Anatomy of Racism* (Minneapolis: University of Minnesota, 1990), pp. 3–17.

51. That race thinking can be far more stipulative than observational is an important lesson of the story that Barzun tells about race thinking in France. Gobineau and his followers apparently needed to be able to assume that their personal worth had a natural guarantee in their descent—see Barzun, *Race*, pp. 85–86, 281–84.

52. The breed–race distinction has always been fogged, as far as I can tell. In writing on race in this century one finds formulas like "race in a biological sense" and "race in a sociological sense," for instance, but a couple of major problems are caused by drawing the distinction in this way. First, breed is at best a doubtful object of biological inquiry (so that in some quarters the proposition "'Race' does not exist" has become a commonplace); the breed center of meaning is constructed by the imputing and accepting of breed identity, which is a "sociological" reality. Second, since "race in a sociological sense" (whether as breed identity or as race character) is thoroughly entangled with "culture," the desire to draw a culture–race distinction tends to claim character qualification for culture and thus to push race back into breed. For the history of modern thinking about race, see Michael Banton's books *The Idea of Race* (London: Tavistock, 1977) and *Racial Theories* (Cambridge: Cambridge University Press, 1987).

53. See James W. Loewen, *The Mississippi Chinese: Between Black and White*, 2d ed. (Prospect Heights, Ill.: Waveland, 1988).

54. Hence Hannah Arendt interprets the Nazis' radical version of genocide as "an attack upon human diversity as such, that is, upon a characteristic of the 'human status' without which the very words 'mankind' or 'humanity' would be devoid of meaning" (Arendt, *Eichmann in Jerusalem: A Report on the Banality of Evil* [New York: Viking, 1964], pp. 268–69).

55. On the emotional roots of gender, see Chapter 6. Anthony Appiah gives an interesting discussion of the relative looseness of breed identity construed as an "ethical" (personally chosen) rather than natural identity in " 'But Would That Still Be Me?' Notes on Gender, 'Race,' Ethnicity, as Sources of 'Identity,' " *Journal of Philosophy* 87 (October 1990): 493–99. One sees here how Appiah is torn between insisting on the metaphysical incoherence of human-kind identities (due to the physical indefiniteness of their centers of meaning) and acknowledging in each case a *ratio* of social and personal cogency.

56. Breed-typing is suspect, for the purely descriptive purposes of physical anthropology, because it blinkers our view of the complex realities of physical variation. It makes us see discrete types where there is continuous variation, concordance of heritable traits where there is discordance, and genetic causation where the environment is the greater influence. See the critiques collected in Ashley Montagu, ed., *The Concept of Race* (London: Collier, 1964). But even if the concept of breed had no value at all for scientific taxonomy, that would not mean that race has no real basis. Perceived differences and resemblances are its basis, and the issue of what humanity will look like in the future is its emotional and normative charge.

57. According to the *American Heritage Dictionary*.

58. See above, p. 14.

59. David Hume, "Of the Standard of Taste," in Ralph Cohen, ed., *Essential Works of David Hume* (New York: Bantam, 1965), p. 462.

60. On childhood, see Philippe Ariès, *Centuries of Childhood: A Social History of Family Life*, tr. Robert Baldick (New York: Knopf, 1962). The practical implications of an analogous perspective on old age are being developed by George Maddox, for example, in *Aging and Well-being* (Bryn Mawr, Pa.: Boettner Research Institute, 1988).

61. David Felder maintains that traditional black African societies have a conception of time that is fundamentally different on this point. Time is not primarily divided into "before" and "after" the moving "present," but rather into the qualities of immediacy (the single occurrence unrelated to larger patterns) and habitualness (a pervading of time that betokens a thickness and stability of being). On this view, getting older is not merely moving down a line or through a series but becoming more real (Felder, "African Con-

ceptualization of Time: Clues from Black English," *Western Journal of Black Studies* 2 [1978]: 208–11). It isn't that this way of looking at age is foreign to Westerners—for "growing up" is seen as an actualization, and "august" older people strike us with the added-up weight of their years—but our emphasis on youth, corresponding to our love and trust of change, makes us increasingly indifferent to the habitual and cumulative.

62. See Richard B. Miller, "Neoteny and the Virtues of Childhood," *Metaphilosophy* 20 (July/October 1989): 319–31. On the biological issue of neoteny, Miller draws on Stephen Jay Gould's *Ontogeny and Phylogeny* (Cambridge, Mass.: Harvard University Press, 1977).

63. Two excellent references on the development of the modern thought of "sexuality" are Michel Foucault, *The History of Sexuality*, vol. 1, tr. Robert Hurley (New York: Random House, 1978); and David Halperin, "One Hundred Years of Homosexuality," in *One Hundred Years of Homosexuality* (London: Routledge, 1990), pp. 15–40.

64. See above, p. 11.

65. See Eve Sedgwick's discussion of the implications of "minoritizing" and "universalizing" presumptions about sexual orientation, in Sedgwick, *Epistemology of the Closet* (Berkeley: University of California Press, 1990).

66. Hence, in the first wave of social-scientific investigation of sexual orientation, "much ingenuity was lavished on the multiplication of techniques for deciphering what a person's 'sexual orientation' really was—independent, that is, of beguiling appearances" (Halperin, *One Hundred Years of Homosexuality*, p. 16 and n. 8.)

67. John Boswell, for instance, writes, "If the categories 'homosexual/heterosexual' and 'gay/straight' are the inventions of particular societies rather than real aspects of the human psyche, there is no gay history" (quoted in Halperin, *One Hundred Years of Homosexuality*, p. 18.) Why (I ask) must the humanly "real" be historically unchanging? Halperin wants to affirm a historically changing human reality, but he doesn't fully break with the prejudice that only the universal and unchanging are "true" and "real"; he still refers to a human identity (like sexual identity) that is not universal and unchanging as "arbitrary," though he insists it is not "absurd" but rather "among the cultural codes which, in any society, give human beings access to themselves as meaningful subjects of their experiences and which are thereby objectivated—that is, realized in actuality" (ibid., p. 43); moreover, he insightfully confesses inability to believe in his own critical theory of sexuality as deeply as he believes in the ideals of the sexual culture in which he has grown up (53). How then can a sexual ideology/idealism be "arbitrary"? You might as well call Oedipus an "arbitrary" tragic character because Lear and Willy Loman are also in the literature.

68. "Within lesbian contexts, the 'identification' with masculinity that appears as butch identity is not a simple assimilation of lesbianism back into

the terms of heterosexuality. As one lesbian femme explained, she likes her boys to be girls, meaning that 'being a girl' contextualizes and resignifies 'masculinity' in a butch identity. . . . In other words, the object [and clearly, there is not just one] of lesbian-femme desire is neither some decontextualized female body nor a discrete yet superimposed masculine identity, but the destabilization of both terms as they come into erotic interplay. Similarly, some heterosexual or bisexual women may well prefer . . . that their girls be boys" (Butler, *Gender Trouble*, p. 123).

69. I am leaving out the complication that important differences may exist between the internal structures of the gay and lesbian sexual worlds, at least as they are presently constituted. For example, it is now commonly remarked that a sex-class division between young, receptive persons and older, dominant persons is more characteristic of gays than of lesbians, and that a central concern for depth and duration of relationships is more characteristic of lesbians than gays.

70. Monique Wittig, *The Lesbian Body*, tr. David LeVay (New York: Morrow, 1975); idem, "One Is Not Born a Woman," *Feminist Issues* 1 (Winter 1981); idem, "The Mark of Gender," in N. K. Miller, ed., *The Poetics of Gender* (New York: Columbia University Press, 1986), pp. 63–73.

71. Foucault notes that the preference for love of boys among certain ancient Greeks was characteristically based on a distinction between grades of love, the noble versus the base, rather than on the sex of the love object as such (cf. Pausanius' speech in Plato's *Symposium* 181b–d) (Foucault, *History of Sexuality*, vol. 2, *The Use of Pleasure*, pt. 4, chap. 1). But we cannot reasonably think that the two loves did not get sex-specific qualities from the fact that the object of the higher kind *had* to be a boy, while the love of women *had* to be of the lower kind. Among examples of the "system of domination" interpretation are insightful essays by Adrienne Rich, "Compulsory Heterosexuality and Lesbian Existence," in *Blood, Bread, and Poetry* (New York: Norton, 1986), pp. 23–75; and Gore Vidal, "Pink Triangle and Yellow Star," in *The Second American Revolution and Other Essays (1976–1982)* (New York: Random House, 1983), pp. 167–84. It is far from my intention to dismiss these powerful critiques of heterosexism on the grounds that they show insufficient sympathy for heterosexual taste; but it is fair to point out that they draw force from this feature of the standoff between the orientations.

72. Disposition to intimacy is exactly what the primary homophobic persecutors, straight males, are weakest in *in general*, if masculinity is oriented to ego separation as Gilligan and others argue (see Chapter 5).

73. I adapt Gayle Rubin's widely applied notion of a "sex–gender system"; see Rubin, "The Traffic in Women," in R. R. Reiter, ed., *Toward an Anthropology of Women* (New York: Monthly Review, 1975), pp. 175–210.

74. Compare Freud's conclusion: "Thus from the point of view of psychoanalysis the exclusive sexual interest felt by men for women is also a prob-

lem that needs elucidating and is not a self-evident fact" (Freud, *Three Essays on the Theory of Sexuality*, tr. James Strachey, Standard Edition, vol. 7 [London: Hogarth, 1953], p. 146).

75. Jean-Paul Sartre, *Being and Nothingness*, tr. Hazel Barnes (New York: Philosophical Library, 1956), p. 529 [pt. 4, chap. 1, sec. 2, d].

76. This characterization especially fits Sarah Hoagland's *Lesbian Ethics: Toward New Value* (Palo Alto, Calif.: Institute of Lesbian Studies, 1988).

77. For a nuanced account of the contemporary workings of sexism, racism, classism, homophobia, ageism, and ableism, incorporating various types of psychological and sociological explanation, see Iris Marion Young, *Justice and the Politics of Difference* (Princeton, N.J.: Princeton University Press, 1990), chap. 5.

Chapter 4

1. See Glenn Hausfater and Sarah Blaffer Hrdy, eds., *Infanticide: Comparative and Evolutionary Perspectives* (New York: Aldine, 1984).

2. René Descartes, letter to Princess Elizabeth of June 28, 1643, tr. G.E.M. Anscombe and Peter Geach, in Walter Kaufmann, ed., *Philosophic Classics* (Englewood Cliffs, N.J.: Prentice Hall, 1968), pp. 77–78.

3. Descartes, letter to Princess Elizabeth of May 21, 1643, in Kaufmann, *Philosophic Classics*, pp. 75–76.

4. Benedict de Spinoza, *Ethics*, pts. 1 and 2.

5. I borrow the term *installation* from Julián Marías, who uses it in a different but complementary way: "I can only project—and this means project myself—from what I was *already* doing, from that 'in which' I already was. We could say that no human project is 'primary' or initial, or, in other words, that human life never starts off from zero. This is what I call *installation*. I cannot live in a forward direction except *out of* a previous manner of being—previous in respect to *each* project and each thing I do—in which I am 'installed'" (Marías, *Metaphysical Anthropology: The Empirical Structure of Human Life*, tr. F. M. López-Morillas [University Park: Pennsylvania State University Press, 1971], p. 83).

6. The line of thinking that follows is essentially speculative, though it is supported by descriptions of experience. One would be obliged to employ a rigorous phenomenological method in this area if there existed such a method free of controversial grounding speculations of its own. For an instructive review of substantive and methodological issues in the philosophy of embodiment, see Richard Zaner, *The Context of Self: A Phenomenological Inquiry Using Medicine as a Clue* (Athens: Ohio University Press, 1981), which incorporates (in chap. 1) a study of Hans Jonas's classic, *The Phenomenon of Life: Toward a Philosophical Biology* (New York: Harper and Row, 1966).

7. In *Posthumous Meditations* (Indianapolis, Ind.: Hackett, 1982), W. A. McMullen tries to show the logical possibility of disembodied yet personal existence as a telepathic–psychokinetic intentional center. According to his Cartesian argument, the *content* of experience and the *efficacy* of agency can still be conceived even after the body is subtracted. I think this argument cheats by failing to take seriously enough the question of how experience and agency are realized. There is much we can say about how the human body works as a focusing lens for experience and as an implementer of will—also about how the structures of experience and will reflect the structure of the body in which these are realized—but the disembodied alternative is sheer enigma. (Of course, God could make violin music without violins, but then what do we make of the fact that it's *violin* music?) As for God, a related conceptual problem is posed by the notion of an immaterial divine being's own existence as an intender. The God of theism needs a body, so to speak, not merely as a sop to the imagination but to be Someone to deal with as distinct from Something (like a spiritual principle) to take into account. Philosophical theism has not been sure whether it could let God be an intender, and thus whether it could remain theism (as distinct from ontology).

8. See Mark Johnson's study of image-schematic structures of meaning arising from embodied experience in *The Body in the Mind* (Chicago: University of Chicago Press, 1987).

9. Iris Marion Young, "Pregnant Embodiment: Subjectivity and Alienation," in *Throwing Like a Girl and Other Essays in Feminist Philosophy and Social Theory* (Bloomington: Indiana University Press, 1990), pp. 164–65.

10. In Plato's figure of a charioteer and two steeds (*Phaedrus* 246), representing the possibility of disharmony within the soul, note the inevitable separation between the point from which intentions (reins) radiate and bodies whose movements will or won't be centered.

11. The mutual qualification of body and intention is not to be confused with the mutual qualification of sex and gender in the historical sense that people's bodies have taken certain forms due to gendered practices, at the same time that gendered practices have taken opportunities presented by sexed bodies. This other "dialectical" sex–gender relationship is asserted by Alison Jaggar in "Human Biology in Feminist Theory: Sexual Equality Reconsidered," in C. C. Gould, ed., *Beyond Domination* (Totowa, N.J.: Rowman and Allanheld, 1983).

12. Margaret Mead, *Male and Female* [1949] (New York: Mentor, 1955).

13. Some of the complex entanglement of innate, historical, and cultural-symbolic causes of gender identity is indicated by Mead: "There seems to be a differential sensitivity in the skins of males and females. . . . Skin-shock is one of the major shocks of birth. . . . Whether or not this initial experience differs for the two sexes in any basic way, their later realization

of their sex can reinvolve the experience they know has occurred. . . . What actual traces remain of the specificities of the birth-shock in the nervous system we do not know, but a careful examination of the ways in which new-born babies are handled . . . shows that these early ways of treating them are strictly congruent with later handling and later phantasies . . . whether the boy learns something different from his mother's voice because he has remembered, at some very deep level, a lesser shock upon his skin, or because he realizes that he can experience birth only once, while the girl pre-lives at that moment the day her own baby will be thrust out into the world—in either case, the birth experience becomes part of the symbolic equipment of women, who are formed to bear children, and of men, who will never bear them" (Mead, *Male and Female*, pp. 54–55).

14. Good examples of recent work on sex-related morphological difference are Michel A. Hofman and Dick F. Swaab, "The Sexually Dimorphic Nucleus of the Preoptic Area in the Human Brain: A Comparative Morphometric Study," *Journal of Anatomy* 164 (1989): 55–72; and Laura S. Allen et al., "Two Sexually Dimorphic Cell Groups in the Human Brain," *Journal of Neuroscience* 9 (1989): 497–506. For an introduction to the questions raised by De Lacoste-Utamsing and Holloway's 1982 report of sexual dimorphism in the corpus callosum, see Stephanie Clarke et al., "Forms and Measures of Adult and Developing Human Corpus Callosum: Is There Sexual Dimorphism?" *Journal of Comparative Neurology* 280 (1989): 213–30. An interesting functional dimorphism is reported by David W. Shucard et al. in "Sex Differences in the Patterns of Scalp-Recorded Electrophysiological Activity in Infancy: Possible Implications for Language Development," in Susan U. Phillips et al., eds., *Language, Gender, and Sex in Comparative Perspective* (Cambridge: Cambridge University Press, 1987). Lorraine Code provides a review of feminist criticism of masculinist standards of "objectivity," along with an argument for staying clear of any essential linkage between genders and epistemological standards (Code, *What Can She Know? Feminist Theory and the Construction of Knowledge* [Ithaca, N.Y.: Cornell University Press, 1991], especially chap. 2). Her argument supposes the sex-determinism conception of gender.

15. It would seem that the *history* of actual interactions between men and women has the great and near impact on our motivations, not, abstracted from this history, the interactional frame created by physical sex as such. But the sex frame makes certain historical sequences more likely than others. Given, for instance, male advantages in fighting and the male capacity to rape, it has been much less likely, in any of the sets of circumstances human beings have lived in so far, that women would gain control of men as a class than that men would subjugate women.

16. Andrea Dworkin, *Intercourse* (New York: Free Press, 1987), pp. 125–27.

17. Søren Kierkegaard said that irony is never found in the "womanly nature" because it is an unsympathetic, self-assured stance (Kierkegaard, *Concluding Unscientific Postscript*, tr. David Swenson and Walter Lowrie [Princeton, N.J.: Princeton University Press, 1941], p. 491). Even if this oversimple generalization were true (and in Chapter 5 we shall see that it is at least not entirely arbitrary), the aptitudes of facial expression need not match dispositional tendencies perfectly.

18. For some sex-related differences in language use, see Luce Irigaray's study of three experimental groups, "The Sexual Order of Discourse," in *Langages* 21/85 (March 1987): 81–123.

19. Experiments by K. Hevner (1937) and M. G. Rigg (1940) show that music sounds happier when played at a higher pitch (cited by Robert W. Lundin, *An Objective Psychology of Music*, 3d ed. [Malabar, Fla.: R. Krieger, 1985], pp. 166–68). A cross-cultural check on this conclusion would be interesting, especially in view of Diana Deutsch's finding that music perception is influenced by culturally variable language patterns (reported by William F. Allman, "The Musical Brain," *U.S. News and World Report* 108 [June 11, 1990]: 56–62). The entry of women's voices into Western music, notably in Renaissance secular music, was an event with major long-term aesthetic consequences (and had a major consequence of another kind in stimulating the demand for *castrati* to sing sacred music in certain Catholic countries) (see Stanley Sadie, ed., *The New Grove Dictionary of Music and Musicians* [London: Macmillan, 1980], s.v. "singing").

20. The best feminist analysis of this problem that I know of is Iris Marion Young's "Throwing Like a Girl: A Phenomenology of Feminine Bodily Comportment, Motility, and Spatiality," in *Throwing Like a Girl*.

21. Precisely because many important features of male–female relations are virtually universal, due to our physical constitutions, a cross-cultural study of male and female choice making cannot demonstrate innately different male and female motivation or emotional disposition. At best we can discover a high correlation between the motivations that go with the male and female *positions* in the world, for example, male preference for youthful beauty in prospective mates versus female preference for resource acquisition capability (see David Buss, "Sex Differences in Human Mate Preferences: Evolutionary Hypotheses Tested in 37 Cultures," *Behavioral and Brain Sciences* 12 [March 1989]: 1–49 with peer critiques).

22. On the gendering of conceptual preferences in science—such as for separation versus connection between observers and objects, or for domineering causes versus networks of coexistence—see, for example, Evelyn Fox Keller, *Reflections on Gender and Science* (New Haven, Conn.: Yale University Press, 1985); and Donna Haraway, *Primate Visions* (New York: Routledge, 1989).

23. See Daniel Rancour-Laferriere's prediction of a genetic basis for

unconscious lying to ourselves about our sexual or otherwise selfish motives (Rancour-Laferriere, *Signs of the Flesh* [Berlin: Mouton de Gruyter, 1985], pp. 14–19). There is a useful review of recent evolutionary thinking about self-deception by Richard D. Alexander in *The Biology of Moral Systems* (New York: Aldine de Gruyter, 1987), pp. 117–26.

24. See Melvin Konner's review of the research on physiological bases of violent behavior and other probable gender-relevant factors in *The Tangled Wing: Biological Constraints on the Human Spirit* (New York: Holt, Rinehart and Winston, 1982), pp. 106–26; and also Ruth Bleier's *Science and Gender* (New York: Pergamon, 1984), chap. 4. Bleier notes rightly that "aggressiveness" is an ambiguous and ideologically freighted category in the study of behavior and that specific behaviors thought of as aggressive are generally context dependent.

25. "Conscious" is a crucial qualification: in humans and many other species, females and males do all sorts of things specifically to control paternity.

26. See Sarah Blaffer Hrdy, *The Woman That Never Evolved* (Cambridge, Mass.: Harvard University Press, 1981), chaps. 7, 8; Donald Symons, *The Evolution of Human Sexuality* (New York: Oxford University Press, 1979), chaps. 3, 4; Hrdy's critique of Symons, "The Evolution of Human Sexuality: The Latest Word and the Last," *Quarterly Review of Biology* 54 (1979): 309–14; and Rancour-Laferriere, *Signs of the Flesh*, pp. 63–107.

27. The reader may find it instructive to compare my unifying account with Roger Scruton's discussion of "The Science of Sex" in *Sexual Desire: A Moral Philosophy of the Erotic* (New York: Free Press, 1986), chap. 7, which well represents the program of enforcing a radical disjunction between rational and nonrational behavior. I will give what seem to me to be the weightiest possible reasons for not being satisfied with the orthodox program. It ought not to remain a question of personal inclination whether one emphasizes the similarities or the differences between human and nonhuman life (cf. Scruton, p. 59: "To those philosophers—like Mary Midgley—who repeat that we must look at the similarities, I answer that we must look at the differences"); we must be able to appreciate both similarities and differences in appropriate ways, as guided by a perspicuous overview.

28. See, for instance, Symons's discussions of cultural and political biases in scientific thinking about sexuality in *Evolution of Human Sexuality*, chap. 2 and passim.

29. I take zoomorphisms in their ideal character as neutral descriptions of animal fact, passing over the inevitable anthropomorphism (and gender inflection) in their original formation. But there is another side of the coin. As our oldest art amply shows, we have long been aware of nonhuman animals in forming our self-descriptions, and indeed have been living in a "species-mixed community" (in Mary Midgley's phrase—see *Animals and Why They Matter* [Athens, Georgia: University of Georgia Press, 1984]), so that nonhuman ex-

pressions must be among the grounds on which our basic understandings of perception, emotion, action, and even thinking are formed.

30. Edith Wharton wrote in her diary: "I am secretly afraid of animals— of all animals except dogs, and even of some dogs. I think it is because of the us-ness in their eyes, with the underlying not-us-ness that belies it, and is so tragic a reminder of the lost age when we human beings branched off and left them: left them to eternal inarticulateness and slavery. 'Why?' their eyes seem to ask us" (quoted by Kenneth Clark, "Animals and Men," in J. S. Baky, ed., *Humans and Animals* [New York: H. W. Wilson, 1980], p. 19).

31. I refer to Geertz's review of Symons's *Evolution of Human Sexuality*, "Sociosexology," *New York Review of Books*, January 24, 1980, pp. 3–4.

32. Hrdy, *Woman That Never Evolved*, chap. 1.

33. I give a fuller account of the distinction between the "human science" orientation to final causation and the "theoretical science" orientation to nonfinal formal and efficient causation in *The Concept of the Spiritual: An Essay in First Philosophy* (Philadelphia: Temple University Press, 1988), pp. 270–77.

34. Irenäus Eibl-Eibesfeldt, whose project of "human ethology" operates on the biological side of the boundary here defined, creates confusion by appearing to reach into anthropology: "The supposition that human ethologists consider only the animallike design features of human behavior as their legitimate domain is wrong. We also try to understand the evolution and functional aspects of cultural patterns, in the perspective of their contribution to overall fitness" (Eibl-Eibesfeldt, "Human Ethology: Concepts and Implications for the Sciences of Man," *Behavioral and Brain Sciences* 2 [March 1979]: 23). If "overall fitness" is given its biological signification, then cultural patterns become "behaviors" and organic "capacities" when they are interpreted in relation to it rather than systems of meaning. They become "animallike" in the sense that counts.

35. Among the human kinds, only age difference presents anything like an analogous asymmetry in degree of human richness, a "lower" versus "higher" form of life, to the extent that maturing in age is progress in fulfilling human form. A mature person's mind transcends a younger person's mind: everything means more to the mature person (in the respect of qualitative development if not ardor).

36. Pico della Mirandola, "Oration on the Dignity of Man," tr. E. L. Forbes, in Ernst Cassirer et al., eds., *The Renaissance Philosophy of Man* (Chicago: University of Chicago Press, 1948), pp. 224–25.

37. Mary Wollstonecraft, *A Vindication of the Rights of Woman* [1792], 2d ed. (New York: Norton, 1988), pp. 15, 26, 46–48.

38. I admit it is difficult to say this about a Spinozan deterministic God that is at the same time a mechanistic Nature, but even here I would point out that the human mind's participation in divine perspective is a transcendence

and transformation of that mind's natural situation, an ascent to the universal that sloughs off the more imprisoning qualification of particularity. And freedom is Spinoza's great ethical theme.

39. The seventeenth teaching of the *Bhagavad Gita* sets forth a three-leveled motivational scheme of "lucidity," "passion," and "dark inertia" (in Barbara Stoler Miller's translation). Any detail of one's life can be assessed according to the quality of motivation that predominates in it. (One can read a superficially dissimilar tradition in the same way—noting, for instance, the stress in Hebrew scriptures on the attitudes of righteousness and mercy, or the concentration of some New Testament writers on love as the decisively reliable and enlightening emotion.)

40. Simone Weil wrote: "If people were told: what makes carnal desire imperious in you is not its carnal element. It is the fact that you put into it the essential part of yourselves—the need for Unity, the need for God.—They wouldn't believe it. To them it seems obvious that this quality of imperious need belongs to carnal desire as such. In the same way it seems obvious to the miser that the quality of desirability belongs to gold as such, and not to its exchange value" (Weil, *First and Last Notebooks*, tr. Richard Rees [London: Oxford University Press, 1970], p. 73; quoted by Susan Griffin in *Pornography and Silence: Culture's Revenge Against Nature* [New York: Harper and Row, 1981], p. 134).

41. Symons, *Evolution of Human Sexuality*, p. 46.

42. "The limbic system . . . functions to mediate sensory input and motor output in a manner subjectively recognized as emotional. The human thalamus, a major component of the limbic system, is about twelve times as large, and the chimpanzee thalamus is about five times as large, as the thalamus of a monkey. These thalamic disparities are about the same as the disparities in the size of the cerebral cortex among humans, chimpanzees, and monkeys" (Symons, *Evolution of Human Sexuality*, pp. 45–46).

43. Symons, *Evolution of Human Sexuality*, pp. 31–38. But surely the most important part of the human environment, at any time, is symbolically mediated human sociality itself. It makes a difference whether this mode of life is realized in a small hunting–gathering band or in midtown Manhattan, but the difference is dwarfed by the constant. If we inherit certain emotional tendencies that suited the hunting–gathering life much better than they fit into our more complicated world, still our ability to deal with our problems by symbolic negotiation and thereby to hold a community of conscious agents together is the key to our survival in either setting.

44. Symons, *Evolution of Human Society*. Most significantly, Symons's argument is substantially untouched by Philip Kitcher's criticisms of sociobiology (*Vaulting Ambition: Sociobiology and the Quest for Human Nature* [Cambridge, Mass.: M.I.T. Press, 1985]) that are sometimes invoked to justify a complete dismissal of the evolutionary perspective on human sexuality. For a

good view of the reception of Symons's work among biologists and psychologists, see his abstract, peer critiques, and his reply in *Behavioral and Brain Sciences* 3 (June 1980): 171–214.

45. Buss, "Sex Differences in Human Mate Preferences." Symons is more diffident about a root principle of female sexual choice (*Evolution of Human Sexuality*, chap. 6).

46. On the basis of his study of women's reactions to male strippers, Jack McDaniel disputes the claim of sex difference in modes of arousability ("The Naked Truth About Gender" [internally published at Millsaps College, 1991]). But I think Symons successfully defends his position against the male-stripper argument in "An Evolutionary Approach: Can Darwin's View of Life Shed Light on Human Sexuality?" in J. H. Geer and W. T. O'Donohue, eds., *Theories of Human Sexuality* (New York: Plenum, 1987), pp. 102–6.

47. On homosexuality, see Symons, *Evolution of Human Sexuality*, pp. 292–305. One wishes that more cross-cultural and historical data were available here; I am leery of taking generalizations about North American urban gay and lesbian life (and one wave of such generalizations at that, namely from the late 1960s and early 1970s) as definitive of what happens to sexual behavior when heterosexual compromises are not in force.

Donald Stone Sade makes a point that is relevant to Symons's supposition that homosexuals reveal innate sexual natures more clearly because they are freed from "heterosexual compromises": "If evolution has ensured that cultural constraints will always be imposed upon reproduction, then studies of sexuality in the absence of some such constraints do not reveal basic motivations, but rather the behavior of part of a mechanism when an equally important part of it is removed. The imprinting of ducklings upon inanimate objects does not mean that ducklings are adapted to follow moving boxes and flashing lights, but rather that the scientist is observing the consequence of rupturing the intact mechanism, which includes both the mother and the duckling" (Sade, critique of Symons's book in *Behavioral and Brain Sciences* 3 [June 1980]: 198–99). Symons's reply (ibid., 203–11) is to warn against the appeal to group selection, which too often sees harmony where there is competition between individuals. It is also worth noting that Sade's perspective could be brought to bear with great conservative force—casting homosexuals or working women as rupturers of "the intact mechanism"!— but we are not compelled to connect questions of evolutionary adaptation with contemporary social questions so simplistically.

48. Symons, *Evolution of Human Sexuality*, pp. 225–26. I am not sure that the possibility has been ruled out that men are more pettish and violent *in general,* as part of their adaptation to fighting, and express this in matters of sex no more or less than in other matters. If this is the case, then a "male sexual nature" would not be unreal—it would be the sexual manifestation of "male nature"—but it would not require or rest so heavily on a reproductive-

interest explanation. As Plato puts it: "Those who are servants of Ares . . . when they have been seized by Love and think they have been wronged in any way by the beloved, become murderous and are ready to sacrifice themselves and the beloved" (*Phaedrus* 252d, tr. H. N. Fowler). Alternatively, male jealousy ultimately caused by the male reproductive interest may fuel fighting behavior and be an important part of its explanation. (Men have often described themselves as fighting to protect their women.)

49. I draw this version of psychoanalytic theory from Dorothy Dinnerstein, *The Mermaid and the Minotaur: Sexual Arrangements and Human Malaise* (New York: Harper and Row, 1976), chap. 3. Valuable suggestions concerning the relationship between evolutionary biology and psychoanalysis are offered by Rancour-Laferriere, *Signs of the Flesh*, starting with pp. 9–19.

50. Spinoza, *Ethics*, tr. Samuel Shirley (Indianapolis, Ind.: Hackett, 1982), p. 143 (part 3, "Definition of the Emotions," #6).

51. In the essay "Jealousy, Attention, and Loss," Leila Tov-Ruach observes that "without the attentive cooperation of others, individuality starves. . . . The continuity of attention to the core *me* assuages the fears that our traits alter and disappear as they tragically do in just those situations where we need others most, in illness, in age, and in situations of social ostracism" (in A. O. Rorty, ed., *Explaining Emotions* [Berkeley: University of California Press, 1980], pp. 480–81). Although Tov-Ruach's description of the need for unfragmented attention to a "core *me*" fits women's and men's situations equally well, the greater stress on individual autonomy in masculinity as we know it (see the next chapter's discussion of Gilligan's views on psychological development) lends her point special application to the masculine. Tov-Ruach goes on to assert, plausibly, that because men are more typically subjected to "endless judgment," they have a greater stake in securing "unjudgmental attentive acceptance," of which sexual relations are a uniquely powerful assurance (482–83).

52. See Martin Daly and Margo Wilson, *Homicide* (New York: Aldine de Gruyter, 1988), chap. 9; and Konner, *The Tangled Wing*; p. 175ff (on two such murders).

53. Charles J. Lumsden and Edward O. Wilson, *Genes, Mind, and Culture: The Coevolutionary Process* (Cambridge, Mass.: Harvard University Press, 1981). See also Kitcher's very damaging argument that Lumsden and Wilson have not yet produced a worthwhile version of this type of explanation (*Vaulting Ambition*, chap. 10).

54. Dinnerstein argues (*Mermaid and the Minotaur*, p. 279 n. 1) that species survival would now require the "breeding out" of maladaptive sex-linked "atavisms" like male belligerence, if it were the case that such traits are biologically transmitted.

55. For a discussion of how intention and spirit are materialized outside the human body, see my *Concept of the Spiritual*, chap. 7.

56. See David Barash, *The Whisperings Within* (New York: Harper and Row, 1979), pp. 151–55; Kitcher's critique, (*Vaulting Ambition*, pp. 252–56), which unfortunately does not take us very far into the problem because it attacks the weakest elements in Barash's remarks; and Edward O. Wilson, *On Human Nature* (Cambridge, Mass.: Harvard University Press, chap. 5, on fear of strangers.

57. Carl Degler documents the importance of the light/dark distinction in the avowedly nonracist society of Brazil (Degler, *Neither Black Nor White: Slavery and Race Relations in Brazil and the United States* [New York: Macmillan, 1971]).

58. Affirmation of generic diversity points to the norm of a *heterogenous* public sphere—an idea explored at length by Iris Marion Young in *Justice and the Politics of Difference* (Princeton, N.J.: Princeton University Press, 1990). In chap. 6 of that work Young usefully distinguishes the "heterogenous public" from the familiar model of interest-group pluralism.

59. Here is a reason sometimes given against minimizing sex difference: "Different does not mean worse or better, it means different. And in fact the greater the difference is, the less easy does it become to dismiss one of the differing parties as a mere inadequate version of the other. This is clearly enough seen in the case of differing individuals, and also in that of differing cultures. And the case of the sexes is on the same footing" (Mary Midgley, "On Not Being Afraid of Natural Sex Differences," in Morwenna Griffiths and Margaret Whitford, eds., *Feminist Perspectives in Philosophy* [Bloomington: Indiana University Press, 1988], p. 37).

Chapter 5

1. Immanuel Kant, *Observations on the Feeling of the Beautiful and the Sublime* [1764], tr. John T. Goldthwait (Berkeley: University of California Press, 1960), p. 46. Page references in the text will be to this edition. For Joseph Addison's ideas on the beautiful and sublime, see especially his praise of Longinus (*Spectator*, no. 409), his Saturday series on Milton (beginning with *Spectator*, no. 279), and his "Essay on the Pleasures of the Imagination" (*Spectator*, nos. 411–21). Kant's analysis of beauty and sublimity is very similar to Addison's in no. 412. For Edmund Burke's thinking, see *A Philosophical Enquiry into the Origin of Our Ideas of the Sublime and the Beautiful*, 2d ed. [1759] (Menston, England: Scolar Press, 1970). I learned from a note in this edition of Burke that Francis Hutcheson, John Baillie, Joseph Spence, Robert Lowth, and William Hogarth all published works on the beautiful or sublime earlier in the eighteenth century.

2. "Observe how the physical leads us unawares to the moral, and how the sweetest laws of love are born little by little from the coarse union of

the sexes" (Jean-Jacques Rousseau, *Emile*, tr. Allan Bloom [New York: Basic Books, 1979], p. 360). Observe, too, how this refinement-thinking as it were pulls "the physical" up to a relatively higher status, since "the physical" is to be developed rather than escaped. Bloom suggests in his introduction to *Emile* that we should trace the history of the idea of sublimation from Rousseau "through Kant, Schopenhauer, and Nietzsche (who first introduced the actual term), and to Freud (who popularized it)" (16). As for gender generalizations, it is also noteworthy that Kant refers to Addison and Steele's *Spectator* in his *Observations*: "The English *Spectator* maintains that no more insulting reproach could be made to man than if he is considered a liar, and to a woman none more bitter than if she is held unchaste" (83). Goldthwait refers this to *Spectator* no. 6 by Steele, prescribing Modesty and Integrity as the chief Ornaments of each Sex (n. 7 to sec. 3 of the *Observations*); but since Kant is commenting on how people actually feel, he must be thinking of no. 99, where Addison writes that "the great Violation of the Point of Honour from Man to Man, is giving the Lie. . . . The Reason perhaps may be, because no other Vice implies a Want of Courage so much as the making of a Lie" (see note 22 to Chapter 3). See also Addison's characterization of Milton's Adam and Eve in no. 363.

3. See p. 16 above.

4. Immanuel Kant, *The Doctrine of Virtue*, tr. Mary Gregor (New York: Harper and Row, 1964), sec. 24 (Akademie 448). See Keith Ward, *The Development of Kant's View of Ethics* (Oxford: Basil Blackwell, 1972), pp. 22–23 and (on the same idea in Kant's *Dreams of a Spirit-Seer*) 37–38.

5. Friedrich Nietzsche, *The Birth of Tragedy Out of the Spirit of Music* [1872/1886], tr. Walter Kaufmann (New York: Random House, 1967).

6. Burke argues that "pain and pleasure in their most simple and natural manner of affecting, are each of a positive nature, and by no means necessarily dependent on each other for their existence" (Burke, *Philosophical Enquiry*, pt. I, sec. 2). This is an important point to him as enabling a distinction between the pain-relative feeling of the sublime and the pleasure-relative feeling of the beautiful. The "positive natures" of pain and pleasure can be phenomenologically distinct, however, as Burke requires, and yet it may still be the case that when and how I experience pain—what makes me afraid, what constitutes deprivation, and so forth—is relative to when and how I experience pleasure.

7. Nancy Jay quotes from John Dewey's *Logic* on the possible chaos in a set that is defined only as "Not-A"—"'If, say, "virtue" be assigned to A as its meaning, then Not-A includes not only vice, but triangles, horseraces, symphonies, and the precessions of the equinoxes'" (Jay, "Gender and Dichotomy," *Feminist Studies* 7 [Spring 1981]: 44–45). Jay discerns the logic of the "infinitation of the negative" in gender thinking. We return to the problem in Chapter 6.

8. A fuller discussion of the superordination of the interintentional frame of reference will be found in my *Concept of the Spiritual* (Philadelphia: Temple University Press, 1988), chap. 3.

9. Plato, *Phaedrus* 256b (tr. H. N. Fowler).

10. Immanuel Kant, *Lectures on Ethics* [as given in the later 1770s], tr. Louis Infield (London: Methuen, 1979), pp. 164–67.

11. I am indebted here to a fine, sustained analysis of these dimensions of love, framed with reference to the traditional love-principles "agape" (generous, gratuitous, personalistic) and "eros" (property-based), by Alan Soble in *The Structure of Love* (New Haven, Conn.: Yale University Press, 1990).

12. Edmund Spenser, "Epithalamion," ll.174–78, 191–95 (spelling modernized).

13. George Eliot, *Adam Bede* [1859] (New York: Airmont, 1966), pp. 11–12.

14. "If desire could liberate itself, it would have nothing to do with the preliminary marking by the sexes" (Monique Wittig, "Paradigm," in Elaine Marks and George Stambolian, eds., *Homosexualities and French Literature* [Ithaca, N.Y.: Cornell University Press, 1979], p. 114; quoted in Judith Butler, *Gender Trouble: Feminism and the Subversion of Identity* [New York: Routledge, 1990], p. 26).

15. It has been suggested that a leading cause of gender-system discomfort in the eighteenth century was the rise of a lively, heterogenous "urban public" sphere in which persons of different classes and sexes shared public discussion (see the remarks and citations by Iris Marion Young in "Impartiality and the Civic Public," *Praxis International* 5 [January 1986]: 387). The eighteenth-century salon would thus be not only an occasion for the gender discourse of Rousseau and Kant but a disturbance they want to quell. (Addison and Steele are in the same position in relation to the mixed-sex readership of their periodical essays, as the playwrights on whom they often comment are also evidently catering to a mixed-sex audience.)

16. I refer to Sherry Ortner and Harriet Whitehead's prestige thesis canvassed above, p. 19.

17. Mary Wollstonecraft, *A Vindication of the Rights of Woman* [1792], 2d ed. (New York: Norton, 1988), pp. 26–27 (referring to Alexander Pope, *Moral Essays* 2.51–52).

18. I owe this observation to Judith Page (personal communication).

19. Burke, *Philosophical Enquiry*, pp. 205–6. A similar male bias in measuring "momentous concern to society" can be seen in David D. Gilmore's account of the importance of the male role: "Because male tasks so often involve contests and bloodletting rather than gentleness and patience, and because of their consequent win-or-lose nature, these tasks are often harshly evaluated as to performance. If women fail to collect vegetables, people may go hungry for a short period. But if men retreat in terror on the battlefield,

or if they stop hunting, the tribe may well face destruction" (Gilmore, *Manhood in the Making: Cultural Concepts of Masculinity* [New Haven, Conn.: Yale University Press, 1990], p. 120).

20. Think of the actions associated with the two sexes when you read this definition of the sublime: "Whatever is fitted in any sort to excite the ideas of pain, and danger, that is to say, whatever is in any sort terrible, or is conversant about terrible objects, or operates in a manner analogous to terror, is a source of the *sublime;* that is, it is productive of the strongest emotion which the mind is capable of feeling. I say the strongest emotion, because I am satisfied the ideas of pain are much more powerful than those which enter on the part of pleasure" (Burke, *Philosophical Enquiry*, pp. 58–59). Well, perhaps one thinks of childbirth as a female locus of danger, terror, pain, and momentousness. But that Burke associated all this with males is evident in a remark he appends to the already-quoted passage on the superiority of the sterner virtues: "The authority of a father, so useful to our well-being, and so justly venerable upon all accounts, hinders us from having that entire love for him that we have for our mothers, where the parental authority is almost melted down into the mother's fondness and indulgence" (207).

21. In biological perspective, female beauty can be interpreted as an indicator to males of reproductive potential. Apart from this, the fact that females are generally smaller, smoother, and finer-featured than males is a strictly phenomenological link with children, so that the meaning of "beauty" overlaps after all with that of reproduction. (The retention of juvenile features in adulthood, the "cuteness factor," is socially advantageous in a number of species.) But Kant makes a point of setting this kind of evidence aside (76).

22. In this instance, it will be feared that assigning strength to the masculine reinforces women's dependent status and liability to violation. Another consideration, however, is that a gender value system might be indispensable in guiding the realization (and control) of naturally given possibilities of interaction between women and men, part of which is the greater danger of men physically abusing women. (For men, the complementary greater danger is of exclusion from intimate relationship as centrally realized and modeled by the mother–child dyad.) The marking out and norming of the male type of physical strength (and likewise of female powers) could be a necessity for civilization. At the same time, we can educate women not to accept passive victim roles in relation to men, we can promote women's competence in self-defense, and we can design more of our machines to be operable by healthy women—all in awareness of the strength asymmetry in the interactional frame, not in denial of it.

23. Simone de Beauvoir, *The Second Sex* [1949], tr. H. M. Parshley (New York: Knopf, 1953); Betty Friedan, *The Feminine Mystique* [1963], new ed. (New York: Norton, 1983); and Shulamith Firestone, *The Dialectic of Sex:*

The Case for Feminist Revolution, rev. ed. (New York: Bantam, 1971). For the works in feminine ethics see note 25 to Chapter 3.

24. An impressive argument that the second horn of this dilemma is a defining principle of the whole modern period—a "sexist," post-"gender" era—is given by Ivan Illich in *Gender* (New York: Pantheon, 1982). Friedrich Engels argued earlier that "the peculiar character of the supremacy of the husband over the wife in the modern family . . . will only be seen in the clear light of day when both possess legally complete equality of rights" (Engels, *The Origin of the Family, Private Property and the State* [1884], tr. Alick West [Harmondsworth: Penguin, 1985], p. 105).

25. Carol Gilligan, *In a Different Voice: Psychological Theory and Moral Development* (Cambridge, Mass.: Harvard University Press, 1982). Page references in the text are to this edition.

26. I relay Sara Ruddick's precise summary of Gilligan's later qualifications of the descriptive claim: "Although the voice of care was discovered from studying women, the variance of the two voices among men and women is neither dichotomous nor symmetrical. Almost every person reasons in both the voice of justice and the voice of love. For some people neither voice predominates. Most women and men, however, tend to favor one kind of reasoning as they identify, interpret, and resolve moral dilemmas. Among men for whom one voice is predominant, the voice is, with few exceptions, the voice of justice. When one voice is predominant for women, it may be either the voice of justice or of love. But whenever the voice of love predominates in some one, that person, with few exceptions, is a woman" (Ruddick, "Remarks on the Sexual Politics of Reason," in E. Feder Kittay and D. T. Meyers, eds., *Women and Moral Theory* [Totowa, N.J.: Rowman and Littlefield, 1986], pp. 240–41). See the articles in pt. 1 of Carol Gilligan et al., eds., *Mapping the Moral Domain* (Cambridge, Mass.: Harvard University Press, 1988).

27. Carol Gilligan, "Moral Orientation and Moral Development," in Kittay and Meyers, *Women and Moral Theory*, p. 20.

28. Lawrence Kohlberg, *Essays on Moral Development*, vol. 2: *The Psychology of Moral Development: The Nature and Validity of Moral Stages* (New York: Harper and Row, 1984), p. 232. (This section of Kohlberg's book was co-written with Charles Levine and Alexandra Hewer.)

29. Ibid., pp. 349–50.

30. For a precise understanding of the part of the sex-basing of character that is appropriately thought of as "situation," or of the different meanings "situation" would take on if the concept were applied to the whole sex-basing of character, one needs an analysis like the one given above in Chapter 4, under the heading "Qualifications of Intention by Sex."

31. These are somewhat discounted as "traditional associations" (69), yet they are implied by the other gender features she cites; and besides, *all* of

the ingredients of genders are artifacts of tradition.

32. Friedrich Schleiermacher, *Christmas Eve: Dialogue on the Incarnation* [1805], tr. T. N. Tice (Richmond, Va.: John Knox, 1967); cited from Elizabeth Clark and Herbert Richardson, eds., *Women and Religion* (New York: Harper and Row, 1977), p. 183.

33. Gilligan, "Moral Orientation and Moral Development," p. 20.

34. Owen Flanagan notes that even if any moral situation can be construed in either the justice or care perspective, there might be good normative or psychological reasons to prefer one perspective to the other; situational "saliencies (e.g., anonymity among parties, prior explicit contracts) [may be] more or less sufficient to generate one construal (e.g., a justice construal) rather than some other" (Flanagan and Kathryn Jackson, "Justice, Care, and Gender: The Kohlberg–Gilligan Debate Revisited," *Ethics* 97 [April 1987]: 624–26). Undoubtedly situational saliencies do in fact prompt our construals, but to allow that such prompting is ever *morally* necessary is to preempt the crucial contribution that any genuinely moral perspective *might* make to any moral deliberation.

35. In what follows, I summarize from chaps. 1 to 3 of Gilligan, *In a Different Voice*.

36. Gilligan and Jane Attanuci write in 1988: "If moral maturity consists of the ability to sustain concerns about justice and care, and if the focus phenomenon [i.e., resolving moral problems by focusing exclusively on one of the two orientations] indicates a tendency to lose sight of one set of concerns, then the encounter with orientation difference can tend to offset errors in moral perception" (Gilligan and Attanuci, "Two Moral Orientations," in Gilligan, *Mapping the Moral Domain*, pp. 84–85).

37. See Kant's *Groundwork of the Metaphysic of Morals*, tr. H. J. Paton (New York: Harper and Row, 1964), Akademie 423, and *The Doctrine of Virtue*, tr. Mary Gregor (New York: Harper and Row, 1964), Akademie 392, 401, 447 et seq.

38. This one bold line is not, of course, the whole pattern. Evidently men are not simply free from pregnancy, because they make parental commitments, and it impinges on them in other ways; and women's lives are and can be made separate from pregnancy in various ways. These facts open up the space for the freedom of gender from sex.

39. Kant, *Critique of Practical Reason*, tr. L. W. Beck (Indianapolis, Ind.: Bobbs Merrill, 1956) 1.1.3.

40. Ibid., pp. 89–90 (Akademie 87).

41. Kant, *Doctrine of Virtue*, Akademie 479–81.

42. Susan Griffin, *Pornography and Silence: Culture's Revenge Against Nature* (New York: Harper and Row, 1981), p. 51.

43. For a review of the issues and a critique of the Griffin–Dworkin line (in its pretention to be a definitive interpretation of pornography), see

Alan Soble, *Pornography: Marxism, Feminism, and the Future of Sexuality* (New Haven, Conn.: Yale University Press, 1986).

44. Hegel's famous "everlasting irony" remark about women, like many other entries in the commonplace-book of misogyny, colors the positive principle of family attachment with the pathology of heterocracy: "Since the community only gets an existence through its interference with the happiness of the Family, and by dissolving [individual] self-consciousness into the universal, it creates for itself in what it suppresses and what is at the same time essential to it an internal enemy—womankind in general. Womankind—the everlasting irony [in the life] of the community—changes by intrigue the universal end of the government into a private end. . . . In general, she maintains that . . . the worth of the son lies in his being the lord and master of the mother who bore him, that of the brother as being the one in whom the sister finds man on a level of equality, that of the youth as being one through whom the daughter, freed from her dependence [on the family] obtains the enjoyment and dignity of wifehood. The community, however, can only maintain itself by suppressing this spirit of individualism" (Hegel, *Phenomenology of Spirit*, tr. A. V. Miller [Oxford: Oxford University Press, 1977], p. 288 [VI, A, b]).

45. In various cultures, stories are passed on by men about an earlier rule of women that men had to overcome. Concern about heterocracy is a motive for these traditions that Joan Bamberger does not consider in her study "The Myth of Matriarchy: Why Men Rule in Primitive Society," in Michelle Z. Rosaldo and Louise Lamphere, eds., *Woman, Culture and Society* (Stanford, Calif.: Stanford University Press, 1974), pp. 263–80. This factor also deserves a place in Dorothy Dinnerstein's powerful analysis of our feelings about feminine and masculine power in *The Mermaid and the Minotaur: Sexual Arrangements and Human Malaise* (New York: Harper and Row, 1976), chap. 8.

46. Two rather different interpretations of the male interest in female chastity deserve to be noted. Most obvious is the male concern to assure paternity. But Otto Weininger, who turned his face from procreation entirely, argued that the virtue of virginity is not really esteemed by women at all but is "the projection of man's own ideal of spotless purity on the object of his love" (Weininger, *Sex and Character* [1903], tr. unknown, from sixth German ed. [London: W. Heinemann, 1906], p. 333). On the degree of alienation that would be *inherent* in gender virtue see p. 54 and note 30 to Chapter 3.

47. Gilmore, *Manhood in the Making*, p. 38.

48. According to Sue Campbell's interesting analysis in "The Aristotelian Mean and the Vices of Gender," the feminine virtues are typically at the passive end of the acceptable "mean" range in morally significant capacities, bordering vicious defects, while the masculine virtues are at the active end of the "mean" range, bordering vicious excesses (*Eidos* 6 [December 1987]: 177–200). It seems to me that in some cases the passive–active con-

trast does not capture very well the nature of the posited complementarity between feminine and masculine virtues—for instance, "discretion" is not the passive complement of a more active "frankness," and only a weaker sort of "flexibility" is more passive than "firmness." The variable here might be *self-assertion* rather than passiveness or activeness as such; but I think it is often most illuminating to apply the potentiation–determination contrast in such cases (see the discussion of the film *High Noon* in Chapter 5 and in the section "Generationality, Potentiation, and Determination" in Chapter 7).

49. See Linda K. Kerber, "Some Cautionary Words for Historians" [the first part of a forum on *In a Different Voice*], *Signs* 11 (1986): 304–10.

50. A good analysis of practical asymmetry in the family is given by M. Rivka Polatnick in "Why Men Don't Rear Children: A Power Analysis," in Joyce Trebilcot, ed., *Mothering: Essays in Feminist Theory* (Totowa, N.J.: Rowman and Allanheld, 1983), pp. 21–40; see also Susan Moller Okin, *Justice, Gender, and the Family* (New York: Basic Books, 1989). On Michael Walzer's conceptualization of a distinct but intimately related ethical problem, the distributions of different goods in different practical spheres are unjustifiably linked so as to create trans-sphere dominance for one group (Walzer, *Spheres of Justice* [New York: Basic Books, 1983]).

51. Kohlberg, *Essays on Moral Development*, p. 348.

52. See the analysis of Eichmann's perversion of Kantian ethics given by Hannah Arendt in *Eichmann in Jerusalem: A Report on the Banality of Evil* (New York: Viking, 1964), chap. 8 ("Duties of a Law-Abiding Citizen"). As for criminals claiming autonomy, I think first in this context of the "libertine," the Marquis de Sade.

53. "The concept of androgyny is problematic from the perspective of gender schema theory because it is based on the presupposition that there is a feminine and a masculine within us all, that is, that 'femininity' and 'masculinity' have an independent and palpable reality and are not cognitive constructs derived from gender-schematic processing. Focusing on androgyny thus fails to prompt serious examination of the extent to which gender organizes both our perceptions and our social world" (Sandra Bem, "Gender Schema Theory and Its Implications for Child Development," *Signs* 8 [Summer 1983]: 614).

54. As Joyce Trebilcot shows in "Two Forms of Androgynism," in Mary Vetterling-Braggin, ed., *"Femininity," "Masculinity," and "Androgyny"* (Totowa, N.J.: Rowman and Allanheld, 1982), pp. 161–69.

55. For an exquisitely exacerbating account of the "melancholia" of gender-identity formation (i.e., as a loss of sexual possibility), see Judith Butler, *Gender Trouble*, chap. 2; on envy, see Eva Feder Kittay, "Womb Envy: An Explanatory Concept," in Trebilcot, *Mothering*, pp. 94–128.

56. The word *androgyny* is sometimes used to mean a surpassing of gender qualities instead of a combining of them. The best defense for this usage

would be that it is rhetorically adapted to the limitations of common prevailing perceptions, thus "provisional" (Mary Anne Warren, "Is Androgyny the Answer to Sexual Stereotyping?" in Vetterling-Braggin, *"Femininity," "Masculinity," and "Androgyny,"* p. 182). But when Warren writes further, "The most serious danger is that of forgetting that psychological androgyny is only a metaphor. The traits being combined are not *really* feminine or masculine" (183), she obscures the point that femininity and masculinity are already metaphorical appropriations of femaleness and maleness to name human possibilities. If she means just that, that femaleness and maleness are metaphorical vehicles for the traits in question, then I see no implication that this way of talking about personal traits can be superseded by a truer way. At least our living conditions, specifically our relation to sexual reproduction, would have to change very drastically for sex to lose its privileged role in the description of certain general character differences.

57. The relationship between gender and theoretical dualities will be studied in Chapter 6.

58. My interpretation of the significance of "drag" differs profoundly from that of Butler (by whom I was inspired to introduce this point), but I am sure she hits part of the truth when she writes that drag "reveals the distinctness of those aspects of gendered experience which are falsely naturalized as a unity through the regulatory fiction of heterosexual coherence. *In imitating gender, drag implicitly reveals the imitative structure of gender itself—as well as its contingency.* Indeed, part of the pleasure, the giddiness of the performance is in the recognition of a radical contingency in the relation between sex and gender in the face of cultural configurations of causal unities that are regularly assumed to be natural and necessary" (Butler, *Gender Trouble*, pp. 137–38).

59. Maria Lugones argues that ontological pluralism with respect to selves is necessary if we are to understand simultaneously how oppression stamps the subjectivity of the oppressed and how the subjects of a particular oppression may have experiences outside that framework, including the experience of liberation (Lugones, "Structure/Antistructure and Agency Under Oppression," *Journal of Philosophy* 83 [October 1990]: 500–507).

60. I draw this idea from Abigail Rosenthal, who works it out cogently in *A Good Look at Evil* (Philadelphia: Temple University Press, 1987).

61. On feminine subjectivity, see my discussion of Kristeva and Irigaray's views under "Social-Scientific Gender-Duality Theories" in the next chapter, and (much more fully) Elizabeth Grosz, *Sexual Subversions: Three French Feminists* (Sydney: Allen and Unwin, 1989). For an unforgettable expression of positive gender thinking on this point, I turn again to José Ortega y Gasset: "The instant we see a woman, we seem to have before us a being whose inward humanity is characterized, in contrast to our own male humanity and that of other men, by being essentially confused. . . . Woman is [a delight] to man by virtue of her confused being. Man, on the contrary, is

made up of clarities. . . . Perhaps everything that he thinks is sheer nonsense; but within himself, he sees himself clearly. Hence in the masculine inwardness everything normally has strict and definite lines" (Ortega y Gasset, *Man and People*, tr. Willard Trask [New York: Norton, 1957], pp. 130–31). Compare Irigaray: "Why is setting oneself up as a solid more worthwhile than flowing as a liquid from between the two [lips?] . . . My life is nothing but the mobile flexibility, tenderness, uncertainty of the fluid" (Irigaray, *Passions elementaires* [Paris: Minuit, 1982], pp. 18, 28; cited and apparently translated by Naomi Schor in "This Essentialism Which Is Not One: Coming to Grips with Irigaray," *differences* 1 [Summer 1989]: 49).

62. Sigmund Freud, *New Introductory Lectures on Psychoanalysis* [1933], lecture 31. For the antithesis, see Norman O. Brown, *Life Against Death* (Middletown, Conn.: Wesleyan University Press, 1959).

63. On the disciplinary force of gender narratives both popular and scientific see Butler (inspired here by Foucault), *Gender Trouble*. Some of the material in Gilligan's interviews reads like gender storytelling in aid of moral clarification. For instance, one "Diane" says: "I think I have a real drive, a real maternal drive, to take care of someone—to take care of my mother, to take care of children . . . to take care of the world. When I am dealing with moral issues, I am sort of saying to myself constantly, 'Are you taking care of all the things that you think are important, and in what ways are you wasting yourself and wasting those issues?'" (Gilligan, *In a Different Voice*, p. 99.)

64. Phyllis Trible, *God and the Rhetoric of Sexuality* (Philadelphia: Fortress, 1978), chap. 4 ("A Love Story Gone Awry").

65. *High Noon* (Stanley Kramer–United Artists, 1952), directed by Fred Zinnemann from a screenplay by Carl Foreman.

66. A fine observer of Westerns, Robert Warshow, sees the Western male and the saloon girl as independent of *love:* "Those women in the Western movies who share the hero's understanding of life are prostitutes (or, as they are usually presented, barroom entertainers)—women, that is, who have come to understand in the most practical way how love can be an irrelevance, and therefore 'fallen' women. . . . The important thing about a prostitute is her quasi-masculine independence: nobody owns her, nothing has to be explained to her, and she is not, like a virtuous woman, a 'value' that demands to be protected. When the Westerner leaves the prostitute for a virtuous woman—for love—he is in fact forsaking a way of life" (Warshow, "The Westerner," in Daniel Talbot, ed., *Film: An Anthology* [Berkeley: University of California Press, 1970], p. 150 [originally in the March 1954 issue of *Partisan Review*]). My point is that the procreative project of marriage is what differentiates this "love," "virtue," and "value."

67. *Stagecoach* (Walter Wanger–United Artists, 1939), directed by John Ford, scripted by Dudley Nichols.

68. Our evaluation of Amy in this respect would have been seriously

affected by a passage in the shooting script that did not appear in the film. Foreman had Amy telling Helen Ramirez, "I'm a feminist. You know, women's rights—things like that" (in George P. Garrett, O. B. Hardison, Jr., and Jane R. Gelfman, eds., *Film Scripts Two* [New York: Appleton-Century-Crofts, 1971], p. 142). Perhaps Foreman was uncertain about this dimension of Amy. He remarks in his preface to the script, "Amy [Kane] is, without knowing it, one of the new women of the period, women who are beginning to rebel against the limitations and restrictions of the Victorian epoch" (ibid., p. 41).

69. If, as Gilmore says (summarizing the ideas of one school of gender identity theory), "the struggle for masculinity is a battle" against "regressive wishes and fantasies" for "the prelapsarian idyll of childhood," and if marriage, in the context of the Western, has the potential meaning of reunion with the mother, then Kane's reinitiation is necessary to secure his socially demanded adult male character (Gilmore, *Mankind in the Making*, pp. 28–29).

70. Amy can be taken to illustrate (if not confirm) Sherry Ortner's hypothesis that women are more likely to be seen as closer to "nature" than "culture" and thus are more likely to be assigned the role of mediating between the two spheres (Ortner, "Is Female to Male as Nature Is to Culture?" in Rosaldo and Lamphere, *Woman, Culture, and Society*, pp. 67–87). As a pacifist, Amy stands for principles of communion and care that transcend the social structures of justice and honor in which Will is embedded. "Every society must have social categories that transcend personal loyalties, but every society must also generate a sense of ultimate moral unity for all its members above and beyond those social categories" (83). Like Antigone, Amy exalts intrafamilial concern to a culture-redeeming universal law. But then she steps down from this higher vantage point to perform feminine mediation of a sort that Ortner did not contemplate.

71. King James Version. The evildoers try to burn Kane up in a stable, but their fire comes to nothing.

72. For the social drama interpretation, see Warshow, "Westerner," p. 158. For the social-psychological view, see Erik Erikson, *Childhood and Society* (New York: Norton, 1950), and, before that, the work of the anthropologist Ralph Linton.

Chapter 6

1. Ella Wheeler Wilcox, "To Lift or to Lean"; cited (without shame) from John Bartlett, *Familiar Quotations*, 14th ed. (Boston: Little, Brown, 1968), p. 825.

2. Jessica Benjamin, *The Bonds of Love: Psychoanalysis, Feminism, and the Problem of Domination* (New York: Pantheon, 1988), pp. 112–13. Parent–child identification is reciprocal; for an account of the special features of

parental identification with children, see Joseph Kupfer, "Can Parents and Children Be Friends?" *American Philosophical Quarterly* 27 (January 1990): 21–22.

3. Iris Marion Young, *Justice and the Politics of Difference* (Princeton, N.J.: Princeton University Press, 1990), p. 124.

4. Emile Durkheim, *The Elementary Forms of the Religious Life*, tr. J. Ward Swain (New York: Free Press, 1965), p. 55. Nancy Jay points out the connection between resistance to social change and continuity-denying dualizing in "Gender and Dichotomy," *Feminist Studies* 7 (Spring 1981): 51–54. Timothy Perper argues that the sacred–profane dichotomy as described by Durkheim has been the basic pattern for female–male dealings in Western culture, "pure" marital relations and impure sexuality being opposed in this way (Perper, *Sex Signals: The Biology of Love* ([Philadelphia: Institute for Scientific Information, 1985], chap. 8). For a more nuanced view, see Michel Foucault, *The History of Sexuality*, especially vol. 2, *The Use of Pleasure*, tr. Robert Hurley (New York: Random House, 1985), and vol. 3, *The Care of the Self*, tr. Robert Hurley (New York: Random House, 1986).

5. I borrow from Jay ("Gender and Dichotomy," p. 44f.) the notion of negative infinitizing; I think she overlooks positive infinitizing.

6. A line that curves or wrinkles in two-dimensional space still counts as one-dimensional (and as a sure splitter) as long as we don't allow it to cross itself. The fact that a two-dimensional space is required to represent its curves is only interesting if we choose to treat the line as a two-dimensional feature; for example, if we want to see whether the shortest distance between line points A and B is traveled inside or outside the line. Analogously, the three-dimensional universe at any moment is relativistically "wrinkled" in relation to time, but future is still split from past everywhere in it.

7. The concept is borrowed from Karl Rahner, though given a different turn (see, for example, Rahner, "Christianity and the Non-Christian Religions" in John Hick and Brian Hebblethwaite, eds., *Christianity and Other Religions* [Philadelphia: Fortress, 1980], p. 75). The existential interpretation of the category of Christianity goes back at least to the apologetics of Justin Martyr.

8. Hence this Brown–Freud thought: "The Freudian theory of the instincts is persistently dualistic because it starts from the fact of conflict in mental life and aims at explaining that fact . . . whether the antagonism, or as Freud calls it the ambivalence, is between sex and self-preservation, or between sex and aggression, or between life and death, in every case Freud postulates an ultimate duality grounded in the very nature of life itself" (Norman O. Brown, *Life Against Death* [Middletown, Conn.: Wesleyan University Press, 1959], p. 79).

9. This is the psychological norm advanced by Jessica Benjamin in *Bonds of Love*.

10. So David Maybury-Lewis argues in "The Quest for Harmony," his introduction to an anthropological survey of dualistic social organization in David Maybury-Lewis and Uri Almagor, eds., *The Attraction of Opposites: Thought and Society in the Dualistic Mode* (Ann Arbor: University of Michigan Press, 1989), pp. 1–17.

11. Jacques Derrida, "Choreographies" (interview with Christie McDonald), in Christie McDonald, ed., *The Ear of the Other*, tr. Peggy Kamuf (Lincoln: University of Nebraska Press, 1985), pp. 184–85. Derrida's goal is actually to rescue the existential import of difference: "But there is another neutralization which can simply neutralize the sexual opposition, and not sexual difference, liberating the field of sexuality for a very *different* sexuality, a more multiple one. At that point there would be no more sexes . . . there would be one sex for each time. One sex for each gift. A sexual difference for each gift" (Derrida, "Women in the Beehive: A Seminar with Jacques Derrida," in Alice Jardine and Paul Smith, eds., *Men in Feminism* [New York: Methuen, 1987], p. 199). But in the posited wilderness of total sexual indeterminacy there is no Here other than the transparent and weightless generalized Here of the indeterminate subject, and one cannot have any sense of what to give or what one is receiving.

12. G.W.F. Hegel, *Philosophy of Right*. Adapted from T. M. Knox's translation (Oxford: Oxford University Press, 1952), p. 114.

13. G.W.F. Hegel, *Phenomenology of Spirit*, VI.A.a ("Human and Divine Law: Man and Woman"). Hegel says here, in an interpretation guided by Sophocles' *Antigone*, that neither of the gender-linked principles of spiritual form is absolutely valid by itself. Through the woman, spirit rises from the unconscious to consciousness (Antigone speaking for the "divine law" of sacred family obligation); through the man (Cleon wielding the sword) there is a "downward movement" of public human law "to the danger and trial of death" (A. V. Miller's translation [Oxford: Oxford University Press, 1977], p. 278).

14. See especially Emmanuel Levinas, *Totality and Infinity* [1961], tr. Alfonso Lingis (Pittsburgh: Duquesne University Press, 1969).

15. Here I give my own conclusions drawn from reading Levinas's *Totality and Infinity*, sec. 6, B; cf. his *Time and the Other* [1947], pt. 4, "Eros," tr. Richard Cohen (Pittsburgh: Duquesne University Press, 1987), pp. 89–90. My interpretation is at least partly licensed by his remark in a 1981 interview that philosophical use of gender categories should "signify that participation in the masculine and feminine belongs to every human being" (Levinas, *Ethique et Infini: Dialogues avec Philippe Nemo* [Paris: Fayard, 1982], p. 71 [my translation]; p. 68 in *Ethics and Infinity*, tr. Richard Cohen [Pittsburgh: Duquesne University Press, 1985]. In *Totality and Infinity* the genders are often identified with the sexes. But it is more my choice than Levinas's to give prominence to a distinction between two basic modalities of ethical relation;

on responsibility-to and responsibility-for, see my *Concept of the Spiritual: An Essay in First Philosophy* (Philadelphia: Temple University Press, 1988), pp. 88–89.

16. See, for example, Levinas, "Language and Proximity" [1967] in *Collected Philosophical Papers*, tr. Alfonso Lingis (Dordrecht, Neth.: Martinus Nijhoff, 1987), pp. 109–26.

17. Carol Gilligan, *In a Different Voice: Psychological Theory and Moral Development* (Cambridge, Mass.: Harvard University Press, 1982), p. 174.

18. *Testimony of Christ's Second Appearing*, 4th ed. (Albany, N.Y.: Van Benthuysen, 1956), pp. 503–4; cited in Rosemary Radford Ruether, *Woman-guides: Readings Toward a Feminist Theology* (Boston: Beacon, 1985), pp. 34–35.

19. Robley Edward Whitson, *The Shakers: Two Centuries of Spiritual Reflection* (New York: Paulist, 1983), p. 210.

20. On "Mother" and "Father–Mother" naming of God by Jewish and Christian Gnostics, see Elaine Pagels, "What Became of God the Mother? Conflicting Images of God in Early Christianity," in Carol C. Christ and Judith Plaskow, eds., *Womanspirit Rising: A Feminist Reader in Religion* (New York: Harper and Row, 1979), pp. 107–19.

21. Linda Mercadante shows that the feminine was, in fact, subordinated to the masculine in the development of Shaker thought, and that the liberating potential of the Shakers' gender-balancing approach was impaired by their reliance on "reified" gender stereotypes (Mercadante, *Gender, Doctrine, and God: The Shakers and Contemporary Theology* [Nashville, Tenn.: Abingdon, 1990]).

22. Actually Genesis 2–3 implies that Eve is the original leader whose post-Fall subordination to Adam is a punishment; 1 Timothy 2:13–14 veers to this thought after repeating Paul's point about the temporal priority of Adam's creation.

23. For a modern defense of Paul's position (which has guided my interpretation of Paul), see Karl Barth, *Church Dogmatics* [1951], III/2, para. 45, sec. 3; and III/4, para. 54, sec. 1.

24. For a most suggestive critical discussion of patriarchal metaphor in Christian theology, see Sallie McFague, *Metaphorical Theology* (Philadelphia: Fortress, 1982), especially chap. 5. Here McFague develops a model of God as "friend" for relief from exclusive emphasis on the precedence ("lordship") of the divine.

25. Beauvoir's feminine "immanence," the imprisonment of women in the natural reproductive cycle, compares very strangely with any plausible notion of divine world-mothering. It is "stagnation" and "brutishness" that "produces nothing new"; male-associated transcendence, however, "bursts out of the present" and "opens the future" (Beauvoir, *The Second Sex* [1949], tr. H. M. Parshley [New York: Vintage, 1974], pp. xxxiii, 71). Of course

Beauvoir did not invent this strange straitjacket for femininity, alienating the most interesting features of maternity to males; rather, she shows how our culture has done it. But her thinking remains cramped in this way. Dorothy Dinnerstein sees that this undervaluation of the human feminine is caused by a poisoned attitude toward the flesh in general; her argument for rectifying the asymmetry is latently theological, an invocation of a goodness of mortal life that must amount finally to divine immanence (Dinnerstein, *The Mermaid and the Minotaur: Sexual Arrangements and Human Malaise* [New York: Harper and Row, 1976], chaps. 7, 9). Beauvoir: "The Good cannot be considered something that *is*." Dinnerstein: "Why not? one wonders" (223). See also n. 54 below.

26. On religion as infantile, see Freud, *The Future of an Illusion* [1927]; on infancy as religious, see Brown, *Life Against Death*, p. 32, and Dinnerstein, *Mermaid and the Minotaur*, p. 165n.

27. For a review of the actual range of family structures (including some lacking "marriage" as Westerners understand it), see Claude Lévi-Strauss, "The Family," in Harry Shapiro, ed., *Man, Culture, and Society* (London: Oxford University Press, 1971), pp. 333–57.

28. Juliet Mitchell, "Introduction I," in Jacques Lacan et al., *Feminine Sexuality* (New York: Norton, 1982), pp. 6–7.

29. Foucault opened the historical question of how "subject of Desire" came to be a central figure for human self-interpretation. See Judith Butler's discussion in *Subjects of Desire: Hegelian Reflections in Twentieth-Century France* (New York: Columbia University Press, 1987), pp. 217–38. See also the sharply polemical Foucault-allied critique of the Freudian "totalization" of Desire by Gilles Deleuze and Felix Guattari, *Anti-Oedipus: Capitalism and Schizophrenia*, tr. Robert Hurley, Mark Seem, and Helen Lane (New York: Viking, 1977), especially pp. 42–50.

30. Sigmund Freud, "Splitting of the Ego in the Process of Defense," in *The Complete Psychological Works: Standard Edition*, vol. 23, tr. James Strachey (London: Hogarth Press, 1964), pp. 273–78; Jacques Lacan, "The Mirror Stage as Formative of the Function of the I as Revealed in Psychoanalytic Experience," in *Ecrits*, tr. Alan Sheridan (New York: Norton, 1977), pp. 1–7.

31. Nancy Chodorow and Dorothy Dinnerstein argue that equalizing women's and men's contributions to earliest child care would contribute to removing at least the most noxious asymmetries of our gender scheme, which currently depend on a certain emotional reaction to a dominant female presence in infancy (Chodorow, *The Reproduction of Mothering* [Berkeley: University of California Press, 1978]; and Dinnerstein, *Mermaid and the Minotaur*). If mothering and fathering are structural functions, then the proposal is to make both women and men mother–fathers, with perhaps a bit more mother on the side of women, generally, because they actually give birth and nurse, and a bit more father on the side of men, because they don't. Without a bit

more of one function one way and of the other the other way, what could
serve as a foundation of gender differentiation? Except on the assumption of
that continuing duality, what content could be given "gender" in this assertion of Chodorow's: "Personal connection to and identification with both
parents would enable a person to choose those activities she or he desired,
without feeling that such choices jeopardized their gender identity" (218)?
In any case, any differentiation of sex-linked qualities on another basis (if a
basis separate from the exigencies of reproduction is thinkable) would resur-
face in the "maternal" and the "paternal" as women and men played their
reproductive parts.

32. Thus Brown: "The androgynous or hermaphroditic ideal of the unconscious reflects the aspiration of the human body to overcome the dualisms
which are its neurosis, ultimately to reunify Eros and the death instinct. The
dualism of masculine–feminine is merely the transposition into genital terms
of the dualism of activity and passivity; and activity and passivity represent
unstable fusions of Eros and Death at war with each other" (Brown, *Life
Against Death*, p. 132).

33. See, for example, Protogenes' argument in Plutarch's *Dialogue on
Love*, discussed by Michel Foucault in *The History of Sexuality*, vol. 3, *The Care
of the Self*, pp. 199–201.

34. Thus, for instance, Eve Sedgwick is justified in saying that heterosexism is "heterophobic" in the sense that "it denies the very possibility of
difference in desires, in objects" (Sedgwick, *Epistemology of the Closet* [Berkeley:
University of California Press, 1990], pp. 196–97). My point is that heterosexuality is implicitly heterosexism, and homosexuality is implicitly homosexism, although the great asymmetry of power between the two groups makes
heterosexism a far more important political factor. But the heterosexual fear
of homosexism, which gets expressed in complaints about homosexual domination of certain industries or professions, is equally warranted (at the present
level of analysis) as homosexual fear of heterosexism, even though the practical proportions of threat are so unequal in our society. I insist, however, that
to say that sexual orientation commitments are opposed to each other in an
important sense does not mean that persons of one sexual orientation must
be intolerant of persons of another.

35. Jacques Lacan, Seminaire 18.6, pp. 9–10; quoted by Jacqueline
Rose, "Introduction II," in Lacan et al., *Feminine Sexuality*.

36. Mitchell, "Introduction I," p. 20, and Rose, "Introduction II," p. 54,
in Lacan et al., *Feminine Sexuality*.

37. Elizabeth Grosz points out conflicting political implications of
Kristeva's and Irigaray's positions (Grosz, *Sexual Subversions: Three French
Feminists* [Sydney: Allen and Unwin, 1989], chaps. 2–5). Despite its definite
links with maternity, Kristeva's feminine is more abstracted from the lives of
women as such, so that she can treat it as a universal aspect of human sub-

jectivity; accordingly, she resists identifying it with women too closely and keeps a distance from feminism. But Irigaray's feminine, despite its status as a social-psychic construction rather than a biological fact, is very closely tied to female sexuality and thus more the property and platform of women. One could say that Kristeva appears to be more interested in the liberation of the subject from phallocentric "identity," Irigaray more in the liberation of women from phallocentric culture—yet I think that this exclusive way of putting it is unfair to both positions. The two mutually implicating poles of the conversation between these positions are the central meaning of gender (e.g., femininity in everyone) and the sexual center of meaning (e.g., the female basis of femininity).

38. Julia Kristeva, "Oscillation Between Power and Denial" (interview with Xavière Gauthier), tr. M. A. August, in Elaine Marks and Isabelle de Courtivron, eds., *New French Feminisms* (New York: Schocken, 1981), p. 166.

39. Kristeva gives this incidental indication: "Because of the decisive role that women play in the reproduction of the species, and because of the privileged relationship between father and daughter, a woman takes social constraints even more seriously, has fewer tendencies toward anarchism, and is more mindful of ethics. This may explain why our negativity is not Nietzschean anger" (Kristeva, "Woman can never be defined," in Marks and de Courtivron, *New French Feminisms*, p. 138). The parallel with Adorno is traced out by Drucilla Cornell and Adam Thurschwell, "Feminism, Negativity, Subjectivity," in Seyla Benhabib and Drucilla Cornell, eds., *Feminism as Critique* (Minneapolis: University of Minnesota Press, 1987), pp. 143–62, 185–89. Levinas had defined femininity as a positive radical Otherness in his lectures of 1946–47, *Time and the Other*, p. 85. Beauvoir objected to the masculinism of the formula (*Second Sex*, p. xix n. 3), but at that time (1949) it was not yet apparent how Levinas would make a radical positive Otherness the centerpiece of an ethical first-philosophy (cf. his 1961 work *Totality and Infinity*)—a development that Kristeva and Irigaray would both take advantage of.

40. Possibly Lacan is getting at a similar transcendent positive when he speaks of a feminine *jouissance* "supplementary" (not complementary) to the *jouissance* proper to the phallic function ("God and the *Jouissance* of The Woman," in Lacan et al., *Feminine Sexuality*, p. 144). He relentlessly denies that this *jouissance* can be spoken of intelligibly, seeming to abuse the would-be feminine subject pretty grievously in doing so, but perhaps we should not let this distract us from the positive implications of his idea (which get explicit positive valuation in his linkage of femininity with the speechless kind of religious mysticism [146–47]); and see how this is echoed by Luce Irigaray, *Speculum of the Other Woman*, tr. G. C. Gill (Ithaca, N.Y.: Cornell University Press, 1985), pp. 191–92.

41. Kristeva, *Revolution in Poetic Language*, tr. Margaret Waller (New York: Columbia University Press, 1974), pt. 1. Anent Lacan's stress on bi-

nary opposition, Cornell and Thurschwell write: "The structuralist attempt to contain gender within its categories represents a misunderstanding of the limits of any categorical account" (Cornell and Thurschwell, "Feminism, Negativity, Subjectivity," p. 156). Charles Scott observes in Lacan "the singularity of the Father's Rule in understanding Language, a singularity that appears to offer domination of difference rather than its free allowance . . . [repressing] the capacity of language to be a dwelling that grants differences and never takes sides" (Scott, "The Pathology of the Father's Rule," *Thought* 61 [March 1986]: 128).

42. Luce Irigaray, "Cosi Fan Tutti," in Irigaray, *This Sex Which Is Not One*, tr. Catherine Porter (Ithaca, N.Y.: Cornell University Press, 1985), p. 90.

43. Irigaray, *Speculum of the Other Woman*, p. 143. More recently she has investigated the distinctive empirical features of women's speech (cf. Irigaray et al., "Le sexe linguistique," *Languages* 21 [March 1987]).

44. Irigaray, "This Sex Which Is Not One," in Irigaray, *This Sex Which Is Not One*, pp. 26–29.

45. Ibid., p. 31.

46. C. G. Jung, "Anima and Animus" and "The Syzygy," in *Aspects of the Feminine*, tr. R.F.C. Hull (Princeton, N.J.: Princeton University Press, 1982), pp. 77–100, 168–79.

47. Friedrich Engels, *The Origin of the Family, Private Property, and the State* [1884]; for Claude Lévi-Strauss, see especially *The Elementary Structures of Kinship*, rev. ed., tr. J. H. Bell, J. R. von Sturmer, and Rodney Needham (Boston: Beacon, 1969), chap. 29; and idem, "Family."

48. This dimension is stressed by Juliet Mitchell in *Woman's Estate* (New York: Pantheon, 1971); and by Susan Brownmiller in *Against Our Will: Men, Women, and Rape* (New York: Simon and Schuster, 1975).

49. Karl Marx and Friedrich Engels, *The German Ideology*, in Robert Tucker, ed., *The Marx–Engels Reader* (New York: Norton, 1978), p. 159.

50. Lévi-Strauss, "Family," p. 348.

51. Lévi-Strauss, *Elementary Structures of Kinship*, p. 478.

52. Gayle Rubin, "The Traffic in Women," in R. R. Reiter, ed., *Toward an Anthropology of Women* (New York: Monthly Review, 1975), p. 198.

53. The relation between "reproduction" and "production" will be studied more closely in Chapter 7. Marx could have used the notion of "production" to include procreation, but his focus tended to narrow to the creation of material objects (see Linda Nicholson, "Feminism and Marx: Integrating Kinship with the Economic," in Benhabib and Cornell, *Feminism as Critique*, p. 17.)

54. Beauvoir observed that Woman "is the wished-for intermediary between nature, the stranger to man, and the fellow being who is too closely

identical" (*Second Sex*, p. 159). Cf. Sherry Ortner's observation (in 1974): "Woman's intermediate position may have the implication of greater symbolic ambiguity. Shifting our image of the culture/nature relationship once again, we may envision culture in this case as a small clearing within the forest of the larger natural system. From this point of view, that which is intermediate between culture and nature is located on the continuous periphery of culture's clearing; and though it may thus appear to stand both above and below (and beside) culture, it is simply outside and around it. We can begin to understand then how a single system of cultural thought can often assign to woman completely polarized and apparently contradictory meanings, since extremes, as we say, meet. That she often represents both life and death is only the simplest example one could mention" (Ortner, "Is Female to Male as Nature Is to Culture?" in Michelle Z. Rosaldo and Louise Lamphere, eds., *Woman, Culture and Society* [Stanford, Calif.: Stanford University Press, 1974], p. 85).

55. Emile Durkheim, *The Division of Labor in Society* [1893], tr. George Simpson (New York: Macmillan, 1933).

56. Irene Fast argues that the fundamental psychic problem for the child, which gender identification addresses equally in boys and girls, is incompleteness as such rather than lack of a penis or womb (Fast, *Gender Identity: A Differentiation Model* [Hillsdale, N.J.: Erlbaum Associates, 1984]).

57. Sherry B. Ortner and Harriet Whitehead, "Introduction," in *Sexual Meanings: The Cultural Construction of Gender and Sexuality* (Cambridge: Cambridge University Press, 1981), p. 16.

58. Ibid., p. 19. "Feminine" status is sometimes prestigious in relation to "neuter" status, but usually in a way that only confirms the preeminence of the masculine. "In Konkani, an Indian language, women of low status because of youth or widowhood are referred to by neuter pronouns, only married women getting the courtesy of the feminine" (Deborah Cameron, *Feminism and Linguistic Theory* [Houndmills: Macmillan, 1985], p. 65; citing Marielouise Janssen-Jurreit, *Sexism: The Male Monopoly of History and Thought*, tr. Verne Moberg [New York: Pluto Press, 1982], p. 29).

59. "On the biological level a species is maintained only by creating itself anew; but this creation results only in repeating the same Life in more individuals." [What about *who* the individuals are? They're not all stamped out of one mold!] "But man assures the repetition of Life while transcending Life through Existence; by this transcendence he creates values that deprive pure repetition of all value. . . . The female, to a greater extent than the male, is the prey of the species; and the human race has always sought to escape its specific destiny. The support of life became for man an activity and a project through the invention of the tool: but in maternity woman remained closely bound to her body, like an animal" (Beauvoir, *Second Sex*, pp. 72–73). One could read the glorification of the tool and escape from the "natural" as conflating human

existence with the masculine project; but the deeper and correct claim is that the value-creating "project" requires migration to a new Here away from a starting point that will be a transcended There.

60. Rubin, "Traffic in Women," p. 204.

Chapter 7

1. On the variability of biological femaleness and maleness, however, see note 10 to Chapter 3.

2. Sara Ruddick, *Maternal Thinking: Toward a Politics of Peace* (Boston: Beacon Press, 1989), p. 42.

3. Compare how in Diane Ehrensaft's argument "the word 'mothering' is used specifically to refer to the day-to-day *primary* care of a child, to the consciousness of being *directly* in charge of the child's upbringing. . . . One mother aptly characterizes shared parenting thus: 'To a child Mommy is the person who takes care of me, who tends my daily needs, who nurtures me in an unconditional and present way. Manda has two mothers; one is a male, Mommy David, and the other a female, Mommy Alice'" (Ehrensaft, "When Women and Men Mother," in Joyce Trebilcot, ed., *Mothering: Essays in Feminist Theory* [Totowa, N.J.: Rowman and Allanheld, 1983], pp. 47–48). Ruddick makes a similar move in defining "mothering," which she confesses "evades" the "ineluctably female" part of "maternal work" (Ruddick, *Maternal Thinking*, p. 48).

4. Couvade is a ritual symbolic labor enacted by males when their children are born. The classic discussion is by Bruno Bettelheim, *Symbolic Wounds* [1954] (New York: Collier, 1962). Among the Arapesh, "the verb to 'bear a child' is used indiscriminately of either a man or a woman, and child-bearing is believed to be as heavy a drain upon the man as upon the woman" (Margaret Mead, *Sex and Temperament in Three Primitive Societies* [1935] [New York: William Morrow, 1963], p. 32). Carol Tavris and Carole Wade rightly suggest that the expanded role of the Western father in Lamaze-method childbirth is a parallel (Tavris and Wade, *The Longest War: Sex Differences in Perspective*, 2d ed. [San Diego: Harcourt Brace Jovanovich, 1984], p. 190 n. 7).

5. The gender contradiction in calling on men to share "mothering"—that is, in requiring males to behave in a way that is, by definition, female-based—seems insupportable. Not that males may not have motherly experiences, feelings, and tendencies. But the sorts of parenting that males *generally* do has got to count as "fathering." Thus if males did come to generally share what is called "mothering," the result would be that "fathering" would overlap with and more nearly resemble "mothering."

6. Jeffner Allen, "Motherhood: The Annihilation of Women," in Trebilcot, *Mothering*, p. 315.

7. Ibid., p. 316.

8. Mary Wollstonecraft, *A Vindication of the Rights of Woman* [1792], 2d ed. (New York: Norton, 1988), p. 145.

9. Jacques Bels reviews what I think are the essentially marginal acknowledgments of procreation by Heraclitus, Plato, Democritus, and Epicurus in his article "Procréation et philosophie: Notes sur la conception de la procréation dans la philosophie de l'Antiquité," *Revue Philosophique de Louvain* 84 (November 1986): 445–59.

10. Shulamith Firestone, *The Dialectic of Sex: The Case for Feminist Revolution*, rev. ed. (New York: Bantam, 1971), chaps. 4, 10.

11. Karl Marx and Friedrich Engels, *The German Ideology*, tr. S. Rayzanskaya, in Robert Tucker, ed., *The Marx–Engels Reader*, 2d ed. (New York: Norton, 1978), p. 164; Engels, *The Origin of the Family, Private Property and the State* [1884], preface to the 1st ed., tr. Alick West (Harmondsworth: Penguin, 1985).

12. Two recommended introductions to these issues are Alison Jaggar and William McBride, "'Reproduction' as Male Ideology," *Women's Studies International Forum* 8 (1985): 185–96, arguing for the former option; and Linda Nicholson, "Feminism and Marx: Integrating Kinship with the Economic," in Seyla Benhabib and Drucilla Cornell, eds., *Feminism as Critique* (Minneapolis: University of Minnesota Press, 1987), pp. 16–30, 164–65, representing the latter. See also Alison Jaggar, *Feminist Politics and Human Nature* (Totowa, N.J.: Rowman and Allanheld, 1983), pp. 152–55.

13. Lynda Lange, "Toward a Theory of Reproductive Labor," unpublished 1979 paper, quoted in Jaggar, *Feminist Politics and Human Nature*, p. 152.

14. Jaggar, *Feminist Politics and Human Nature*, p. 153. See also Barbara Katz Rothmann, "The Products of Conception: The Social Context of Reproductive Choices," *Journal of Medical Ethics* 11 (December 1985): 188–92.

15. Hannah Arendt, *The Human Condition* (Chicago: University of Chicago Press, 1958), chaps. 3–5. Page references in text are to this edition.

16. See also my *Concept of the Spiritual* (Philadelphia: Temple University Press, 1988), pp. 166–72.

17. Emmanuel Levinas, *Totality and Infinity* [1961], tr. Alfonso Lingis (Pittsburgh: Duquesne University Press, 1969), p. 266; see also pp. 267–69 and his *Time and the Other* [1947], tr. Richard Cohen (Pittsburgh: Duquesne University Press, 1987), pp. 91–92. Contrast the view of Nietzsche's Zarathustra: "'I want heirs'—thus speaks all that suffers; 'I want children, I do not want *myself*.' Joy, however, does not want heirs, or children—joy wants itself, wants eternity, wants recurrence, wants everything eternally the same." (Nietzsche, *Thus Spoke Zarathustra* 4.19.9, tr. Walter Kaufmann, *The Portable Nietzsche* [New York: Viking, 1968], p. 434.)

18. Among many moving testimonies to the normal ambivalence of

traditional motherhood, see Adrienne Rich, "Anger and Tenderness," in *Of Woman Born*, 2d ed. (New York: Norton, 1986), chap. 1.

19. Ann Ferguson, "On Conceiving Motherhood and Sexuality: A Feminist Materialist Approach," in Trebilcot, *Mothering*, pp. 153–82.

20. I am indebted for this point to Edith Wyschogrod's discussion of work and labor (part of an argument for the crucial corporeality of saintliness) in *Saints and Postmodernism: Revisioning Moral Philosophy* (Chicago: University of Chicago Press, 1990), pp. 72–85.

21. I mean "hero" broadly, as anyone risking or giving up life for the sake of someone else's well-being. Childbirth is so dangerous that the mother is one such "hero."

22. Joseph Kupfer puts this point in moral terms: "When his adult child cares for him, the parent directly experiences some of the very virtues he helped cultivate. In a sense, the parent returns to care for himself, externalized and embodied in his adult child. In Aristotelian terms, the craftsman's product is plying the craft on the craftsman himself" (Kupfer, "Can Parents and Children Be Friends?" *American Philosophical Quarterly* 27 [January 1990]: 25).

23. Arthur Schopenhauer, *The World as Will and Representation* [1859], chap. 44.

24. In *Humanae Vitae* [1968], Pope Paul VI wrote thus: "To make use of the gift of conjugal love while respecting the laws of the generative process means to acknowledge oneself not to be the arbiter of the sources of human life, but rather the minister of the design established by the Creator. In fact, just as man does not have unlimited dominion over his body in general, so also, with particular reason, he has no such dominion over his generative faculties as such, because of their intrinsic ordination towards raising up life, of which God is the principle" (in Robert Baker and Frederick Elliston, eds., *Philosophy and Sex* [Buffalo, N.Y.: Prometheus, 1976], p. 138).

25. This point is made by Oliver O'Donovan in *Begotten or Made?* (Oxford: Clarendon, 1984), p. 1. On the other hand, it seems that the artificial fabrication of a human being is not absolutely impossible. It is the nature of the result of a process, not the nature of the process, that should determine the standing of the result, and I cannot discover an a priori connection between "natural" generation (or a technically interventionist variation thereof) and a human-in-principle result. If procreation happened in this way, however, we would be ethically bound to bring it under adapted norms of parenthood (which Dr. Frankenstein conspicuously failed to do, so that his monster was condemned to pathetically inadequate experiences of being parented); and insofar as we would still be obliged to regard parental choice and commitment as necessary conditions for beginning new human life, we would continue to think of parents' relation to their children as an investment of their substance.

26. Marguerite Duras, "A Woman's Work," *Harper's* 280 (February 1990): 43. This is part of her portrait of the childishness of men; children,

too, want always to be seen as "heroes," and children and men both have this attitude partly because of their freedom from procreative responsibility.

27. Rich, *Of Woman Born*, pp. 174–75.

28. Concerning opposition to birth control, Rich writes: "There has always been, and there remains, intense fear of the suggestion that women shall have the final say as to how our bodies are to be used. It is as if the suffering of the mother, the primary identification of woman *as* the mother—were so necessary to the emotional grounding of human society that the mitigation or removal of that suffering, that identification, must be fought at every level" (ibid., p. 30). My answer to her implicit question here is that it is the introduction of *choice with respect to suffering* into this fateful arena that is threatening, not the removal of suffering per se, or the identification of women as mothers per se.

29. Margaret Mead plausibly suggests one psychological cause of variation in our imaginings of the dangers of childbirth: "Men who feel copulation as aggressive may have different phantasies about the dire effects on their wives of their dreadful uncontrolled aggressive desires from men who feel copulation as pleasant, who may share in a cultural phrasing which insists that the child 'sleeps quietly until it is time to be born, then puts its hands above its head and comes out'" (Mead, *Male and Female* [1949] [New York: Mentor, 1955], p. 180).

30. Rolf George makes a revealing study of the ethical implications of everyone's dependence on the young in "Who Should Bear the Cost of Children?" *Public Affairs Quarterly* 1 (January 1987): 1–42.

31. An argument for patrilineality might be that it offsets the relative effacement of men in procreation caused by the mother's necessary centrality in childbearing. But the suppression of matrilineality can be seen as horrifically incongruous precisely because of the mother's extraordinary self-investment.

32. Susan Moller Okin elaborates the point that family life is a "school of justice" in Okin, *Justice, Gender, and the Family* (New York: Basic Books, 1989). She notes John Rawls's undeveloped recognition of the dependence of moral order on family life in Rawls, *A Theory of Justice* (Cambridge, Mass.: Harvard University Press, 1971), pp. 463, 490.

33. John Locke, *Two Treatises of Government* [1690], the second book, chap. 6.

34. Karl Marx, from the third of the *Economic and Philosophical Manuscripts* [1844], tr. T. B. Bottomore, in Erich Fromm, ed., *Marx's Concept of Man* (New York: Ungar, 1966), p. 126.

35. José Ortega y Gasset, *Man and People*, tr. Willard Trask (New York: Norton, 1957), pp. 130, 138.

36. C. S. Lewis, *The Four Loves* (New York: Harcourt Brace Jovanovich, 1971), p. 108.

37. Ruddick complains that the Christian story's veiling of the "bodily

realities on which the birth relationship depends . . . renders natality senti-
mental," and that Arendt's account has the same problem (Ruddick, *Maternal Thinking*, p. 212 and n. 35). I agree that there is a danger of sentimentaliz-
ing birth but still maintain that birth points beyond itself with unique insis-
tence because it is a beginning of life. Thus there would be a contradiction
in attempting to *completely* undo the effacement of childbearing by riveting
attention on what the mother experiences in it.

38. Evelyn Fox Keller, *Reflections on Gender and Science* (New Haven:
Yale University Press, 1985), chap. 8.

39. Important qualifications: In traditional societies, men have often
been as much subject to the coercion of family-sponsored marriages as women
have. And even under modern conditions, in spite of the fact that women are
more generally expected to try to "catch" husbands than men to "catch" wives,
men are pressured into marriage (though not procreation) by homophobia,
and into procreation by family hopes for heirs.

40. See Thomas Aquinas, *Summa Theologica* II–II, 153, 2.

41. See above, pp. 234–36.

42. Pope Paul VI, *Humanae Vitae*, p. 140.

43. Three supplementary remarks may speak to questions that arise in
the reader's mind at this point:

1. There is, as a matter of fact, legal killing that is not directly protective of
   life but rather of political freedom or property. But when we consider
   that political domination and theft are ultimately assured only by the
   use of lethal force—that to resist tyranny or invasion or theft, which
   one is entitled to do, might well bring about one's own death—then it
   becomes evident that the justification for such killing traces back to the
   principle of self-defense.
2. The cases of euthanasia that we tend to approve of are understood to be
   for the purpose of making the dying process more humane, rather than
   actually initiating that process, so that this type of killing is not seen as
   true killing.
3. The application of this argument to suicide is ambiguous. One "plays
   God" and betrays the community in a different way when committing
   suicide than when killing someone else, and yet the commonality in the
   two kinds of killing is sufficiently strong that I do not want to put in a
   qualification that excludes suicide. Pushing this question further is not
   to the present purpose.

44. Mary Anne Warren, "On the Moral and Legal Status of Abortion,"
Monist 57 (January 1973): 43–61.

45. Don Marquis has argued that the lives of the unborn are morally
considerate because they possess valuable "futures-like-our" (Marquis, "Why

Abortion Is Immoral," *Journal of Philosophy* 86 [April 1989]: 183–202). Peter McInerny has replied that a fetus, lacking qualifications of personal identity, cannot have the morally relevant relationship to its future that Marquis supposes (McInerny, "Does a Fetus Already Have a Future-Like-Ours?" *Journal of Philosophy* 87 [May 1990]: 264–68). Both arguments make the mistake of discussing the moral considerateness of life in abstraction from the issue of the composition of society. It is only because a zygote, embryo, or fetus has a future that includes the life of a *different, distinctive* person that the moral community is bound to protect its life.

46. In "An Almost Absolute Value in History," John Noonan pinned the difference in moral status between sex cells and zygotes to the vast difference in their probabilities of yielding human life. If this reasoning were correct, then the moral situation would change dramatically if we gained the ability to predict conjunctions between particular sex cells in given coital acts. But it doesn't. Richard Galvin is right to criticize Noonan's reliance on epistemic as opposed to real probability, but the Galvin–Noonan discussion is still not decisive because neither the epistemic nor the real probability of human life arising at any given point is the morally central factor. The central question is whether an *entity* exists (see following note) that *will for all we know* (i.e., we do not know that it will not) *become* a human individual. See Galvin, "Noonan's Argument Against Abortion: Probability, Possibility and Potentiality," *Journal of Social Philosophy* 19 (Summer 1988): 80–89.

47. Starting from a biological report by Bedate and Cefalo, Thomas Bole argues that the zygote cannot be regarded as a human individual in any sense because it does not contain in itself the whole determination of a human individual's biological form; which biological individual the zygote will become, or even whether it will be an individual or a number of individuals or merely a hydatidiform mole, is contingent on interaction between zygotic and extrazygotic molecules (Bole, "Metaphysical Accounts of the Zygote as a Person," *Journal of Medicine and Philosophy* 14 [1989]: 647–53). Even granting a real indeterminacy of the zygote's identity, however, the fact remains that apart from our intervention we expect a zygote to *become* a particular person, or perhaps several persons. (In contrast, the maximally informed contraceptive-user's expectation can only be that certain sex cells would *form* a particular person or persons.) What if some important part of genetic identity, like one's sex, were determined over the course of the first year after birth by factors like diet and temperature? We would not deny that a six-month-old's life is continuous with a morally considerate future life, notwithstanding the openness of its identity at that age, because we would hold the continuous development of the organism before our mind's eye.

48. Mary Anne Warren, "The Moral Significance of Birth," *Hypatia* 4 (Fall 1989): 63.

49. Judith Jarvis Thomson, "A Defense of Abortion," in Baker and Ellis-

ton, *Philosophy and Sex*, pp. 306–7. Warren ("Moral Significance of Birth") constructs a similar scenario with a space explorer who falls into the hands of aliens able to turn cells of his [sic] body into new human beings. Here, too, one must ask, what if everyone depended for their lives on such a process?

50. For this argument, see Alison Jaggar, "Abortion and a Woman's Right to Decide," in Baker and Elliston, *Philosophy and Sex*, pp. 324–37. The moral community's interest in preventing individuals from changing (for private reasons) the composition of the community by subtraction is weightier than any social interest acknowledged by Jaggar; furthermore, it is constant, unlike the economic and demographic contingencies that Jaggar admits might in some cases warrant social control of abortion. But this point constitutes an objection to her argument only if it is construed as a *moral* argument, whereas she offers it as a (well-justified) *political* argument. Here "moral community" and "society" are not conceptually interchangeable, even though we cannot speak of one without involving the other.

51. As nongestators, males are freer to see what is to be seen by identifying with unborn life. That is to state positively a point that can also be given a critical turn. For instance, Mary Daly speaks of a "fetal identification syndrome" in male ethicists. She illustrates this by quoting Ralph Potter: "When a fetus is aborted no one asks for whom the bell tolls. . . . But do not feel indifferent and secure. The fetus symbolizes you and me and our tenuous hold upon a future here at the mercy of our fellow men" (Daly, *Beyond God the Father* [1973] [Boston: Beacon Press, 1985], p. 111). Daly says that males identify with a right-to-life-holding fetus because "they sense as their own condition the role of controller, possessor, inhabitor of women. Draining female energy, they *feel* 'fetal'" (Daly, *Gyn/Ecology: The Metaethics of Radical Feminism* [Boston: Beacon Press, 1982], pp. 58–59). John Wilcox has a complementary insight: he sees a myth of "demonic nature" in Thomson's sort of abortion parable that indicates women's oppressed procreative position (Wilcox, "Nature as Demonic in Thomson's Defense of Abortion," *New Scholasticism* 63 [Fall 1989]: 463–84).

52. Carol Gilligan, *In a Different Voice: Psychological Theory and Moral Development* (Cambridge, Mass.: Harvard University Press, 1982), p. 100.

53. Ibid., p. 118. Page references in the text henceforth are to this edition.

54. The difficulty is revealed by John Stuart Mill's inability to conceive happiness as a supreme value without taking account of criteria for "higher" happiness that inhere in the more "elevated faculties" of human beings (Mill, *Utilitarianism*, chap. 2). Indeed it belongs to our "elevated faculty" of moral reasonableness that we apply the utility principle disinterestedly to all, not selfishly—that I let the pleasures of others count equally with my own—and Mill's utilitarianism trades on this as a given.

55. For example, Sarah contrasts the fantastic "pros for having the baby"

like "having the adoring love of this beautiful Gerber baby" to the realistic cons of losing a good job, having to go on welfare, and being estranged from her parents (Gilligan, *In a Different Voice*, p. 92).

56. This moral dialectic is missing as a reflective theme (although it is very evidently *in force*) in Mary O'Brien's otherwise programmatically admirable "dialectics of reproduction" (O'Brien, *The Politics of Reproduction* [London: Routledge and Kegan Paul, 1981]).

Conclusion

1. Judith Butler, *Gender Trouble: Feminism and the Subversion of Identity* (London: Routledge, 1990), p. 104.

2. G. K. Chesterton, *Orthodoxy* (London: John Lane, 1909), pp. 69–70.

3. See pp. 49–52 and pp. 190–92 above.

4. See, for example, Romans 12:3–8, 14.

5. Simone de Beauvoir, *The Second Sex* [1949], tr. H. M. Parshley (New York: Knopf, 1953), pp. 813–14. Compare Friedrich Engels's projection— more negatively libertarian, on the surface, yet obviously assuming the continuing importance of sex difference—of "a new generation . . . of men who never in their lives have known what it is to buy a woman's surrender with money or any other social instrument of power; a generation of women who have never known what it is to give themselves to a man from any other considerations than real love. . . . When these people are in the world, they will care precious little what anybody today thinks they ought to do; they will make their own practice and their corresponding public opinion about the practice of each individual—and that will be the end of it" (Engels, *The Origin of the Family, Private Property and the State* [1884], tr. Alick West [Harmondsworth: Penguin, 1985], p. 114).

6. See note 30 to Chapter 3 on Irigaray's claim of intersexual "regeneration."

7. Andrea Dworkin, *Intercourse* (New York: Free Press, 1987); Immanuel Kant, *Observations on the Feeling of the Beautiful and the Sublime* [1764], sec. 3.

8. My understanding of social extension parallels that of Gramsci, but for the reason I give I cannot accept his vision of a unity of theory and practice. See his discussion of philosophy in the *Prison Notebooks*, which may be found in Roger Gottlieb, ed., *An Anthology of Western Marxism* (Oxford: Oxford University Press, 1989), pp. 120–37.

Index

375

GENDER THINKING

THINKING

Steven G. Smith